TODAY'S SCRIPTURE GUIDANCE

"YOU ARE A CHILD OF CHRIST"

Book III

Section C

By

A servant of Jesus Christ

Dedication

This book is written to give God glory and to lift the name of our Lord and Savior, Jesus Christ. It is dedicated to anyone who desires to understand the Word of God and those who desire to live their life to the Will of God. Amen.

About the Author

Anthony Teran Miller is a servant of Jesus Christ. I am not worthy of being Jesus's servant, but Jesus is worthy to be served! Amen. Jesus has called me to serve, so I serve Him. Hallelujah! In the business world, I have had a successful career as a Senior Leader in four Fortune 300 companies. Yet, I knew that I was not serving Jesus. I accepted Jesus when I was eight years old, and I have been active in the church for many of my adult years, but I knew that I was not doing what God had designed me to do. I was focused more on pleasing man and achieving the world's view of success than I was on serving Jesus.

I began to hear the voice of my Master, Jesus, challenging me to do more for Him. I ignored Him. I kept telling myself that I wanted to serve Him, but I continued to serve Him the way I wanted to, with my primary focus still on the world. Then one day, I lost my job as Vice President of the very large company that I was working for; and a few nights later, Jesus's voice spoke to me loud and clear! Jesus gave me an exact assignment to serve Him daily. I woke up and ran down to my home office and wrote down everything that Jesus had called me to do. And on the night that Jesus called me, I became a servant of Jesus Christ! Hallelujah!

I pray that Today's Scripture Guidance moves you in the manner that God calls it to. And to God be the glory! Amen

Table of Contents

Scripture Guidance for all servants of Jesus Christ

"All Scripture is given by the inspiration of God, and is useful for teaching, rebuking, correcting, and training in righteousness,

so that the servant of God may be well equipped for every good work."

(2 Timothy 3:16-17)

"Each of you should use whatever gift you have received (from God) to serve others, as faithful stewards of God's grace in various forms.

If anyone speaks, they should do so as one who speaks the very words of God. If anyone serves, they should do so with the strength God provides; so that in all things God may be praised through Jesus Christ. To Him be the glory and the power for ever and ever. Amen!"

(1 Peter 4:10-11)

"This is what we speak, not in words taught us by human wisdom, but in words taught by the Holy Spirit; explaining spiritual realities with Spirit taught words."

(1 Corinthians 2:13)

"I became a servant of this Gospel by the gift of God's grace given me through the working of His power.

Although I am the least of all the Lord's people, this grace was given me; to preach to the Gentiles the boundless riches of Christ,

and to make plain to everyone the administration of this mystery, which for the ages past was kept hidden in God, who created all things."

(Ephesians 3:7-9)

To God be the glory! Forever and Ever! Amen.

Day 181

The Lord God says: "These people come near to Me with their mouth and honor Me with their lips, but their hearts are not with Me. Their worship of Me is based on merely human rules they have been taught."

"Woe to those who go to great depths to hide their plans from the Lord, who do their work in darkness and think, 'Who sees us? Who will know?'

You (these people) turn things upside down, as if the Potter (God) were thought to be like the clay (these people)! Shall what is formed (the people) say to the One (God) who formed it, 'You did not make me?' Can the pot (these people) say to the Potter (Almighty God), 'You know nothing?'"

(Isaiah 29:13 & 15-16)

In today's Scripture, the great servant of God, the prophet Isaiah, speaks to people that claim to worship God, to show the hypocrisy that God sees in these people, that they worship Him with their words, not their hearts. Amen! That was true at the time of Isaiah, and that is true today! Amen again! And if you are worshiping God only with words, you are not worshiping God, because God does not accept your worship! God only accepts worship to Him that is coming from the heart! Amen! None of us can fool God with our words, for God looks at our hearts as we speak. Amen again! God knows why your mouth is moving. God hears what you say, and God watches how you live! How you live is dictated by your heart. And God wants your heart! God also has a warning for people. Stop saying one thing to God, and then go live your life in sinful ways, thinking God does not see you. You cannot fool God, and you cannot hide from God! God sees your everything! Amen! You are not fooling God when you praise Him with your mouth, but live according to a sinful heart! Amen again! Yes, God wants to hear you worship and praise Him, but only if you truly mean it! Hallelujah! And God sees today, what He saw at the time of Isaiah, people speaking to Him with their mouths, not their hearts! Glory Hallelujah, tell the truth! And if this is you, God is not happy with you, and He wants you to know it! You cannot fool God, who made you, and sees you! And that is the truth! For Almighty God sees your heart! Glory to God! Our Scripture begins with this message to these people, **The Lord God says: "These people come near to Me with their mouth and honor Me with their lips, but their hearts are not with Me. Their worship of Me is based on merely human rules they have been taught."** God does not accept these people as His people! God cannot be fooled! Amen! Our Word now gives a warning to these people, saying, **"Woe to those who go to great depths to hide their plans from the Lord, who do their work in darkness and think, 'Who sees us? Who will know?'"** God knows how you plan to sin, and God sees your sins at all times! God knows what you are planning and what you are doing! You cannot hide from God, and God cannot be fooled! Amen again! And finally, the Word of God says to these people, **"You (these people) turn things upside down, as if the Potter (God) were thought to be like the clay (the people)! Shall what is formed (these people) say to the One (God) who formed it, 'You did not make me?' Can the pot (these people) say to the Potter (Almighty God), 'You know nothing?'"** God created you, and knows everything about you, so how can anyone fool God! Hallelujah! No one can fool God with what they say, or how they live. Amen.

Today, our Scripture is speaking to all people who try to fool God. You know what you are doing, and God knows what you are doing! Amen! Stop trying to fool God with your worship. God sees your heart, and God knows what you are doing. Stop trying to fool God! It is not working, because it cannot work. God is God! Amen again! And if this is you, God is not happy with you, and He wants you to know it! You cannot fool God, who made you, and sees you! And that is the truth! For Almighty God sees your heart! Glory to God! The prophet Isaiah, speaks to people that claim to worship God, to show the hypocrisy that God sees in these people, that they worship Him with their words, not their hearts. Amen! And if you are worshiping God only with words, you are not worshiping God, because God does not accept your worship! God only accepts worship to Him that is coming from the heart! Amen! None of us can fool God with our words, for God looks at our hearts as we speak. Amen again! God hears what you say, and God watches how you live! How you live is dictated by your heart.

And God wants your heart! Our Scripture begins with this message to these people, **The Lord God says: "These people come near to Me with their mouth and honor Me with their lips, but their hearts are not with Me. Their worship of Me is based on merely human rules they have been taught."** God does not accept these people as His people! God cannot be fooled! Amen! This is happening today! So many people are turning their words to God in phony worship. It has become almost mandatory for people to say to others: 'Our hearts and prayers are with you.', and there are no plans at all to pray! Tell the truth! It has just become a "proper" human rule to say! And there are far too many "church folks" who go to church because of traditions in their family, or in their society. God sees this, and if you are one of these people, God is convicting you today! God is not pleased with you, and you know who you are! God knows who you are! Stop trying to fool God with your worship! God does not accept your worship! You better change your ways, and start worshiping God with your heart! For you are not fooling God, and right now, God does not accept you as His people! And that is the truth! Amen.

Today, our Word is speaking to all people who try to fool God. You know what you are doing, and God knows what you are doing! Amen! Stop trying to fool God with your worship. God sees your heart, and God knows what you are doing. God also has a warning for people. Stop saying one thing to God, and then go live your life in sinful ways, thinking God does not see you. You cannot fool God, and you cannot hide from God! God sees your everything! Amen! You are not fooling God when you praise Him with your mouth, but live according to a sinful heart! Amen again! God sees today, what He saw at the time of Isaiah, people speaking to Him with their mouths in the light, while planning to do their sins in the dark! Glory Hallelujah, tell the truth! And if this is you, God is not happy with you, and He wants you to know it! You cannot fool God, who made you, and sees you! And that is the truth! Glory to God! God does not accept these people as His people! God cannot be fooled! Amen! Our Word now gives a warning to these people, saying, **"Woe to those who go to great depths to hide their plans from the Lord, who do their work in darkness and think, 'Who sees us? Who will know?'"** God knows how you plan to sin, and God sees your sins at all times! God knows what you are planning and what you are doing! You cannot hide from God, and God cannot be fooled! Amen again! God sees this, and if you are one of these people, God is convicting you today! God is not pleased with you, and you know who you are! God knows who you are! Stop planning your sins, and stop sinning in the dark! God sees you, and God knows what you are doing! You better change your ways, and come out of the dark where you are sinning! God sees your sins at all times. You cannot hide from God, while you sin in the dark! Tell the truth! For you are not fooling God, and right now, God does not accept you as His people! And that is the truth! Amen.

Today, the Word of God is speaking to all people who try to fool God. You know what you are doing, and God knows what you are doing! Amen! Stop trying to fool God with your worship. God sees your heart, and God knows what you are doing. And stop saying one thing to God, and then go live your life in sinful ways, thinking God does not see you. You cannot fool God, and you cannot hide from God! God sees your everything! Amen! You are not fooling God when you praise Him with your mouth, but live according to a sinful heart, while planning to do your sins in the dark!! Amen again! Glory Hallelujah, tell the truth! And if this is you, God is not happy with you, and He wants you to know it! You cannot fool God, who made you, and sees you! And that is the truth! Glory to God! God does not accept these people as His people! God cannot be fooled! Amen! And finally, the Word of God says to these people, **"You (these people) turn things upside down, as if the Potter (God) were thought to be like the clay (the people)! Shall what is formed (these people) say to the One (God) who formed it, 'You did not make me?' Can the pot (these people) say to the Potter (Almighty God), 'You know nothing?'"** God created you, and knows everything about you, so how can anyone fool God! Hallelujah! No one can fool God with what they say, or how they live. God sees this, and if you are one of these people, God is convicting you today! God is not pleased with you, and you know who you are! God knows who you are! You are not the Potter, you are the pot! And God the Potter will judge you based on what He sees as righteous, you do not get to tell God anything! Hallelujah! God is a righteous God! And God sees you, and God knows what you are doing! You better change your ways, and come out of the dark where you are sinning! God sees your sins at all times. You cannot hide from God, while you sin in the dark! Tell the truth! For you are not fooling God, and right now, God does not accept you as His people! And that is the truth! Amen.

Today, our Scripture Guidance is for all people who live their life trying to fool God. You know who you are, and God knows who you are. Amen! Stop trying to fool God with your worship. God sees your heart, and God knows what you are doing. And stop saying one thing to God, and then go live your life in sinful ways, thinking God does not see you. You cannot fool God, and you cannot hide from God! God sees your everything! Amen! If this is you, God is not happy with you, and He wants you to know it! You cannot fool God, who made you, and sees you! And that is the truth! Glory to God! God will not accept these people as His people! God cannot be fooled! Amen.

Day 182

"Dear children (born again Believers), let us not love with (just) words or speech, but with actions and in truth.

This is how we know that we belong to the Truth (Jesus), and how we set our hearts at rest in His presence."

(1 John 3:18-19)

In today's Scripture, the great servant of Jesus, the apostle John, speaks to Believers who have been born again into Jesus. Amen! When you accepted Jesus as your Lord and Savior, you were redeemed to God! Your old self, in God's eyes, is dead and reborn to God through the blood of Jesus! Amen again! This guidance is for Believers! This message is only for those that have been born again through Jesus, to God the Father! Glory! Through the blood of Jesus, Believers are adopted by God, and therefore are His children. Glory Hallelujah! And John is giving direction to God's children about showing love to others, just as Jesus showed love to us, and how God so loved the world! Amen! God commands His children to show love! Amen again! Our Scripture begins with, **"Dear children (born again Believers),"** This instruction is only for Believers, God's children through Jesus Christ! No one else! Amen! Our Word gives all Believers these instructions, "let us not love **with (just) words or speech, but with actions and in truth. This is how we know that we belong to the Truth (Jesus)," Believers** are commanded to love others, with their actions! It is how you live your life with love toward others that shows the world that you belong to Jesus! Amen again! And the Word of God concludes that by showing love to others, that is how we show the world we belong to Jesus, **"and how we set our hearts at rest in His presence."** When we show others love with our actions, Jesus will be pleased, and through this, we will have peace in Him. Glory Hallelujah! This guidance is for Believers! This message is only for those that have been born again through Jesus, to God the Father! Glory! Amen.

Today, our Scripture is speaking to Believers. This is not a message to the world, this is specific instruction for Believers, God's children, through the name of Jesus! John is speaking to Believers who have been born again into Jesus. Amen! When you accepted Jesus as your Lord and Savior, you were redeemed to God! Your old self, in God's eyes, is dead, and reborn to God through the blood of Jesus! Amen again! This message is only for those that have been born again through Jesus, to God the Father! Glory! Believers have been adopted by God, and therefore are His children. Glory Hallelujah! And John is giving direction to God's children about showing love to others, just as Jesus showed love to us, and how God so loved the world! Amen! God commands His children to show love! Amen again! Our Scripture begins with, **"Dear children (born again Believers),"** This instruction is only for Believers, God's children through Jesus Christ! No one else! Amen! You are now a part of God's family, and God has certain expectations for each one of His children. Glory to God!

God does not have the same expectation for sinners who are not redeemed by Him. God loves them, but they are not His children! Hallelujah, tell the truth! As a Believer, you have been given glory from God, and you have been set apart from the world, so God sees you differently from the rest of the world. Glory Hallelujah! If you are a Believer, you are God's child! Amen! You are special to God! Amen again! So this guidance is for Believers! This message is only for those that have been born again through Jesus, to God the Father! Glory! Amen.

Today, our Word is speaking to Believers. This is specific instruction for Believers, God's children, through the name of Jesus! John is speaking to Believers who have been born again into Jesus. Amen! When you accepted Jesus, you were redeemed to God! Your old self, in God's eyes, is dead, and reborn to God through the blood of Jesus! Amen again! This message is only for those that have been born again through Jesus! Glory! Believers have been adopted by God, and therefore are His children. Glory Hallelujah! And this is the holy direction to God's children about showing love to others, just as Jesus showed love to us, and how God so loved the world! God commands His children to show love! This instruction is only for Believers, God's children through Jesus Christ! No one else! Amen! Our Word gives all Believers this instruction, **"let us not loves with (just) words or speech, but with actions and in truth. This is how we know that we belong to the Truth (Jesus),"** Believers are commanded to love others, with their actions! It is how you live your life with love toward others that shows the world that you belong to Jesus! Amen again! God commands His children to live their life with love toward others. God is not moved by talk, God is moved by actions, which are driven by the heart! The mouth will often speak on its own, but your heart drives how you live! And God knows if you truly belong to Jesus, by the way you live and treat others! And that is also how the people in the world will know that you belong to Jesus, by how they see you treat others! Amen! So don't just talk love, live love with your actions toward others. Amen again! Give glory to God! This guidance is for Believers! This message is only for those that have been born again through Jesus, to God the Father! Glory! Amen.

Today, the Word of God is speaking to Believers. This is specific instruction for God's children through the name of Jesus! John is speaking to Believers who have been born again into Jesus. Amen! You have been redeemed by God! Your old self, in God's eyes, is dead, and reborn to God through the blood of Jesus! Amen again! This message is only for those that have been born again through Jesus! Glory! Believers have been adopted by God, and therefore are His children. Glory Hallelujah! And this is the holy direction to God's children about showing love to others, just as Jesus showed love to us, and how God so loved the world! God commands His children to show love! This instruction is only for Believers, God's children through Jesus Christ! No one else! Amen! Believers are commanded to love others, with their actions! It is how you live your life with love toward others that shows the world that you belong to Jesus! Amen again! And the the Word of God concludes that by showing love to others, that is how we show the world we belong to Jesus, **"and how we set our hearts at rest in His presence."** When we show others love with our actions, Jesus will be pleased, and through this, we will have peace in Him. Glory Hallelujah! If you truly want Jesus in your life, treat others with love! Jesus loves to see His followers show love to others, just as Jesus showed love to others! Amen! And when you consistently show love to others, Jesus has joy in you, and you will have Him in your presence to keep your heart at peace! Hallelujah! This guidance is for Believers! This message is only for those that have been born again through Jesus, to God the Father! Glory! Amen.

Today, our Scripture Guidance is for Believers! This message is only for those that have been born again through Jesus, to God the Father! Glory! Through the blood of Jesus, Believers are adopted by God, and therefore are His children. So therefore, live your life showing love for others, just as Father God showed His love for you by sending you Jesus to save you! This guidance is for Believers! Amen.

Day 183

"The Lord (God) reigns, let the nations tremble, let the earth shake.

Great is the Lord in Zion' He is exalted over all the nations.

Let them (all people) praise your great and awesome Name, You are holy.

The King (Almighty God) is mighty, He loves justice, and You have established equality, in Jacob (Israel) You have done what is just and right.

Exalt the Lord our God and worship at His footstool, He is holy.

Moses and Aaron were among His priests, Samuel was among those who call on His name."

"Lord our God, You answered them, You were a forgiving God, though you punished their sins.

Exalt the Lord our God and worship at His Holy Mountain, for the Lord our God is holy."

(Psalm 99:1-6 & 8-9)

In today's Scripture, the author writes a song celebrating the great and holy God! Amen! God is great, and God is holy! Amen again! And all people should recognize that and celebrate that! God is great, and God is holy! Hallelujah! And the author also celebrates that there are special benefits that God gives to His people! Amen! God offers His people justice and equality in His eyes! Glory! God also corrects His people when we fall off His righteous path for us, and God forgives us of our sins when we repent to Him. Amen again! God is great, and God is holy! The Psalms were written over three thousand years ago, yet this psalm is still true today! And we should be celebrating what the author celebrated, God is great, and God is holy, and hallelujah, God's people have benefits from God! Glory Hallelujah! You are being challenged! Are you celebrating the One and Only great and holy God? And if you are a Believer in Jesus Christ, do you recognize and celebrate that you have special benefits from God for being His people? These are real questions that each of us must answer! Are you celebrating God? Amen! Our Scripture begins with a statement of fact to all people, **"The Lord (God) reigns, let the nations tremble, let the earth shake. Great is the Lord in Zion' He is exalted over all the nations. Let them (all people) praise your great and awesome Name, You are holy."** There is only One God, and God is in control over all people on Earth! Praise Him! Amen! Our Word now speaks to God's people, saying, **"The King (Almighty God) is mighty, He loves justice, and You have established equality, in Jacob (Israel), You have done what is just and right. Exalt the Lord our God and worship at His footstool, He is holy. Moses and Aaron were among His priests, Samuel was among those who call on His name. Lord our God, You answered them, You were a forgiving God,**

though you punished their sins." God gives benefits to His people! Worship Him! God will correct you and forgive you of your sins! Praise Him! Amen again! And the Word of God encourages God's people to, **"Exalt the Lord our God and worship at His Holy Mountain, for the Lord our God is holy."** If you believe in Jesus Christ as your Lord and Savior, bow down and worship God! And celebrate that God is your Father, and you are His child! Celebrate! For the Lord God Almighty is great, and Almighty God is holy! Celebrate today! Amen.

Today, our Scripture is a song celebrating the great and holy God! Amen! God is great, and God is holy! Amen again! And all people should recognize that and celebrate that! God is great, and God is holy! Hallelujah! This psalm is still true today! And we should be celebrating what the author celebrated, God is great, and God is holy. Amen again! You are being challenged! Are you celebrating the One and Only great and holy God? This is a real question that each of us must answer! Are you celebrating God? Amen! Our Scripture begins with a statement of fact to all people, **"The Lord (God) reigns, let the nations tremble, let the earth shake. Great is the Lord in Zion' He is exalted over all the nations. Let them (all people) praise your great and awesome Name, You are holy."** There is only One God, and God is in control over all people on Earth! Praise Him! Amen! Too many people today take God for granted, and too many people today ignore God. How could anyone alive ignore God? And how can Believers in Jesus Christ take God for granted? But we do! Tell the truth! God is the reason for all things, and anything! God is King over all things, all nations, and all people! Yet too many times, we wait for some great new thing, or we wait for some horrific new challenge, to truly recognize God. Amen! Yet God is great, and God is awesome, all the time! Are you celebrating God, for being God? Amen again! For the Lord God Almighty is great, and Almighty God is holy! All the time! And that is the truth! Celebrate today! Amen.

Today, our Word is a song celebrating the great and holy God! Amen! God is great, and God is holy! Amen again! And all people should recognize that and celebrate that! God is great, and God is holy! Hallelujah! And we should be celebrating what the author celebrated, God is great, and God is holy. Amen again! You are being challenged! Are you celebrating God? Amen! The author also celebrates that there are special benefits that God gives to His people! Amen! God offers His people justice and equality in His eyes! Glory! God also corrects His people when we fall off His righteous path for us, and God forgives us of our sins when we repent to Him. Amen again! God is great, and God is holy! And we should be celebrating what the author celebrated, God is great, and God is holy, and hallelujah, God's people have benefits from God! Glory Hallelujah! You are being challenged! Are you celebrating the One and Only great and holy God? And if you are a Believer in Jesus Christ, do you recognize and celebrate that you have special benefits from God for being His people? These are real questions that each of us must answer! Are you celebrating

God! There is only One God, and God is in control over all people on Earth! Praise Him! Amen! Our Word now speaks to God's people, saying, **"The King (Almighty God) is mighty, He loves justice, and You have established equality, in Jacob (Israel) You have done what is just and right. Exalt the Lord our God and worship at His footstool, He is holy. Moses and Aaron were among His priests, Samuel was among those who call on His name. Lord our God, You answered them, You were a forgiving God, though you punished their sins."** God gives benefits to His people! Worship Him! God will correct you and forgive you of your sins! Praise Him! Amen again! As a Believer, you need to recognize and celebrate the benefits that God gives His people. You are special to God, and God treats you special! Hallelujah! But how special do you treat your God? Tell the truth! Are you celebrating God, for being your God? If you are saved by the blood of Jesus, you are God's child, and God is your Father God! Amen again! For the Lord God Almighty is great, and Almighty God is holy! All the time! And that is the truth! Celebrate today! Amen.

Today, the Word of God is a song celebrating the great and holy God! Amen! God is great, and God is holy! Amen again! And all people should recognize that and celebrate that! God is great, and God is holy! Hallelujah! Each of us should be celebrating what the author celebrated, God is great, and God is holy. Amen again! You are being challenged! Are you celebrating God? Amen! And there are special benefits that God gives to His people! Amen! God offers His people justice and equality in His eyes! Glory! God also corrects His people when we fall off His righteous path for us, and God forgives us of our sins when we repent to Him. Amen again! God is great, and God is holy! We should be celebrating that God is great and God is holy, and hallelujah, God's people have benefits from God! Glory Hallelujah! You are being challenged! Are you celebrating the One and Only great and holy God? And if you are a Believer in Jesus Christ, do you recognize and celebrate that you have special benefits from God for being His people? These are real questions that each of us must answer! Are you celebrating God! There is only One God, and God is in control over all people on Earth! Praise Him! Amen! And God gives benefits to His people! Worship Him! God will correct you and forgive you of your sins! Praise Him! Amen again! And the Word of God encourages God's people to, **"Exalt the Lord our God and worship at His Holy Mountain, for the Lord our God is holy."** If you believe in Jesus Christ as your Lord and Savior, bow down and worship God! And celebrate that God is your Father, and you are His child! Celebrate! Lift God up and praise His holy Name! God sits on His Throne in Heaven above, and God looks out for you! God blesses you! God protects you! You are His child in the name of Jesus! Glory Hallelujah! Are you celebrating God, for being God? Amen again! For the Lord God Almighty is great, and Almighty God is holy! All the time! And that is the truth! Celebrate today! Amen.

Today, the psalm is a song celebrating the great and holy God! Amen! God is great, and God is holy! Amen again! And all people should recognize that and celebrate that! Amen again! Each of us should be celebrating what the author celebrated, God is great, and God is holy. Hallelujah! You are being challenged! Are you celebrating God? Glory Hallelujah! Celebrate! Are you celebrating God, for being God? Give glory to God! Celebrate! For the Lord God Almighty is great, and Almighty God is holy! All the time! And that is the truth! Celebrate today! Amen.

Day 184

"See to it, brothers and sisters, that none of you has a sinful, unbelieving heart that turns (you) away from the living God.

But encourage one another daily, as long as it is called 'Today', so that none of you may be hardened by sin's deceitfulness.

We (Believers) have come to share in Jesus Christ, if indeed we hold our original conviction firmly to the end (of our life)."

(Hebrews 3:12-14)

In today's Scripture, the author writes to those who have accepted Jesus Christ as their Lord and Savior, warning them about falling back to sinful hearts, which can lead them to disbelief. Amen. For it is not enough to speak your belief in Jesus at one time in your life, but allow the evil in the world to turn you to live a life of disbelief! In other words, the same faith you had in Jesus that led you to accept Him, must be the same faith in Him at the end of your life! Amen again! This is a warning to Believers today! Too many Believers have accepted Jesus at one time in their life, but have lived in so much sin, that sin has turned them away from Jesus! And living a life of sin, and ignoring your faith in Jesus, shows Jesus that you do not believe in Him! Our Scripture Guidance is trying to help someone today! You are calling yourself a Believer, because you committed to Him at one point in your life, but you have lived completely in sin, denying

Jesus through the rest of your life! And by doing so, you have turned away from the living God! If this is you, this message is for you! You need to get back to your faith in Jesus before it is too late! Because Believers receive glory from God if they have faith in Jesus at the end of their life! Tell the truth! Our Scripture begins with a message that is only for Believers in Jesus Christ, saying, **"See to it, brothers and sisters, that none of you has a sinful, unbelieving heart that turns (you) away from the living God."** God has made a Covenant with you, but it is an "if/then" covenant. If you believe in Jesus as your Lord and Savior, God will forgive your sins and give you everlasting life with Him! Do not break the Covenant by losing your "if"! Amen! The Word tells Believers not to have a sinful, unbelieving heart, **"But encourage one another daily, as long as it is called 'Today,' so that none of you may be hardened by sin's deceitfulness."** Each Believer should encourage each other through fellowship, daily! By doing this, we build each other's faith in Jesus! Amen again! And the Word of God confirms the "if/then" New Covenant of God, **"We (Believers) have come to share in Jesus Christ, if indeed we hold our original conviction firmly to the end (of our life)."** Each Believer must live their life true to the original commitment of faith! We started our Covenant with God when we made a commitment to faith that Jesus is our Lord and Savior, and God wants that same commitment to Jesus throughout your life! Glory! Your faith in Jesus begins with your acceptance of Him, but you must also have that faith in Jesus to the end of your life! God views your commitment to Jesus by how you live! The same faith you had in Jesus that led you to accept Him, must be the same faith in Him at the end of your life! Amen.

Today, our Scripture is speaking to Believers in Jesus Christ as their Lord and Savior, warning them about falling back to sinful hearts, which can lead them to disbelief. Amen. For it is not enough to speak your belief in Jesus at one time in your life, but allow the evil in the world to turn you to living a life of disbelief! In other words, the same faith you had in Jesus that led you to accept Him, must be the same faith in Him at the end of your life! Amen again! Too many Believers have accepted Jesus at one time in their life, but have lived in so much sin, that sin has turned them away from Jesus! And if you are living a life of sin, and ignoring your faith in Jesus, you are showing Jesus that you do not believe in Him! You are calling yourself a Believer, because you committed to Him at one point in your life, but you have lived completely in sin, denying Jesus throughout the rest of your life! And by doing so, you have turned away from the living God! If this is you, this message is for you! You need to get back to your faith in Jesus, before it is too late! Because Believers receive glory from God if they have faith in Jesus at the end of their life! Tell the truth! Our Scripture begins with a message that is only for Believers in Jesus Christ, saying, **"See to it, brothers and sisters, that none of you has a sinful, unbelieving heart that turns (you) away from the living God."** God has made a Covenant with you, but it is an "if/then" covenant. If you believe in Jesus as your Lord and Savior, God will forgive your sins and give you everlasting life with Him! Do not break the Covenant by losing your "if"! Amen! This message is for every Believer! Do not allow your heart to be so sinful, that you live your life without faith in Jesus. For that will turn you away from God...and His Covenant with you! Amen again! You have been warned, and you are being encouraged! Keep your faith in Jesus throughout your life! You have come to share in Jesus's glory if, indeed, you hold your conviction firmly to the end of your life! Amen.

Today, our Word is speaking to Believers in Jesus Christ as their Lord and Savior, warning them about falling back to sinful hearts, which can lead them to disbelief. Amen. It is not enough to speak your belief in Jesus at one time in your life, but allow the evil in the world to turn you to living a life of disbelief! The same faith you had in Jesus that led you to accept Him, must be the same faith in Him at the end of your life! Amen again! And if you are living a life of sin, and ignoring your faith in Jesus, you are showing Jesus that you do not believe in Him! You are calling yourself a Believer, because you committed to Him at one point in your life, but you have lived completely in sin, denying Jesus throughout the rest of your life! And by doing so, you have turned away from the living God! This message is for you! You need to get back to your faith in Jesus, before it is too late! Because Believers receive glory from God if they have faith in Jesus at the end of their life! Tell the truth! God has made a Covenant with you, but it is an "if/then" covenant. If you believe in Jesus as your

Lord and Savior, God will forgive your sins and give you everlasting life with Him! Do not break the Covenant by losing your "if"! Amen! The Word tells Believers not to have a sinful, unbelieving heart, **"But encourage one another daily, as long as it is called 'Today,' so that none of you may be hardened by sin's deceitfulness."** Each Believer should encourage each other through fellowship, daily! By doing this, we build each other's faith in Jesus! Amen again! As a Believer, if you live your life in constant fellowship with other Believers, you can encourage them to remain faithful to Jesus, and you will be encouraged by them to remain faithful to Jesus! That encouragement will help you to turn away from the temptations and lies of sin! Hallelujah! You have been warned, and you are being encouraged! Keep your faith in Jesus throughout your life! You have come to share in Jesus's glory if, indeed, you hold your conviction firmly to the end of your life! Amen.

Today, the Word of God is speaking to Believers in Jesus Christ as their Lord and Savior, warning them about falling back to sinful hearts, which can lead them to disbelief. Amen. It is not enough to speak your belief in Jesus at one time in your life, but allow the evil in the world to turn you to living a life of disbelief! The same faith you had in Jesus that led you to accept Him, must be the same faith in Him at the end of your life! Amen again! And if you are living a life of sin, and ignoring your faith in Jesus, you are showing Jesus that you do not believe in Him! You call yourself a Believer, but now you have to live completely in sin, denying

Jesus in the way you live your life! You have turned away from the living God! This message is for you! You need to get back to your faith in Jesus, before it is too late! Because Believers receive glory from God if they have faith in Jesus at the end of their life! Tell the truth! God has made a Covenant with you, but it is an "if/then" covenant. If you believe in Jesus as your Lord and Savior, God will forgive your sins and give you everlasting life with Him! Do not break the Covenant by losing your "if"! Amen! Each Believer should encourage each other through fellowship, daily! By doing this, we build each other's faith in Jesus! Amen again! And the Word of God confirms the "if/then" New Covenant of God, **"We (Believers) have come to share in Jesus Christ, if indeed we hold our original conviction firmly to the end (of our life)."** Each Believer must live their life true to the original commitment of faith! We started our Covenant with God when we made a commitment to faith that Jesus is our Lord and Savior, and God wants that same commitment to Jesus throughout your life! Glory! Too many Believers accepted Jesus when they were young, or at a time when the Word moved them, but then chose to live sinful lives, because they loved sin more than Jesus! This is a hard truth, that you must admit, so that you can seek forgiveness and return to your original faith in Jesus! Amen! You have been warned, and you are being encouraged! Keep your faith in Jesus throughout your life! You have come to share in Jesus's glory if, indeed, you hold your conviction firmly to the end of your life! Amen.

Today, Believers are being issued a warning! It is not enough to speak your belief in Jesus at one time in your life, but allow the evil in the world to turn you to living a life of disbelief! The same faith you had in Jesus that led you to accept Him, must be the same faith in Him at the end of your life! Amen again! And if you are living a life of sin, and ignoring your faith in Jesus, you are showing Jesus that you do not believe in Him! Your faith in Jesus begins with your acceptance of Him, but you must also have that faith in Jesus to the end of your life! God views your commitment to Jesus by how you live! The same faith you had in Jesus that led you to accept Him, must be the same faith in Him at the end of your life! You have been warned, and you are being encouraged! Keep your faith in Jesus throughout your life! You have come to share in Jesus's glory if, indeed, you hold your conviction firmly to the end of your life! Amen.

Day 185

Jesus told this parable: "A man had a fig tree growing in his vineyard, and he went to look for fruit on it, but did not find any.

So he said the man who took care of the vineyard, 'For 3 years now I've been coming to look for fruit on this fig tree, and haven't found any. Cut it down! Why should it use up the soil?'

'Sir,' the man replied, 'leave it alone for one more year, and I will dig around it and fertilize it. If it bears fruit next year, fine! If not, then cut it down.'"

(Luke 13:6-9)

In today's Scripture, the great servant of Jesus, the author Luke, shares a parable that Jesus spoke about the need for people to repent (and accept Jesus) or perish. In this particular passage, Jesus is guiding His servants about ministering to those individuals who have not repented, even though the Gospel of Jesus has been spoken to them. Our guidance is to not give up on these people, and continue to teach them, but at some point, the servant of Jesus must move on to teach others, so that other people have the chance to hear the Gospel of Jesus and repent! Amen! Jesus knows that not everyone will repent when we think they have had enough time hearing the Word, and there are times that His servant may want to give up on them, but Jesus is encouraging us to continue to teach them. But at some point, move on to someone else! For you should not use up all your "water and fertilizer" on a tree that will not bear fruit! Amen again! Our Scripture begins with, **Jesus told this parable: "A man had a fig tree growing in his vineyard, and he went to look for fruit on it, but did not find any. So he said the man who took care of the vineyard, 'For 3 years now I've been coming to look for fruit on this fig tree, and haven't found any. Cut it down!"** There are times when each servant of Jesus will work and teach people the Gospel of Jesus, and they will not accept Jesus! You will be frustrated, but do not give up! Not yet! Amen! Our Word gives this guidance to the servants of Jesus, through the response of the servant in this parable, **'Sir,' the man replied, 'leave it alone for one more year, and I will dig around it and fertilize it. If it bears fruit next year, fine!'** When someone does not accept Jesus, even though they have had ample opportunity through your teaching, go to God and ask for Him for more time, and His help! Seek help from God, before you give up on someone! Amen again! However, the Word of God says about the tree (person) who is given more time that if they bear fruit (repent and accept Jesus), fine, **"If not, then cut it down.'"** At some point, the servant of Jesus has to move on, for that person has had ample opportunity to accept Jesus. So move on! At that point, the servant of Jesus has done what Jesus called them to do! Hallelujah! Move on! Amen.

Today, our Scripture is speaking to the servants of Jesus Christ. There will be times that you have brought the Word of God and the Gospel of Jesus Christ to a person, and that person has not yet accepted Jesus. Luke shares a parable that Jesus spoke regarding the expectations of His servants. Jesus is guiding His servants about ministering to those individuals who have not repented, even though the Gospel of Jesus has been spoken to them. Our guidance is to not give up on these people and continue to teach them, but at some point, the servant of Jesus must move on to teach others so that other people have the chance to hear the Gospel of Jesus and repent! Amen! Jesus knows that not everyone will repent when they hear the Gospel, and that His servant may want to give up on them, but Jesus is encouraging us to continue to teach them. But at some point, move on to someone else! For you should not use up all your "water and fertilizer" on a tree that will not bear fruit! Amen again! Our Scripture begins with, **Jesus told this parable: "A man had a fig tree growing in his vineyard, and he went to look for fruit on it, but did not find any. So he said the man who took care of the vineyard, 'For 3 years now, I've been coming to look for fruit on this fig tree, and haven't found any. Cut it down!"** There are times when each servant of Jesus will work and teach people the Gospel of Jesus, and they will not accept Jesus! You will be frustrated, but do not give up! Not yet! Amen! Yes, you have given that person ample time, and you have done what Jesus has asked you to do for some time. You have had enough! But do not give up on them yet! Amen! Seek help from God, before you give up on someone! Amen again! And if they accept Jesus, fine! But if they do not accept Jesus after all that, then move on! At that point, the servant of Jesus has done what Jesus called them to do! Hallelujah! Move on! Amen.

Today, our Word is speaking to the servants of Jesus Christ. There will be times when you have brought the Word of God and the Gospel of Jesus Christ to a person, and that person has not yet accepted Jesus. In this parable, Jesus spoke about His expectations of His servants. Jesus is guiding His servants about ministering to those individuals who have not repented, even though the Gospel of Jesus has been spoken to them. Do not give up on them yet! Continue to teach them, but at some point, you must move on to teach others, so that other people have the chance to hear the Gospel of Jesus and repent! Amen! Jesus knows that not everyone will repent when they hear the Gospel, and that His servant may want to give up on them, but Jesus is encouraging us to continue to teach them. But at some point, move on to someone else! Do not use all your servant time fertilizing a tree that will not bear fruit! Amen again! There are times when each servant of Jesus will work and teach people the Gospel of Jesus, and they will not accept Jesus! You will be frustrated, but do not give up! Not yet! Amen! Our Word gives this guidance to the servants of Jesus, through the response of the servant in this parable, **'Sir,' the man replied, 'leave it alone for one more year, and I will dig around it and fertilize it. If it bears fruit next year, fine!'** When someone does not accept Jesus, even though they have had ample opportunity through your teaching, go to God and ask for Him for more time, and His help! Seek help from God, before you give up on someone! Amen again! Ask for guidance from the Holy Spirit that may give you a new way to present the Gospel in a way that moves that person to repent! Don't give up yet, pray and keep teaching. And if they accept Jesus, fine! But if they do not accept Jesus after all that, then move on! At that point, the servant of Jesus has done what Jesus called them to do! Hallelujah! Move on! Amen.

Today, the Word of God is speaking to the servants of Jesus Christ. There will be times when you have brought the Word of God and the Gospel of Jesus Christ to a person, and that person has not yet accepted Jesus. In this parable, Jesus is speaking to His servants. Jesus is guiding His servants about those individuals who will not repent, even though you have taught them over and over again, the Gospel of Jesus Christ. Still, do not give up on them yet! Continue to teach them, but at some point, you must move on to teach others, so that others have the chance to hear the Gospel of Jesus and repent! Amen! Jesus knows that not everyone will repent when they hear the Gospel, but Jesus is encouraging you to continue to teach them. But at some point, move on to someone else! Do not use all your servant time fertilizing a tree that will not bear fruit! Amen again! There are times when each servant of Jesus will work and teach people the Gospel of Jesus, and they will not accept Jesus! You will be frustrated, but do not give up! Not yet! Amen! When someone does not accept Jesus, even though they have had ample opportunity through your teaching, go to God and ask for Him for more time, and His help! Seek help from God, before you give up on someone! Amen again! However, the Word of God says about the tree (person) who is given more time that if they bear fruit (repent and accept Jesus), fine, **"If not, then cut it down.'"** At some point, the servant of Jesus has to move on, for that person has had ample opportunity to accept Jesus. God gives each person free will to make the decision to accept Jesus, or not to accept Jesus. So move on! At that point, the servant of Jesus has done what Jesus called them to do! Hallelujah! Move on! Amen.

Today, Jesus is speaking to His servants. Jesus knows that not everyone will repent when they hear the Gospel, and that His servant may want to give up on them, but Jesus is encouraging us to continue to teach them. But at some point, move on to someone else! Do not use all your servant time fertilizing a tree that will not bear fruit! Amen again! There are times when each servant of Jesus will work and teach people the Gospel of Jesus, and they will not accept Jesus! You will be frustrated, but do not give up! Not yet! Continue to teach them. Pray for them! Seek help from God and guidance from the Holy Spirit! Do all those things! And if they accept Jesus, fine! But if they do not accept Jesus after all that, then move on! At that point, the servant of Jesus has done what Jesus called them to do! Hallelujah! Move on! Amen.

Day 186

At this time, Jesus says, "I praise you, Father (God), Lord of Heaven and Earth, because You have hidden these things from the wise and learned, and revealed to little children (Believers).

Yes, Father, for this is what You were pleased to do.

All things have been committed to Me by My Father. No one knows the Son (Jesus) except the Father (God), and no one knows the Father except the Son, and those to whom the Son chooses to reveal Him.

Come to Me (the Son), all you who are weary and burdened (from sin), and I will give you rest (peace from the Father)."

(Matthew 11:25-28)

In today's Scripture, the great servant of Jesus, the apostle Matthew, shares what he witnessed when Jesus preached to the people in the towns of Galilee. In this particular passage of Jesus teaching the people, Jesus reveals to the crowd that the Father, Almighty God, is revealed in His Son, Jesus! Amen! And that those who come to God's Son, would receive rest through His Son from God. Amen again! Hallelujah! This message is for all people, and Jesus taught it Himself! Glory Hallelujah! Or Scripture begins with, **At this time, Jesus says, "I praise you, Father (God), Lord of Heaven and Earth, because You have hidden these things from the wise and learned, and revealed to little**

children (Believers). Yes, Father, for this is what You were pleased to do." Jesus first gives glory to God, and reveals that it is God's plan that the Gospel of Jesus be revealed and that it would only be revealed to those who gave themselves to Jesus! For faith in Jesus pleases God! Amen! Our Word then has Jesus giving an invitation to all people to be saved, by coming through Him, saying, **"All things have been committed to Me by My Father. No one knows the Son (Jesus) except the Father (God), and no one knows the Father except the Son, and those to whom the Son chooses to reveal Him. Come to Me (the Son), all you who are weary and burdened (from sin),"** This is the full revelation of God's plan for redemption and salvation! Hallelujah! Each person has an opportunity to be saved, but you can only be saved by acknowledging that Jesus is the Son of God, and repenting your sins to Him! Amen again! And the Word of God concludes the invitation with this everlasting promise from the mouth of Jesus. That if you come to Him and repent your sins, Jesus will take the burdens of your sins off of you, and promises you, **"and I will give you rest (peace from the Father)."** Glory! Jesus will give you eternal rest! Jesus will redeem you to God, and God will give you peace, by guaranteeing you everlasting life with Him! Glory Hallelujah! This is the Gospel of Jesus Christ! Amen! This is the New Covenant of God! This is God's plan for you! And hallelujah, the Father, Almighty God, is revealed in His Son, Jesus! Amen.

Today, our Scripture is speaking to everyone. God has a plan of redemption and everlasting glory with Him, for all that believe that Jesus is His Son, and for those that repent their sins to Jesus. Hallelujah! This is the Gospel of Jesus Christ! Amen! This is the New Covenant of God! This is God's plan for you! And hallelujah, the Father, Almighty God, is revealed in His Son, Jesus! Glory Hallelujah! The apostle Matthew shares what he witnessed when Jesus preached to the people in the towns of Galilee. Jesus reveals to the crowd that the Father, Almighty God, is revealed in His Son, Jesus! Amen! And that those who come to God's Son, would receive rest through His Son, from God. Amen again! Hallelujah! This message is for all people, and Jesus taught it Himself! Glory Hallelujah! Or Scripture begins with, **At this time, Jesus says, "I praise you, Father (God), Lord of Heaven and Earth, because You have hidden these things from the wise and learned, and revealed to little children (Believers). Yes, Father, for this is what You were pleased to do."** Jesus first gives glory to God, and reveals that it is God's plan that the Gospel of Jesus be revealed, and that it would only be revealed to those who gave themselves to Jesus! For faith in Jesus pleases God! Amen! This is the Gospel of Jesus Christ! Amen! This is the New Covenant of God! This is God's plan for you! And hallelujah, the Father, Almighty God, is revealed in His Son, Jesus! Amen.

Today, our Word is speaking to everyone. God has a plan of redemption and everlasting glory with Him, for all that believe that Jesus is His Son, and for those that repent their sins to Jesus. Hallelujah! This is the Gospel of Jesus Christ! Amen! This is the New Covenant of God! This is God's plan for you! And hallelujah, the Father, Almighty God, is revealed in His Son, Jesus! Glory Hallelujah! Matthew shares what he witnessed when Jesus preached to the people in the towns of Galilee. Jesus reveals to the crowd that the Father, Almighty God, is revealed in His Son, Jesus! Amen! And that those who come to God's Son, would receive rest through His Son, from God. Amen again! Hallelujah! This message is for all people, and Jesus taught it Himself! Glory Hallelujah! Jesus first gives glory to God, and reveals that it is God's plan that the Gospel of Jesus be revealed, and that it would only be revealed to those who gave themselves to Jesus! For faith in Jesus pleases God! Amen! Our Word then has Jesus giving an invitation to all people to be saved, by coming through Him, saying, **"All things have been committed to Me by My Father. No one knows the Son (Jesus) except the Father (God), and no one knows the Father except the Son, and those to whom the Son chooses to reveal Him. Come to Me (the Son), all you who are weary and burdened (from sin),"** This is the full revelation of God's plan for redemption and salvation! Hallelujah! Each person has an opportunity to be saved, but you can only be saved by acknowledging that Jesus is the Son of God, and repenting your sins to Him! Amen again! This is the Gospel of Jesus Christ! Amen! This is the New Covenant of God! This is God's plan for you! And hallelujah, the Father, Almighty God, is revealed in His Son, Jesus! Amen.

Today, the Word of God is speaking to everyone. God has a plan of redemption and everlasting glory with Him, for all that believe that Jesus is His Son, and for those that repent their sins to Jesus. Hallelujah! This is the Gospel of Jesus Christ! Amen! This is the New Covenant of God! This is God's plan for you! And hallelujah, the Father, Almighty God, is revealed in His Son, Jesus! Glory Hallelujah! Jesus is revealing to you that the Father, Almighty God, is revealed in His Son, Jesus! Amen! And that if you come to God's Son, then you will receive rest through His Son, from God. Amen again! Hallelujah! This message is for you, and Jesus taught it Himself! Glory Hallelujah! Jesus first gives glory to God, and reveals that it is God's plan that the Gospel of Jesus be revealed, and that it would only be revealed to those who gave themselves to Jesus! For faith in Jesus pleases God! Amen! This is the full revelation of God's plan for redemption and salvation! Hallelujah! Each person has an opportunity to be saved, but you can only be saved by acknowledging that Jesus is the Son of God, and repenting your sins to Him! Amen again! And the Word of God concludes the invitation with this everlasting promise from the mouth of Jesus. That if you come to Him and repent your sins, Jesus will take the burdens of your sins off of you, and promises you, **"and I will give you rest (peace from the Father)."** Glory! Jesus will give you eternal rest! Jesus will redeem you to God, and God will give you peace, by guaranteeing you everlasting life with Him! Glory Hallelujah! This is the Gospel of Jesus Christ! Amen! This is the New Covenant of God! This is God's plan for you! And hallelujah, the Father, Almighty God, is revealed in His Son, Jesus! Amen.

Today, Jesus is speaking to you! God has a plan of redemption and everlasting glory with Him, for all that believe that Jesus is His Son, and for those that repent their sins to Jesus. Hallelujah! This message is for you, and Jesus taught it Himself! Glory Hallelujah! Jesus first gives glory to God, and reveals that it is God's plan that the Gospel of Jesus be revealed, and that it would only be revealed to those who gave themselves to Jesus! For faith in Jesus pleases God! Amen! This is the full revelation of God's plan for redemption and salvation! Hallelujah! Each person has an opportunity to be saved, but you can only be saved by acknowledging that Jesus is the Son of God, and repenting your sins to Him! Amen again! Jesus will give you eternal rest! Jesus will redeem you to God, and God will give you peace, by guaranteeing you everlasting life with Him! Glory Hallelujah! This is the Gospel of Jesus Christ! Amen! This is the New Covenant of God! This is God's plan for you! And hallelujah, the Father, Almighty God, is revealed in His Son, Jesus! Amen.

Day 187

"To those who through the righteousness of our God and Savior Jesus Christ have received a faith as precious as ours:

Grace and peace be yours in abundance through the knowledge of God and of Jesus our Lord.

His divine power has given us everything we need for a godly life through our knowledge of Him, who called us by His own glory and goodness.

Through these He has given us His very great and precious promises, so that through them you may participate in the divine nature, having escaped the corruption in the world caused by evil desires."

(2 Peter 1:1-4)

In today's Scripture, the great servant of Jesus, the apostle Peter, is writing to Believers to confirm that each believer has been called, and that through Jesus, God has made available everything that we need to live a holy life while still on this earth. Amen! And through the grace and power of God, each Believer has been given promises by God, so that we can participate in God's divine righteousness that keeps us separate from those who live in evil! Amen again! We need to understand that each Believer is called to accept Jesus! And God has given each Believer His divine power, in the form of His Holy Spirit! And through the promise of

God, each Believer is set apart from the world, having escaped the punishment of eternal death through their faith in Jesus Christ! Glory Hallelujah! As a Believer, you have been called, you have been given power from God, and you have been set apart from the world, so that you may walk a life with God, and have eternal life with God! Glory Hallelujah! Our Scripture says to Believers, **"To those who through the righteousness of our God and Savior Jesus Christ have received a faith as precious as ours:"** This message is for Believers! You have been chosen by God to know Jesus, and God has given you the capacity of faith! Amen! Our Word continues speaking to Believers, saying, **"Grace and peace be yours in abundance through the knowledge of God and of Jesus our Lord. His divine power has given us everything we need for a godly life through our knowledge of Him, who called us by His own glory and goodness."** This message is for Believers! God gives you His grace, and His peace through your faith in Him through Jesus Christ! And God also gives you His power to live a righteous life based on the knowledge of His Word. Amen again! And the Word of God confirms to Believers, that, **"Through these, He has given us His very great and precious promises, so that through them you may participate in the divine nature, having escaped the corruption in the world caused by evil desires."** This message is for Believers! God has given you great promises! God allows for you to participate in His divine nature, through the gift of His Holy Spirit in you! God blesses you with abundance because of His love for you! And God forgives you of your sins in the name of Jesus, keeping you from everlasting corruption in Hell! Glory Hallelujah! This message is for Believers! Amen.

Today, our Scripture is speaking to Believers. The apostle Peter is writing to Believers to confirm that each believer has been called, and that through Jesus, God has made available everything that we need to live a holy life while still on this earth. Amen! And through the grace and power of God, each Believer has been given promises by God, so that we can participate in God's divine righteousness that keeps us separate from those who live in evil! Amen again! Each Believer is called to accept Jesus! And God has given each Believer His divine power, in the form of His Holy Spirit! And each Believer is set apart from the world, having escaped the punishment of eternal death through their faith in Jesus Christ! Glory Hallelujah! As a Believer, you have been called, you have been given power from God, and you have been set apart from the world, so that you may walk a life with God, and have eternal life with God! Glory Hallelujah! Our Scripture says to Believers, **"To those who through the righteousness of our God and Savior Jesus Christ have received a faith as precious as ours:"** This message is for Believers! You have been chosen by God to know Jesus, and God has given you the capacity of faith! Amen! It is God's plan, through His mercy and righteousness, that you heard the Gospel of Jesus! God chose you to hear His Word! It was God's voice that brought you to Jesus! God! It was not you, your Mother, the Pastor, or any other human!

God chose you, and God gave you an understanding of His Word, and God prompted you to accept Jesus! Hallelujah! It was not even the Holy Spirit, because you did not have the Holy Spirit in you at that time. It was God! Glory to God! This message is for Believers! Amen.

Today, our Word is speaking to Believers. Peter writes that each believer has been called, and that through Jesus, God has made available everything that we need to live a holy life on this earth. Amen! And through the grace and power of God, each Believer has been given promises by God, so that we can participate in God's divine righteousness that keeps us separate from those who live in evil! Amen again! Each Believer is holy to God! Each Believer is called to accept Jesus! And God has given each Believer His divine power, in the form of His Holy Spirit! And each Believer is set apart from the world, having escaped the punishment of eternal death through their faith in Jesus Christ! Glory Hallelujah! This message is for Believers! You have been chosen by God to know Jesus, and God has given you the capacity of faith! Amen! So that you may walk a life with God, and have eternal life with God! Glory Hallelujah! Our Word continues speaking to Believers, saying, **"Grace and peace be yours in abundance through the knowledge of God and of Jesus our Lord. His divine power has given us everything we need for a godly life through our knowledge of Him, who called us by His own glory and goodness."** This message is for Believers! God gives you His grace, and His peace through your faith in Him through Jesus Christ! And God also gives you His power to live a righteous life based on the knowledge of His Word. Amen again! How wonderful it is that God gives you His grace! How amazing it is that God gives you His peace! And with God's grace and peace comes His power to live your life according to His righteousness! Hallelujah! Through your faith in Jesus, you receive the knowledge of God! And you have it all because God called you to have it all! Give glory to God! This message is for Believers! Amen.

Today, the Word of God is speaking to Believers. You have been called by God to know Jesus, and through Jesus, God has made available everything that you need to live a holy life on this earth. Amen! And through the grace and power of God, you have been given promises by God, so that you can participate in God's divine righteousness that keeps you separate from those who live in evil! Amen again! You are holy to God! And God has given you His divine power in the form of His Holy Spirit! You have been set apart from the world, having escaped the punishment of eternal death through your faith in Jesus Christ! Glory Hallelujah! This message is for Believers! You have been chosen by God to know Jesus, and God has given you the capacity of faith! Amen! So that you may walk a life with God, and have eternal life with God! Glory Hallelujah! God gives you His grace, and His peace through your faith in Him through Jesus Christ! And God also gives you His power to live a righteous life based on the knowledge of His Word. Amen again! And the Word of God confirms to Believers, that, **"Through these, He has given us His very great and precious promises, so that through them you may participate in the divine nature, having escaped the corruption in the world caused by evil desires."** This message is for Believers! God has given you great promises! God allows for you to participate in His divine nature, through the gift of His Holy Spirit in you! God blesses you with abundance because of His love for you! And God forgives you of your sins in the name of Jesus, keeping you from everlasting corruption in Hell! Glory Hallelujah! God even lives in you, through His Holy Spirit that He put in you! Glory, glory, glory, give God all the glory! This message is for Believers! Amen.

Today, this message is for Believers! If you are a Believer in Jesus Christ, you are a Believer because God chose you to believe! Amen! God gave you the capacity to understand the Gospel of Jesus, and to have faith in the promise of God! Amen again! And because of your faith in Jesus, God gives you an abundance of His grace, and His peace! Hallelujah! God has put His Holy Spirit inside of you to guide you and protect you! Glory Hallelujah! And because you believe in Jesus Christ as your Lord and Savior, God has made you promises! You can live this life in the righteousness of God, and you will escape the penalty of sin, while joining Jesus in the eternal Kingdom of God! Glory! This message is for Believers! Amen.

Day 188

"For this very reason, make every effort to add to your faith goodness, and to goodness, knowledge,

and to knowledge, self-control, and to self-control, perseverance, and to perseverance, godliness,

and to godliness, mutual affection, and to mutual affection, love.

For if you possess these qualities in increasing measure, they will keep you from being ineffective and unproductive in your knowledge of our Lord Jesus Christ.

But whoever does not have them is nearsighted and blind, forgetting that they have been cleansed from their past sins."

(2 Peter 1:5-9)

In today's Scripture, the great servant of Jesus, the apostle Peter, is writing to Believers to confirm that each believer has been called, and that through Jesus, God has made available everything that we need to live a holy life while still on this earth. Amen! And through the grace and power of God, each Believer has been given promises by God, so that we can participate in God's divine righteousness that keeps us separate from those who live in evil! Amen again! And through the promise of God, each Believer is set apart from the world, having escaped the punishment of eternal death through their faith in Jesus Christ! Glory Hallelujah! However, Peter also guides each Believer that God expects us to grow in our walk in faith with Jesus, to mature as Christians. Amen! In fact, Peter lists the virtues that will produce a well-rounded and fruitful Christian life. Amen again! Our Scripture says to Believers that because God has set us apart for Him through our faith in Jesus, that, **"For this very reason, make every effort to add to your faith goodness, and to goodness, knowledge, and to knowledge, self-control, and to self-control, perseverance, and to perseverance, godliness, and to godliness, mutual affection, and to mutual affection, love."** This message is for Believers! You have been chosen by God to know Jesus, and God has given you the capacity of faith! Now God expects you to grow through your faith in Jesus! Amen! Our Word continues speaking to Believers, saying, **"For if you possess these qualities in increasing measure, they will keep you from being ineffective and unproductive in your knowledge of our Lord Jesus Christ."** This message is for Believers! Although your faith in Jesus gives you many blessings from God, including His Holy Spirit, you still need to grow so that your faith will begin to bring fruit to the vine that is Jesus! Amen again! And the Word of God gives this warning to Believers, **"But whoever does not have them is nearsighted and blind, forgetting that they have been cleansed from their past sins."** This message is for Believers! If you do not grow in your faith and walk with Jesus, you are in danger of losing your strength to fight against the temptation of sins, and could fall back to your evil way of life. Tell the truth! This message is for Believers! Amen.

Today, our Scripture is speaking to Believers. Peter tells us that each Believer has been called by God to know Jesus, and through Jesus, God has made available everything that we need to live a holy life while still on this earth. Amen! Through the grace and power of God, each Believer has been given promises by God, so that we can participate in God's divine righteousness that keeps us separate from those who live in evil! Amen again! And each Believer is set apart from the world, having escaped the punishment of eternal death through their faith in Jesus Christ! Glory Hallelujah! However, Peter also guides each Believer that God expects us to grow in our walk in faith with Jesus, to mature as Christians. Amen! In fact, Peter lists the virtues that will produce a well-rounded and fruitful Christian life. Amen again! Our Scripture says to Believers that because God has set us apart for Him through our faith in Jesus, that, **"For this very reason, make every effort to add to your faith goodness, and to goodness, knowledge, and to knowledge, self-control, and to self-control, perseverance, and to perseverance, godliness, and to godliness, mutual affection, and to mutual affection, love."** This message is for Believers! You have been chosen by God to know Jesus, and God has given you the capacity of faith! Now God expects you to grow through your faith in Jesus! Amen! And when you grow through prayer and studying the Word of God, you will spiritually grow these virtues that will help you in life, and to attract other people to Jesus! Now that is growing in your faith! Hallelujah! So, although your faith in Jesus gives you many blessings from God, including His Holy Spirit, you still need to grow so that your faith will begin to bring fruit to the vine that is Jesus! Amen again! This message is for Believers! Amen.

Today, our Word is speaking to Believers. Each Believer has been called by God to know Jesus, and God has made available everything that we need to live a holy life on this earth. Amen! Each Believer has been given promises by God, so that we can participate in God's divine righteousness that separates us from those who live in evil! Amen again! Each Believer is holy to God! And God has given each Believer His divine power, in the form of His Holy Spirit! For each Believer is set apart from the world, having escaped the punishment of eternal death through their faith in Jesus Christ! Glory Hallelujah! This message is for Believers! You have been chosen by God to know Jesus, and have faith in Jesus, so that you may walk a life with God, and have eternal life with God! Glory Hallelujah! However, God expects each of us to grow in our walk in faith with Jesus, and to mature as Christians. Amen! Our Word continues speaking to Believers, saying, **"For if you possess these qualities in increasing measure, they will keep you from being ineffective and unproductive in your knowledge of our Lord Jesus Christ."** This message is for Believers! Although your faith in Jesus gives you many blessings from God, including His Holy Spirit, you still need to grow so that your faith will begin to bring fruit to the vine that is Jesus! Amen again! Give glory to God! Our Word does not suggest that you need to focus on building each of these virtues. However, our guidance is to focus on growing our knowledge of God's Word, and that the focus on His Word will drive us to possess the qualities to be productive as a servant of Jesus Christ! Hallelujah! And your increased knowledge of the Word, and the qualities that come from that knowledge, will affect the way you live your life! And that will make you an effective disciple of Christ! Glory Hallelujah! Although your faith in Jesus gives you many blessings from God, including His Holy Spirit, you still need to grow so that your faith will begin to bring fruit to the vine that is Jesus! Amen again! This message is for Believers! Amen.

Today, the Word of God is speaking to Believers. Each Believer has been called by God to know Jesus, and God has made available everything that we need to live a holy life on this earth. Amen! Each Believer has been given promises by God, so that we can participate in God's divine righteousness that separates us from those who live in evil! Amen again! Each Believer is holy to God! And God has given each Believer His divine power, in the form of His Holy Spirit! For each Believer is set apart from the world, having escaped the punishment of eternal death through their faith in Jesus Christ! Glory Hallelujah! This message is for Believers! You have been chosen by God to know Jesus! Glory Hallelujah! However, God expects each of us to grow in our walk in faith with Jesus, and to mature as Christians. Amen! So that you may walk a life with God, and have eternal life with God! Glory Hallelujah! Although your faith in Jesus gives you many blessings from God, including His Holy Spirit, you still need to grow so that your faith will begin to bring fruit to the vine that is Jesus! Amen again! And the Word of God gives this warning to Believers, **"But whoever does not have them is nearsighted and blind, forgetting that they have been cleansed from their past sins."** This message is for Believers! If you do not grow in your faith and walk with Jesus, you are in danger of losing your strength to fight against the temptation of sins, and could fall back to your evil way of life. Tell the truth! When a Believer does not grow in their faith, the enemy can attack, and close your eyes to the Truth that is Jesus! And sin can once again take over your life! And that is the truth! So, although your faith in Jesus gives you many blessings from God, including His Holy Spirit, you still need to grow so that your faith will begin to bring fruit to the vine that is Jesus! Amen again! This message is for Believers! Amen.

Today, this message is for Believers! If you are a Believer in Jesus Christ, God gives you an abundance of His grace, and His peace! Hallelujah! God has put His Holy Spirit inside of you to guide you and protect you! Glory Hallelujah! And because you believe in Jesus Christ as your Lord and Savior, God has made you promises! However, God expects us to grow in our walk in faith with Jesus, and to mature as Christians. Amen! And your growth in your faith will develop virtues that will produce a well-rounded and fruitful Christian life. But if you do not grow in your faith and walk with Jesus, you are in danger of losing your strength to fight against the temptation of sins, and you could fall back to your evil way of life. Amen! Although your faith in Jesus gives you many blessings from God, including His Holy Spirit, you still need to grow so that your faith will begin to bring fruit to the vine that is Jesus! Amen again! This message is for Believers! Amen.

Day 189

"Jesus entered Jericho and was passing through.

A man was there by the name of Zacchaeus, he was a chief tax collector and was wealthy.

He wanted to see who Jesus was, but because he was short, he could not see over the crowd.

So he ran ahead and climbed a sycamore fig tree to see Him, since Jesus was coming that way.

When Jesus reached the spot, He looked up and said to him, 'Zacchaeus come down immediately, I must stay at your house today.'

So Zacchaeus came down at once and welcomed Him gladly."

(Luke 19:1-6)

In today's Scripture, the great servant of Jesus, the author Luke, is writing about the time that Jesus noticed a man that was trying to see Him, but could not because he was small, and the crowd to see Jesus blocked him. Yet, the man was determined to see Jesus! Amen. Our Scripture begins with, **"Jesus entered Jericho and was passing through."** Jesus will give you an opportunity to see Him, for Jesus will pass through with His presence in your life! Amen! Our Word continues and tells us, **"A man was there by the name of Zacchaeus, he was a chief tax collector and was**

wealthy. He wanted to see who Jesus was, but because he was short, he could not see over the crowd. So he ran ahead and climbed a sycamore fig tree to see Him, since Jesus was coming that way." When Jesus is in your presence, do whatever it takes to see Him! Do not let Jesus pass you by! Amen again! And the Word of God proclaims to us, that, **"When Jesus reached the spot, He looked up and said to him, 'Zacchaeus come down immediately, I must stay at your house today.' So Zacchaeus came down at once and welcomed Him gladly."** When Jesus sees that you truly want to be with Him, He will call you, and stay with you! Hallelujah! Jesus wants you to want Him! And when He sees your complete desire to be with Him, He will call you and stay with you! Glory Hallelujah! Now, what will you do to see Jesus when He is passing through in your life? Amen.

Today, our Scripture is speaking to everyone! There will be times in your life when Jesus comes by to see you. He will make Himself available to you. For those who do not know Jesus as their Savior, Jesus is passing through so that you can acknowledge Him, and be saved! Amen! For Believers, Jesus is passing through so that you can acknowledge Him, and serve Him! Amen again! But, you must seek Jesus when He is passing through! You must have a desire to see Him! And when Jesus sees your desire to be with Him, He will call you and stay with you! Glory Hallelujah! The author Luke is writing about the time that Jesus noticed a man that was trying to see Him, but could not because he was small, and the crowd to see Jesus blocked him. Yet, the man was determined to see Jesus! Amen. Our Scripture begins with, **"Jesus entered Jericho and was passing through."** Jesus will give you an opportunity to see Him, for Jesus will pass through with His presence in your life! Amen! Jesus will make Himself available to you, for He will pass through. He will place Himself in your life so that you can see Him. But you have to do something! You have to make the first step to Him! Amen! If you lay back, and do not seek Jesus, Jesus will just keep on passing through! But make no mistake about it; Jesus will bring His presence! Amen again! Now, what will you do to see Jesus when He is passing through in your life? Amen.

Today, our Word is speaking to everyone! There will be times in your life when Jesus comes by to see you. He will make Himself available to you. For those who do not know Jesus as their Savior, Jesus is passing through so that you can acknowledge Him, and be saved! Amen! For Believers, Jesus is passing through so that you can acknowledge Him, and serve Him! Amen again! But, you must seek Jesus when He is passing through! You must have a desire to see Him! Jesus wants to see that you have a desire to be with Him! Jesus wants you to be desperate to have Him in your life! And when Jesus sees that you truly want to see Him, He will call you and stay with you! Glory Hallelujah! Luke writes about the time that Jesus noticed a man that was trying to see Him, but could not because he was small, and the crowd to see Jesus blocked him. Jesus will give you an opportunity to see Him, for Jesus will pass through with His presence in your life! Amen! Our

Word continues, and tells us, "**A man was there by the name of Zacchaeus, he was a chief tax collector and was wealthy. He wanted to see who Jesus was, but because he was short, he could not see over the crowd. So he ran ahead and climbed a sycamore fig tree to see Him, since Jesus was coming that way.**" When Jesus is in your presence, do whatever it takes to see Him! Do not let Jesus pass you by! Amen again! Jesus is there for you, He is right there! But you have to let Him see your desire to be with Him! Jesus is not impressed by what you have, He will not notice you for that! And Jesus does not care how hard it is for you to see Him, your desire to be with Him should make you do whatever it takes to have Jesus notice you! Zacchaeus, a short man, climbed a sycamore fig tree. Sycamore fig trees are thirty to forty feet tall! And Zacchaeus climbed it, to see Jesus! How tall is your tree? What will you do to see Jesus! Hallelujah! Jesus is right there! Jesus is in your presence! Glory is right there for you! Glory Hallelujah! Now, what will you do to see Jesus when He is passing through in your life? Amen.

Today, the Word of God is speaking to everyone! There will be times in your life when Jesus comes by to see you. He will make Himself available to you. If you do not know Jesus as your Savior, Jesus is passing through so that you can acknowledge Him, and be saved! Amen! And if you are already a Believer, Jesus is passing through so that you can acknowledge Him, and serve Him! Amen again! But, you must seek Jesus when He is passing through! You must have a desire to see Him! Jesus wants to see that you have a desire to be with Him! Jesus wants to know that you will do anything to have Him in your life! And when Jesus sees that you truly want to see Him, He will call you and stay with you! Glory Hallelujah! Jesus will give you an opportunity to see Him, for Jesus will pass through with His presence in your life! Amen! And when Jesus is in your presence, do whatever it takes to see Him! Do not let Jesus pass you by! Amen again! And the Word of God proclaims to us that, **"When Jesus reached the spot, He looked up and said to him, 'Zacchaeus come down immediately, I must stay at your house today.' So Zacchaeus came down at once and welcomed Him gladly."** When Jesus sees that you truly want to be with Him, He will call you and stay with you! Hallelujah! Jesus wants you to want Him! And when He sees your complete desire to be with Him, He will call you and stay with you! Glory Hallelujah! There is a reward when Jesus sees you seeking Him! You will be saved by Jesus! Glory! And you will be able to serve Jesus! Glory, Hallelujah! Jesus is right there, and if you seek Him, He will call your name to be with Him! You will have Jesus save you, or you will have Jesus as your Master, and you His servant! Glory, glory, glory! Now, what will you do to see Jesus when He is passing through in your life? Amen.

Today, our Scripture Guidance is for everyone! Jesus will bring His presence into your life. He will make Himself available to you. Amen! You can seek Him, and be saved! Glory! Or will you let the crowd block you? You can do whatever it takes for Him to see you, and serve Him! Hallelujah! Or is your tree too tall to climb?

You are being challenged today, Jesus is coming through. Now, what will you do to see Jesus when He is passing through in your life? Amen.

Day 190

"To those who have been called, who are loved in God the Father, and kept forever in Jesus Christ:

Mercy, peace, and love be yours in abundance."

"Now to Him who is able to keep you from stumbling and to present you before His glorious presence without fault and with great joy,

to the only God our Savior be glory and majesty, power and authority, through Jesus Christ our Lord, before all ages, now and forevermore! Amen."

(Jude1-2 & 24-25)

In today's Scripture, the author Jude, who is possibly the brother of Jesus, writes to Believers to warn them about false teachers who distort the Word of God, to convince Believers that because they have been saved through the blood of Jesus, that they now have a license to sin. That is a lie! Amen! However, that is not the focus of our Scripture Guidance today. Our focus is the greeting that Jude gives to Believers, and the concluding message to Believers. For these are messages that each Believer should give to their fellow Believers! Amen again! As Believers, we should recognize and acknowledge other Believers with a welcome and blessing of love and peace. Hallelujah! And we should depart each other with the encouragement that God is constantly with them through Jesus Christ, and send them off with the protection that only God can give them! Glory Hallelujah! For each Believer is part of a very special family, God's family! So God's love and peace, and His everlasting protection and salvation, is with each Believer always in the name of Jesus! Glory! So we are being encouraged to speak it, and share it with each other! Glory to God! Our Scripture begins with this greeting to each Believer, **"To those who have been called, who are loved in God the Father, and kept forever in Jesus Christ: Mercy, peace, and love be yours in abundance."** Each Believer has been selected by God to receive salvation from God! So greet them by reminding them that God's mercy, peace, and love is with them through their acceptance of Jesus Christ as their Lord and Savior! And this is with them forever! For they are part of God's family! Amen! And the Word says to share this with each Believer when they depart, **"Now to Him who is able to keep you from stumbling, and to present you before His glorious presence without fault and with great joy,"** Remind each Believer of the protection that they have from God, wherever they go in their life, and through salvation! For God is your Father in the name of Jesus, while living on this earth and throughout your eternal life! For they are part of God's family! Amen again! And finally, the Word of God wants each Believer to remind every Believer of who their Father is, **"to the only God our Savior be glory and majesty, power and authority, through Jesus Christ our Lord, before all ages, now and forevermore! Amen."** Through your faith in Jesus, Almighty God is your Father! And it is your Father God who has the power and the authority to keep each Believer with Him always and forever! Glory! For they are part of God's family! Amen.

Today, our Scripture is speaking to Believers. Each and every Believer in Jesus Christ, is part of God's family! And each Believer is being encouraged to acknowledge each other with greetings that are welcoming as members of God's family and to depart with encouragement that reassures God's everlasting protection, as part of God's family. Hallelujah! For they are part of God's family. Glory Hallelujah! As Believers, we should recognize and acknowledge other Believers with a welcome and blessing of love and peace. Hallelujah! For each Believer is part of a very special family, God's family! So God's love and peace is with each Believer always in the name of Jesus! Glory! So we are being encouraged to speak it, and share it with each other! Glory to God! Our Scripture begins with this greeting to each Believer, **"To those who have been called, who are loved in God the Father, and kept forever in Jesus Christ: Mercy, peace and love be yours in abundance."** Each Believer has been selected by God to receive salvation from God! So greet them by reminding them that God's mercy, peace, and love is with them through their acceptance of Jesus Christ as their Lord and Savior! And this is with them forever! For they are part of God's family! Amen! Each Believer was called by God to be in His family! Each Believer is kept forever in God's family through their faith in

Jesus! Hallelujah! Each Believer receives God's mercy and God's peace, and each Believer can welcome each other by acknowledging to them that they have God's blessings in abundance! Glory Hallelujah! So greet your family with love and peace, and send them off with God's protection! After all, they are family! Amen.

Today, our Word is speaking to Believers. Each and every Believer in Jesus Christ, is part of God's family! And each Believer is being encouraged to acknowledge each other with greetings that are welcoming as members of God's family, and to depart with encouragement that reassures God's everlasting protection, as part of God's family. Hallelujah! For they are part of God's family. Glory Hallelujah! As Believers, we should depart each other with the encouragement that God is constantly with them through Jesus Christ, and send them off with the protection that only God can give them! Glory Hallelujah! For each Believer is part of a very special family, God's family! So God's love and peace, and His everlasting protection and salvation, is with each Believer always in the name of Jesus! Glory! So we are being encouraged to speak it, and share it with each other! Glory to God! And the Word says to share this with each Believer when they depart, **"Now to Him who is able to keep your from stumbling, and to present you before His glorious presence without fault and with great joy,"** Remind each Believer of the protection that they have from God, wherever they go in their life, and through salvation! For God is your Father in the name of Jesus, while living on this earth, and throughout your eternal life! For they are part of God's family! Amen again! And it is God who can strengthen you against the temptations of sin. It is God that allow you into His Kingdom and into His presence without fault. And all this is because you have accepted Jesus as your Lord and Savior, just as each and every Believer in Jesus has! Hallelujah! So greet your family with love and peace, and send them off with God's protection! After all, they are family! Amen.

Today, the Word of God is speaking to Believers. Each and every Believer in Jesus Christ, is part of God's family! And each Believer is being encouraged to acknowledge each other with greetings that are welcoming as members of God's family, and to depart with encouragement that reassures God's everlasting protection, as part of God's family. Hallelujah! For they are part of God's family. Glory Hallelujah! And each Believer is part of a very special family, God's family! So God's love and peace, and His everlasting protection and salvation, is with each Believer always in the name of Jesus! Glory! So we are being encouraged to speak it, and share it with each other! Glory to God! And we should remind each Believer of the protection that they have from God, wherever they go in their life, and through salvation! For God is your Father in the name of Jesus, while living on this earth, and throughout your eternal life! For they are part of God's family! Amen again! And finally, the Word of God wants each Believer to remind every Believer of who their Father is, **"to the only God our Savior be glory and majesty, power and authority,**

through Jesus Christ our Lord, before all ages, now and forevermore! Amen." Through your faith in Jesus, Almighty God is your Father! And it is your Father God who has the power and the authority to keep each Believer with Him always and forever! Glory! For they are part of God's family! As you depart from each other, remind each other to live their life focusing on God, who is the only one that will do what He says He will do! Glory! Only God can promise, and authorize His promise to you, and that promise is forever and ever! Glory Hallelujah! Only God! So greet your family with love and peace, and send them off with God's protection! After all, they are family! Amen.

Today, our Scripture Guidance is for Believers. Each and every Believer in Jesus Christ is part of God's family! And going forward, you should welcome your fellow Believer with the acknowledgement of God's peace and love for them, and you should send them off with the comfort of God's everlasting protection and salvation. Hallelujah! Each Believer you talk to, or see, is part of your family, which is part of God's family, through the blood of Jesus Christ!! So greet your family with love and peace, and send them off with God's protection! After all, they are family! Amen.

Day 191

"Praise the Lord, all you servants of the Lord who minister by night in the house of the Lord.

Lift up your hands in the sanctuary and praise the Lord.

May the Lord bless you from Zion, He who is the Maker of Heaven and earth."

(Psalm 134:1-3)

In today's Scripture, the author writes a psalm that is an exchange between the members of the church that leave the Temple (church) of God after an evening worship service, and those servants that God has in place to take care of the church between services. Amen! The members of the church first encourage those who keep the church between services, to continue to praise God in the church, and the psalm also gives a response from the servants of God (Jesus) that care for the church that asks God to continue to bless the church members. Amen again! And this psalm is challenging God's people today! Too many churches conclude their worship services, and the members just leave! We do not give a lot of thought, or prayer for those that will take care of the church between services. Tell the truth! Not only should we thank God for them, and offer prayer for them to remain diligent in doing the work in the church, we should pray that they remember that in the House of God, there should be praise to God! Hallelujah! The Scripture Guidance to Believers, who attend the Worship Service, is that we should leave the House of God in celebration and prayer, encouraging and praying that those who take care of the church, continue to praise God while they are in the House of God! Glory Hallelujah! And in turn, those who take care of the church, who are servants of God (Jesus), should always ask God to continue to bless the church members. Hallelujah again! Our Scripture begins with the church members encouraging the servants of God (Jesus) in the church, saying, **"Praise the Lord, all you servants of the Lord who minister by night in the house of the Lord."** There should always be the praise of God in His house! Not just during the Worship Service! Amen! The Word continues encouraging church members encouraging the workers in the church to praise God, and, **"Lift up your hands in the sanctuary and praise the Lord."** People in God's house should always be excited to praise Him while in His house! And lifting one's hands while praising God shows excitement to God! And not just during the Worship Service! Amen again! And the Word of God concludes with guidance to His servants to ask for blessings for the church members, by responding to them with, **"May the Lord bless you from Zion, He who is the Maker of Heaven and earth."** God's (Jesus) servants should always ask for God to continue to bless His people! For this is part of serving God (Jesus), to seek blessings for His people, every day! Not just during the Worship Service! Hallelujah! Amen.

Today, our Scripture is speaking to the people of God. We are being given an example of guidance that should happen at the end of Worship Service in the House of God. The author writes a psalm that is an exchange between the members of the church that leave the Temple (church) of God after an evening worship service, and those servants that God has in place to take care of the church between services. Amen! The members of the church encourage those who keep the church between services, to continue to praise God in the church between services. Amen again! And this psalm is challenging God's people today! Too many churches conclude their worship services, and the members just leave! We do not give a lot of thought, or prayer for those that will take care of the church between services. Tell the truth! Not only should we thank God for them, we should leave the House of God in celebration and prayer, encouraging, and praying that those who take care of the church, continue to praise God while they are in the House of God! Glory Hallelujah! Our Scripture begins with the church members encouraging the servants of God (Jesus) in the church, saying, **"Praise the Lord, all you servants of the Lord who minister by night in the house of the Lord."** There should always be the praise of God in His house! Not just during the Worship Service! Amen! The people of God in the church are responsible for encouraging praise for God at all times! Even if you are not in the church at all times, you can pray for those that are in the church between Worship Services, taking care of the church! Thank them for their service, and encourage them to keep praising God as they do the work of the church, for they will still be in the House of God! For there should always be praise from people whenever they are in the House of God! Not just during the Worship service! Amen.

Today, our Word is speaking to the people of God. We are being given an example of guidance that should happen at the end of the Worship Service in the House of God. The author writes a psalm that is an exchange between the members of the church and those servants that God has in place to take care of the church. Amen! The members of the church encourage those who keep the church, to continue to praise God while serving in the church, even though the Worship Service is over, and the congregation is gone. Amen again! This psalm is challenging God's people today! Too many churches conclude their worship services, and the members just leave! We do not give a lot of thought, or prayer for those that will take care of the church between services. Tell the truth! We should thank God for them, while encouraging, and praying that those who take care of the church, continue to praise God while they are in the House of God! Glory Hallelujah! For there should always be the praise of God in His house! Not just during the Worship Service! Amen! The Word continues encouraging church members encouraging the workers in the church to praise God, and **"Lift up your hands in the sanctuary and praise the Lord."** People in God's house should always be excited to praise Him while in His house! And lifting one's hands while praising God shows excitement to God! And not just during the Worship

Service! Amen again! God's people should enter His House with excitement! When God's people are in His House, we should be excited to be in His presence! And lifting our hands while praising God shows God we are excited to be in His House, and excited to praise Him! So encourage those that will be in His House taking care of His House between Worship Services, to lift their hands and praise Him! For there should always be excitement in the praise from people whenever they are in the House of God! Not just during the Worship service! Amen.

Today, the Word of God is speaking to the people of God. We are being given an example of guidance that should happen at the end of the Worship Service in the House of God. This psalm is an exchange between the members of the church and those servants that God has in place to take care of the church. Amen! The members of the church should encourage those who keep the church, to continue to praise God while serving in the church, even though the Worship Service is over, and the congregation is gone. Amen again! Too many churches conclude their worship services, and the members just leave! Tell the truth! We should thank God for these servants, while encouraging, and praying that those who take care of the church, continue to praise God while they are in the House of God! Glory Hallelujah! For there should always be the praise of God in His house! Not just during the Worship Service! Amen! People in God's house should always be excited to praise Him while in His house! And lifting one's hands while praising God shows excitement to God! And not just during the

Worship Service! Amen again! And now, the Word of God is challenging those that take care of the church, who are servants of God (Jesus), that you should always ask God to continue to bless the church members. Hallelujah! The Word of God concludes with guidance to His servants to ask for blessings for the church members, by responding to them with, **"May the Lord bless you from Zion, He who is the Maker of Heaven and earth."** God's (Jesus) servants should always ask for God to continue to bless His people! For this is part of serving God (Jesus), to seek blessings for His people, every day! Not just during the Worship Service! Hallelujah! All of God's people should seek blessings from God for all of His people! Because only Almighty God can supply blessings, so seek Him to bless each other! Glory Hallelujah! So when you depart Worship Service, ask God to continue to bless each of His people! For God's people should always ask God to bless His people, every day! Not just during the Worship service! Amen.

Today, our Scripture Guidance is for the people of God. We are being given an example of guidance that should happen at the end of the Worship Service in the House of God. We have a responsibility to encourage people that there should always be praise in the House of God. Not just during the Worship Service! So as you leave Worship Service, remember to encourage others, because there should always be praise of God in His house! Remember to encourage others, because there should always be excitement when we praise God in His house! And remember to always ask God to continue to bless His people, for this is part of serving God (Jesus)! Glory Hallelujah! Amen.

Day 192

"Rejoice in the Lord always. I will say it again: Rejoice!"

"Do not be anxious about anything, but in every situation, by prayer and petition, with Thanksgiving, present your requests to God.

And the peace of God, which transcends all understanding, will guard your hearts and minds in Christ Jesus."

(Philippians 4:4 & 6-7)

In today's Scripture, the great servant of Jesus, the apostle Paul, writes to Believers encouraging each of us to live joyfully in faith, because of their belief in Jesus Christ as their Lord and Savior, that God Almighty will be with them in every circumstance in their life. Amen! This message is only for Believers! All any of us have to do is seek God in prayer with anything that we are going through, and God will give us His peace while we go through it! Amen again! So knowing that, Paul tells us to rejoice! Rejoice in Jesus! Rejoice! For as a Believer, you have something that non-Believers do not have. You have Jesus on your side! This also means that you have Almighty God on your side! Rejoice! And no matter what the situation, you have the peace of God guarding your hearts and minds! Rejoice, give your situations to God, and rejoice! Say it again: Rejoice! Amen! Our Scripture begins by speaking to Believers to, **"Rejoice in the**

Lord always. I will say it again: Rejoice!" Believers have Jesus, and with Jesus, you have benefits from God! Rejoice! Amen! Our Word continues with this guidance to Believers, **"Do not be anxious about anything, but in every situation, by prayer and petition, with thanksgiving, present your requests to God."** Believers have Jesus, and through Jesus, we can speak to Almighty God in every situation. All you have to do is seek Him with Thanksgiving, and ask Him to bring you through your situation. Because with Jesus, you have the benefit of God as your Father! So do not be anxious about anything. Rejoice! Amen again! And the Word of God gives a promise to Believers who seek Him in every situation, **"And the peace of God, which transcends all understanding, will guard your hearts and minds in Christ Jesus."** Believers have Jesus, and Believers will receive the peace of God to guard them from being anxious, about anything! In every situation, no matter what the situation, Believers are guaranteed peace from God, when you present your situations to Him through the name of Jesus! Hallelujah! So do not be anxious about anything. Rejoice!

Today, our Scripture is speaking to Believers. And this message is only for Believers! The apostle Paul writes to Believers encouraging each of us to live joyfully in faith, because of their belief in Jesus Christ as their Lord and Savior... that God Almighty will be with them in every circumstance in their life. Amen! All any Believer has to do is seek God in prayer with anything that we are going through, and God will be faithful to give us His peace while we go through it! Amen again! So rejoice! Rejoice in Jesus! Rejoice! As a Believer, you have something that non-Believers do not have. You have Jesus on your side! This also means that you have Almighty God on your side! Rejoice! And no matter what the situation, you have the peace of God guarding your hearts and minds! Rejoice, give your situations to God, and rejoice! Amen! Our Scripture begins by speaking to Believers to, **"Rejoice in the Lord always. I will say it again: Rejoice!"** Believers have Jesus, and with Jesus, you have benefits from God! Rejoice! Amen! Keep your faith in Jesus always, even under difficult circumstances, or even suffering, because you have Jesus! And Jesus gives you benefits from God that others just do not have! Today, the world is bringing you difficult problems, and quite frankly, man does not have a clue to handle these problems. And people everywhere are anxious! And fear is probably in your heart also! Tell the truth! But still, rejoice! Rejoice that you have Jesus! And hallelujah, with Jesus, you have benefits from God! Glory Hallelujah! So do not be anxious about anything. Rejoice! Amen.

Today, our Word is speaking to Believers. And this message is only for Believers! Believers are being encouraged to live joyfully in faith, knowing that because of your belief in Jesus Christ... that God Almighty will be with you in every circumstance in your life. Amen! All any Believer has to do is seek God in prayer with any situation, and God will be faithful to give us His peace while we go through it! Amen again! So rejoice! Rejoice in Jesus! As a Believer, you have Jesus on your side! Hallelujah! This also means that you have Almighty God on your side! Rejoice! And no matter what the situation, you have the peace of God guarding your hearts and minds! Believers have Jesus, and with Jesus, you have benefits from God! Rejoice! Amen! Our Word continues with this guidance to Believers, **"Do not be anxious about anything, but in every situation, by prayer and petition, with thanksgiving, present your requests to God."** Believers have Jesus, and through Jesus, we can speak to Almighty God in every situation. All you have to do is seek Him with Thanksgiving, and ask Him to bring you through your situation. Because with Jesus, you have the benefit of God as your Father! Do not be anxious about anything. Rejoice! Amen again! God is your Father! And that is why you can have Thanksgiving right now! God is your Father, Almighty God! And all you have to do is take your situation to God your Father, and seek His help! No matter what the situation, and in every situation, take it to God! Hallelujah! Rejoice! You have Jesus, and through Jesus, you can seek God! That is the benefit that you have through your faith in Jesus as your Lord and Savior. You can speak to God in every situation! So do not be anxious about anything. Rejoice! Amen.

Today, the Word of God is speaking to Believers. This message is for you! You are being encouraged to live joyfully in faith, knowing that because of your belief in Jesus Christ, God Almighty will be with you in every circumstance in your life. Amen! All you have to do is seek God in prayer through the name of Jesus for any situation, and God will be faithful to give you His peace while you go through it! Amen again! So rejoice! Rejoice in Jesus! As a Believer, you have Jesus on your side! Hallelujah! And you have Almighty God on your side! So rejoice! And no matter what the situation, you have the peace of God guarding your heart and mind! You have Jesus, and with Jesus, you have benefits from God! Rejoice! Amen! You have Jesus, and through Jesus, you can speak to Almighty God in every situation. All you have to do is seek Him with Thanksgiving, and ask Him to bring you through your situation. Because with Jesus, you have the benefit of God as your Father! Rejoice! Amen again! And the Word of God gives a promise to Believers who seek Him in every situation, **"And the peace of God, which transcends all understanding, will guard your hearts and minds in Christ Jesus."** Believers have Jesus, and Believers will receive the peace of God to guard them from being anxious, about anything! In every situation, no matter what the situation, Believers are guaranteed peace from God, when you present your situations to Him through the name of Jesus! Hallelujah! This does not mean that God will immediately remove the issue that is in your situation, but it does mean that God will be with you, and you will have His peace that will drive away your anxiety! For Believers, just like all people, we will all go through situations. The difference is that you, as a Believer, can have the peace of God, while you go through your situation! Amen! And remember, like all tough situations, this, too, will pass! Do not be anxious about anything! You have Jesus! You have benefits from God! You can speak to God, and give Him your issues, and the peace of God will be with you as you go through your situations! So do not be anxious about anything. Rejoice! Amen.

Today, this message is only for Believers! No matter what the situation, rejoice in the Lord always! Do not be anxious about anything! Just seek God in the name of Jesus, and give your situations to God! And Almighty God, your Father, through the name of Jesus, will take away your anxiety, and replace it with His peace! Glory Hallelujah! For as a Believer, you have something that non-Believers do not have. You have Jesus on your side! So rejoice in the Lord always! I will say it again: Rejoice! Amen.

Day 193

"To the lady (church) chosen by God, and to her children (church members), whom I love in the Truth (Jesus), and not only I, but also all who know the Truth (Jesus),

which lives in us, and will be with us, forever.

Grace, mercy and peace from God the Father, and from Jesus Christ, the Father's Son, will be with us in truth and love.

It has given me great joy to find some of your children (Believers) walking in the Truth, just as the Father (Almighty God) has commanded us."

(2 John 1-4)

In today's Scripture, the great servant of Jesus, the apostle John, writes to a church to encourage the church to stay grounded in their faith that Jesus Christ is the Truth, the only way to forgiveness of sins, and the only Way to redemption and salvation with God! Amen! At that time, just like today, there are people in the church who do not believe the Truth of Jesus, and are in the church to teach against the Truth! Amen again! And John is encouraging each Believer to stay faithful to the Truth, to only speak the Truth, and to turn a deaf ear to those in the church that do not confess the Truth of Jesus. Each Believer must understand that not every member in the church, truly believe that Jesus is the Son of God and Lord and Savior! Tell the truth! So the church, and Believers in the church, are being encouraged to live their life in the Truth, with faith in Jesus! And to have joy and fellowship with other Believers in the church. Hallelujah! But also to be aware, and beware, of those who do not truly speak the truth of Jesus. Our Scripture begins with, **"To the lady (church) chosen by God, and to her children (church members), whom I love in the Truth (Jesus), and not only I, but also all who know the Truth (Jesus), which lives in us, and will be with us, forever."** Always recognize that the church and its leaders are chosen by God to establish and teach the Truth! But know that not all "church members" are Believers! So be aware, and beware! Our Word gives Believers a message of blessings, saying that, **"Grace, mercy and peace from God the Father, and from Jesus Christ, the Father's Son, will be with us in truth and love."** For Believers that truly know Jesus, God gives those Believers His gifts, and He gives them to you in truth and love, through your faith in Jesus! Hallelujah! And the Word of God concludes that when a servant of Jesus sees a congregation of Believers living their life in the Truth of Jesus, they will respond in the same way as the Apostle John, that, **"It has given me great joy to find some of your children (Believers) walking in the Truth, just as the Father (Almighty God) has commanded us."** For a servant of Jesus receives joy in Believers living in the Truth that is Jesus! Glory Hallelujah! Amen. But be aware of those in your church who do not speak, or live, the Truth that is Jesus! For they are out there, and they want to lie in your church! Not all "church members" are Believers! So be aware, and beware! Amen.

Today, our Scripture is speaking to church leaders and Believers in the church. You are being encouraged to stay grounded in your faith that Jesus Christ is the Truth, and the only way to forgiveness of sins, and the only Way to redemption and salvation with God! Amen! And John is encouraging each Believer to stay faithful to the Truth, to only speak the Truth, and to turn a deaf ear to those in the church that do not confess the Truth of Jesus. Today there are people in the church who do not believe the Truth of Jesus, and are in the church to teach against the Truth! Amen again! Each Believer must understand that not every member in the church, truly believes that Jesus is the Son of God and Lord and Savior! So the church, and Believers in the church, are being encouraged to live their life in the Truth, with faith in Jesus! And to have joy and fellowship with other Believers in the church. Hallelujah! But also to be aware, and beware, of those who do not truly speak the truth of Jesus. Our Scripture begins with, **"To the lady (church) chosen by God, and to her children (church members), whom I love in the Truth (Jesus), and not only I, but also all who know the Truth (Jesus), which lives in us, and will be with us, forever."** Always recognize that the church and its leaders are chosen by God to establish and teach the Truth! But know that not all "church members" are Believers! And be aware of those in your church who do not speak, or live, the Truth that is Jesus! You must be aware that there are some people in your church who work for Satan, who are there to lie and disrupt the church from the Truth! For they are out there, and they want to lie in your church! Not all "church members" are Believers! So be aware, and beware! Amen.

Today, our Word is speaking to church leaders and Believers in the church. You are being encouraged to stay grounded in your faith that Jesus Christ is the Truth, and the only way to forgiveness of sins, and the only Way to redemption and salvation with God! Amen! Believers are being encouraged to stay faithful to the Truth, and to only speak the Truth, and to turn a deaf ear to those in the church that do not confess the Truth of Jesus. Amen again! Each Believer must understand that not every member in the church, truly believes that Jesus is the Son of God and Lord and Savior! So the church, and Believers in the church, are being encouraged to live their life in the Truth, with faith in Jesus! And to have joy and fellowship with other Believers in the church. Hallelujah! But also to be aware, and beware, of those who do not truly speak the truth of Jesus. Always recognize that the church and its leaders are chosen by God to establish and teach the Truth! But know that not all "church members" are Believers! So be aware, and beware! Our Word gives Believers a message of blessings, saying that, **"Grace, mercy and peace from God the Father, and from Jesus Christ, the Father's Son, will be with us in truth and love."** For Believers that truly know Jesus, God gives those Believers His gifts, and He gives them to you in truth and love, through your faith in Jesus! Hallelujah! Believers in

Jesus as their Lord and Savior will receive the gift of God's grace! Hallelujah! Believers in Jesus as their Lord and Savior will receive the gift of God's mercy! Glory Hallelujah! And Believers in Jesus as their Lord and Savior will receive the gift of God's peace! Glory! And God gives you these gifts in truth and love, because you believe in Jesus as your Lord and Savior! Glory to God! These gifts go to Believers, not "church members"! Be aware of those in your church who do not speak, or live, the Truth that is Jesus! For they are out there, and they want to lie in your church! Not all "church members" are Believers! So be aware, and beware! Amen.

Today, the Word of God is speaking to church leaders and Believers in the church. You are being encouraged to stay faithful to the Truth, to only speak the Truth, and to turn a deaf ear to those in the church that do not confess the Truth of Jesus. Amen! You must understand that not every member in the church, truly believes that Jesus is the Son of God and Lord and Savior! So you are being encouraged to live your life in the Truth, with faith in Jesus! And to have joy and fellowship with other Believers in the church. Hallelujah! But also to be aware, and beware, of those who do not truly speak the truth of Jesus. Always recognize that the church and its leaders are chosen by God to establish and teach the Truth! But know that not all "church members" are Believers! So be aware, and beware! For Believers that truly know Jesus, God gives those Believers His gifts, and He gives them to you in truth and love, through your faith in Jesus! Hallelujah! And the Word of God concludes that when a servant of Jesus sees a congregation of Believers living their life in the Truth of Jesus, they will respond in the same way as the Apostle John, that, "**It has given me great joy to find some of your children (Believers) walking in the Truth, just as the Father (Almighty God) has commanded us.**" For a servant of Jesus receives joy in Believers living in the Truth that is Jesus! Glory Hallelujah! Amen. And each Believer should find joy in a church congregation that walks and lives according to the Truth that is Jesus! There is great joy in being part of such a church body! Hallelujah! But be aware! Not all "church members" are Believers! So be aware, and beware! Amen.

Today, our Scripture Guidance is for church leaders and Believers in the church. Stay faithful to the Truth, and only speak the Truth, and turn a deaf ear to those in the church that do not confess the Truth of Jesus. Amen! You must understand that not every member in the church, truly believes that Jesus is the Son of God and Lord and Savior! So you are being encouraged to live your life in the Truth, with faith in Jesus! Celebrate and worship in your church! Have joy and fellowship in your church! Hallelujah! Give glory to God in your church! But be aware of those in your church who do not speak, or live, the Truth that is Jesus! For they are out there, and they want to lie in your church! Not all "church members" are Believers! So be aware, and beware! Amen.

Day 194

"Jesus came as High Priest of the good things to come, with the greater and more perfect Tabernacle, not made with hands, that is, not of this creation.

(He came to the altar) Not with the blood of goats and calves, but with His own "perfect" blood He entered the Most Holy Place (in Heaven) once for all, having obtained eternal redemption."

"And for this reason Jesus is the Mediator of the New Covenant, by means of (His) death, for the redemption of the transgressions under the Old Covenant, that those who are called may receive the promise of the eternal inheritance."

(Hebrews 9:11-12 & 15)

In today's Scripture, the author is speaking to Believers, and all people that hear the Gospel of Jesus, that Jesus is absolutely the supreme and only, Mediator of God's grace toward people. Amen! Jesus is the High Priest that took His own blood to the altar of God, so that we could be permanently forgiven of sin, and be redeemed by God for eternity. Amen again! There is no other way to be forgiven and redeemed by God! Hallelujah! The only sacrifice that God will accept to forgive the sins of any person... is the blood of Jesus! Glory Hallelujah! For the blood of Jesus comes from the human body of Jesus, a body that did not commit sin!

That is why Jesus's blood is perfect! Our sins are forgiven when we accept Jesus, who took His perfect blood to the altar of God for you! Glory! And for that reason, Jesus is all you need! Thank you, Jesus! Our Scripture begins with, **"Jesus came as High Priest of the good things to come, with the greater and more perfect Tabernacle, not made with hands, that is, not of this creation. (He came to the altar) Not with the blood of goats and calves, but with His own "perfect" blood He entered the Most Holy Place (in Heaven) once for all, having obtained eternal redemption."** Jesus came to this earth to give His human blood as a sacrifice for your sins! And Jesus also came as the High Priest to take His own blood to God, and present it on the altar of God in Heaven. Amen! Our Word also tells us that, **"And for this reason, Jesus is the Mediator of the New Covenant, by means of (His) death, for the redemption of the transgressions under the Old Covenant,"** Because Jesus paid the price for our sins, He is now our High Priest to mediated forgiveness of sins for us, from Almighty God! That is the New Covenant of God! Amen again! And the Word of God concludes that all of this is available through Jesus, so, **"that those who are called may receive the promise of the eternal inheritance."** For all Believers are called by God to come to and accept Jesus as their Lord and Savior! Hallelujah! Give glory to God! For it is God who calls you to Jesus, and it is God's New Covenant that His mercy presents to us, and hallelujah, it is God who sent Jesus to shed His blood for you, and to present His blood to God so that you could be forgiven and redeemed to

God! Tell the truth! Hallelujah! Thank you, Jesus! Jesus is absolutely the supreme and only Mediator of God's grace toward you. And that is the truth! Amen.

Today, our Scripture is speaking to all people. Jesus is all you need to be forgiven of your sins and to be redeemed by God for eternity. Jesus is all you need! The author of Hebrews is speaking to Believers, and all people that hear the Gospel of Jesus, that Jesus is absolutely the supreme and only, Mediator of God's grace toward people. Amen! Jesus is the High Priest that took His own blood to the altar of God, so that we could be permanently forgiven of sin, and be redeemed by God for eternity. Amen again! There is no other way to be forgiven and redeemed by God! Hallelujah! The only sacrifice that God will accept to forgive the sins of any person, is the blood of Jesus! Glory Hallelujah! For the blood of Jesus comes from the human body of Jesus, and Jesus's blood is perfect! Our sins are forgiven when we accept Jesus, who took His perfect blood to the altar of God for you! Glory! And for that reason, Jesus is all you need! Thank you, Jesus! Our Scripture begins with, **"Jesus came as High Priest of the good things to come, with the greater and more perfect Tabernacle, not made with hands, that is, not of this creation. (He came to the altar) Not with the blood of goats and calves, but with His own "perfect" blood. He entered the Most Holy Place (in Heaven) once and for all, having obtained eternal redemption."** Jesus came to this earth to give His human blood as a sacrifice for your sins! And Jesus also came as the High Priest to take His own blood to God, and present it on the altar of God in Heaven. Amen! Jesus not only came to this earth to die for you, but Jesus also arose from the dead so that He could take His perfect blood to God and put it on God's Tabernacle in Heaven. Jesus did that for you! And He only had to do it one time! So that you could receive eternal salvation with God! Hallelujah! Thank you, Jesus! And for that reason, Jesus is absolutely the supreme and only Mediator of God's grace toward you. Amen.

Today, our Word is speaking to all people. Jesus is all you need to be forgiven of your sins and to be redeemed by God for eternity. Jesus is all you need! Jesus is absolutely the supreme, and only, Mediator of God's grace toward people. Amen! Jesus is the High Priest that took His own blood to the altar of God, so that we could be permanently forgiven of sin, and be redeemed by God for eternity. Amen again! There is no other way to be forgiven and redeemed by God! Hallelujah! The only sacrifice that God will accept to forgive the sins of any person... is the blood of Jesus! Glory Hallelujah! Because Jesus's blood is perfect! Our sins are forgiven when we accept Jesus, who took His perfect blood to the altar of God for you! Glory! And for that reason, Jesus is all you need! Thank you, Jesus! Jesus came to this earth to give His human blood as a sacrifice for your sins! And Jesus also came as the High Priest to take His own blood to God, and present it on the altar of God in Heaven. Amen! Our Word also tells us that, **"And for this reason, Jesus is the Mediator of the New Covenant, by means of (His) death, for the redemption of the transgressions**

under the Old Covenant," Because Jesus paid the price for our sins, He is now our High Priest to mediated forgiveness of sins for us, from Almighty God! That is the New Covenant of God! Amen again! That is why Jesus came to earth, so that He could present a sacrifice for you to God, and then become our High Priest that goes to God to seek mercy for us! Jesus went to God for you when you initially accepted Him as your Lord and Savior, and Jesus goes to God for you each time you sin and confess your sins to Him! Jesus is constantly mediating God's grace for you! Hallelujah! Thank you, Jesus! And for that reason, Jesus is absolutely the supreme and only Mediator of God's grace toward you. Amen.

Today, the Word of God is speaking to all people. Jesus is all you need to be forgiven of your sins, and to be redeemed to God for eternity. Jesus is all you need! Jesus is absolutely the supreme, and only, Mediator of God's grace toward people. Amen! Jesus is the High Priest that took His own blood to the altar of God so that you could be permanently forgiven of sin, and be redeemed to God for eternity. Amen again! And the only sacrifice that God will accept to forgive your sins... is the blood of Jesus! Glory Hallelujah! Because Jesus's blood is perfect! Your sins are forgiven when you accept Jesus, who took His perfect blood to the altar of God for you! Glory! And for that reason, Jesus is all you need! Thank you, Jesus! Jesus came to this earth to give His human blood as a sacrifice for your sins! And Jesus also came as the High Priest to take His own blood to God, and present it on the altar of God in Heaven, for you! Amen! Because Jesus paid the price for your sins, He is now your High Priest to mediate forgiveness of sins for you, from Almighty God! That is the New Covenant of God! Amen again! And the Word of God concludes that all of this is available through Jesus, so, **"that those who are called may receive the promise of the eternal inheritance."** For all Believers are called by God to come to, and accept Jesus as their Lord and Savior! Hallelujah! Give glory to God! For it is God who calls you to Jesus, and it is God's New Covenant that His mercy presents to us, and hallelujah, it is God who sent Jesus to shed His blood for you, and to present His blood to God so that you could be forgiven and redeemed to God! Tell the truth! Hallelujah! Thank you, Jesus! And for that reason, Jesus is absolutely the supreme and only Mediator of God's grace toward you. Amen. And that is the truth! Amen.

Day 195

"In fact, when we were with you (Believers), we (the servants of Jesus) kept telling you that we would be persecuted. And it turned out that way, as you well know.

For this reason, when I could stand it no longer, I sent to find out about your faith. I was afraid that in some way the tempter (Satan) had tempted you and that our labors had been in vain.

But Timothy, (the servant of Jesus who had helped establish the church), has come to us from you, and has brought good news about your faith and love.

Therefore Brothers and sisters, in all our distress and persecution we were encouraged about you because of your faith.

For now we really live (in joy), since you are standing firm in the Lord."

(1 Thessalonians 3:4-8)

In today's Scripture, the great servant of Jesus, the apostle Paul, writes to Believers to praise them for their spiritual maturity and perseverance of faith in Jesus, even though there had been great difficulties and temptations that had happened since Paul had left. Amen! And because of these horrible events and times, Paul was worried that Believers had lost their faith. But instead, Believers had strengthened their faith in Jesus, even during these difficult times. Hallelujah! And today, Believers are being challenged! We are going through some absolutely difficult times! And Satan sees these difficult times as an opportunity to test your faith in Jesus! Tell the truth! Many Believers are in isolation, and are cut off from the world, and their normal ways. Satan is looking at you, and Satan is trying to tempt you at a time when he thinks you are afraid and weak, because of what you are going through. But Satan is a liar! So strengthen your faith in Jesus right now! Because it is your faith in Jesus that will get you through these difficult times! And that is the truth! Glory Hallelujah! Our Scripture begins with the servant of Jesus speaking to Believers about difficult times, saying, "In fact, when we were with you (Believers), we (the servants of Jesus) kept telling you that we would be persecuted. And it turned out that way, as you well know. For this reason, when I could stand it no longer, I sent to find out about your faith. I was afraid that in some way the tempter (Satan) had tempted you and that our labors might have been in vain." Believers have always been told there would be difficult times in life, but now those times are here! And Satan is using these difficult times to tempt you! Amen! Our Word continues with the servant of Jesus saying, **"But Timothy (the servant of Jesus who had helped establish the church) has come to us from you, and has brought good news about your faith and love."** Your continued faith in Jesus is good news! Amen again! And the Word of God concludes with the servant of Jesus saying to Believers, **"Therefore, Brothers and sisters, in all our distress and**

persecution, we were encouraged about you because of your faith. For now, we really live (in joy), since you are standing firm in the Lord." There is great joy in your faith in Jesus! And it is your faith in Jesus that will help others to have faith in Jesus. And hallelujah, it is that faith in Jesus that will bring you through the difficult times! Glory Hallelujah! So stand firm in your faith in Jesus! Stand firm! Amen.

Today, our Scripture is speaking to Believers. The world is going through some very difficult times, and these difficult times are testing the faith of Believers and these times are even affecting the continuity of the church! Amen! And because of these difficult times, Satan sees an opportunity to challenge your faith with evil temptations and thoughts! Amen again! But this is nothing new! And you are being encouraged today to know that Believers in Jesus have stood on their faith to get through difficult times all through the history of Christianity! This, too, will pass! And this is an opportunity to grow in your faith in Jesus. Glory Hallelujah! The apostle Paul writes to Believers to praise them for their perseverance of faith in Jesus, even though there had been great difficulties that had happened since Paul had left. Amen! And because of these horrible events and times, Paul was worried that Believers had lost their faith. But instead, Believers had strengthened their faith in Jesus, even during these difficult times. Hallelujah! Believers are being challenged! We are going through some absolutely difficult times! And Satan sees these difficult times as an opportunity to test your faith in Jesus! Tell the truth!

Many Believers are in isolation, and are cut off from the world and their normal ways. And Satan is trying to tempt you at a time when he thinks you are afraid and weak. But Satan is a liar! So strengthen your faith in Jesus right now! Because it is your faith in Jesus that will get you through these difficult times! And that is the truth! Glory Hallelujah! Our Scripture begins with the servant of Jesus speaking to Believers about difficult times, saying, **"In fact, when we were with you (Believers), we (the servants of Jesus) kept telling you that we would be persecuted. And it turned out that way, as you well know. For this reason, when I could stand it no longer, I sent to find out about your faith. I was afraid that in some way the tempter (Satan) had tempted you and that our labors might had been in vain."** Believers have always been told there would be difficult times in life, but now those times are here! And Satan is using these difficult times to tempt you! Amen! But hallelujah, you know the Truth, that is Jesus! And Satan cannot do a thing to you as long as you keep your faith! And that is the truth! So stand firm in your faith in Jesus! Stand firm! Amen.

Today, our Word is speaking to Believers. The world is going through some very difficult times, and these difficult times are testing the faith of Believers and these times are even affecting the continuity of the church! Amen! And Satan sees an opportunity to challenge your faith with evil temptations! Amen again! But this is nothing new! This, too, will pass! And this is an opportunity to grow in your faith in Jesus. Glory Hallelujah! Paul writes to

Believers to praise them for their perseverance of faith in Jesus, even though there had been great difficulties. Amen! And Paul was worried that Believers had lost their faith. But instead, Believers had strengthened their faith in Jesus, even during these difficult times. Hallelujah! Believers are being challenged today! We are going through some absolutely difficult times! Satan sees these difficult times as an opportunity to test your faith in Jesus! Tell the truth! Many Believers are in isolation and are cut off from their normal ways. And Satan is trying to tempt you at a time when he thinks you are afraid and weak. But Satan is a liar! So strengthen your faith in Jesus right now! Because it is your faith in Jesus that will get you through these difficult times! And that is the truth! Glory Hallelujah! Believers have always been told there would be difficult times in life, but now those times are here! And Satan is using these difficult times to tempt you! Amen! Our Word continues with the servant of Jesus saying, **"But Timothy, (the servant of Jesus who had helped establish the church), has come to us from you, and has brought good news about your faith and love."** Your continued faith in Jesus is good news! Amen again! It is your faith and love of Jesus that will give you strength, and it will also give strength to the church and other Believers. Glory Hallelujah! And the servants of Jesus will see you standing in your faith, and they will receive joy because of your faith! Your faith in Jesus during these incredibly bad times, is good news! Hallelujah! So stand firm in your faith in Jesus! Stand firm! Amen.

Today, the Word of God is speaking to Believers. The world is going through some very difficult times, and these difficult times are testing the faith of Believers. Amen! Satan sees an opportunity to challenge your faith! Amen again! But this is nothing new! This, too, will pass! And this is an opportunity to grow in your faith in Jesus. Glory Hallelujah! Believers are being challenged today! We are going through some absolutely difficult times! Satan sees these difficult times as an opportunity to test your faith in Jesus! Tell the truth! Many Believers are in isolation, and are cut off from their normal ways. And Satan is trying to tempt you, but Satan is a liar! So strengthen your faith in Jesus right now! Because it is your faith in Jesus that will get you through these difficult times! And that is the truth! Glory Hallelujah! Believers have always been told there would be difficult times in life, but now those times are here! And Satan is using these difficult times to tempt you! Amen! Your continued faith in Jesus is good news! Amen again! And the Word of God concludes with the servant of Jesus saying to Believers, **"Therefore, Brothers and sisters, in all our distress and persecution, we were encouraged about you because of your faith. For now, we really live (in joy), since you are standing firm in the Lord."** There is great joy in your faith in Jesus! And it is your faith in Jesus that will help others to have faith in Jesus. And hallelujah, it is that faith in Jesus that will bring you through the difficult times! That is why Believers can find joy and strength in each other's faith! Your faith will always bring you through difficult times. And it is your faith that will also defeat Satan! Glory Hallelujah! So stand firm in your faith in Jesus! Stand firm! Amen.

Today, our Scripture Guidance is for Believers. We are going through some of the worst times that the world has ever seen, and Satan sees an opportunity to challenge your faith! Satan thinks that because of these difficulties, you may be weak in your faith. Well, make Satan a liar! For that is all He is! Amen! Stand strong in your faith in Jesus! Believers have always been told there would be difficult times in life, but now those times are here! And Satan is using these difficult times to tempt you! Amen! But hallelujah, your continued faith in Jesus is good news! Amen again! Your faith will always defeat Satan! There is great joy in your faith in Jesus! And it is your faith in Jesus that will help others to have faith in Jesus. And hallelujah, it is that faith in Jesus that will bring you through the difficult times! Glory Hallelujah! So stand firm in your faith in Jesus! Stand firm! Amen.

Day 196

After Rachel gave birth to Joseph, Jacob said to Laban (Rachel's Father), "Send me on my way so I can go back to my own homeland.

Give me my wives and children, for whom I have served you (for), and I will be on my way. You know how much work I have done for you."

Then Laban said to Jacob, "If I have found favor in your eyes, please stay. I have learned by experience that the Lord has blessed me because of you."

He also said to Jacob, "Name your wages, and I will pay them (if you stay)."

"And we know that in all things God works for the good of those who love Him, who have been called according to His purpose."

(Genesis 30:25-28 & Romans 8:28)

In today's Scripture, the great servant of God, Moses, writes the history of Jacob, as given to Moses by God. Amen! Since Moses was not yet alive during the life of Moses, what Moses writes to us was given to Him by the Spirit of God! Amen again! Jacob was the son of Isaac, who was the son of Abraham. Amen again! Jacob fled from his land because his brother Esau wanted to kill him, because Jacob had tricked his Father Isaac into giving Jacob the blessing that should have gone to Esau, the firstborn son. So Jacob fled to the land of his mother's (Rebekah) brother, whose name is Laban. Jacob had been forbidden by his Father of marrying Canaanite women, but instead to marry a woman from his mother's family, which would be from the daughters of his uncle Laban. Well, Jacob ended up working for Laban, and also marrying his two daughters, Leah and Rachel. And Jacob ended up having twelve children. Our Scripture begins with, **After Rachel gave birth to Joseph, Jacob said to Laban (Rachel's Father), "Send me on my way so I can go back to my own homeland. Give me my wives and children, for whom I have served you (for), and I will be on my way. You know how much work I have done for you."** Once a servant of God (Jesus) finishes their commitment to man, they will want to move on. Amen. Our Word continues, **Then Laban said to Jacob, "If I have found favor in your eyes, please stay. I have learned by experience that the Lord has blessed me because of you."** People will realize the value of having a servant of God (Jesus) in their lives, for they will be blessed because of the presence of the servant! Amen again! And the Word of God concludes with, He also said to Jacob, **"Name your wages, and I will pay them (if you stay)."** God will open up opportunities for His servants! Hallelujah! For our Scripture Guidance says, **"And we know that in all things God works for the good of those who love Him, who have been called according to His purpose."** Glory Hallelujah! And that is forever the truth of the Word of God! Glory to God! You are being encouraged today! You may feel trapped in an unfair situation, or it may seem that people are taking advantage of you. But know this, if you love God and you are working on God's purpose, what seems like a bad situation, will work out for your good! Amen.

Today, our Scripture is speaking to those who love God and are working in His purpose. You may be in a bad situation, and it may seem like people are trying to take advantage of you, but keep on working on His purpose! For what you are going through is all part of God's plan, and He will use this bad situation for your good! Amen! That is a promise from the Word of God! Amen again! Moses writes the history of Jacob. Jacob's brother Esau wanted to kill him. So Jacob fled to the land of his mother's (Rebekah) brother, whose name is Laban. Well, Jacob ended up working for Laban, and also marrying his two daughters, Leah and Rachel. And Jacob ended up having twelve children. Jacob had worked for Laban much longer than Laban had originally demanded. And now Jacob was ready to leave Laban and live life on his own with his family. Our Scripture begins with, **After Rachel gave birth to Joseph, Jacob said to Laban (Rachel's Father), "Send me on my way so I can go back to my own homeland. Give me my wives and children, for whom I have served you (for), and I will be on my way. You know how much work I have done for you."** Once a servant of God (Jesus) finishes their commitment to man, they will want to move on. Amen! There will be times when you know you have done more than enough in a situation, and you are ready to leave. However, that does not mean it is the right time for you to leave! Many times we miss out on blessings because we are impatient! We want to use our own timeline! We want to leave because we are frustrated with our work environment, or lack of recognition for what we have done. We want to move on! Amen.

Today, our Word is speaking to those who love God and are working for His purpose. You may be in a bad situation, and it may seem like people are trying to take advantage of you, but keep on working on His purpose! For what you are going through is all part of God's plan, and He will use this bad situation for your good! Amen! That is a promise from the Word of God! Amen again! Jacob had fled to the land of his mother's brother, whose name is Laban. Jacob ended up working for Laban, and also marrying his two daughters, Leah and Rachel. Jacob had worked for Laban much longer than Laban had originally demanded. And now Jacob was ready to leave Laban, and live life on his own with his family. Once a servant of God (Jesus) finishes their commitment to man, they will want to move on. Amen! Our Word continues, **Then Laban said to Jacob, "If I have found favor in your eyes, please stay. I have learned by experience that the Lord has blessed me because of you."** People will realize the value of having a servant of God (Jesus) in their lives, for they will be blessed because of the presence of the servant! Amen again! When a servant of God (Jesus) works in man's world, man will see the goodness of that servant's work. And they will not want to lose the blessing that God moves to them through the work of His servant. So even though they may be unfair to you, their desire to keep getting what you give them will make them want to keep you around. For you have value, and they know it! Amen.

Today, the Word of God is speaking to those who love God and are working on His purpose. You may be in a bad situation, and it may seem like people are trying to take advantage of you, but keep on working on His purpose! For what you are going through is all part of God's plan, and He will use this bad situation for your good! Amen! That is a promise from the Word of God! Amen again! Jacob had fled to the land of his mother's brother, whose name is Laban. Jacob ended up working for him and marrying his two daughters. Jacob had worked for Laban much longer than Laban had originally demanded. And now Jacob was ready to leave Laban and live life on his own with his family. Once a servant of God (Jesus) finishes their commitment to man, they will want to move on. Amen! However, people will realize the value of having a servant of God (Jesus) in their lives, for they will be blessed because of the presence of the servant! Amen again! The Word of God concludes with, **He (Laban) also said to Jacob, "Name your wages, and I will pay them (if you stay)."** God will open up opportunities for His servants! Hallelujah! God is utilizing the unfairness of man, to set you up for the goodness of God! Amen! Laban paid Jacob very little, yet later on, Jacob will have more wealth than Laban! God used Laban's unfairness, to grow Jacob beyond anything that Jacob could imagine! Because it was God that had Laban see Jacob's value, and keep Jacob with him. Because God had already named Jacob's wages if he stayed in God's purpose! Amen.

Today, our Scripture Guidance is for those who love God and are working in His purpose. You may be in a bad situation, and it may seem like people are trying to take advantage of you, but keep on working on His purpose! For what you are going through is all part of God's plan, and He will use this bad situation for your good! Amen! That is a promise from the Word of God! Amen again! God's people need to understand that once a servant of God (Jesus) finishes their commitment to man, the servant will want to move on. Amen! However, people will realize the value of having a servant of God (Jesus) in their lives, for they will be blessed because of the presence of the servant! Amen again! But God will open up opportunities for His servants! Hallelujah! For our Scripture Guidance says, **"And we know that in all things God works for the good of those who love Him, who have been called according to His purpose."** Glory Hallelujah! And that is forever the truth of the Word of God! Glory to God! You are being encouraged today! You may feel trapped in an unfair situation, or it may seem that people are taking advantage of you. But know this, if you love God and you are working on God's purpose, what seems like a bad situation, will work out for your good! And even though you feel that what is happening to you is unfair, God has already named your wages if you continue to stay in His purpose! God has already named the good that is coming out of this bad situation! For the Word of God has made you a promise! That God works for the good of all things, for those who love Him and do His purpose! Glory! Amen.

Day 197

(God said to His servant) "Therefore, son of man, say to your people, 'If someone who is righteous disobeys, that person's former righteousness will count for nothing. And if someone who is wicked repents, that person's former wickedness will not bring condemnation. The righteous person who sins will not be allowed to live even though they were formerly righteous."

"Yet your people say, "That the way of the Lord is not just.' But it is their way that is not just.

If a righteous person turns from their righteousness and does evil, they will die for it.

And if a wicked person turns way from their wickedness and does what is just and right, they will live for doing so.

Yet people say, 'The way of the Lord is not just.' But I will judge each of you according to your own ways."

(Ezekiel 33:12 & 17-20)

In today's Scripture, the great servant of God, the priest and prophet Ezekiel, shares God's words to His people about His righteous judgment of people. Amen! God will judge all people, and God judges them based on His righteousness! Amen again! People will often think that God is not fair to them, because they want God to judge them based on their own set of judgment rules. Tell the truth! But your judgment of yourself, or others, based on your evaluation of rules, means nothing! You have no judgment power over yourself, and certainly over nobody else! You are to be judged by God, and only God! And by His evaluation of your life, and how you live your life! And hallelujah, that is the truth! Yet, people have, and will always, question the fairness of God. So God responds to that to Ezekiel, and had him share His words with us. Hallelujah! Our Scripture begins with, **(God said to His servant) "Therefore, son of man, say to your people, 'If someone who is righteous disobeys, that person's former righteousness will count for nothing. And if someone who is wicked repents, that person's former wickedness will not bring condemnation. The righteous person who sins will not be allowed to live even though they were formerly righteous."** However, today, people have Jesus! And through Jesus, we can be credited with righteousness! Today, if Believers who have been credited with righteousness because of their faith in Jesus, turn away from Jesus and live a life of sin without repenting, or denying that Jesus is their Savior, they will receive everlasting death! Even though they once confessed with their mouth that Jesus is their Savior. And if a wicked person, who has sinned all of their life, repents their sins and accepts Jesus, then hallelujah, they will not be condemned to everlasting death, but will receive everlasting life! Amen! Our Word continues with God saying to His servant, **"Yet your people say, "That the way of the Lord is not just.' But it is their way that is not just."** Just because we disagree with God does not make God wrong! God is always right, so it is you and I who are not just! Amen again! And the Word of God concludes to each person, **"If a righteous person turns from their righteousness and does evil, they will die for it. And if a wicked person turns away from their wickedness and does what is just and right, they will live for doing so. Yet people say, 'The way of the Lord is not just.' But I will judge each of you according to your own ways."** God is the only judge of each person, and God will always judge each of us based on His righteousness and based on how each of us lives our lives. God is God, and He will judge you, so live life according to His rules! Amen! You will be judged by God, and only God! And by His evaluation of your life, and how you live your life! God will judge you based on His rules, and only His rules! And hallelujah, that is the truth! The way of the Lord is just! Glory to God! Amen.

Today, our Scripture is speaking to God's people. The priest and prophet Ezekiel shares God's words to His people about His righteous judgment of all people. Amen! God will judge all people, and God judges them based on His righteousness! Amen again! People want God to judge them based on their own set of judgment rules. Tell the truth! But your judgment of yourself, or others, based on your evaluation of rules, means nothing! You are to be judged by God, and only God! And by His evaluation of your life, and how you live your life! That is the truth! Yet, people have, and will always, question the fairness of God. So God responds through Ezekiel, and had him share His words with us. Hallelujah! Our Scripture begins with, **(God said to His servant)**

"Therefore, son of man, say to your people, 'If someone who is righteous disobeys, that person's former righteousness will count for nothing. And if someone who is wicked repents, that person's former wickedness will not bring condemnation. The righteous person who sins will not be allowed to live even though they were formerly righteous." However, today, people have Jesus! And through Jesus, we can be credited with righteousness! Today, if Believers who have been credited with righteousness because of their faith in Jesus turn away from Jesus and live a life of sin without repenting, or denying that Jesus is their Savior, they will receive everlasting death! Even though they once confessed with their mouth that Jesus is their Savior. And if a wicked person, who has sinned all of their life, repents their sins and accepts Jesus, then hallelujah, they will not be condemned to everlasting death, but will receive everlasting life! Amen! Now whether you think that is fair or not, that does not matter, because you are not the one who will judge! You could live most of your life confessing Jesus, and deny Him on the last day of your life, and you will be judged and sent to everlasting condemnation in Hell! And another person could live their entire life wicked and in denial of Jesus, but confess their sins and accept Jesus on the last day of their life, and that person will be judged by God and receive everlasting life with God in Heaven! But know this, each and every person will be judged by God! Amen! You will be judged by God, and only God! And by His evaluation of your life, and how you live your life! Amen again! God will judge you based on

His rules, and only His rules! And hallelujah, that is the truth! The way of the Lord is just! Glory to God! Amen.

Today, our Word is speaking to God's people. God will judge all people, and God judges them based on His righteousness! Amen! People want God to judge them based on their own set of judgment rules. Amen again! Tell the truth! But your judgment of yourself, or others, based on your evaluation of rules, means nothing! You are to be judged by God, and only God! And evaluates your life, and how you live your life! That is the truth! Yet, people have, and will always, question the fairness of God. So God responds through Ezekiel, and had him share His words with us. Hallelujah! However, today, people have Jesus! And through Jesus, we can be credited with righteousness! And today, if Believers who have been credited with righteousness because of their faith in Jesus, turn away from Jesus and live a life of sin without repenting, or deny that Jesus is their Savior, they will receive everlasting death! Even though they once confessed with their mouth that Jesus is their Savior. And if a wicked person, who has sinned all of their life, repents their sins and accepts Jesus, then hallelujah, they will not be condemned to everlasting death, but will receive everlasting life! Amen! Our Word continues with God saying to His servant, **"Yet your people say, "That the way of the Lord is not just.' But it is their way that is not just."** Just because we disagree with God does not make God wrong! God is always right, so it is you and I who are not just! Amen again! Only God is righteous, and all will be judged based on His righteousness! You will be judged by God, and only God! And by His evaluation of your life, and how you live your life! You may think that the way of the Lord is not just, but what you think is just only matters if you agree and live your life based on what God thinks is just! Hallelujah! For God will judge you based on His rules, and only His rules! And hallelujah, that is the truth! The way of the Lord is just! Glory to God! Amen.

Today, our Word is speaking to God's people. God will judge all people, and God judges them based on His righteousness! Amen! People want God to judge them based on their own set of judgment rules. Amen again! Tell the truth! But your judgment of yourself, or others, based on your evaluation of rules, means nothing! You are to be judged by God, and only God! And evaluates your life, and how you live your life! That is the truth! Yet, people have, and will always, question the fairness of God. However, today, people have Jesus! And through Jesus, we can be credited with righteousness! And today, if Believers who have been credited with righteousness because of their faith in Jesus, turn away from Jesus and live a life of sin without repenting, or denying that Jesus is their Savior, they will receive everlasting death! Even though they once confessed with their mouth that Jesus is their Savior. And if a wicked person, who has sinned all of their life, repents their sins and accepts Jesus, then hallelujah, they will not be condemned to everlasting death, but will receive everlasting life! Amen! You may disagree with God, but that does not, and will never make God wrong! God is always right, so it is you and I who are not just! Amen again! And the Word of God concludes to each person, **"If a righteous person turns from their righteousness and does evil, they will die for it. And if a wicked person turns away from their wickedness and does what is just and right, they will live for doing so. Yet people say, 'The way of the Lord is not just.' But I will judge each of you according to your own ways."** God is the only judge of each person, and God will always judge each of us based on His righteousness, and based on how each of us lives our lives. God is God, and He will judge you, so live life according to His rules! Amen! You will be judged by God, and only God! And by His evaluation of your life, and how you live your life! God will judge you based on His rules, and only His rules! And hallelujah, that is the truth! The way of the Lord is just! Glory to God! Amen.

Today, our Scripture Guidance is for Believers. God will judge all people, and God judges them based on His righteousness! Amen! People want God to judge them based on their own set of judgment rules. Amen again! But God will judge you based on the rules He put forth in the Gospel of Jesus Christ! For hallelujah, today, people have Jesus! And through Jesus, we can be credited with righteousness! So you must live your life with the faith that Jesus Christ is the Son of God and your Lord and Savior! And you must confess your sins through Jesus, and never turn away from the righteousness that you have received from God through your faith in Jesus! Amen again! For God will judge you based on those rules. Tell the truth! You have no judgment power over yourself, and certainly over nobody else! You are to be judged by God, and only God! And by His evaluation of your life, and how you live your life! God will judge your righteousness, and you can only receive righteousness from God is through your faith in Jesus Christ! For the Word of God says that God gives righteousness to people, saying, **"This righteousness is given through faith in Jesus Christ to all who believe. There is no difference between Jew and Gentile, for all have sinned and fall short of the glory of God, and all are justified freely by his grace through the redemption that came by Christ Jesus." (Romans 3:22-24)** And hallelujah, that is the truth! The way of the Lord is just! Amen.

Day 198

"Better (are) the poor whose walk is blameless, than a fool whose lips are perverse."

"The poor are shunned by all their relatives, how much more do their friends avoid them! Though the poor pursue them (family and friends) with pleading, they are nowhere to be found."

"Whoever is kind to the poor, lends to the Lord, and He will reward them for what they have done."

"What a person desires (in their life) is unfailing love, (and to attain that it is) better to be poor than a liar."

(Proverbs 18:1, 7, 17 & 22)

In today's Scripture, the author, most likely King Solomon, writes to God's people to emphasize the importance of living wisely, and in fear of God, as opposed to living in the foolish way of an evil world. Amen! In our Scripture passage, the proverbs focus on the poor, particularly on how we often evaluate the poor, and how we treat the poor. Amen again! For throughout the history of the world, we often judge people by the material things that have been obtained in life. And for the people who are poor, most people with more, disregard them as not worthy. Tell the truth! This was true at the time of Solomon, and unfortunately, we have that same perception of poor people today! And as God's people, we are being challenged! How do you view people who are considered poor, and more importantly, how do you treat them? This message and question is to God's people! Hallelujah! Our Scripture begins with a proverb, saying to God's people, **"Better (are) the poor whose walk is blameless, than a fool whose lips are perverse."** A poor person who walks with God, is better in the eyes of God, than a rich fool who speaks evil! Amen! Our Word continues with a statement about how most people treat the poor people that they know, **"The poor are shunned by all their relatives, how much more do their friends avoid them! Though the poor pursue them (family and friends) with pleading, they are nowhere to be found."** And these are people you know! These are people you claim to love! Amen again! Yet the Word of God makes a promise to His people, that, **"Whoever is kind to the poor, lends to the Lord, and He will reward them for what they have done."** God is watching how you treat poor people! And God promises to bless those that help the poor people on earth! Glory! And our Scripture Guidance concludes with this fact, **"What a person desires (in their life) is unfailing love, (and to attain that it is) better to be poor than a liar."** People live their life desiring to have unconditional love that will never fail them, and that kind of love comes from God! Being rich and a liar will lead to a desire for evil, while being poor and humble will lead to a desire to have the love of God! And having the love of God through Jesus Christ is the greatest wealth that you can have! So be careful how you evaluate and treat poor people.

Today, our Scripture is speaking to God's people. Be careful how you evaluate, and how you treat, poor people. The author of Proverbs writes to God's people to emphasize the importance of living wisely, and in fear of God, as opposed to living in the foolish way of an evil world. Amen! In our Scripture passage, the proverb focuses on the poor, particularly on how we often evaluate the poor, and how we treat the poor. Amen again! For throughout the history of the world, we often judge people by the material things that have been obtained in life. And for the people who are poor, most people with more, disregard them as not worthy. And that is foolish and unwise! Unfortunately, many Believers have that same perception of poor people today! Tell the truth! And Believers are being challenged! How do you view people who are considered poor, and more importantly, how do you treat them? What is your truth? Our Scripture begins with a proverb, saying to God's people, **"Better (are) the poor whose walk is blameless, than a fool whose lips are perverse."** A poor person who walks with God, is better in the eyes of God, than a rich fool who speaks evil! Amen! God does not look at your material goods, or your status in the world. God looks at your righteousness! If you are righteous through your faith in Jesus Christ, you are rich in everlasting life! Glory! That poor person who is righteous, is richer than any wealthy person without Jesus could ever be! And that is the truth! So be careful how you evaluate and treat poor people. For God is watching you! Amen.

Today, our Word is speaking to God's people. Be careful how you evaluate, and how you treat, poor people. The author writes to God's people to emphasize the importance of living wisely, and in fear of God, as opposed to living in the foolish way of an evil world. Amen! This series of proverbs focuses on the poor, on how we often evaluate the poor, and how we treat the poor. Amen again! We often judge people by the material things that have been obtained in life. And for the people who are poor, most people with more, disregard them as not worthy. And that is foolish and unwise! However, many Believers have that same perception of poor people today! Tell the truth! And Believers are being challenged! How do you view people who are considered poor, and more importantly, how do you treat them? What is your truth? As Believers, we should know that a poor person who walks with God, is better in the eyes of God, than a rich fool who speaks evil! Amen! Yet many Believers do not want to be around poor people, while they often celebrate the lives of rich people! Is that you? Our Word continues with a statement about how most people treat the poor people that they know, **"The poor are shunned by all their relatives, how much more do their friends avoid them! Though the poor pursue them (family and friends) with pleading, they are nowhere to be found."** And these are people you know! These are people you claim to love! Amen again! If one of your relatives is poorer than you, how often do you go to see them, and spend time with them? Or do you expect the poorer person to come where you are? And do you find ways to avoid them, even though they ask to see you? What about friends, do you avoid the ones that are poor, while seeing the ones who are not poor? These are tough questions, but ones you are being challenged to answer! Is that you? So be careful how you evaluate and treat poor people. For God is watching you! Amen.

Today, the Word of God is speaking to God's people. Be careful how you evaluate and how you treat, poor people. The author emphasizes the importance of living wisely, and in fear of God, as opposed to living in the foolish way of an evil world. Amen! This series of proverbs focuses on the poor, and how we treat the poor. Amen again! We often judge people by what they have been obtained in life. And for the people who are poor, we disregard them as not worthy. And that is foolish and unwise! Yet, many Believers have that same perception of poor people today! Tell the truth! And you are being challenged! How do you view people who are considered poor, and more importantly, how do you treat them? What is your truth? As a Believers in Jesus Christ, you should know that a poor person who walks with God, is better in the eyes of God, than a rich fool who speaks evil! Amen! Yet many Believers do not want to be around poor people, while they often celebrate the lives of rich people! We even shun family and friends if they are poor. And these are people you know! These are people you claim to love! Amen again! Is that you? Do you treat poor people like that? Yet the Word of God makes a promise to His people, that, **"Whoever is kind to the poor, lends to the Lord, and He will reward them for what they have done."** God is watching how you treat poor people! And God promises to bless those that help the poor people on earth! Glory! When you treat poor people well, you are acting on behalf of God! And God promises that He will reward you for doing so. Glory Hallelujah! So be careful how you evaluate and treat poor people. For God is watching you! Amen.

Today, our Scripture Guidance is for God's people. Be careful how you evaluate, and how you treat, poor people. Believers in Jesus are expected to live wisely, and in fear of God, as opposed to living in the foolish way of an evil world. Amen! Our proverbs focus on the poor, and how we treat the poor. Amen again! We often judge people by what they have been obtained in life. And for the people who are poor, we disregard them as not worthy. And that is foolish and unwise! Tell the truth! And you are being challenged! How do you view people who are considered poor, and more importantly, how do you treat them? What is your truth? As a Believers in Jesus Christ, you should know that a poor person who walks with God, is better in the eyes of God, than a rich fool who speaks evil! Amen! Yet many Believers do not want to be around poor people, while they often celebrate the lives of rich people! We even shun family and friends if they are poor. And these are people you know! These are people you claim to love! Amen again! Well, God is watching how you treat poor people! And God promises to bless those that help the poor people on earth! Glory! Is that you? How do you treat poor people? And our Scripture Guidance concludes with this fact, **"What a person**

desires (in their life) is unfailing love, (and to attain that it is) better to be poor than a liar." People live their life desiring to have unconditional love that will never fail them, and that kind of love comes from God! Being rich and a liar will lead to a desire for evil, while being poor and humble will lead to a desire to have the love of God! And having the love of God through Jesus Christ is the greatest wealth that you can have! So be careful how you evaluate and treat poor people. For God is watching you! Amen.

Day 199

"I became a servant of this Gospel by the gift of God's grace given me through the working of His power.

Although I am the least of all the Lord's people, this grace was given me, to preach to the Gentiles the boundless riches of Christ,

and to make plain to everyone the administration of this mystery, which for the ages past was kept hidden in God, who created all things.

His intent was that now, through the church, the manifold wisdom of God should be made known to the rulers and authorities in the heavenly realms,

according to His eternal purpose that He accomplished in Christ Jesus our Lord.

In Him we may approach God with freedom and confidence."

(Ephesians 3:7-12)

In today's Scripture, the great servant of Jesus, the apostle Paul, writes to the Gentiles (which is every person who is not Jewish), about God's marvelous and merciful plan to include Gentles in His offer of redemption and grace through His Son Jesus! Amen! Before Jesus came to earth and revealed His Gospel of redemption to God, and salvation with God, God's plan for all people had not been revealed. Amen again. For the prophecy of the Messiah was only given to the Jewish people, who, therefore thought that the Messiah, was only for them! But hallelujah, God had a plan for all people! Glory Hallelujah! And Jesus had selected Paul to be a big part of revealing and then spreading God's plan to the Gentiles throughout the world. Glory to God! Our Scripture begins with the servant of Jesus proclaiming God's purpose for him, **"I became a servant of this Gospel by the gift of God's grace given me through the working of His power. Although I am the least of all the Lord's people, this grace was given me, to preach to the Gentiles the boundless riches of Christ, and to make plain to everyone the administration of this mystery, which for the ages past was kept hidden in God, who created all things."** Servants of Jesus are selected by God, and gifted by God, to do the Will of God! And God always has an exact purpose for those He chooses to serve Jesus! Amen! Our Word continues to reveal God's purpose for Jesus's servant, saying of God's purpose is, **"His intent was that now, through the church, the manifold wisdom of God should be made known to the rulers and authorities in the heavenly realms, according to His eternal purpose that He accomplished in Christ Jesus our Lord."** God's purpose is that through Jesus, God's wisdom for earth would be accomplished on earth! Amen again! And the Word of God concludes with what His purpose, that was accomplished through Jesus, now means for those who accept Jesus, that with Jesus, **"In Him we may approach God with freedom and confidence."** The servant of

Jesus is to reveal to all people, that through the name of Jesus, we can now have a relationship with God on earth, and an everlasting relationship with God in Heaven! Glory! Amen.

Today, our Scripture is speaking to all people. God chooses people to serve Jesus, so that each servant can help tell the people throughout the world about His plan for all people. And that plan is Jesus! Hallelujah! The great servant of Jesus, the apostle Paul, writes to all people, about God's marvelous and merciful plan to include all people in His offer of redemption and grace through His Son Jesus! Amen! Before Jesus came to earth and revealed His Gospel of redemption to God, and salvation with God, God's plan for all people had not been revealed. Amen again. For the prophecy of a Messiah had only been given to the Jewish people. But God had a plan for all people! Glory Hallelujah! And Jesus had assigned Paul to be a big part of revealing and then spreading God's plan to people throughout the world. Glory to God! Our Scripture begins with the servant of Jesus proclaiming God's purpose for him, **"I became a servant of this Gospel by the gift of God's grace given me through the working of His power. Although I am the least of all the Lord's people, this grace was given me, to preach to the Gentiles the boundless riches of Christ, and to make plain to everyone the administration of this mystery, which for the ages past was kept hidden in God, who created all things."** Servants of Jesus are selected by God, and gifted by God, to do the Will of God! And God always has an exact purpose for those He chooses to serve Jesus! Amen! Each servant of Jesus was chosen and designed by God to do a specific purpose, according to His Will. And God has given each servant of Jesus specific gifts, so that His Will, will be done! Hallelujah! And Jesus calls His servants, and gives them their specific assignment to support God's Will to unveil the mystery of God's Word to people all over the world. Glory! God has a plan for all people, and that plan is Jesus! Glory Hallelujah! Now go serve Jesus, and tell the rest of the world about Him! Amen.

Today, our Word is speaking to all people. God chooses people to serve Jesus, so that each servant can help tell the people throughout the world about His plan for all people. And that plan is Jesus! Hallelujah! The apostle Paul was responsible for telling Gentiles about God's marvelous and merciful plan to include all people in His offer of redemption and grace through His Son Jesus! Amen! Before Jesus came to earth, God's plan for all people had not been revealed. Amen again. For the prophecy of a Messiah had only been given to the Jewish people. But God had a plan for all people! Glory Hallelujah! And Jesus had assigned Paul to begin revealing, and then spreading, God's plan to people throughout the world. Glory to God! Paul did not know that he was a part of God's plan, until Jesus revealed it to him. But God knew! Hallelujah! For servants of Jesus are selected by God, and gifted by God, to do the Will of God! And God always has an exact purpose for those He chooses to serve Jesus! Amen! Our Word continues to reveal God's purpose for Jesus's servant, saying of God's purpose is, **"His intent was that now, through the church, the manifold wisdom**

of God should be made known to the rulers and authorities in the heavenly realms, according to His eternal purpose that He accomplished in Christ Jesus our Lord." God's purpose is that through Jesus, God's wisdom for earth would be accomplished on earth! Amen again! God has always had a plan that could allow all people, who have sinned, to be forgiven for their sins and be redeemed by God. Yet His plan would not be revealed until Jesus came to this earth, and revealed it! Jesus was the first person to teach and reveal God's plan. Jesus was the first servant that God chose to reveal His plan. And then Jesus accomplished God's plan when He sacrificed Himself on the cross, and rose from death after the third day! Glory! And God's intent is still that His plan for redemption is spread across the world to all people! That is why there are servants of Jesus! Amen! God has a plan for all people, and that plan is Jesus! Glory Hallelujah! Now go serve Jesus, and tell the rest of the world about Him! Amen.

Today, the Word of God is speaking to all people. God chooses people to serve Jesus, so that each servant can help tell the people throughout the world about His plan for all people. And that plan is Jesus! Hallelujah! Paul was responsible for telling God's marvelous and merciful plan to include all people in His offer of redemption and grace through His Son Jesus! Amen! Before Jesus came to earth, God's plan for all people had not been revealed. Amen again. But God had a plan for all people! Glory Hallelujah! And Jesus had assigned Paul to begin revealing, and then spreading, God's plan to people throughout the world. Glory to

God! Paul did not know that he was a part of God's plan, until Jesus revealed it to him. But God knew! Hallelujah! For servants of Jesus are selected by God, and gifted by God, to do the Will of God! And God always has an exact purpose for those He chooses to serve Jesus! Amen! For God's purpose is that through Jesus, God's wisdom for earth would be accomplished on earth! Amen again! And the Word of God concludes with what His purpose, which was accomplished through Jesus, that with Jesus, **"In Him we may approach God with freedom and confidence."** The servant of Jesus is to reveal to all people, that through the name of Jesus, we can now have a relationship with God on earth, and an everlasting relationship with God in Heaven! Glory! That is why there are servants of Jesus Christ! To continue to let all people know that through Jesus, any person can be with God, today and forever! Glory to God, and glory with God! Glory! God has a plan for all people, and that plan is Jesus! Glory Hallelujah! Now go serve Jesus, and tell the rest of the world about Him! Amen.

Today, God has a plan for all people that was accomplished through Jesus on earth, and the purpose of each servant of Jesus is to reveal God's plan, and Jesus's accomplishment to all people! Hallelujah! God has a plan for all people, and that plan is Jesus! Glory Hallelujah! Now go serve Jesus, and tell the rest of the world about Him! Amen.

Day 200

(Jesus said to His Disciples) "Nevertheless I tell you the truth. It is to your advantage that I go away (to Heaven), for if I do not go away, the Helper (the Holy Spirit) will not come to you, but if I depart, I will send Him to you.

And when He has come, He will convict the world of sin, and of righteousness, and of judgment:

of sin, because they do not believe in Me,

of righteousness, because I go to My Father and you see Me no more,

of judgment, because the ruler of this world is judged."

(John 16:7-11)

In today's Scripture, the great servant of Jesus, the apostle John, shares with us Jesus's conversations with His disciples in the upper room, during the Lord's Supper. Amen! This would be the last time that Jesus would be with all twelve of His disciples, for this is also the night that Judas would leave the room, to betray Jesus. Amen again! So since Jesus knew that this would be their last night together, these conversations on different subjects, would serve as His final discourse to the Twelve. Hallelujah! And John's Gospel gives us the most information about what Jesus said that night. Glory Hallelujah! Again, there were many topics that Jesus covered with them, including that He would ask His Father,

Almighty God, to send a Helper to be with His servants forever, and that Helper is the Holy Spirit **(John 14:15-16)**! Amen! In our particular passage, Jesus tells His Believers that He must leave earth, so that the Holy Spirit could be sent to earth. Jesus also speaks to the work that the Holy Spirit will do on earth. Amen again! Our Scripture begins with, **(Jesus said to His Disciples) "Nevertheless I tell you the truth. It is to your advantage that I go away (to Heaven), for if I do not go away, the Helper (the Holy Spirit) will not come to you, but if I depart, I will send Him to you."** Jesus knew that the Holy Spirit would not come into the world, until He had been crucified and buried, raised from the dead, and had risen to Heaven. Jesus knew these things because His Father had revealed it to Him! Amen! Our Word continues with the role of the Holy Spirit on earth, **"And when He has come, He will convict the world of sin, and of righteousness, and of judgment: of sin, because they do not believe in Me, of righteousness, because I go to My Father and you see Me no more,"** This is the purpose, and the work, of the Holy Spirit in the world. Amen again! And the Word of God concludes with Jesus also confirming that the Holy Spirit coming into the world also convicts the world, **"of judgment, because the ruler of this world is judged."** The Holy Spirit on earth also represents the victory of Jesus over Satan, because, with Jesus's victory, Satan will be judged and destroyed for eternity! Glory Hallelujah! That is the Will of God! That is the work of the Holy Spirit on earth! Amen.

Today, our Scripture is speaking to Jesus's disciples. If you believe in Jesus as your Lord and Savior, this Scripture is for you. Hallelujah! The apostle John shares with us Jesus's conversations with His disciples in the upper room, during the Lord's Supper. Amen! This would be the last time that Jesus would be with all twelve of His disciples, for this is the night that Judas would betray Jesus. Amen again! Jesus knew that this would be their last night together, so these conversations are on different subjects. Hallelujah! Again, there were many topics that Jesus covered with them, including that He would ask His Father to send a Helper to be with His servants forever, and that Helper is the Holy Spirit! Amen! Jesus tells His Believers that He must leave earth, so that the Holy Spirit could be sent to earth. Jesus also speaks to the work that the Holy Spirit will do on earth. Amen again! Our Scripture begins with, **(Jesus said to His Disciples) "Nevertheless I tell you the truth. It is to your advantage that I go away (to Heaven), for if I do not go away, the Helper (the Holy Spirit) will not come to you, but if I depart, I will send Him to you."** Jesus knew that the Holy Spirit would not come into the world, until He had been crucified and buried, raised from the dead, and had risen to Heaven. Jesus knew these things because His Father had revealed it to Him! Amen! For Jesus also knew His assignment from God! Jesus knew the plan before He was sent to earth and became flesh! God assigned Jesus, and Jesus knew from God that when He had completed His assignment on earth, that He would send the Holy Spirit to His Believers! Hallelujah! Jesus had to complete His assignment first, and leave the earth, before He could send the Holy Spirit! Glory Hallelujah! That is the Will of God! That is the work of the Holy Spirit on earth! Amen.

Today, our Word is speaking to Jesus's disciples. If you believe in Jesus as your Lord and Savior, this Word is for you. Hallelujah! John shares with us Jesus's conversations with His disciples during the Lord's Supper. Amen! This would be the last time that Jesus would be with all twelve of His disciples. Amen again! Jesus knew that this would be their last night together, so these conversations are on different subjects. Hallelujah! Jesus told His followers that He would ask His Father to send a Helper to be with His servants forever, and that Helper is the Holy Spirit! Amen! Jesus tells His Believers that He must leave earth, so that the Holy Spirit could be sent to earth. Jesus also speaks to the work that the Holy Spirit will do on earth. Amen again! Jesus knew that the Holy Spirit would not come into the world, until He had been crucified and buried, raised from the dead, and had risen to Heaven. Jesus knew these things because His Father had revealed it to Him! Amen! Our Word continues with the role of the Holy Spirit on earth, **"And when He has come, He will convict the world of sin, and of righteousness, and of judgment: of sin, because they do not believe in Me, of righteousness, because I go to My Father and you see Me no more,"** This is the purpose, and the work, of the Holy Spirit in the world. Amen again! The Holy Spirit that is sent to each Believer to help Believers, also works through Believers to convict sin of the people in the world! The Holy Spirit works through Believers to impart God's righteousness to the people in the world. The Holy Spirit takes on that role, which was also the role of Jesus! Hallelujah! For the Holy Spirit, just like Jesus, is a part of God! Glory Hallelujah! That is the Will of God! That is the work of the Holy Spirit on earth! Amen.

Today, the Word of God is speaking to Jesus's disciples. If you believe in Jesus as your Lord and Savior, the Word of God is speaking to you! Hallelujah! John shares with us Jesus's conversations with His disciples during the Lord's Supper. Amen! Jesus knew that this would be their last night together, so these conversations are on different subjects. Hallelujah! Jesus told His followers that He would ask His Father to send a Helper to be with His servants forever, and that Helper is the Holy Spirit! Amen! Jesus tells His Believers that He must leave earth, so that the Holy Spirit could be sent to earth. Jesus also speaks to the work that the Holy Spirit will do on earth. Amen again! Jesus knew that the Holy Spirit would not come into the world, until He had been crucified and buried, raised from the dead, and had risen to Heaven. Jesus knew these things because His Father had revealed it to Him! Amen! And there is a purpose, and work, that the Holy Spirit will do in the world. Amen again! And the Word of God concludes with Jesus also confirming that the Holy Spirit coming into the world also convicts the world, **"of judgment, because the ruler of this world is judged."** The Holy Spirit on earth also represents the victory of Jesus over Satan, because, with Jesus's victory, Satan will be judged and destroyed for eternity! And that is the truth! Hallelujah! When Jesus rose from the dead, he defeated death! And when Jesus rose from the earth to Heaven, Satan knew then that He had been judged, and that He would not, and could not conquer the world! Thank you, Jesus! And when the Holy Spirit of God arrived on earth through the Believers of Jesus Christ, Satan knew that it would only be a matter of time before Jesus came back to claim the earth, and for God to send Satan to eternal damnation in Hell! Glory Hallelujah! That is the Will of God! That is the work of the Holy Spirit on earth! Amen.

Today, the Holy Spirit is sent to each Believer to help them live righteous on earth. But the Holy Spirit is also sent to earth to convict the world and signal defeat for Satan! That is the Will of God! That is the work of the Holy Spirit on earth! Amen.

Day 201

During the high priesthood of Annas and Caiaphas, the Word of God came to John son of Zechariah in the wilderness.

He went into all the country around the (river) Jordan, preaching a baptism of repentance for the forgiveness of sins.

The people were waiting expectantly, and were all wondering if John might possibly be the Messiah (that had been spoken of by the prophets in the Old Testament).

John answered them all, "I baptize you with water. But One who is more powerful than I will come, the straps of whose sandals I am not worthy to untie. He will baptize you with the Holy Spirit and fire."

(Luke 3:2-3 &15-16)

In today's Scripture, the great servant of Jesus, Luke, re-tells the history of John the Baptist, as John prepared the way for Jesus. Amen! John was given the assignment by God to preach repentance of sin to the people of God. Yet, because of this, some people wondered if John was the Messiah. But John wasted no time in letting all people know that he was not. Amen again! For no matter how great a servant of Jesus is in the eyes of people, there is only One Messiah! Hallelujah! And that Messiah is Jesus! The message for us today is that as we serve Jesus, there will be some people that want to give the servant glory. You must waste no time with such talk, you must let people know right away that you are not worthy of praise. For no matter how well you may serve Jesus, there is only One Messiah! And to God goes all the glory! Hallelujah! Our Scripture begins with, **During the high priesthood of Annas and Caiaphas, the Word of God came to John, son of Zechariah, in the wilderness. He went into all the country around the (river) Jordan, preaching a baptism of repentance for the forgiveness of sins.** The servant of Jesus will always be assigned according to the Will of God! No one serves Jesus on their own will. Amen! Our Word continues saying that, **The people were waiting expectantly, and were all wondering if John might possibly be the Messiah (that had been spoken of by the prophets in the Old Testament).** The servant of Jesus will often amaze others when they utilize the gifts that God has given them, when they are serving Jesus and doing the Will of God. For God has given gifts that, when utilized by the Holy Spirit to serve Jesus, that are amazing! Amen again! Yet the Word of God says that when people began to wonder if the servant was the Master, **John answered them all, "I baptize you with water. But One who is more powerful than I will come, the straps of whose sandals I am not worthy to untie. He will baptize you with the Holy Spirit and fire."** The servant should always be sure that people know that they are a servant, not the Master! For the only Master, who is the only Messiah, is Jesus! Glory Hallelujah! Today, we are all being reminded to be grateful for the servants of Jesus, but praise and worship the Master, Jesus! Amen.

Today, our Scripture is speaking to Believers. Sometimes we are so excited by the servant of Jesus that we praise the servant, instead of praising the Master. Amen! And the servant must remember that when people start to praise them, they must immediately correct them, and direct them to praise the Master, Jesus! Amen again! Luke re-tells the history of John the Baptist. John was given the assignment by God to preach repentance of sin to the people of God. Yet because John served and did his assignment so well, some people wondered if John was the Messiah. And John wasted no time in letting all people know that he was not. Amen again! For no matter how great a servant of Jesus is in the eyes of people, there is only One Messiah! Hallelujah! And that Messiah is Jesus! All of Jesus's servants must remember, that as we serve Jesus, there will be some people that want to give the servant glory. You must waste no time with such talk, you must let people know right away that you are not worthy of praise. For no matter how well you may serve Jesus, there is only One Messiah! And to God goes all the glory! Hallelujah! Our Scripture begins with, **During the high priesthood of Annas and Caiaphas, the Word of God came to John, son of Zechariah, in the wilderness. He went into all the country around the (river) Jordan, preaching a baptism of repentance for the forgiveness of sins.** The servant of Jesus will always be assigned according to the Will of God! No one serves Jesus on their own will. Amen! All servants of Jesus have been chosen by God, and each servant of Jesus has a purpose that is chosen by God. Hallelujah! And all servants of Jesus are called to serve. John was called by God; all other servants of Jesus are called by Jesus! Servants of Jesus are always assigned according to the Will of God. Amen.

Today, our Word is speaking to Believers. Sometimes we are so excited by the servant of Jesus that we praise the servant, instead of praising the Master. Amen! Well, the servant must remember that when people start to praise them, they must immediately correct them, and direct them to praise the Master, Jesus! Amen again! Luke re-tells the history of John the Baptist. John was given the assignment by God to preach repentance of sin. Yet because John served and did his assignment so well, some people wondered if John was the Messiah. John wasted no time in letting all people know that he was not. Amen again! For no matter how great a servant of Jesus is in the eyes of people, there is only One Messiah! Hallelujah! And that Messiah is Jesus! The servants of Jesus must remember, that as we serve Jesus, there will be some people that want to give the servant glory. You must let people know right away that you are not worthy of praise. For no matter how well you may serve Jesus, there is only One Messiah! And to God goes all the glory! Hallelujah! The servant of Jesus will always be assigned according to the Will of God! No one serves Jesus on their own will. Amen! Our Word continues saying that, **The people were waiting expectantly, and were all**

wondering if John might possibly be the Messiah (that had been spoken of by the prophets in the Old Testament). The servant of Jesus will often amaze others when they utilize the gifts that God has given them, when they are serving Jesus and doing the Will of God. For God has given gifts that when utilized by the Holy Spirit to serve Jesus, that are amazing! Amen again! And because of these gifts, many Believers are excited by the servant of Jesus, and that is the Will of God, but the excitement should be for Jesus! Hallelujah! The gifts that are given to the servant by God, are to be utilized to encourage you to follow Jesus, and the Word of God! Too many Believers focus on the servant of Jesus! They begin to follow the servant, so much so that they are disappointed when the servant is not there. Tell the truth! The servant may amaze you, but the servant is not the Messiah! Amen!

Today, the Word of God is speaking to Believers. Sometimes we are so excited by the servant of Jesus that we praise the servant, instead of praising the Master. Amen! Well, the servant must remember that when people start to praise them, they must immediately correct them, and direct them to praise the Master, Jesus! Amen again! John the Baptist was given the assignment by God to preach repentance of sin. John served and did his assignment so well, that some people wondered if John was the Messiah. John wasted no time in letting all people know that he was not. Amen again! For no matter how great a servant of Jesus is in the eyes of people, there is only One Messiah! Hallelujah! And that Messiah is Jesus! Well, as we serve Jesus, there will be some people that want to give the servant glory. You must let people know right away that you are not worthy of praise. For no matter how well you may serve Jesus, there is only One Messiah! And to God goes all the glory! Hallelujah! The servant of Jesus will always be assigned according to the Will of God! No one serves Jesus on their own will. Amen! The servant of Jesus will often amaze others when they utilize the gifts that God has given them, when they are serving Jesus and doing the Will of God. For God has given gifts that, when utilized by the Holy Spirit to serve Jesus, that are amazing! Amen again! Yet the Word of God says that when people began to wonder if the servant was the Master, John answered them all, **"I baptize you with water. But One who is more powerful than I will come, the straps of whose sandals I am not worthy to untie. He will baptize you with the Holy Spirit and fire."** The servant should always be sure that people know that they are a servant, not the Master! For the only Master, who is the only Messiah, is Jesus! Glory Hallelujah! And it is the absolute responsibility of the servant of Jesus, to ensure that they are seen as only the servant! That is one reason each servant of Jesus must serve, humbly! Because each servant of Jesus is flesh, and flesh desires praise! Amen! So stay humble and remember that God gave you gifts, and an assignment, to be a servant of Jesus Christ! Hallelujah! So when people become excited about your gifts, praise your Master Jesus! And as soon as you hear someone praise you, stop them, and have them praise Jesus! Stay humble, servant of Jesus! Always make sure that all people know that you are a servant, not the Master! For the only Master, who is the only Messiah, is Jesus! Glory Hallelujah! Praise Jesus, and give glory to God! Amen.

Day 202

"Now these are (God's) people who came back from the captivity of the exiles whom Babylon had taken and had returned to Jerusalem and Judah, each to their own town."

"The whole company (that returned) numbered 42,360 people.

"When the seventh month came and the Israelites had settled (back) into their own towns, the people assembled together as one (large group) in Jerusalem.

Then Joshua (son of Jozadak) and his fellow priests, along with Zerubbabel (son of Sealtiel) and his associates began to build the altar of the God of Israel (Almighty God), to sacrifice burnt offerings on it, in accordance with what is written in the Law of Moses.

Despite their fear (of the enemies) around them, they built the altar on it's foundation, and sacrificed burnt offerings on it (to God)."

(Ezra 2:1, 64 & 3:1-3)

In today's Scripture, the author (most likely Ezra), recalls the time that the people of God had returned from captivity, and exile from Babylonia. God had punished His people for their sins, and had moved Babylonia to attack Judah, capture His people, and take them to Babylonia. Yet God had always had the plan to bring a "remnant" of His people back to Judah, and to have them restore

His temple and return to worshiping Him. Amen! The restoration of God's people and His Temple would be done, even though the Jewish people were still under Gentile rule, and were very fearful. Amen again! And God's mercy to deliver them from captivity would bring the Jewish people together, and even though they still feared man, their faith in God would pull them through! Hallelujah! And that is our guidance today! As we go through very difficult times captured by an unseen enemy, God will deliver His people! Amen! And even though we are still afraid, God's people must band together with their faith in God to restore His church, and return to worshiping Him! Amen again! For even in the worst times, God has a plan for His people! Hallelujah! But we must come together as one (His people), and worship Him! Glory Hallelujah! Give glory to God! Our Scripture begins with, **"Now these are (God's) people who came back from the captivity of the exiles whom Babylon had taken and had returned to Jerusalem and Judah, each to their own town. The whole company (that returned) numbered 42,360 people."** God will bring His people back from their "captivity". Amen! Our Word continues saying, **"When the seventh month came, and the Israelite's had settled (back) into their own towns, the people assembled together as one (large group) in Jerusalem. Then Joshua (son of Jozadak) and his fellow priests, along with Zerubbabel (son of Sealtiel) and his associates, began to build the altar of the God of Israel (Almighty God), to sacrifice burnt offerings on it, in accordance with what is written in the**

Law of Moses." When God brings His people out of captivity, we must form as one (His people), and restore worship in His Temple (Church). Amen again! And the Word of God concludes this about His people, that, **"Despite their fear (of the enemies) around them, they built the altar on its foundation, and sacrificed burnt offerings on it (to God)."** There will be fear when we are delivered from our "captivity", but do not let fear control you! Hallelujah! Come together and worship God in His Temple! For God is the only One that is in control! Worship Him without fear, of anyone, or anything! Amen.

Today, our Scripture is speaking to God's people. We all are feeling "captured" by an unseen, yet powerful enemy! But hallelujah, God is going to deliver His people from captivity! Glory Hallelujah! This is not the first time that God's people have been in captivity, and it probably will not be the last time. But still, God is always in control! Glory to God! The author writes of the time that the people of God had returned from captivity and exile in Babylonia. God had punished His people for their sins, and had moved Babylonia to attack Judah, capture His people, and take them to Babylonia. Yet God had always had a plan to bring His people back to Judah, and to have them return to worshiping Him. Amen! The restoration of God's people and His Temple would be done, even though the Jewish people were still very fearful. Amen again! And God's mercy to deliver them from captivity would bring the Jewish people together, and even though they still feared man, their faith in God would pull them through! Hallelujah! As we go through very difficult times captured by an unseen enemy, God will deliver His people! Amen! And even though we are still afraid, God's people must band together with their faith in God to restore His church, and return to worshiping Him! Amen again! For even in the worst times, God has a plan for His people! Hallelujah! Give glory to God! Our Scripture begins with, **"Now these are (God's) people who came back from the captivity of the exiles whom Babylon had taken and had returned to Jerusalem and Judah, each to their own town. The whole company (that returned) numbered 42,360 people."** God will bring His people back from their "captivity"! Amen! It is a very difficult time when we feel captured, or put in captivity by an "enemy". We are away from the "physical" house of God, and from the place where we typically come together as one to worship God. But even this, too, will pass! God already has spoken His plan for His people to return from captivity. Hallelujah! And when that time comes, make sure you return to God's Temple! Give glory to God! Come together and worship God in His Temple! For God is the only One that is in control! Worship Him without fear, of anyone, or anything! Amen.

Today, our Word is speaking to God's people. We all are feeling "captured" by an unseen, yet powerful enemy! But hallelujah, God is going to deliver His people from captivity! Glory Hallelujah! God is always in control! Glory to God! The author writes of the time that the people of God had returned from captivity and exile in Babylonia. God had punished His people for their sins, and had moved Babylonia to attack Judah, capture His people, and take them to Babylonia. Yet God had always had a plan to bring His people back to Judah, and to have them return to worshiping Him. Amen! God's mercy to deliver them from captivity would bring the Jewish people together, and even though they still feared man, their faith in God would pull them through! Hallelujah! As we go through very difficult times captured by an unseen enemy, God will deliver His people! Amen! And even though we are still afraid, God's people must band together with their faith in God to restore His church, and return to worshiping Him! Amen again! For even in the worst times, God has a plan for His people! Hallelujah! Give glory to God! God will bring His people back from their "captivity". Amen! Our Word continues saying, **"When the seventh month came, and the Israelites had settled (back) into their own towns, the people assembled together as one (large group) in Jerusalem. Then Joshua (son of Jozadak) and his fellow priests, along with Zerubbabel (son of Sealtiel) and his associates, began to build the altar of the God of Israel (Almighty God) to sacrifice burnt offerings on it, in accordance with what is written in the Law of Moses."** When God brings His people out of captivity, we must form as one (His people), and restore worship in His Temple (Church). Amen again! We must all admit that during our "captivity," we have gotten out of the habit of going to God's Temple (your church), to worship God. Now you do not have to be in a physical structure to worship God. You can worship God anywhere! Hallelujah! But there is strength gained when Believers come together in the House of the Lord to fellowship and worship! Tell the truth! Yet, Satan will do all he can to get you from joining other Believers to be as one, because the strength that you receive from that fellowship and worship, defeats Satan! And that is the truth! Glory Hallelujah! So when you get out of this captivity, come together and worship God in His Temple! For God is the only One that is in control! Worship Him without fear, of anyone, or anything! Amen.

Today, our the Word of God is speaking to God's people. You are feeling "captured" by an unseen, yet powerful enemy! But hallelujah, God is going to deliver you from captivity! Glory Hallelujah! God is always in control! Glory to God! The author writes of the time that the people of God had returned from captivity and exile in Babylonia. God had punished His people for their sins, and allowed them to be taken to Babylonia. Yet God had always had a plan to bring His people back to Judah, and to have them return to worshiping Him. Amen! God's mercy to deliver them from captivity would bring the Jewish people together, and even though they still feared man, their faith in God would pull them through! Hallelujah! As we go through very difficult times captured by an unseen enemy, God will deliver His people! Amen! And even though we are still afraid, God's people must band together with their faith in God to restore His church, and return to worshiping Him! Amen again! For even in the worst times, God has a plan for His people! Hallelujah! Give glory to

God! God will bring His people back from their "captivity". Amen! And when God brings His people out of captivity, we must form as one (His people), and restore worship in His Temple (Church). Amen again! And the Word of God concludes this about His people, that, **"Despite their fear (of the enemies) around them, they built the altar on its foundation, and sacrificed burnt offerings on it (to God)."** There will be fear when we are delivered from our "captivity", but do not let fear control you! Hallelujah! We must understand that fear is a weapon of Satan! God did not give you a spirit of fear! **(2 Timothy 1:7)** Amen! In fact, "I can do all this through him who gives me strength." **(Philippians 4:13).** Amen again! So as soon as you get out of "captivity", go to God's temple! Fellowship with your family, God's family! Celebrate that you are no longer in captivity, because of the mercy of your Father, Almighty God! Despite your enemies, have no fear! Glory Hallelujah! Come together and worship God in His Temple! For God is the only One that is in control! Worship Him without fear, of anyone, or anything! Amen.

Today, we are in captivity by an unseen enemy. But hallelujah, God is going to deliver you from captivity! Trust that, because that is the truth! God has a plan for His people! Hallelujah! Give glory to God! God will bring His people back from their "captivity". Amen! And when God brings His people out of captivity, we must form as one (His people), and restore worship in His Temple (Church). Amen again! There will be fear when we are delivered from our "captivity", but do not let fear control you! Despite your enemies, have no fear! Glory Hallelujah! Come together and worship God in His Temple! For God is the only One that is in control! Worship Him without fear, of anyone, or anything! Amen.

Day 203

Jesus said to His host (who invited Him to dinner), "When you give a luncheon or dinner, do not invite your friends, your brothers or sister, your relatives, or your rich neighbors, if you do, they may invite you back and so you will be repaid.

But when you give a banquet, invite the poor, the crippled, the lame, the blind,

and you will be blessed. Although they cannot repay you, you will be repaid at the resurrection of the righteous."

(Luke 14:12-14)

In today's Scripture, the servant of Jesus, Luke, shares with us the time that Jesus had been invited to eat in the house of a prominent Pharisee. When Jesus noticed that the guests were also prominent people, who were looking to be noticed by seating themselves at the tables that were considered to be the places of honor, Jesus told them a parable to teach them that one should not pick their own place of honor, but should pick the least important place, and allow the host to move them to higher places of honor. Amen! Jesus then spoke to the host of the dinner. And the guidance that Jesus gave to the host, applies to the hosts of gatherings today. Amen again! Our Scripture begins with, Jesus said to His host (who invited Him to dinner), **"When you give a luncheon or dinner, do not invite your friends, your brothers**

or sister, your relatives, or your rich neighbors, if you do, they may invite you back, and so you will be repaid." As a host of the Gospel of Jesus, the servants of Jesus should not only share the Gospel of Jesus with those who already know Him. Amen! Our Word continues with this guidance from Jesus to the host of His Gospel, **"But when you give a banquet, invite the poor, the crippled, the lame, the blind, and you will be blessed."** The servants of Jesus must go out and seek those who do not know the Gospel of Jesus, so they may have the opportunity to eat from the bounty of God! And for each person that you feed the Gospel of Jesus that has never tasted the Word before, you will be blessed! Amen again! And the Word of God tells us that Jesus says, that when we reach those that do not know the Gospel of Jesus, that, **"Although they cannot repay you, you will be repaid at the resurrection of the righteous."** The servants of Jesus may never know if those that they have fed the Gospel of Jesus will accept Jesus, they will receive glory with God in Heaven! Glory Hallelujah! Jesus is speaking to His servants today! Do not be content to just share the Gospel of Jesus with Believers. Seek those who do not know the Gospel of Jesus, so that they have the opportunity to know Him. And do not worry that you may not see the people you expose to Jesus, accept Jesus. For hallelujah, you will receive glory from Almighty God when you arrive in Heaven at the glorious return of Jesus to claim His Believers! Glory Hallelujah! Amen. Jesus is speaking to you! You are the host of Jesus's banquet! Amen.

Today, our Scripture is speaking to the servants of Jesus Christ. You are being encouraged to seek those who do not know the Gospel of Jesus, and give those people the opportunity to know Him. Amen! The servants of Jesus are being guided by Jesus to go beyond those that already know Jesus, to reach those who do not. Amen again! Luke shares with us the time that Jesus had been invited to eat in the house of a prominent Pharisee. When Jesus noticed that the guests were also prominent people, who were seating themselves at the tables that were considered to be the places of honor. So Jesus told them a parable to teach them that one should not pick their own place of honor, but should pick the least important place, and allow the host to move them to higher places of honor. Amen! Jesus also spoke to the host of the dinner. And the guidance that Jesus gave to the host, applies to the hosts of gatherings today. Amen again! Our Scripture begins with, **Jesus said to His host (who invited Him to dinner), "When you give a luncheon or dinner, do not invite your friends, your brothers or sister, your relatives, or your rich neighbors, if you do, they may invite you back, and so you will be repaid."** As a host of the Gospel of Jesus, the servants of Jesus should not only share the Gospel of Jesus with those who already know Him. Amen! While it is wonderful, and part of God's Will that the servants of Jesus encourage Believers by sharing the Gospel with them, Jesus is challenging us that if we only feed those who have already eaten at the banquet, we will never give an opportunity to feed someone who has never eaten! Amen! And every Believer that we serve the Gospel to can serve it back to you, so they can repay you! However, you can control who you invite to eat the fruit of the Gospel of Jesus, and Jesus is speaking to you! Hallelujah! You are the host of Jesus's banquet! Amen.

Today, our Word is speaking to the servants of Jesus Christ. You are the host of the Gospel of Jesus! And you are being encouraged to seek those who do not know the Gospel of Jesus and give those people the opportunity to know Him. Amen! The servants of Jesus are being guided by Jesus to go beyond those that already know Jesus, to reach those who do not. Amen again! Luke shares with us the time that Jesus had been invited to eat in the house of a prominent Pharisee. When Jesus noticed that the guests were also prominent people, who were seating themselves at the tables that were considered to be the places of honor. So Jesus told them a parable to teach them that one should not pick their own place of honor. Amen! Jesus also spoke to the host of the dinner. And the guidance that Jesus gave to the host, applies to the hosts of gatherings today. Amen again! As a host of the Gospel of Jesus, the servants of Jesus should not only share the Gospel of Jesus with those who already know Him. Amen! Our Word continues with this guidance from Jesus to the host of His Gospel, **"But when you give a banquet, invite the poor, the crippled, the lame, the blind, and you will be blessed."** The servants of Jesus must go out and seek those who do not know the Gospel of Jesus, so they may have the opportunity to eat from the bounty of God! And for each person that you feed the Gospel of Jesus that has never tasted the Word before, you will be blessed! Amen again! The greatest service that you can give as a servant of Jesus, is to introduce someone to the Gospel of Jesus! Hallelujah! For when someone finally tastes the bounty of God through Jesus Christ, they are more likely to want more of it! So seek someone who does not know Jesus, and invite them to the banquet that is provided through the Gospel of Jesus. Glory Hallelujah! Jesus is speaking to you! You are the host of Jesus's banquet! Amen.

Today, the Word of God is speaking to the servants of Jesus Christ. You are the host of the Gospel of Jesus! And you are being encouraged to seek those who do not know the Gospel of Jesus, and give those people the opportunity to know Him. Amen! You are being guided by Jesus to go beyond those that already know Jesus, to reach those who do not. Amen again! Jesus is speaking to you, because you serve as the host to His banquet. Hallelujah! And the guidance that Jesus gave to the host, applies to the hosts of gatherings today. Amen again! As a host of the Gospel of Jesus, the servants of Jesus should not only share the Gospel of Jesus with those who already know Him. Amen! The servants of Jesus must go out and seek those who do not know the Gospel of Jesus, so they may have the opportunity to eat from the bounty of God! And for each person that you feed the Gospel of Jesus that has never tasted the Word before, you will be blessed! Amen again! And the Word of God tells us that Jesus says, that when we reach those that do not know the Gospel of Jesus, that, **"Although they cannot repay you, you will be repaid at the resurrection of the**

righteous." The servants of Jesus may never know if those that they have fed the Gospel of Jesus will accept Jesus, they will receive glory with God in Heaven! Glory Hallelujah! The work that Jesus calls His servants to do is to teach His Gospel to those who do not know it. In fact, Jesus said to His disciples (servants), "Go and make disciples of all nations, baptizing them in the name of the Father and of the Son, and of the Holy Spirit **(Matthew 28:19)**." Glory! To do that, the servants of Jesus must invite people who do not know Jesus, to His banquet. Tell the truth! Jesus is speaking to you! You are the host of Jesus's banquet! Amen.

Today, Jesus is speaking to His servants! You are the host of the banquet that is the Gospel of Jesus! Do not be content to just share the Gospel of Jesus with Believers. Seek those who do not know the Gospel of Jesus, so that they have the opportunity to know Him. And do not worry that you may not see the people you expose to Jesus, accept Jesus. For hallelujah, you will receive glory from Almighty God when you arrive in Heaven at the glorious return of Jesus to claim His Believers! Glory Hallelujah! Jesus is speaking to you! You are the host of Jesus's banquet! Amen.

Day 204

"Since sexual immorality is occurring, each man should have sexual relations with his own wife, and each woman with her own husband.

The husband should fulfill his marital duty to his wife, and likewise the wife to her husband.

The wife does not have authority over her own body, but yields it to her husband. In the same way, the husband does not authority over his own body, but yields it to his wife.

Do not deprive each other except perhaps by mutual consent, and for a time, so that you may devote yourselves to prayer. Then come together again so that Satan will not tempt you because of your lack of self-control."

(1 Corinthians 7:2-5)

In today's Scripture, the great servant of Jesus, the apostle Paul, responds to Believers with his thoughts that address problems in the church, and answers questions that have come to him from the members of the church. Amen! These problems and questions had come from the church to Paul, at a time when the church was being torn apart by different groups within the church, and from the spiritual immaturity of the Believers in the church. Amen again! For even then, the church had problems! And today, the church has problems! Tell the truth! There are different groups within the church, who join together, based on what they conclude to be the problems in the church. And often, their answers to the problems in the church, is not based on spiritual truth, but based on their own opinion! And that is the truth! Believers in the church are still being divided by opinion and spiritual immaturity. In our particular passage, Paul addresses questions concerning married life. Part of the reason that Believers should marry, is so that they can have sex regularly with each other, without succumbing to sexual temptations… which lead to unmarried sex! Hallelujah! Our Scripture begins with the servant of Jesus giving guidance to Believers who are married, saying, **"Since sexual immorality is occurring, each man should have sexual relations with his own wife, and each woman with her own husband. The husband should fulfill his marital duty to his wife, and likewise the wife to her husband."** Married couples should have regular sexual activities with each other, as long as there is sexual desire in either spouse. That is marital duty! Amen! The Word continues with the servant of Jesus's reasoning to Believers, that in marriage, **"The wife does not have authority over her own body, but yields it to her husband. In the same way, the husband does not have authority over his own body, but yields it to his wife."** In marriage, both the husband and the wife have sexual rights, and exclusive possession of the other spouse's body and sexual desires. Amen again! And the Word of God concludes with the servant of Jesus cautioning each spouse in the marriage, **"Do not deprive each other except perhaps by mutual consent, and for a time,**

so that you may devote yourselves to prayer. Then come together again so that Satan will not tempt you because of your lack of self-control." Believers in a marriage must understand that sexual drive is God-given! Sex is a need of the adult human, and depriving your spouse of a basic need, makes it easier to be tempted by Satan, to seek their sexual need from someone else! For the sexual drive in humans is very strong, and Satan constantly sends sexual temptations throughout the day, week, month, year, and lifetime, seeking to take advantage of the weakness of husbands and wives who are being denied sexual fulfillment by their spouse. Amen.

Today, our Scripture is speaking to Believers who are married. Take care of the sexual needs of your spouse, by giving of yourself! And take care of your own sexual needs, only through your spouse! Hallelujah! For that is an important part of your marital duty! Amen! Do not give into temptations that lead to sex without marriage, for it is better to marry than to burn with passion **(1 Corinthians 7:9).** Amen again! The apostle Paul responds to Believers with his thoughts that address problems in the church, and answers questions that have come to him from the members of the church. Amen! This was at a time when the church was being torn apart by different groups within the church, and from the spiritual immaturity of the Believers in the church. Amen again! For even then, the church had problems! And today, the church has problems! Tell the truth! There are different groups within the church, who join together, and often their answers to the problems in the church, is not based on spiritual truth, but based on their own opinion! And that is the truth! In our particular passage, Paul addresses questions concerning married life. Part of the reason that Believers should marry, is so that they can have sex regularly with each other, without succumbing to sexual temptations, which lead to unmarried sex! Hallelujah! Our Scripture begins with the servant of Jesus giving guidance to Believers who are married, saying, **"Since sexual immorality is occurring, each man should have sexual relations with his own wife, and each woman with her own husband. The husband should fulfill his marital duty to his wife, and likewise the wife to her husband."** Married couples should have regular sexual activities with each other, as long as there is sexual desire in either spouse. That is marital duty! Amen! For the sexual drive in humans is very strong, and Satan constantly sends sexual temptations throughout the day, week, month, year, and lifetime, seeking to take advantage of the weakness of husbands and wives who are being denied sexual fulfillment by their spouse. Amen.

Today, our Word is speaking to Believers who are married. Take care of the sexual needs of your spouse, by giving of yourself! And take care of your own sexual needs, only through your spouse! Hallelujah! For that is an important part of your marital duty! Amen! Do not give into temptations that lead to sex without marriage, for it is better to marry than to burn with passion. Amen again! Paul responds to Believers with his thoughts that address problems in the church. Amen! The church was being torn apart by different groups within the church, and from the spiritual immaturity of the Believers in the church. Amen again! And today, the church has problems! Tell the truth! There are different groups within the church, that give their answers to the problems in the church, which is often not based on spiritual truth, but based on their own opinion! And that is the truth! Paul addresses questions concerning married life. Part of the reason that Believers should marry, is so that they can have sex regularly with each other, without succumbing to sexual temptations that lead to unmarried sex! Hallelujah! Married couples should have regular sexual activities with each other, as long as there is sexual desire in either spouse. That is marital duty! Amen! The Word continues with the servant of Jesus's reasoning to Believers, that in marriage, **"The wife does not have authority over her own body, but yields it to her husband. In the same way, the husband does not have authority over his own body, but yields it to his wife."** In marriage, both the husband and the wife have sexual rights, and exclusive possession of the other spouse's body and sexual desires. Amen again! For the sexual drive in humans is very strong, and Satan constantly sends sexual temptations throughout the day, week, month, year, and lifetime, seeking to take advantage of the weakness of husbands and wives who are being denied sexual fulfillment by their spouse. Amen.

Today, the Word of God is speaking to Believers who are married. Take care of the sexual needs of your spouse, by giving of yourself! And take care of your own sexual needs, only through your spouse! Hallelujah! For that is an important part of your marital duty! Amen! Do not give into temptations that lead to sex without marriage, for it is better to marry than to burn with passion. Amen again! And today, this is a problem in the marriages of Believers! Tell the truth! Believers that are married are constantly being tempted by Satan, to have sex with someone else other than their spouse. And that is the truth! Well, part of the reason that Believers should marry, is so that they can have sex regularly with each other, without succumbing to sexual temptations that lead to unmarried sex. Hallelujah! Married couples should have regular sexual activities with each other, as long as there is sexual desire in either spouse. That is marital duty! Amen! In marriage, both the husband and the wife have sexual rights, and exclusive possession of the other spouse's body and sexual desires. Amen again! And the Word of God concludes with the servant of Jesus cautioning each spouse in the marriage, **"Do not deprive each other except perhaps by mutual consent, and for a time, so that you may devote yourselves to prayer. Then come together again so that Satan will not tempt you because of your lack of self-control."** Believers in a marriage must understand that sexual drive is God-given! Sex is a need of the adult human, and depriving your spouse of a basic need, makes it easier to be tempted by Satan, to seek their sexual need from someone else! For the sexual drive in humans is very strong, and Satan constantly sends sexual temptations throughout the day, week, month, year, and lifetime, seeking to take advantage of the weakness of husbands and wives who are being denied sexual fulfillment by their spouses. For the sexual drive in humans is very strong, and Satan constantly sends sexual temptations throughout the day, week, month, year, and lifetime, seeking to take advantage of the weakness of husbands and wives who are being denied sexual fulfillment by their spouses. Amen.

Today, Believers who are married, are being warned! Take care of the sexual needs of your spouse, by giving of yourself! And take care of your own sexual needs, only through your spouse! Hallelujah! For that is an important part of your marital duty! Too many Believers do not realize, or want to admit, that they, and/or their spouse, is not having enough sex! Whether or not enough sex is happening is in the eyes of each individual spouse! You may think that you are doing enough, but you may not! And your spouse may be thinking that they are doing enough, but you may think they are not! But one thing each spouse can be sure of, Satan is watching, and Satan is throwing temptation after temptation at your spouse! And you already know that Satan is throwing temptation after temptation, at you! So you are being warned today if you are married! Take care of the sexual needs of your spouse, by giving of yourself! And take care of your own sexual needs, only through your spouse! Hallelujah! That is an important part of your marital duty! For the sexual drive in humans is very strong, and Satan constantly sends sexual temptations throughout the day, week, month, year, and lifetime, seeking to take advantage of the weakness of husbands and wives who are being denied sexual fulfillment by their spouses. Amen.

Day 205

The sisters (Mary and Martha) sent word to Jesus, "Lord the one you love (Lazarus) is sick."

When He heard this, Jesus said, "This sickness will not end in death. No, it is for God's glory, so that God's Son may be glorified through it."

Jesus, once more deeply moved, came to the tomb (of Lazarus). It was a cave with a stone laid across the entrance.

"Take away the stone," Jesus said.

"But Lord," said Martha, the sister of the dead man, "by this time there is a bad odor, for he has been (buried) there four days."

Then Jesus said, "Did I not tell you that if you believe, you will see the glory of God?"

(John 11:3-4 & 38-40)

In today's Scripture, the great servant of Jesus, the apostle John, tells us of the time that Jesus was told that his good friend, Lazarus, was sick, and would eventually die. Amen! This account of Lazarus is only told in the Gospel of John. John's Gospel of Jesus focuses on Jesus as the Messiah, and Son of God, so John presented seven signs of Jesus's identity as the Son of God. These signs were in the form of the miracles that Jesus performed, which no man could perform! Amen again! And Lazarus presented Jesus an opportunity to show people that He was much more than a man, and in fact, that He, indeed, is the Son of God! Hallelujah! Tell the truth! Lazarus would be the seventh sign of Jesus's miracles that appear in the Gospel of John. Glory Hallelujah! Jesus is the Messiah, and Son of God! And that is the Truth! Glory to God! Our Scripture begins with, **The sisters (Mary and Martha) sent word to Jesus, "Lord the one you love (Lazarus) is sick." When He heard this, Jesus said, "This sickness will not end in death. No, it is for God's glory, so that God's Son may be glorified through it."** The Son of God already knew that Lazarus had died, and the Son of God knew that He would raise Lazarus from death! For the Son of God knew that by raising Lazarus from death, He would glorify God, and show people a miracle so that they would know that the man Jesus is the Son of God! Amen! Our Word continues with Jesus approaching the dead Lazarus, **Jesus, once more deeply moved, came to the tomb (of Lazarus). It was a cave with a stone laid across the entrance. "Take away the stone," Jesus said. "But Lord," said Martha, the sister of the dead man, "By this time, there is a bad odor, for he has been (buried) there four days."** The Son of God can redeem a dead person to life, and see hope when others see no hope! For the Son of God makes the impossible happen! Amen again! And the Word of God concludes with a promise from the One and only Son of God, that He makes to all people who come to Him, **Then Jesus said, "Did I not tell you that if you believe, you will see the glory of God?"** Jesus is the Son of God, and all impossible things are possible through Him, but you have to believe Him to see the glory of God! Tell the Truth! Glory Hallelujah! Jesus is the Messiah, and Son of God! And that is the Truth! Glory to God! Amen.

Today, our Scripture is speaking to all people! Jesus is the Son of God, but you have to believe Him to see the glory of God! Tell the Truth! Glory Hallelujah! Jesus is the Messiah, and Son of God! And that is the Truth! Glory to God! The apostle John tells us of the time that Jesus was told that his good friend, Lazarus, was sick, and would eventually die. Amen! John's Gospel of Jesus focuses on Jesus as the Messiah, and Son of God, so John presented seven signs of Jesus to identify Him as the Son of God. These signs were miracles that Jesus performed, which no man could ever perform! Amen again! And Lazarus presented Jesus an opportunity to show people that He was much more than a man, and in fact, that He, indeed, is the Son of God! Hallelujah! Tell the truth! Jesus is the Messiah, and Son of God! And that is the Truth! Glory to God! Our Scripture begins with, **The sisters (Mary and Martha) sent word to Jesus, "Lord the one you love (Lazarus) is sick." When He heard this, Jesus said, "This sickness will not end in death. No, it is for God's glory, so that God's Son may be glorified through it."** The Son of God already knew that Lazarus had died, and the Son of God knew that He would raise Lazarus from death! For the Son of God knew that by raising Lazarus from death, He would glorify God, and show people a miracle so, that they would know that the man Jesus is the Son of God! Amen!

Jesus already knew that Lazarus was dead before He heard that Lazarus was sick. And Jesus already knew that Lazarus's death would be used to show people that Jesus is the Son of God! For as the Son of God, God had already shown Jesus what would take place. That is why, when Jesus heard that Lazarus was sick, He did not hurry to heal Him! Lazarus's death was an opportunity for Jesus to do the impossible, and as the Son of God, Jesus would glorify His Father! Hallelujah! Tell the Truth! Glory Hallelujah! Jesus is the Messiah, and Son of God! And that is the Truth! Glory to God! Amen.

Today, our Word is speaking to all people! Jesus is the Son of God, but you have to believe Him to see the glory of God! Tell the Truth! Glory Hallelujah! Jesus is the Messiah, and Son of God! And that is the Truth! Glory to God! John tells us that Jesus was told that his good friend, Lazarus, was sick, and would eventually die. Amen! John focuses on Jesus as the Messiah, and Son of God, so John presented seven signs of Jesus to identify Him as the Son of God. These signs were miracles that Jesus performed, which no man could ever perform! Amen again! And Lazarus presented Jesus an opportunity to show people that He was much more than a man, that He, indeed, is the Son of God! Hallelujah! Tell the truth! Jesus is the Messiah, and Son of God! And that is the Truth! Glory to God! And the Son of God already knew that Lazarus had died, yet the Son of God knew that He would raise Lazarus from death! For Jesus, the Son of God, knew that by raising Lazarus from death, He would glorify God, and show people a miracle, so that they would know that the man Jesus is the Son of God! Amen! Our Word continues with Jesus approaching the dead Lazarus, **Jesus, once more deeply moved, came to the tomb (of Lazarus). It was a cave with a stone laid across the entrance. "Take away the stone," Jesus said. "But Lord," said Martha, the sister of the dead man, "by this time, there is a bad odor, for he has been (buried) there four days."** The Son of God can redeem a dead person to life, and see hope when others see no hope! For the Son of God makes the impossible happen! Amen again! Jesus, the Son of God, purposely waited to arrive at the tomb of Lazarus four days after his death. Because at the time of Jesus on earth, the Jewish people believed that the soul of a person stayed near the body for three days after death, hoping that the soul could re-enter a dead body. But after three days, the Jewish people believed that all hope for the soul was gone. And that is why the Son of God did not arrive until the fourth day! So that Jesus, the Son of God, could make the impossible happen! Hallelujah! Tell the Truth! Glory Hallelujah! Jesus is the Messiah, and Son of God! And that is the Truth! Glory to God! Amen.

Today, the Word of God is speaking to all people! Jesus is the Son of God, but you have to believe Him to see the glory of God! Tell the Truth! Glory Hallelujah! Jesus is the Messiah, and Son of God! And that is the Truth! Glory to God! Jesus was told that his good friend, Lazarus, was sick, and would eventually die. Amen! John focuses on Jesus as the Messiah, and Son of God, so John presented seven miracles that Jesus performed, which no man could ever perform! Amen again! And Lazarus presented Jesus an opportunity to show people that He was, indeed, the Son of God! Hallelujah! Tell the truth! Jesus is the Messiah, and Son of God! And that is the Truth! Glory to God! The Son of God already knew that Lazarus had died, yet the Son of God knew that He would raise Lazarus from death! For Jesus, the Son of God, knew that by raising Lazarus from death, He would glorify God, and show people a miracle, so that they would know that the man Jesus is the Son of God! Amen! For only the Son of God could redeem a dead person to life, and see hope when others see no hope! For the Son of God makes the impossible happen! Amen again! And the Word of God concludes with a promise from the One and only Son of God, that He makes to all people who come to Him, **Then Jesus said, "Did I not tell you that if you believe, you will see the glory of God?"** Jesus is the Son of God, and all impossible things are possible through Him, but you have to believe Him to see the glory of God! Hallelujah! All people must first accept Jesus, and believe that He is the Son of God, before they will see the glory of God! That is what the Gospel of Jesus, and the New Covenant of God is all about! Amen! Before you can receive the grace of God, you must first believe that Jesus is the Son of God! Without that happening, you will not see the glory of God! Tell the Truth! Glory Hallelujah! Jesus is the Messiah, and Son of God! And that is the Truth! Glory to God! Amen.

Today, our Scripture Guidance is for all people! Jesus is the Son of God! And you have to believe in Him as the Son of God, and your Messiah, to see the glory of God! Tell the truth today! Glory Hallelujah! Jesus is the Messiah, and Son of God! And that is the Truth! Believe in Him, and you will see the glory of God! Amen.

Day 206

So they took away the stone (at Lazarus tomb). Then Jesus looked up and said, "Father, I thank You that You have heard Me.

I knew that You always hear Me, but I said this for the benefit of the people standing here, that they may believe that You sent Me."

When He had said this, Jesus called in a loud voice, "Lazarus, come out!"

The dead man (Lazarus) came out, his hands and feet wrapped with strips of linen, and cloth around his face. Jesus said to them, "Take off the grave clothes and let him go."

Therefore many of the Jews who had come to visit Mary, and had seen what Jesus did, believed in Him.

(John 11:41-45)

In today's Scripture, the great servant of Jesus, the apostle John, tells us of the time that Jesus raised his good friend Lazarus from the dead. Amen! This account of Lazarus is only told in the Gospel of John. John's Gospel of Jesus focuses on Jesus as the Messiah, and Son of God, so John presented seven signs of Jesus's identity as the Son of God. These signs were in the form of the miracles that Jesus performed, which no man could perform! Amen again! And Lazarus presented Jesus an opportunity to show people that

He was much more than a man, and in fact, that He, indeed, is the Son of God! Hallelujah! Tell the truth! For Lazarus, death had been preordained by God, so that Jesus would raise a dead man to life in front of people. This is so very important because Jesus preached that He would be raised from death, and that He had the authority of God to raise people from eternal death, to be with God! Glory Hallelujah! And only Jesus can do this, because Jesus is the Messiah, and Son of God! And that is the Truth! Glory to God! Our Scripture begins with, **So they took away the stone (at Lazarus's tomb). Then Jesus looked up and said, "Father, I thank You that You have heard Me. I knew that You always hear Me, but I said this for the benefit of the people standing here, that they may believe that You sent Me."** The Son of God already knew that He would raise Lazarus from death! Yet Jesus wanted the people to see Him talk to God, and call Him Father! Jesus wanted people to see that He was connected to God, and that through God, He could do the impossible! And that by raising Lazarus from death, He would glorify God, and show people a miracle, so that they would know that the man Jesus is the Son of God! Amen! Our Word continues with Jesus commanding the impossible to happen, **When He had said this, Jesus called in a loud voice, "Lazarus, come out!" The dead man (Lazarus) came out, his hands and feet wrapped with strips of linen, and cloth around his face. Jesus said to them, "Take off the grave clothes and let him go."** Only the Son of God can redeem a dead person to life! For the Son of God makes the impossible happen!

Amen again! And the Word of God concludes that people now know that Jesus is the Messiah and Son of God, saying, **Therefore many of the Jews who had come to visit Mary, and had seen what Jesus did, believed in Him.** Jesus is the Son of God, and all impossible things are possible through Him, but you have to believe Him to see the glory of God! Tell the Truth! Glory Hallelujah! Jesus is the Messiah, and Son of God! And that is the Truth! Glory to God! Amen.

Today, our Scripture is speaking to all people! Jesus is the Son of God, but you have to believe Him to see the glory of God! Tell the Truth! Glory Hallelujah! Jesus is the Messiah, and Son of God! And that is the Truth! Glory to God! The apostle John tells us of the time that Jesus raised his good friend Lazarus from the dead. Amen! John's Gospel of Jesus focuses on Jesus as the Messiah, and Son of God, so John presented seven signs of Jesus's identity as the Son of God. These signs were in the form of the miracles that Jesus performed, which no man could perform! Amen again! And Lazarus presented Jesus with an opportunity to show people that He is the Son of God! Hallelujah! Tell the truth! For Lazarus, death had been preordained by God, so that Jesus would raise a dead man to life in front of people. Jesus preached that He would be raised from death, and that He had the authority of God to raise people from eternal death, to be with God! Glory Hallelujah! And only Jesus can do this, because Jesus is the Messiah, and Son of God! And that is the Truth! Glory to God! Our Scripture begins with, **So they took away the stone (at Lazarus's tomb). Then**

Jesus looked up and said, "Father, I thank You that You have heard Me. I knew that You always hear Me, but I said this for the benefit of the people standing here, that they may believe that You sent Me." The Son of God already knew that He would raise Lazarus from death! Yet Jesus wanted the people to see Him talk to God, and call Him Father! Jesus wanted people to see that He was connected to God, and that through God, He could do the impossible! And that by raising Lazarus from death, He would glorify God, and show people a miracle, so that they would know that the man Jesus is the Son of God! Amen! Jesus also knew that if people saw Him speaking to God as His Father, before He performed the miracle, people would see that God the Father had given Jesus authority to raise the dead. And the miracle would confirm that Jesus is the Son of God! Hallelujah! So Lazarus's death was an opportunity for Jesus to do the impossible, and as the Son of God, Jesus would glorify His Father! Glory Hallelujah! Tell the Truth! Jesus is the Messiah, and Son of God! And that is the Truth! Glory to God! Amen.

Today, our Word is speaking to all people! Jesus is the Son of God, but you have to believe Him to see the glory of God! Tell the Truth! Glory Hallelujah! Jesus is the Messiah, and Son of God! And that is the Truth! Glory to God! John tells us of the time that Jesus raised his good friend Lazarus from the dead. Amen! John's Gospel of Jesus focuses on Jesus as the Messiah, and Son of God, so John presented signs that were in the form of miracles that Jesus performed, which no man could perform! Amen again! And

Lazarus's death presented Jesus an opportunity to show people that He is the Son of God! Hallelujah! Tell the truth! Lazarus death had been preordained by God, so that Jesus would raise a dead man to life in front of people. Jesus preached that He had the authority from God to raise people from eternal death, to be with God! Glory Hallelujah! The Son of God already knew that He would raise Lazarus from death! Yet Jesus wanted the people to see Him talk to God, and call Him Father! Jesus wanted people to see that He was connected to God, and that through God, He could do the impossible! Amen! Our Word continues with Jesus commanding the impossible to happen, **When He had said this, Jesus called in a loud voice, "Lazarus, come out!" The dead man (Lazarus) came out, his hands and feet wrapped with strips of linen, and cloth around his face. Jesus said to them, "Take off the grave clothes and let him go."** Only the Son of God can redeem a dead person to life! For the Son of God makes the impossible happen! Amen again! Jesus, the Son of God, spoke to a dead man, and the dead man heard Him! Hallelujah! The dead man heard the voice, and recognized that voice, to be the Son of God! Hallelujah again! How could a dead man, hear a voice? Because the voice was not the voice of a man, the voice was from the Son of God! And the Son of God gave a commandment, that made the impossible, happen! Amen! And only Jesus, the Son of God, could make the impossible happen! Hallelujah! Tell the Truth! Glory Hallelujah! Jesus is the Messiah, and Son of God! And that is the Truth! Glory to God! Amen.

Today, the Word of God is speaking to all people! Jesus is the Son of God, but you have to believe Him to see the glory of God! Tell the Truth! Glory Hallelujah! Jesus is the Messiah, and Son of God! And that is the Truth! Glory to God! John tells us of the time that Jesus raised his good friend Lazarus from the dead. Amen! John's Gospel of Jesus focuses on Jesus as the Messiah, and Son of God, so John presented signs that were in the form of miracles that Jesus performed, which no man could perform! Amen again! And Lazarus's death presented Jesus an opportunity to show people that He is the Son of God! Hallelujah! Tell the truth! Lazarus's death had been preordained by God, so that Jesus would raise a dead man to life in front of people. Jesus preached that He had the authority of God to raise people from eternal death, to be with God! Glory Hallelujah! The Son of God already knew that He would raise Lazarus from death! Yet Jesus wanted the people to see Him talk to God, and call Him Father! Jesus wanted people to see that He was connected to God, and that through God, He could do the impossible! Amen! Only the Son of God can redeem a dead person to life! For the Son of God makes the impossible happen! Amen again! And the Word of God concludes that people now know that Jesus is the Messiah and Son of God, saying, **Therefore many of the Jews who had come to visit Mary, and had seen what Jesus did, believed in Him.** Jesus is the Son of God, and all impossible things are possible through Him, but you have to believe Him to see the glory of God! Tell the Truth! Glory

Hallelujah! Jesus is the Messiah, and Son of God! And that is the Truth! Glory to God! Amen.

Today, our Scripture Guidance is for all people! Jesus is the Son of God! And you have to believe in Him as the Son of God, and your Messiah, to see the glory of God! Tell the truth today! Glory Hallelujah! Jesus is the Messiah, and Son of God! And that is the Truth! Believe in Him, and you will see the glory of God! Amen.

Day 207

"What good is it, my brothers and sisters, if someone claims to have faith (in Jesus), but has no deeds (work for Jesus). Can such faith save them?

Suppose a brother or a sister is without clothes and daily food.

If one of you says to them, 'Go in peace, keep warm and well fed,' but does nothing about their physical needs, what good is it?

In the same way, faith by itself, if it is not accompanied by action, is dead."

"You see that a person is considered righteous by what they do, and not by faith alone."

"As the body without the Spirit is dead, so faith without deed is dead."

(James 2:14-17, 24 & 26)

In today's Scripture, the author James, a leader of the Jerusalem church (and most likely the brother of Jesus), speaks to Believers about living a Christian life, that is characterized by faith that drives good deeds and good works. Amen! Now James is not saying that a person is saved by good works, because we know that a person can only be saved by their faith in Jesus Christ as their Lord and Savior. Hallelujah! For you are justified by God by your faith alone. However, your faith should not be alone! Genuine faith in Jesus should compel each Believer to produce good deeds through serving Jesus. Amen again! James was challenging Believers then, and the Word is challenging Believers today! Does your faith in Jesus, show in the work that you do for Jesus? You are being challenged! Amen! Our Scripture begins with the servant of Jesus asking each Believer, **"What good is it, my brothers and sisters, if someone claims to have faith (in Jesus), but has no deeds (work for Jesus). Can such faith save them?"** Only faith in Jesus can save you, but genuine faith in Jesus drives His people to serve Him! Amen! Our Word continues with an example to each Believer, saying, **"Suppose a brother or a sister is without clothes and daily food. If one of you says to them, 'Go in peace, keep warm and well fed,' but does nothing about their physical needs, what good is it? In the same way, faith by itself, if it is not accompanied by action, is dead."** This shows false faith in Jesus, because the person who claims to love Jesus... does not show love to their brother or sister! A Believer's faith in action, drives love in action! Amen again! And the Word of God proclaims to Believers, **"You see that a person is considered righteous by what they do, and not by faith alone. As the body without the Spirit is dead, so faith without deed is dead."** God credits righteousness based on what each of us does! You become righteous in the eyes of God by how you live! And your faith in Jesus should drive you to live in a way that serves

Him! Hallelujah! Without any works for Jesus, your faith is not alive the way that Jesus wants it to be! Amen.

Today, our Scripture is speaking to Believers! You are being challenged! Your faith in Jesus should compel you to do work in the name of Jesus! Amen! For without any works for Jesus, your faith is not alive the way that Jesus wants it to be! Amen again! James, a leader of the Jerusalem church, speaks to Believers about living a Christian life, one that is characterized by faith that drives good deeds and good works. Amen! James is not saying that a person is saved by good works, because we know that a person can only be saved by their faith in Jesus Christ as their Lord and Savior. Hallelujah! You are justified by God by your faith alone. However, your faith should not be alone! Genuine faith in Jesus should compel each Believer to produce good deeds through serving Jesus. Amen again! James was challenging Believers then, and the Word is challenging Believers today! Does your faith in Jesus, show in the work that you do for Jesus? Amen! Our Scripture begins with the servant of Jesus asking each Believer, **"What good is it, my brothers and sisters, if someone claims to have faith (in Jesus), but has no deeds (work for Jesus). Can such faith save them?"** Only faith in Jesus can save you, but genuine faith in Jesus drives His people to serve Him! Amen! This is a sensitive subject for many Believers, for so many Believers think that going to church, and sitting in the pews on Sunday, is somehow credited as working for Jesus! Tell the truth! Sitting in church on Sunday is a good thing! It is fellowship, and in many cases, it is worship, but it is not work! You are not doing work for Jesus when you go to church and sit! In fact, you are in church watching other servants of Jesus show their faith, by their work! Believers are being challenged to get past the concept of "all I have to do is go to church"! Your love of Jesus, and your faith in Jesus, should drive you to work for Jesus! Hallelujah! Without any works for Jesus, your faith is not alive the way that Jesus wants it to be! And that is the truth! Amen.

Today, our Word is speaking to Believers! You are being challenged! Your faith in Jesus should compel you to do work in the name of Jesus! Amen! For without any works for Jesus, your faith is not alive the way that Jesus wants it to be! Amen again! James speaks to Believers about living a Christian life, of faith that drives good deeds and good works. Amen! James is not saying that a person is saved by good works, for a person can only be saved by their faith in Jesus as their Lord and Savior. Hallelujah! You are justified by God by your faith alone. However, your faith should not be alone! Your faith in Jesus should compel you to produce good deeds through serving Jesus. Amen again! James was challenging Believers then, and the Word is challenging you today! Does your faith in Jesus, show in the work that you do for Jesus? Amen! Only faith in Jesus can save you, but genuine faith in Jesus drives His people to serve Him! Amen! Our Word continues with an example to each Believer, saying, **"Suppose a brother or a sister is without clothes and daily food. If one of you says to them, 'Go in peace, keep warm and well fed,' but**

does nothing about their physical needs, what good is it? In the same way, faith by itself, if it is not accompanied by action, is dead." This shows false faith in Jesus, because the person who claims to love Jesus, does not show love to their brother or sister! A Believer's faith in action, drives love in action! And love in action, drives work for Jesus! Amen again! Again, when you decide not to work for Jesus, you are actually displaying false faith! Working for Jesus shows your love of Jesus, and your love to your brothers and sisters! For the work that Jesus calls you to do, benefits others! Hallelujah! Your work does not benefit Jesus; Jesus does not need you to be Jesus! Glory Hallelujah! Your faith in Jesus, which drives work for Jesus, is to the benefit of bringing others to Jesus! That displays the love of Jesus inside of you! That is true faith! Your love of Jesus, and your faith in Jesus, should drive you to work for Jesus! Hallelujah! Without any works for Jesus, your faith is not alive the way that Jesus wants it to be! And that is the truth! Amen.

Today, the Word of God is speaking to Believers! You are being challenged! Your faith in Jesus should compel you to do work in the name of Jesus! Amen! For without any works for Jesus, your faith is not alive the way that Jesus wants it to be! Amen again! You should be living a Christian life, of faith that drives you to do good deeds and good works. Amen! Works do not save you, for a person can only be saved by their faith in Jesus as their Lord and Savior. Hallelujah! You are justified by God by your faith alone. However, your faith should not be alone! Your faith in Jesus should compel you to produce good deeds through serving Jesus. Amen again! The Word of God is speaking to you today! Does your faith in Jesus, show in the work that you do for Jesus? Amen! Only faith in Jesus can save you, but genuine faith in Jesus drives His people to serve Him! Amen! Are you living in false faith? For a Believer's faith in action, drives love in action! And love in action, drives work for Jesus! Amen again! And the Word of God proclaims to Believers, **"You see that a person is considered righteous by what they do, and not by faith alone. As the body without the Spirit is dead, so faith without deed is dead."** God credits righteousness based on what each of us does! You become righteous in the eyes of God by how you live! And your faith in Jesus should drive you to live in a way that serves Him! Hallelujah! To say that your faith without works is dead, is a very strong conviction! It is personal, and for most Believers, that cuts deep! Amen! And it is meant to cut deep! Amen again! Too many Believers confess a true faith in Jesus, but their lack of action for Jesus, reflects confession with the mouth, and not the heart! And that is a hard truth, but it is the truth! That is why you are being challenged today! Where is your faith, where is your work? For without any works for Jesus, your faith is not alive the way that Jesus wants it to be! Your love of Jesus, and your faith in Jesus, should drive you to work for Jesus! Hallelujah! Without any works for Jesus, your faith is not alive the way that Jesus wants it to be! And that is the truth! Amen.

Today, you are being challenged! Does your faith in Jesus compel you to do work in the name of Jesus! Amen! Works do not save you, for a person can only be saved by their faith in Jesus as their Lord and Savior. Hallelujah! You are justified by God by your faith alone. However, your faith should not be alone! Only faith in Jesus can save you, but genuine faith in Jesus drives His people to serve Him! Amen! However, your faith in action, drives love in action! And love in action, drives work for Jesus! Amen again! You become righteous in the eyes of God by how you live! And your faith in Jesus should drive you to live in a way that serves Him! Hallelujah! So yes, you are being challenged today! Does your faith in Jesus, show in the work that you do for Jesus? Your love of Jesus, and your faith in Jesus, should drive you to work for Jesus! Hallelujah! Without any works for Jesus, your faith is not alive the way that Jesus wants it to be! And that is the truth! Amen.

Day 208

"Now all has been heard, here is the conclusion of the matter: Fear God and keep His commandments, for this is the duty of all mankind.

For God will bring every deed (you do) into judgment, including every hidden thing, whether it is good or evil."

(Ecclesiastes 12:13-14)

In today's Scripture, the unknown author (possibly King Solomon), writes to God's people to reveal what he has discovered about the meaninglessness of every human endeavor, that is done without God at the center of one's life. Amen! The author utilizes his wisdom to examine the human experience and assess the human situation. The author considers life as he has experienced it, from birth to death. And the author comes to the conclusion that life in this world, and beyond this world, is under the rule and judgment of God! Amen again! This message is for all people! You can live a life focused on God, or you can live a life denying God, but your life is still ruled by God, and how you live your life will be judged by God! And that is the truth! Glory to God! Our Scripture begins with, **"Now all has been heard, here is the conclusion of the matter: Fear God and keep His commandments,"** After all has been said and done, the best way for every single person to live life on earth, is to worship God, and do what God and His Word tell you to do! Every single person!

Amen! The Word of God makes it clear that this guidance is for everyone, saying, **"for this is the duty of all mankind."** Every single person that has ever been born, is born with the duty to worship God and keep His commandments! Every single person! Amen again! And the Word of God concludes with this promise that applies to everyone, **"For God will bring every deed (you do) into judgment, including every hidden thing, whether it is good or evil."** No matter who you are, or what you believe, how you live your life will be judged by God! Hallelujah! Every single person! And God will judge everything that you have ever done! Good, or evil, everything will be judged by God, and that is true for every single person! Amen! So, here is the conclusion of the matter, fear God and keep His commandments to you! Now that is wisdom! Amen.

Today, our Scripture is speaking wisdom to all people. Fear God and keep His commandments to you! Now that is wisdom! Hallelujah! Our author writes to God's people to reveal what he has discovered about the meaninglessness of every human endeavor... that is done without God at the center of one's life. Amen! The author utilizes his wisdom to assess the human situation, considering life as he has experienced it, from birth to death. And the author comes to the conclusion that life in this world, and beyond this world, is under the rule and judgment of God! Amen again! You can live a life focused on God, or you can live a life denying God, but your life is still ruled by God, and how you live your life will be judged by God! And that is the truth!

Glory to God! Our Scripture begins with, **"Now all has been heard, here is the conclusion of the matter: Fear God and keep His commandments,"** After all has been said and done, the best way for every single person to live life on earth, is to worship God, and do what God and His Word tell you to do! Every single person! Amen! And God commands that the way to forgiveness of sin and redemption to Him, is through acceptance of His Son, Jesus, as your Lord and Savior! Glory! That is what God tells us to do! Worship Him and accept Jesus as your Savior! That is the only way to be forgiven when you sin against the way God commands you to live! And when you accept Jesus, you are showing that your fear the wrath of God! Glory Hallelujah! So, here is the conclusion of the matter, fear God and keep His commandments to you! Now that is wisdom! Amen.

Today, our Word is speaking wisdom to all people. Fear God and keep His commandments to you! Now that is wisdom! Hallelujah! Our author writes to reveal what he has discovered about the meaninglessness of every human endeavor... that is done without God at the center of one's life. Amen! The author utilizes his wisdom to assess the human situation, and the author comes to the conclusion that life in this world, and beyond this world, is under the rule and judgment of God! Amen again! You can live a life focused on God, or you can live a life denying God, but your life is still ruled by God, and how you live your life will be judged by God! And that is the truth! Glory to God! After all has been said and done, the best way for every single person to live life on earth, is to worship God, and do what God and His Word tell you to do! Every single person! Amen! The Word of God makes it clear that this guidance is for everyone, saying, **"For this is the duty of all mankind."** Every single person that has ever been born... is born with the duty to worship God and keep His commandments! Every single person! Amen again! God does not discriminate in His expectations. Every person born is expected to keep God's commandments! That is what God expects of you, and everyone else! But God knows that you will not keep all His commandments, for you and I are flesh, and flesh sins! But because God is a merciful God, He gave us a path to forgiveness of our sins, and commanded that we expect Jesus to be forgiven of our sins, and be free of everlasting punishment for breaking His commandments! Hallelujah! God is a merciful God! But you must do His commandment of accepting Jesus to be free of the everlasting punishment of sin! Amen! So, here is the conclusion of the matter, fear God and keep His commandments to you! Now that is wisdom! Amen.

Today, the Word of God is speaking wisdom to all people. Fear God and keep His commandments to you! Now that is wisdom! Hallelujah! Your life is meaningless if you live it without God at the center of your life. Amen! For life in this world, and beyond this world, is under the rule and judgment of God! Amen again! You can live a life focused on God, or you can live a life denying God, but your life is still ruled by God, and how you live your life will be judged by God! And that is the truth! Glory to God! After all has been said and done, the best way for every single person to live life on earth, is to worship God, and do what God and His Word tell you to do! Every single person! Amen! Every single person that has ever been born, is born with the duty to worship God and keep His commandments! Every single person! Amen again! And the Word of God concludes with this promise that applies to everyone, **"For God will bring every deed (you do) into judgment, including every hidden thing, whether it is good or evil."** No matter who you are, or what you believe, how you live your life will be judged by God! Hallelujah! Every single person! And God will judge everything that you have ever done! Good, or evil, everything will be judged by God, and that is true for every single person! Amen! All of us will be judged for our sins, even Believers! But Believers will have Jesus with them as their Mediator, and hallelujah, Jesus will mediate God's mercy to you! Glory Hallelujah! So, here is the conclusion of the matter, fear God and keep His commandments to you! Now that is wisdom! Amen.

Today, our Scripture Guidance gives wisdom to all people. Fear God and keep His commandments to you! Hallelujah! Your life is meaningless if you live it without God at the center of your life. Amen! For life in this world, and beyond this world, is under the rule and judgment of God! Amen again! So the best way for every single person to live life on earth, is to worship God, and do what God and His Word tell you to do! Amen! Every single person that has ever been born, is born with the duty to worship God and keep

His commandments! Amen again! And no matter who you are, or what you believe, how you live your life will be judged by God! Hallelujah! Every single person! So, here is the conclusion of the matter, fear God and keep His commandments to you! Now that is wisdom! Amen.

Day 209

I prayed to the Lord my God and confessed: "Lord, the great and awesome God, who keeps His covenant of love with those who love Him and keep His commandments,

we have sinned and done wrong. We have been wicked and have rebelled, we have turned away from Your commands and laws.

We have not listened to Your servants the prophets, who spoke in Your Name to our kings, or princes and our ancestors, and to all the people of the land.

Lord, you are righteous, but this day we are covered with shame, in all the countries where you have scattered us because of our unfaithfulness to You."

(Daniel 9:4-7)

In today's Scripture, the great servant of God, the prophet Daniel, writes to God's people throughout the world, to remind them that God is the sovereign Ruler over all of the world. Amen! At this time, Daniel and God's people have been taken captive, and put into exile by a powerful enemy, the kingdom of Babylon. And this has been done, because God orchestrated it to be done to His people, because God's people had turned away from God, and sinned against God! Amen again! God's people were captured and exiled because God had had enough of their sins! This did not happen because the enemy was so great, this happened because of the way God's people lived their lives consistently against the commandments of God. Tell the truth! For there is no enemy on earth or in heaven that is more powerful than God, and there is no enemy on earth or in heaven that could do anything against the people of God, without God allowing it to happen. And that is the truth! God is a merciful God, who absolutely loves His people, yet God is a righteous Father, and as a righteous Father, God disciplines His children when they consistently turn away from what He has commanded. Glory to God! And God will not relent from disciplining His people, until His people repent and ask God to forgive them. That was true at the time of Daniel, and that is true today! Amen! And when all of God's people are being punished by God for the collective sins of many against God, it is up to the servants of God (so, therefore, the servants of Jesus), to seek out God in prayer and confess the sins of the people to God and seek His mercy. Amen again! Daniel understood this, and went to God in prayer. Today, God's people are being held captive, and are in exile by a powerful and unseen enemy. And Believers in Jesus Christ, who are servants of Jesus, must seek God in prayer, confess the sins of the people against God, and seek His forgiveness and mercy. Hallelujah! We must humble ourselves before God, and confess the sins that we see that are being committed. Glory Hallelujah! You are being challenged! Will you be the Daniel of today? Seek God, and confess the sins of the people. Our Scripture begins with the servant of God saying, **I prayed to the Lord my God and confessed: "Lord, the great** and awesome God, who keeps His covenant of love with those who love Him and keep His commandments," God is a righteous and loving Father, and God is faithful to His people who love Him. So seek Him! Amen! Our Word continues with the servant of God, confessing to God, "We have sinned and done wrong. We have been wicked and have rebelled, we have turned away from Your commands and laws. We have not listened to Your servants, the prophets, who spoke in Your Name to our kings, our princes and our ancestors, and to all the people of the land." God is a merciful Father, confess your sins and the sins of His people to Him! So seek Him, and confess! Amen again! And the Word of God concludes that the servant of God accepts God's punishment as righteous and just, saying to God, "Lord, you are righteous, but this day we are covered with shame, in all the countries where you have scattered us because of our unfaithfulness to You." God is a just God, for God does not punish His people unless He is disciplining us for our sins, or correcting our paths. So seek Him, and accept God's punishment for sin! Glory Hallelujah! Amen.

Today, our Scripture is speaking to the servants of Jesus. Through Jesus, you are the servants of God! And as His servants, we are to seek God and pray to Him to bring His people through difficult times. Jesus Himself said to His disciples, "Be always on the watch, and pray that you may be able to escape all that is about to happen, and that you may be able to stand before the Son of Man" (Luke 21:36). Amen again! The great servant of God, the prophet Daniel, writes to God's people to remind us that God is the sovereign Ruler over all of the world! Amen! Daniel and God's people had been taken captive, and put into exile by a powerful enemy, the kingdom of Babylon. God's people had turned away from God, and sinned against God! Amen again! And God had had enough of their sins! This did not happen because the enemy was so great, this happened because of the way God's people lived their lives consistently against the commandments of God. Tell the truth! For there is no enemy on earth or in heaven that is more powerful than God! And that is the truth! God is a merciful God, yet God is a righteous Father, and as a righteous Father, God disciplines His children when they consistently turn away from what He has commanded. Glory to God! And God will not relent from disciplining His people, until His people repent and ask God to forgive them. And when all of God's people are being punished by God for the collective sins of many against God, it falls on the servants of God (servants of Jesus), to seek out God in prayer and confess the sins of the people to God and seek His mercy. Amen! Today, God's people are being held captive, and are in exile by a powerful and unseen enemy. And Believers in Jesus Christ, must seek God in prayer, confess the sins of the people against God, and seek His forgiveness and mercy. Hallelujah! We must humble ourselves before God and confess the sins that we see that are being committed, whether we committed the sins or not! Glory Hallelujah! You are being challenged! Seek God, and confess the sins of the people. Our Scripture begins with the servant of God saying, **I prayed to the Lord my God and confessed: "Lord, the great and awesome God, who keeps His covenant of love with those who love Him and keep His commandments,"** God is a righteous and loving Father, and God is faithful to His people who love Him. So seek Him! Amen! As Believers in Jesus Christ, we must pray for the world and the people of the world. It is a responsibility that Jesus gave to His servants, and God gave to His servants before Jesus came to the world. For the servants of God and Jesus know God to be merciful and forgiving, if we seek Him! And you are a Believer in Jesus Christ, and Jesus told you to always be on watch, and pray! So today, pray for all of the people in the world who have sinned, so that we may be able to be forgiven for our sins, and receive mercy from God so that we may be able to stand! Amen.

Today, our Word is speaking to the servants of Jesus. Through Jesus, you are the servants of God! And as His servants, we are to seek God and pray to Him to bring His people through difficult times. Jesus Himself said to His disciples, "Be always on the watch, and pray that you may be able to escape all that is about to happen, and that you may be able to stand before the Son of Man". Amen again! Daniel and God's people had been taken captive, and put into exile by a powerful enemy, the kingdom of Babylon. God's people had turned away from God, and sinned against God! Amen! And God had had enough of their sins! There is no enemy on earth or in heaven that is more powerful than God. And that is the truth! God disciplines His children when they consistently turn away from what He has commanded. Glory to God! And God will not relent from disciplining His people, until His people repent and ask God to forgive them. And it falls on the servants of God (servants of Jesus), to seek out God in prayer and confess the sins of the people to God and seek His mercy. Amen! Today, God's people are being held captive, and are in exile by a powerful and unseen enemy. And Believers in Jesus Christ, must seek God in prayer, confess the sins of the people against God, and seek His forgiveness and mercy. Hallelujah! We must humble ourselves before God and confess the sins that we see that are being committed, whether we committed the sins or not! Glory Hallelujah! You are being challenged! Seek God, and confess the sins of the people. God is a righteous and loving Father, and God is faithful to His people who love Him. So seek Him! Amen! Our Word continues with the servant of God, confessing to God, **"We have sinned and done wrong. We have been wicked and have rebelled, we have turned away from Your commands and laws. We have not listened to Your servants, the prophets, who spoke in Your Name to our kings, our princes and our ancestors, and to all the people of the land."** God is a merciful Father, confess your sins and the sins of His people to Him! So seek Him, and confess! Amen again! Jesus told you to always be on watch, and pray! And **1 John 1:9** says, "If we confess our sins, he is faithful and just and will forgive us our sins and purify us from all unrighteousness." Amen! God is righteous, and God is faithful to forgive our sins, if we seek Him! And you are a Believer in Jesus Christ, and Jesus told you to always be on watch, and pray! So today, pray for all of the people in the world who have sinned, so that we may be able to be forgiven for our sins, and receive mercy from God so that we may be able to stand! Amen

Today, the Word of God is speaking to the servants of Jesus. Through Jesus, you are the servants of God! The Word of God is speaking to you! You are to seek God and pray to Him to bring His people through difficult times. Jesus Himself said to His disciples, "Be always on the watch, and pray that you may be able to escape all that is about to happen, and that you may be able to stand before the Son of Man". Amen again! God's people have turned away from God, and sinned against God! Amen! And God has had enough of their sins! God disciplines His children when they consistently turn away from what He has commanded. Glory to God! And God will not relent until His people repent and ask God to forgive them. And it falls on the servants of God (servants of Jesus), to seek out God in prayer and confess the sins of the people to God, and seek His mercy. Amen! Today, God's people are being held captive, and are in exile by a powerful and unseen enemy. And you must seek God in prayer, confess the sins of the people against God, and seek His forgiveness and mercy. Hallelujah! You must humble yourself before God and confess the sins that we see that are being committed today, whether we committed the sins or not! Glory Hallelujah! You are being challenged! Seek God, and confess the sins of the people. God is a righteous and loving Father, and God is faithful to His people who love Him. So seek Him! Amen! God is a merciful Father, confess your sins and the sins of His people to Him! So seek Him, and confess! Amen again! And the Word of God concludes that the servant of God accepts God's punishment as righteous and just, saying to God, **"Lord, you are righteous, but this day we are covered with shame, in all the countries where you have scattered us because of our unfaithfulness to You."** God is a just God, for God does not punish His people unless He is disciplining us for our sins, or correcting our paths. So seek Him, and accept God's punishment for sin! Glory Hallelujah! Today, the world and most of its people have lived in a way that is against the commandments of God. And God has had enough! And we are being punished, and we should all be ashamed in the presence of God! Tell the truth! And as Believers, we are the servants that must go to God in prayer and confess the sins of the people, and seek His mercy to get us past our current punishment! This should be of no surprise to the servants of Jesus, because Jesus told you to always be on watch, and pray! So today, pray for all of the people in the world who have sinned, so that we may be able to be forgiven for our sins, and receive mercy from God so that we may be able to stand! Amen.

Today, the Word of God is speaking to the servants of Jesus! The Word of God is speaking to you! The people of the world have turned away from God, and sinned against God! Amen! And God has had enough of their sins! Today, God's people are being held captive, and are in exile by a powerful and unseen enemy. And you must seek God in prayer, confess the sins of the people against God, and seek His forgiveness and mercy. Hallelujah! You are being challenged! Seek God, and confess the sins of the people. God is a righteous and loving Father, and God is faithful to His people who love Him. So seek Him! Amen! God is a merciful Father, confess your sins and the sins of His people to Him! So seek Him, and confess! Amen again! And as Believers, we are the servants that must go to God in prayer and confess the sins of the people, and seek His mercy to get us past our current punishment! This should be of no surprise to the servants of Jesus, because Jesus told you to always be on watch, and pray! So today, pray for all of the people in the world who have sinned, so that we may be able to be forgiven for our sins, and receive mercy from God so that we may be able to stand! The servant of God, the prophet Daniel prayed and confessed the sins of the people to God. And God heard him, and had mercy. Hallelujah! Will you be the Daniel of today? Seek God, and confess the sins of the people. Amen.

Day 210

"Now, our God, hear the prayers and petitions of Your servant. For Your sake, Lord, look with favor on Your desolate Sanctuary.

Give ear, our God, and hear; open Your eyes and see the desolation of the city that bears Your Name. We do not make requests of You because we are righteous, but because of Your great mercy.

Lord God, listen! Lord, forgive! Lord, hear and act! For Your sake God, do not delay; because Your city and Your people bear Your Name."

(Daniel 9:17-19)

In today's Scripture, the great servant of God, the prophet Daniel, writes to God's people throughout the world, to remind them that God is the sovereign Ruler over the entire world. Amen! God's people have been taken captive, and put into exile by a powerful enemy, the kingdom of Babylon. And this has been done, because God orchestrated it to be done to His people, because God's people had turned away from God, and sinned against God! Amen again! God's people were captured and exiled because God had had enough of their sins! This happened because of the way God's people lived their lives consistently against the commandments of God. Tell the truth! For there is no enemy on earth or in heaven that could do anything against the people of God, without God allowing it to happen. And that is the truth! God is a merciful God, who absolutely loves His people; yet God is a righteous Father; and as a righteous Father, God disciplines His children when they consistently turn away from what He has commanded. Glory to God! Yet, God is also a merciful God; and God is faithful to forgive His people when they repent and ask God to forgive them. That was true at the time of Daniel, and that is true today! Amen! And when all of God's people are being punished by God for their collective sins, it is up to the servants of God (so, therefore, the servants of Jesus) to seek out God in prayer and confess the sins of the people to God and seek His mercy. Amen again! Daniel understood this; and went to God in prayer. Daniel confessed to God the sins of the people, and on behalf of the people; Daniel is now asking God to forgive the people, because they are God's people! Hallelujah! Believers in Jesus Christ are God's people. Believers in Jesus Christ are God's family! And through Jesus, Believers, we bear God's Name. Hallelujah! Today, God's people are being held captive, and are in exile by a powerful and unseen enemy. And Believers in Jesus Christ, who are servants of Jesus, must seek God in prayer, confess the sins of the people against God, and seek His forgiveness and mercy. Hallelujah! We must humble ourselves before God, and confess the sins that we see that are being committed. Glory Hallelujah! And after we confess the sins of the people to God, we must now seek His forgiveness and mercy. That is what Daniel is doing in our Scripture passage. And Daniel calls on God, calling out that God's people are being hurt; and because God's people bear God's Name, God's Name is being hurt, and His Sanctuary is empty. You are being challenged! Will you be the Daniel of today? Seek God and confess the sins of the people, and plead for His forgiveness and mercy! Our Scripture begins with the servant of God asking for God's attention, saying to God, **"Now, our God, hear the prayers and petitions of Your servant. For Your sake, Lord, look with favor on Your desolate Sanctuary. Give ear, our God, and hear; open Your eyes and see the desolation of the city that bears Your Name."** The servants of Jesus must continue to speak to God, and seek His attention to the matter, that is hurting His people! So seek God, and get His attention! Amen! Our Word continues with the servant of God recognizing that we are not worthy of forgiveness, by acknowledging to God, that, **"We do not make requests of You because we are righteous, but because of Your great mercy."** The servants of God must seek God in a humble manner, knowing that we do not earn forgiveness, we receive forgiveness and mercy from God! God is a merciful Father! So seek God, and His mercy! Amen again! And the Word of God concludes that the servant of God should continue to seek God, and cry out to God, **"Lord God, listen! Lord, forgive! Lord, hear and act! For Your sake, God, do not delay; because Your city and Your people bear Your Name."** The servants of Jesus must call on God with passion! We must be humble when we seek God, but not timid! We are children of God through the name of Jesus, and God grants us the right to call on Him. So seek God, and call out to Him until He answers your prayer! Glory Hallelujah! Amen.

Today, our Scripture is speaking to the servants of Jesus. Through Jesus, you are the servants of God! And as His servants, we are to seek God and pray to Him to bring His people through difficult times. The servants of Jesus are being challenged to pray for God's people, right now! Amen! Today, Believers see the mess that the world is in; and we need to seek mercy from God! Jesus said to His disciples, "Be always on the watch, and pray that you may be able to escape all that is about to happen, and that you may be able to stand before the Son of Man" **(Luke 21:36)**. Amen again! God is a merciful God; yet God is a righteous Father; and as a righteous Father, God disciplines His children when they consistently turn away from what He has commanded. Glory to God! God will not relent from disciplining His people; until His people repent and ask God to forgive them. Amen! Today, God's people are being held captive, and are in exile by a powerful and unseen enemy. And Believers must seek God in prayer, confess the sins of the people against God, and seek His forgiveness and mercy. Hallelujah! We must humble ourselves before God, and confess the sins that we see that are being committed. Glory Hallelujah! And after we confess the sins of the people to God, we must now seek His forgiveness and mercy. That is what Daniel is doing in our Scripture passage. And Daniel calls on God that His people are being hurt, and because God's people bear God's Name,

God's Name is being hurt, and His Sanctuary is empty. You are being challenged to seek God and confess the sins of the people, and plead for His forgiveness and mercy! Our Scripture begins with the servant of God asking for God's attention, saying to God, **"Now, our God, hear the prayers and petitions of Your servant. For Your sake, Lord, look with favor on Your desolate Sanctuary. Give ear, our God, and hear; open Your eyes and see the desolation of the city that bears Your Name."** The servants of Jesus must continue to speak to God, and seek His attention to the matter, that is hurting His people! So seek God, and get His attention! Amen! As Believers in Jesus Christ, we must pray for the people of the world. It is a responsibility that Jesus gave to His servants, and God gave to His servants before Jesus came to the world. For the servants of Jesus know that God is merciful and forgiving, if we seek Him! And we must continue to pray to God to get His attention! So today, pray for all of the people in the world who have sinned; so that we may be able to be forgiven for our sins, and receive mercy from God so that we may be able to stand through these difficult times! Amen.

Today, our Word is speaking to the servants of Jesus. Through Jesus, you are the servants of God! And as His servants, we are to seek God and pray to Him to bring His people through difficult times. The servants of Jesus are being challenged to pray for God's people, right now! Amen! Today, Believers see the mess that the world is in; and we need to seek mercy from God! Amen again! God is a merciful God; yet God is a righteous Father; and as a righteous Father, God disciplines His children when they turn away from what He has commanded. Glory to God! God will not relent from disciplining His people; until His people repent and ask God to forgive them. Amen! Today, God's people are being held captive, and are in exile by a powerful and unseen enemy. And Believers must seek God in prayer, confess the sins of the people, and seek His forgiveness and mercy. Hallelujah! We must humble ourselves before God, and confess the sins that we see that are being committed. Glory Hallelujah! And then, we must seek His forgiveness and mercy. Daniel calls on God, saying that His people are being hurt, and because God's people bear God's Name, God's Name is being hurt, and His Sanctuary is empty. Today, you are being challenged to seek God and confess the sins of the people, and plead for His forgiveness and mercy! The servants of Jesus must continue to speak to God, and seek His attention to the matter, that is hurting His people! So seek God, and get His attention! Amen! Our Word continues with the servant of God, confessing to God, **"We do not make requests of You because we are righteous, but because of Your great mercy."** The servants of God must seek God in a humble manner, knowing that we do not earn forgiveness, we receive forgiveness and mercy from God! God is a merciful Father! So seek God, and His mercy! Amen again! We must understand that when we approach God for forgiveness and mercy, that we are acknowledging our sins, for we are not righteous when we sin! Tell the truth! But God is righteous! God is faithful to forgive our sins when we seek Him, because God is a merciful Father! For that is, and will always be, the truth! Glory to God! For the servants of Jesus know that God is merciful and forgiving, if we seek Him! And we must continue to pray to God to get His attention! So today, pray for all of the people in the world who have sinned; so that we may be able to be forgiven for our sins, and receive mercy from God so that we may be able to stand through these difficult times! Amen.

Today, the Word of God is speaking to the servants of Jesus. Through Jesus, you are the servants of God! And as His servants, we are to seek God and pray to Him to bring His people through difficult times. The servants of Jesus are being challenged to pray for God's people, right now! Amen! Today, Believers see the mess that the world is in; and we need to seek mercy from God! Amen again! God is a merciful God; yet God is a righteous Father; and as a righteous Father, God disciplines His children when they turn away from what He has commanded. Glory to God! God will not relent from disciplining His people; until His people repent and ask God to forgive them. Amen! Today, God's people are being held captive, and are in exile by a powerful and unseen enemy. And Believers must seek God in prayer, and confess the sins of the people, and seek His forgiveness and mercy. Hallelujah! We must humble ourselves before God, and confess the sins that we see that are being committed. Glory Hallelujah! And then, we must seek His forgiveness and mercy. Daniel calls on God, saying that His people are being hurt, and because God's people bear God's Name, God's Name is being hurt, and His Sanctuary is empty. Today, you are being challenged to seek God and confess the sins of the people, and plead for His forgiveness and mercy! The servants of Jesus must continue to speak to God, and seek His attention to the matter, that is hurting His people! So seek God, and get His attention! Amen! The servants of God must seek God in a humble manner, knowing that we do not earn forgiveness, we receive forgiveness and mercy from God! God is a merciful Father! So seek God, and His mercy! Amen again! And the Word of God concludes that the servant of God should continue to seek God, and cry out to God, **"Lord God, listen! Lord, forgive! Lord, hear and act! For Your sake, God, do not delay; because Your city and Your people bear Your Name."** The servants of Jesus must call on God with passion! The servants of Jesus must call on God with urgency! We must be humble when we seek God, but not timid! We are children of God through the name of Jesus, and God grants us the right to call on Him. And sometimes a child has to scream for his Father to hear him! Sometimes a child has to holler for his Father to know that he is in great pain! So seek God, and call out to Him until He answers your prayer! Glory Hallelujah! Amen. Today, the world and most of its people have lived in a way that is against the commandments of God. And God has had enough! And we are being punished, and we should all be ashamed in the presence of God! Tell the truth! And as Believers, we are the servants that must go to God in prayer and confess the sins of the people, and seek His mercy to get us past our current punishment! So today, pray for all of the people in the world who have sinned; so that we may be able to be forgiven for our sins, and receive mercy from God so that we may be able to stand! Amen.

Today, the Word of God is speaking to the servants of Jesus! The Word of God is speaking to you! The people of the world have turned away from God, and sinned against God! Amen! And God has had enough of their sins! Today, God's people are being held captive, and are in exile by a powerful and unseen enemy. And you must seek God in prayer, and confess the sins of the people against God, and seek His forgiveness and mercy. Hallelujah! You are being challenged! Today, the world and most of its people have lived in a way that is against the commandments of God. And God has had enough! And we are being punished, and we should all be ashamed in the presence of God! Tell the truth! And as Believers, we are the servants that must go to God in prayer and confess the sins of the people, and seek His mercy to get us past our current punishment! The servant of God, the prophet Daniel prayed and confessed the sins of the people to God. And God heard him and had mercy. Hallelujah! Will you be the Daniel of today? Today, pray for all of the people in the world who have sinned; so that we may be able to be forgiven for our sins, and receive mercy from God so that we may be able to stand! Seek God, and confess the sins of the people. Amen.

Day 211

"For this reason, (Jesus perfect blood sacrifice), Christ is the Mediator of a New Covenant; that those who are called may receive the promised eternal inheritance, now that He has died as a ransom to set them (us) free from the sins committed under the First (Old) Covenant."

(Hebrews 9:15)

In today's Scripture, the author of the Book of Hebrews writes to demonstrate that Jesus has absolute supremacy; and that Jesus is all that anyone will ever need to mediate and reveal God's forgiveness and grace to us. Amen! This message is to all people. Jesus is the only One who can bear your sins; and take them to the altar of God, where your sins will be forgiven through the grace of God! Amen again! There is no other method; or sacrifice! There is no other Savior; nor Son of God! There is no other man; or Spirit that can do this! There is only One Mediator of God's forgiveness and grace, and that is Jesus! Hallelujah! And Jesus is the Truth! Glory Hallelujah! In our Chapter, the author speaks to the difference between the animal blood sacrifice for sins required in the Old Testament Covenant Law of Moses; and the "perfect blood sacrifice" of Jesus that is required in the New Testament Covenant. The Old Testament blood offering sacrifice was meant as a temporary sacrifice for sin that was acceptable to God. This animal sacrifice process was a copy of the "true" sacrifice process that Jesus would bring to the earth several thousands of years later! How can a copy come before the original? Well, Almighty God has spoken the entire life of mankind already, and we are, in a sense, living the world to the date that God has already spoken as the end of the world! Glory to God! We are living in the same way, as if we are reading a book from page one: for a book that already has been completely written, including the ending! We have just not gotten to the end yet, but God has! That is why God could tell Moses to copy the process before Jesus brought the original! Hallelujah, God is an awesome God! So the New Covenant's perfect blood sacrifice for sins is the true sacrifice, and the animal blood sacrifice in the Old Testament, is a copy of Jesus's true sacrifice! Glory Hallelujah! Our Scripture begins with, **"For this reason, (Jesus's perfect blood sacrifice), Christ is the Mediator of a New Covenant;"** Jesus's blood sacrifice is the basis of forgiveness in God's New Covenant with man; therefore, Jesus mediates God's forgiveness for each person that receives His blood to wash away their sins. Amen! Our Word says that Jesus is the Mediator so **"that those who are called may receive the promised eternal inheritance,"** God decides who will be called to accept Jesus as their Lord and Savior, and only God's mercy can grant a person eternal life in His Kingdom. And on the basis of Jesus's sacrificial and atoning death, Believers are granted this eternal inheritance from God the Father! Jesus is the only Mediator of God's mercy! Amen again! And the Word of God proclaims this truth; that Jesus is the Mediator of the New

Covenant, **"now that He has died as a ransom to set them (us) free from the sins committed under the First (Old) Covenant."** Jesus's death on earth provide the "perfect blood" to be put on the altar of God in Heaven; so that we could be set eternally free from the sins we have committed before we accepted Jesus. And it is only through Jesus that our sins can still be forgiven, by confessing our sins through Jesus, which allows Jesus to continue to mediate forgiveness and mercy from God! Amen! There is only One Mediator of God's forgiveness and grace, and that is Jesus! Hallelujah! And Jesus is the Truth! Glory Hallelujah!

Today, our Scripture is speaking to everybody! All of us are sinners, yet those that believe in Jesus as their Lord and Savior, and confess their sins to Jesus, are forgiven of their sins by God through His mercy. Amen! This message is to all people! Jesus is the only One who can bear your sins; and take them to the altar of God, where your sins will be forgiven through the grace of God! Amen again! There is only One Mediator of God's forgiveness and grace, and that is Jesus! Hallelujah! Hebrews speaks to the difference between the animal blood sacrifice for sins required in the Old Testament Covenant Law of Moses; and the "perfect blood sacrifice" of Jesus that is required in the New Testament Covenant. The Old Testament blood offering sacrifice was meant as a temporary sacrifice for sin that was acceptable to God. This animal sacrifice process was a copy of the "true" sacrifice process that Jesus would bring to the earth several thousands of years later! How can a copy come before the original? Well, Almighty God has spoken the entire life of mankind already! Glory to God! We have just not gotten to the end yet, but God has! That is why God could tell Moses to copy the process before Jesus brought the original! Hallelujah, God is an awesome God! So the New Covenant's perfect blood sacrifice for sins is the true sacrifice, and the animal blood sacrifice in the Old Testament, is a copy of Jesus's true sacrifice! Glory Hallelujah! Our Scripture begins with, **"For this reason, (Jesus's perfect blood sacrifice), Christ is the Mediator of a New Covenant;"** Jesus's blood sacrifice is the basis of forgiveness in God's New Covenant with man; therefore, Jesus mediates God's forgiveness for each person that receives His blood to wash away their sins. Amen! Jesus had to be slaughtered on earth by man; because He is the sacrificial lamb whose blood had to be placed on the everlasting altar that is in God's Temple in Heaven. This perfect blood sacrifice could only come from a man who walked perfectly without sin. Hallelujah! And God knew there was no man on earth who could do that, so He sent His only Son from Heaven, wrapped in human flesh, so that His perfect blood could be offered to God for our sins! Glory Hallelujah! And for this reason, Jesus is the Mediator of the New Covenant! And it is only through Jesus that our sins can still be forgiven, by confessing our sins through Jesus, which allows Jesus to continue to mediate forgiveness and mercy from God! Amen! There is only One Mediator of God's forgiveness and grace, and that is Jesus! Hallelujah! And Jesus is the Truth! Glory Hallelujah!

Today, our Word is speaking to everybody! All of us are sinners, yet those that believe in Jesus as their Lord and Savior, and confess their sins to Jesus, are forgiven of their sins by God through His mercy. Amen! This message is to all people! Jesus is the only One who can bear your sins; and take them to the altar of God, where your sins will be forgiven through the grace of God! Amen again! There is only One Mediator of God's forgiveness and grace, and that is Jesus! Hallelujah! The Old Testament animal blood offering sacrifice was meant as a temporary sacrifice for sin that was acceptable to God. The New Covenant has Jesus's perfect blood as the true, and everlasting sacrifice for sins! Glory Hallelujah! Jesus's blood sacrifice is the basis of forgiveness in God's New Covenant with man; therefore, Jesus mediates God's forgiveness for each person that receives His blood to wash away their sins. Amen! Our Word says that Jesus is the Mediator, so **"that those who are called may receive the promised eternal inheritance,"** God decides who will be called to accept Jesus as their Lord and Savior; and only God's mercy can grant a person eternal life in His Kingdom. And on the basis of Jesus's sacrificial and atoning death, Believers are granted this eternal inheritance from God the Father! Jesus is the only Mediator of God's mercy! Amen again! No one can receive an inheritance from God unless they are born again through the blood of Jesus to God! That is the only way anyone can be in God's family! That is the only way that you can become an adopted child of God, and God becomes your Father. You will only receive the promised eternal inheritance from God, through Jesus! Tell the truth! And it is only through Jesus that our sins can still be forgiven, by confessing our sins through Jesus, which allows Jesus to continue to mediate forgiveness and mercy from God! Amen! There is only One Mediator of God's forgiveness and grace, and that is Jesus! Hallelujah! And Jesus is the Truth! Glory Hallelujah!

Today, the Word of God is speaking to everybody! All of us are sinners, yet those that believe in Jesus as their Lord and Savior, and confess their sins to Jesus, are forgiven of their sins by God through His mercy. Amen! This message is to all people! Jesus is the only One who can bear your sins; and take them to the altar of God, where your sins will be forgiven through the grace of God! Amen again! There is only One Mediator of God's forgiveness and grace, and that is Jesus! Hallelujah! The Old Testament animal blood offering sacrifice was always s temporary sacrifice for sin that was acceptable to God. The New Covenant has Jesus's perfect blood as an everlasting sacrifice for sins! Glory Hallelujah! Jesus's blood sacrifice is the basis of forgiveness in God's New Covenant with man; therefore, Jesus mediates God's forgiveness for each person that receives His blood to wash away their sins. Amen! And God decides who will be called to accept Jesus as their Lord and Savior, and only God's mercy can grant a person eternal life in His Kingdom. And on the basis of Jesus's sacrificial and atoning death, Believers are granted this eternal inheritance from God the Father! Jesus is the only Mediator of God's mercy! Amen again! And the Word of God proclaims this truth; that Jesus is the

Mediator of the New Covenant, **"Now that He has died as a ransom to set them (us) free from the sins committed under the First (Old) Covenant."** Jesus's death on earth provided the "perfect blood" to be put on the altar of God in Heaven; so that we could be set eternally free from the sins we have committed before we accepted Jesus. Jesus paid our ransom to set us free from sin and damnation! Jesus freely gave Himself to be murdered for you, and for me! Hallelujah, thank you, Jesus! And it is only through Jesus that our sins can still be forgiven, by confessing our sins through Jesus, which allows Jesus to continue to mediate forgiveness and mercy from God! Amen! There is only One Mediator of God's forgiveness and grace, and that is Jesus! Hallelujah! And Jesus is the Truth! Glory Hallelujah!

Today, our Scripture Guidance is for everyone! For all have sinned, and fallen short of the glory of God! But hallelujah, we do have a Mediator who can go to God on our behalf, and mediate forgiveness for our sins, and mercy from Almighty God. And that Mediator is Jesus! Amen! And it is only through Jesus that our sins can still be forgiven, by confessing our sins through Jesus, which allows Jesus to continue to mediate forgiveness and mercy from God! Amen! Jesus is the only One who can bear your sins; and take them to the altar of God, where your sins will be forgiven through the grace of God! Amen again! There is no other method; or sacrifice! There is no other Savior; nor Son of God! There is no other man; or Spirit that can do this! There is only One Mediator of God's forgiveness and grace, and that is Jesus! Hallelujah! And Jesus is all you need! And that is the Truth! Glory Hallelujah!

Day 212

"We (the servants of Jesus) are hard pressed on every side, but not crushed; perplexed, but not in despair,

persecuted, but not abandoned; struck down, but not destroyed.

We always carry around in our body the death of Jesus, so that the life of Jesus may also be revealed in our body.

For we who are alive are always being given over to death for Jesus sake, so that His life may also be revealed in our mortal body."

(2 Corinthians 4:8-11)

In today's Scripture, the great servant of Jesus, the apostle Paul, is speaking to encourage Jesus's servants to stay true to the teaching and the work that Jesus has called each of His servants to do, despite the fact that the servant of Jesus will receive punishment from the evil people in the world for serving Jesus. Amen! For just as Paul had experienced suffering from the evil in the world because he served Jesus, each servant of Jesus will experience some suffering when they serve Jesus. Amen again! There really is no way around this, and quite frankly, we should welcome persecution from evil people as a sign that we are truly being effective servants! Hallelujah! For Satan hates the servants of Jesus! Glory Hallelujah! Our Scripture begins with the servant stating the truth about serving Jesus, saying, **"We (the servants** of Jesus) are hard pressed on every side, but not crushed; perplexed, but not in despair, persecuted, but not abandoned; struck down, but not destroyed."** The servants of Jesus will be punished by the evil people in the world, but the world will not be able to stop you from serving Jesus! Amen! Our Word continues with the servant of Jesus acknowledging that Jesus is inside of them, confirming, **"We always carry around in our body the death of Jesus, so that the life of Jesus may also be revealed in our body."** Jesus is inside of each servant; so that the Truth and the Light that is Jesus, is revealed through His servants! Amen again! And the Word of God concludes with the servant of Jesus acknowledging the truth about the role of each servant of Jesus, by proclaiming, **"For we who are alive are always being given over to death for Jesus's sake, so that His life may also be revealed in our mortal body."** Hallelujah! Amen.

Today, our Scripture is speaking to the servants of Jesus Christ. The great servant of Jesus, the apostle Paul, is speaking to encourage Jesus's servants to stay true to the teaching and the work that Jesus has called each of His servants to do. Amen! For just as Paul had experienced suffering from the evil in the world because he served Jesus, each servant of Jesus will experience some suffering when they serve Jesus. Amen again! And quite frankly, we should welcome persecution from evil people as a sign that we are truly being effective servants! Hallelujah! For Satan hates the servants of Jesus! Glory Hallelujah! Our Scripture begins with the servant stating the truth about serving Jesus, saying, **"We (the**

servants of Jesus) are hard pressed on every side, but not crushed; perplexed, but not in despair, persecuted, but not abandoned; struck down, but not destroyed." The servants of Jesus will be punished by the evil people in the world, but the world will not be able to stop you from serving Jesus! Amen! So if you are a servant of Jesus, be encouraged today! Yes, you will be persecuted by Satan and his evil workers, but consider it joy! Because Satan hates you; because you speak the Truth that is Jesus, and Satan knows that it is that Truth, that will destroy him and every lie he has ever told! Glory Hallelujah! And that is the Truth! Amen.

Today, our Word is speaking to; and encouraging, the servants of Jesus Christ. The apostle Paul is speaking to encourage Jesus's servants to stay true to the teaching and the work that Jesus has called each of His servants to do. Amen! Paul had experienced great suffering from the evil in the world because he served Jesus, and each servant of Jesus will experience some suffering when they serve Jesus. Amen again! For Satan hates the servants of Jesus, and Satan will do all he can to disrupt you from serving Jesus! Tell the truth! The servants of Jesus will be punished by the evil people in the world, but the world will not be able to stop you from serving Jesus! Amen! Our Word continues with the servant of Jesus acknowledging that Jesus is inside of them, confirming, **"We always carry around in our body the death of Jesus, so that the life of Jesus may also be revealed in our body."** Jesus is inside of each servant; so that the Truth and the Light that is

Jesus, is revealed through His servants! Amen again! So if you are a servant of Jesus, be encouraged today! Yes, you will be persecuted by Satan and his evil workers, but consider it joy! Because Satan hates you; because you speak the Truth that is Jesus, and Satan knows that it is that Truth that will destroy him and every lie he has ever told! Glory Hallelujah! And that is the Truth! Amen.

Today, the Word of God is encouraging the servants of Jesus Christ. You are being encouraged to stay true to the teaching and the work that Jesus has called each of His servants to do, despite the fact that you will be persecuted by the evil people of the world. Amen! Each servant of Jesus will experience some suffering when they serve Jesus, because you tell the Truth, that is the saving grace of Jesus! Amen again! For Satan hates the servants of Jesus; because the Truth of Jesus destroys all the lies of Satan! And that is the truth! Glory Hallelujah! The servants of Jesus will be punished by the evil people in the world, but the world will not be able to stop you from serving Jesus! Amen! Jesus is inside of each servant; so that the Truth and the Light that is Jesus, is revealed through His servants! Amen again! And the Word of God concludes with the servant of Jesus acknowledging the truth about the role of each servant of Jesus, by proclaiming, **"For we who are alive are always being given over to death for Jesus's sake, so that His life may also be revealed in our mortal body."** Hallelujah! So if you are a servant of Jesus, be encouraged today! Yes, you will be persecuted by Satan and his evil workers, but consider it joy! Because Satan hates you; because you speak the Truth that is Jesus, and Satan knows that it is that Truth, that will destroy him and every lie he has ever told! Glory Hallelujah! And that is the Truth! Amen.

Today, if you are a servant of Jesus Christ, be encouraged! Stay true to the teaching and the work that Jesus has called you to do. Amen! Satan hates you, and that is a good thing! Be encouraged! Yes, you will be persecuted by Satan and his evil workers, but consider it joy! Because Satan hates you; because you speak the Truth that is Jesus, and Satan knows that it is that Truth, that will destroy him and every lie he has ever told! Glory Hallelujah! And that is the Truth! Amen.

Day 213

"The law of the Lord (God) is perfect, refreshing the soul. The statutes of the Lord are trustworthy, making wise the simple.

The precepts of the Lord are right, giving joy to the heart. The commands of the Lord are radiant, giving light to the eyes.

The fear of the Lord is pure, enduring forever. The decrees of the Lord are firm, and all of them are righteous.

They are more precious than gold, than much pure gold; they are sweeter than honey, than honey from the honeycomb.

By them (God's laws and expectations) Your servant is warned; in keeping them there is great reward."

(Psalm 19:7-11)

In today's Scripture, the great servant of God, David, has written a hymn that speaks to the majestic glory of God, specifically celebrating the incredible worth of God's laws, and the value of living to God's expectations. Amen! God has given us His commandments and guidelines throughout His Word so that we can live the best possible life that we can; for there is nothing better for you than to live your life according to God's Will for you. Amen again! How could there be; when it is God who has written your life, and it is God that will judge your life, and send you to your everlasting destination! Hallelujah! So when we live our life, choosing to follow what God tells us, God is pleased!

Glory Hallelujah! And when God is pleased with you, good things await you! Glory! That is why each of us should read and study the Word of God to understand what God expects of us; also to seek God in prayer to receive His Will for our life! Amen! For God has general expectations of all of us, but He also has a specific Will for you! So set your mind and heart to live to God's laws, and live your life according to God's expectations for you! Hallelujah! Glory to God! Our Scripture begins with the truth about God's laws and expectations, saying that, **"The law of the Lord (God) is perfect, refreshing the soul. The statutes of the Lord are trustworthy, making wise the simple. The precepts of the Lord are right, giving joy to the heart. The commands of the Lord are radiant, giving light to the eyes. The fear of the Lord is pure, enduring forever. The decrees of the Lord are firm, and all of them are righteous."** God's laws and expectations for us endure from generation to generation; for God does not change! And they guide us to live a life that is righteous in the eyes of God. And to fulfill God's laws and expectations, you must first love Him, and fear Him! Amen! Our Word proclaims that God's laws and expectations are so valuable to us, that, **"They are more precious than gold, than much pure gold; they are sweeter than honey, than honey from the honeycomb."** There is nothing more valuable than God's laws and expectations, and living according to them brings the sweetest reward while living your life opposite to them brings a bitter reward! Amen again! And the Word of God confirms that there is a purpose to God's laws and expectations for us to live by, saying to each of us that, **"By them (God's laws and expectations) Your servant is warned; in keeping them there is great reward."** God gives His laws and expectations to us for a reason; that we will live righteously and receive His blessings for those that are obedient! Hallelujah! For Almighty God is a righteous Father, and all blessings come from the Father to His children! Glory Hallelujah! And God wants you to live the best possible life that you can; for there is nothing better for you than to live your life according to God's Will for you! Amen.

Today, our Scripture is speaking to God's people. And if you believe in Jesus as your Lord and Savior, you are one of God's people; in fact, you are one of God's children! Glory Hallelujah! God wants to bless you abundantly, but you must live in obedience to your Father. That is why God your Father gives you His laws and His expectations! Because your Father loves you! Glory to God! David has written a hymn that speaks to the majestic glory of God, specifically celebrating the incredible worth of God's laws, and the value of living to God's expectations. Amen! God has given us His commandments and guidelines so that we can live the best possible life that we can; for there is nothing better for you than to live your life according to God's Will for you. Amen again! God has written your life, and it is God that will judge your life, and send you to your everlasting destination! Hallelujah! So when we live our life, choosing to follow what God tells us, God is pleased! Glory Hallelujah! And when God is pleased with you, good things await you! Glory! God has general expectations of all of us, but He also has a specific Will for you! So set your mind and heart to live to God's laws, and live your life according to God's expectations for you! Hallelujah! Glory to God! Our Scripture begins with the truth about God's laws and expectations, saying that, **"The law of the Lord (God) is perfect, refreshing the soul. The statutes of the Lord are trustworthy, making wise the simple. The precepts of the Lord are right, giving joy to the heart. The commands of the Lord are radiant, giving light to the eyes. The fear of the Lord is pure, enduring forever. The decrees of the Lord are firm, and all of them are righteous."** God's laws and expectations for us endure from generation to generation; for God does not change! And they guide us to live a life that is righteous in the eyes of God. And to fulfill God's laws and expectations, you must first love Him, and fear Him! Amen! God has given us His laws and expectations to live righteously on this earth. The only expectation that has changed since the time of David is that God sent His Son Jesus to this earth to redeem us to God, and receive forgiveness for our sins! However, even that was forecast at the time of David that a Messiah would come! Hallelujah! For God has always wanted mankind to know how He wants us to live. And God wants you to live the best possible life that you can; for there is nothing better for you than to live your life according to God's Will for you! Amen.

Today, our Word is speaking to God's people. And through the name of Jesus, you are one of God's people; you are one of God's children! Glory Hallelujah! God wants to bless you abundantly, but you must live in obedience to your Father. That is why God your Father gives you His laws and His expectations! Because your Father loves you! Glory to God! God has given us His commandments and guidelines so that we can live the best possible life that we can. Amen again! God has written your life, and it is God that will judge your life! Hallelujah! So when we live our life, choosing to follow what God tells us, God is pleased! Glory Hallelujah! And when God is pleased with you, good things await you! Glory! God has general expectations of all of us, but He also has a specific Will for you! So set your mind and heart to live to God's laws, and live your life according to God's expectations for you! Hallelujah! Glory to God! God's laws and expectations for us endure from generation to generation; for God does not change! And they guide us to live a life that is righteous in the eyes of God. And to fulfill God's laws and expectations, you must first love Him and fear Him! Amen! Our Word proclaims that God's laws and expectations are so valuable to us that, **"They are more precious than gold, than much pure gold; they are sweeter than honey, than honey from the honeycomb."** There is nothing more valuable than God's laws and expectations; and living according to them brings the sweetest reward, while living your life opposite to them brings a bitter reward! Amen again! There is absolutely nothing on earth that is more valuable than the

Word of God! For nothing else can bring you the righteousness of God! You cannot buy it, and you cannot work for it! But you can live according to God's righteousness by understanding His Word and His expectations for you, and living according to them! Glory Hallelujah! And God wants you to live the best possible life that you can; for there is nothing better for you than to live your life according to God's Will for you! Amen.

Today, the Word of God is speaking to God's people. And through Jesus, you are one of God's people, you are one of God's children! Glory Hallelujah! God wants to bless you abundantly, but you must live in obedience to your Father. That is why God your Father gives you His laws and His expectations! Because your Father loves you! Glory to God! God has written your life, and it is God that will judge your life! Hallelujah! So when you live your life choosing to follow what God tells you, God is pleased! Glory Hallelujah! And when God is pleased with you, good things await you! Glory! God has general expectations of all of us, but He also has a specific Will for you! So set your mind and heart to live to God's laws, and live your life according to God's expectations for you! Hallelujah! Glory to God! God's laws and expectations for us endure from generation to generation; for God does not change! And they guide us to live a life that is righteous in the eyes of God. And to fulfill God's laws and expectations, you must first love Him, and fear Him! Amen! And there is nothing more valuable than God's laws and expectations, and living according to them brings the sweetest reward, while living your life opposite to them brings a bitter reward! Amen again! And the Word of God confirms that there is a purpose to God's laws and expectations for us to live by, saying to each of us that, **"By them (God's laws and expectations) Your servant is warned; in keeping them there is great reward."** God gives His laws and expectations to us for a reason; that we will live righteously and receive His blessings for those that are obedient! Hallelujah! For Almighty God is a righteous Father, and all blessings come from the Father to His children! Glory Hallelujah! God wants you to be blessed, and God wants you to live in obedience to His laws and expectations. So His Word guides us, and His Word warns us! The Holy Spirit that God has put inside of you guides you, and the Holy Spirit warns you! God wants you to receive the greatest possible rewards that He has for you. And God wants you to live the best possible life that you can; for there is nothing better for you than to live your life according to God's Will for you! Amen.

Today, our Scripture Guidance is for God's people; each and every single Believer in Jesus Christ! God wants to bless you abundantly, but you must live in obedience to your Father. However; God knows that no person in their fleshly body can live a life without sin; so God does not require perfection, and that is why He sent His Son Jesus to redeem us to Him! Glory Hallelujah! And yes, you are promised glory through Jesus, and your sins have been forgiven. Still, God wants you to live as closely to His righteousness as you can! Hallelujah! That is why God your Father gives you His laws and His expectations! Because your Father loves you! And God wants you to live the best possible life that you can; for there is nothing better for you than to live your life according to God's Will for you! Amen.

Day 214

"The end of all things is near. Therefore be alert and of sober mind so that you may pray."

"Each of you (Believers) should use whatever gift you have received (from God) to serve others (through serving Jesus), as faithful stewards of God's grace (to you) in various forms.

If anyone speaks (while serving Jesus), they should do so as one who speaks the very words of God. If anyone serves (other people while serving Jesus), they should do so with the strength God provides; so that in all things God may be praised (and glorified) through Jesus Christ. To Him (Almighty God) be the glory and the power for ever and ever. Amen!"

(1 Peter 4:7 & 10-11)

In today's Scripture, the great servant of Jesus, the apostle Peter, writes to Believers with instructions for holy living in a sinful world, that seeks to persecute Believers. Amen! For it is Satan's evil plan to distract Believers from living in a way that influences others to be redeemed to God through Jesus Christ; so, therefore, Satan utilizes people to be obstacles to those who have accepted Jesus as their Lord and Savior, so that those Believers will not serve Jesus and do the Will of God that God has gifted each Believer to do. Amen again! God created each Believer with gifts to utilize to serve Jesus. Yes, every single Believer! And Satan knows this about you! Satan knows that God has designed you to serve Jesus, and be a part of the righteous army that spreads the Truth that will expose the lies of Satan! Hallelujah! That is why Satan hates you; and utilizes whatever carnal tools of this world, including people, to try to keep you from serving Jesus and doing what God designed you to do. But Satan is a liar! Glory to God! In our particular Scripture passage, Peter is speaking to each Believer to get each of us to realize that it is time for us to utilize our gifts; and to realize that God gave each of us our gifts; so that we can serve Jesus through the power of God! Amen! And as long as we serve Jesus with what God has given us, we will be successful in accomplishing what God has planned us to accomplish, all through the name of our Master Jesus! Amen again! Today, you are being challenged! It is time to serve Jesus with the gifts that God has given you to do His Will! Hallelujah! Our Scripture begins with, **"The end of all things is near. Therefore be alert and of sober mind so that you may pray."** It is time for you to be serious and focused! It is time for you to seek the Will of God through prayer! It is time for you to submit yourself to Jesus, and serve Him! It is time! Amen! Our Word says to Believers that, **"Each of you (Believers) should use whatever gift you have received (from God) to serve others (through serving Jesus), as faithful stewards of God's grace (to you) in various forms. If anyone speaks (while serving Jesus), they should do so as one who speaks the very words of God. If anyone serves (other people while serving Jesus), they should**

do so with the strength God provides; so that in all things God may be praised (and glorified) through Jesus Christ." It is time for you to utilize your gifts to serve Jesus! You have specific and powerful gifts from God, and they were given to each Believer! It is time to serve Jesus with the power of God; for your gifts were given to you to glorify God! Amen again! And the Word of God proclaims that each Believer was designed to serve Jesus, and to give glory to God, saying that we serve Jesus so that, **"To Him (Almighty God) be the glory and the power for ever and ever. Amen!"** It is time for each Believer to realize that you have been created and gifted to serve Jesus to glorify God! And that serving Jesus and doing the Will of God, glorifies God! And when each of us glorifies God, we are doing our part to grow the Kingdom of God, and that is why Satan hates us! Glory to God! Right now, it is time for you to serve Jesus and glorify God! Amen.

Today, our Scripture is speaking to Believers. It is time for you to serve Jesus and glorify God! Hallelujah! Glory to God! The apostle Peter writes to Believers with instructions for holy living in a sinful world, for it is Satan's evil plan to distract Believers from living in a way that influences others to be redeemed to God through Jesus Christ. So, therefore,, Satan utilizes people to be obstacles to Believers, so that those Believers will not serve Jesus and do the Will of God. Amen again! It is not enough for you to go to church; God wants you to serve Jesus! Tell the truth! God created each Believer with gifts to serve Jesus. Yes, every single Believer! That is the truth! And Satan knows that God has designed you to serve Jesus, and to speak the Truth that will expose the lies of Satan! Hallelujah! That is why Satan hates you; and utilizes whatever carnal tools of this world, including people, to try to keep you from serving Jesus and doing what God designed you to do. But Satan is a liar! Glory to God! Peter is speaking to each Believer to get each of us to realize that it is time for us to utilize the gifts that God gave us; so that we can serve Jesus through the power of God! Amen! And as long as we serve Jesus, we will be successful in accomplishing what God has planned for us to accomplish! Amen again! Today, you are being challenged! It is time to serve Jesus with the gifts that God has given you to do His Will! Hallelujah! Our Scripture begins with, **"The end of all things is near. Therefore be alert and of sober mind so that you may pray."** It is time for you to be serious and focused! It is time for you to seek the Will of God through prayer! It is time for you to submit yourself to Jesus, and serve Him! It is time! Amen! As the end of time becomes closer and closer, it is time for those who believe in Jesus to mature in their faith; and stand on the Word of God. It is time to be sober, and not be "drunk" on the things of the world. It is time to see the evil in the world, and pray to God for mercy, and that His Will be done! It is time to stop watching others serve Jesus; while you sit on the sideline of the battle! The end of all things on Earth is near! Hallelujah! Right now, it is time for you to serve Jesus and glorify God! Amen.

Today, our Word is speaking to Believers. It is time for you to serve Jesus and glorify God! Hallelujah! Glory to God! The apostle Peter writes to Believers with instructions for holy living in a sinful world, for it is Satan's evil plan to distract Believers from living in a way that influences others to be redeemed to God through Jesus Christ. And Satan utilizes people to be obstacles to Believers so that those Believers will not serve Jesus and do the Will of God. Amen again! It is not enough for you to go to church; God wants you to serve Jesus! Tell the truth! Yes, every single Believer! That is the truth! Satan knows that God has designed you to serve Jesus, and expose the lies of Satan! Hallelujah! That is why Satan hates you and tries to keep you from serving Jesus and doing what God designed you to do. But Satan is a liar! Glory to God! And it is time for each Believer to utilize the gifts that God gave us, and serve Jesus through the power of God! Amen! And as long as we serve Jesus, we will be successful in accomplishing what God has planned for us to accomplish! Amen again! Today, you are being challenged! It is time to serve Jesus with the gifts that God has given you to do His Will! Hallelujah! It is time for you to be serious and focused! It is time for you to seek the Will of God through prayer! It is time for you to submit yourself to Jesus, and serve Him! It is time! Amen! Our Word says to Believers that, **"Each of you (Believers) should use whatever gift you have received (from God) to serve others (through serving Jesus), as faithful stewards of God's grace (to you) in various forms. If anyone speaks (while serving Jesus), they**

should do so as one who speaks the very words of God. If anyone serves (other people while serving Jesus), they should do so with the strength God provides; so that in all things God may be praised (and glorified) through Jesus Christ." It is time for you to utilize your gifts to serve Jesus! You have specific and powerful gifts from God, and they were given to each Believer! It is time to serve Jesus with the power of God; for your gifts were given to you to glorify God! Amen again! God chose you and created you with gifts to serve Jesus and do His Will, and if you are not serving Jesus, you are wasting the gifts that God gave you! Amen! God gave you powerful gifts! And when you use your gifts to serve Jesus, you do so with the power of God! Stop wasting your gifts! Give glory to God by serving Jesus! Hallelujah! Right now, it is time for you to serve Jesus and glorify God! Amen.

Today, the Word of God is speaking to Believers. You are being challenged! It is time for you to serve Jesus and glorify God! Hallelujah! Glory to God! Satan utilizes people to be obstacles to you, so that you will not serve Jesus and do the Will of God. Amen again! It is not enough for you to go to church; God wants you to serve Jesus! Tell the truth! Yes, you! Satan knows that God has designed you to serve Jesus, and expose the lies of Satan! Hallelujah! That is why Satan tries to keep you from serving Jesus and doing what God designed you to do. But Satan is a liar! Glory to God! And it is time for you to utilize the gifts that God gave us, and serve Jesus through the power of God! Amen! And as long as you serve Jesus, you will be successful in accomplishing what

God has planned for you to accomplish! Amen again! Today, you are being challenged! It is time to serve Jesus with the gifts that God has given you to do His Will! Hallelujah! It is time for you to be serious and focused! It is time for you to seek the Will of God through prayer! It is time for you to submit yourself to Jesus, and serve Him! It is time! Amen! It is time for you to utilize your gifts to serve Jesus! You have specific and powerful gifts from God! It is time for you to serve Jesus with the power of God; for your gifts were given to you to glorify God! Amen again! And the Word of God proclaims that each Believer was designed to serve Jesus, and to give glory to God, saying that we serve Jesus so that, **"To Him (Almighty God) be the glory and the power for ever and ever. Amen!"** It is time for each Believer to realize that you have been created and gifted to serve Jesus to glorify God! And that serving Jesus and doing the Will of God, glorifies God! And when each of us glorifies God, we are doing our part to grow the Kingdom of God, and that is why Satan hates us! And you should hate Satan; because Satan hates God, Jesus, and you! So serve Jesus and glorify God! Glory to God! Right now, it is time for you to serve Jesus and glorify God! Amen.

Today, each Believer is being challenged! Are you serving Jesus to glorify God? It is time for you to stop being distracted by Satan! It is time for you to stop worrying about being persecuted! It is time for you to be serious and focused! It is time for you to utilize your gifts to serve Jesus! It is time for you to realize that you have been created and gifted to serve Jesus to glorify God!

Today, right now, it is time for you to serve Jesus and glorify God! Amen.

Day 215

"At that time (the end of days) Michael (the Arch Angel), the prince who protects your people (God's people), will arise. There will be a time of distress (The Tribulation) such has not happened from the beginning of nations until then. But at that time your people (God's people); everyone whose name is found written in the book (of Life), will be delivered.

Multitudes who sleep in the dust (the dead) will arise; some (God's people) to everlasting life (in the Kingdom of God), others to shame and everlasting contempt (in Hell).

Those who are wise will shine like the brightness of the heavens, and those (servants) who lead many to righteousness, (are) like the stars for ever and ever."

"As for you; go your way till the end (of life). You will rest (in death); and then at the end of the days, you will rise to receive your allotted inheritance (from God)."

(Daniel 12:1-3 & 13)

In today's Scripture, the great servant of God, the prophet Daniel, has been given visions by God of what would happen in the world in time to come. Amen. First, Daniel was given what would happen to the world in the immediate future of Daniel's time on Earth, and then Daniel was given what would happen to the world at the end of time on Earth. Amen again! This was approximately 500 years before Jesus was born on Earth! Hallelujah! For God has always sent His plans through His servants to reveal His Will. Glory to God! As you live today, there is no mystery about what is going to happen to the world; God has revealed it! And God has revealed it over and over again through the pages of His Holy Word, the Bible! And God has always given us advance knowledge of what will happen, with the accuracy that only Almighty God can provide, because God has already spoken it! Amen! Daniel's visions are accurate; because the only One who can make them happen is Almighty God who makes all things happen! Hallelujah...and that is the truth! Our Scripture begins with the vision that is revealed to Daniel that, **"At that time (the end of days) Michael (the Arch Angel), the prince who protects your people (God's people), will arise. There will be a time of distress (The Tribulation), such has not happened from the beginning of nations until then. But at that time your people (God's people); everyone whose name is found written in the book (of Life), will be delivered."** At the end of time, there will be great distress, and those who are alive will see horrible things, that have never happened before! Amen! Our Word tells us that at the end of time, **"Multitudes who sleep in the dust (the dead) will arise; some (God's people) to everlasting life (in the Kingdom of God), others to shame and everlasting contempt (in Hell). Those who are wise will shine like the brightness of the heavens, and those (servants) who lead many to righteousness, (are) like the stars forever and ever."** At the end of time, all who have lived and died will arise to be judged for the life that they have lived. For all will be judged, and sentenced to their eternity! Amen again! And the Word of God has a message for God's people, **"As for you, go your way till the end (of life). You will rest (in death); and then at the end of the days, you will rise to receive your allotted inheritance (from God)."** At the end of time, all of God's people have an assurance that God will receive you into His Kingdom, as He has promised you! Glory! And today, that promise is for all people who have been redeemed to God as His people, through the name of Jesus Christ! Glory Hallelujah! So if you believe in Jesus as your Lord and Savior, go your way through the rest of your life believing in Jesus, and you will rise to receive your inheritance in the Kingdom of God! Amen.

Today, our Scripture is speaking to God's people. God is making you a promise! At the end of the time for the flesh of people to walk on this earth, God promises that you will rise to receive your glory, and live with God in His Kingdom forever! This promise is only for God's people. And today, that promise is for all people who have been redeemed to God as His people, through the name of Jesus Christ! Glory Hallelujah! So if you believe in Jesus as your Lord and Savior, you can rest assured knowing that God has made you a promise! And you do not have to worry about what will happen to you at the end of the days, God has made you a promise! Glory! So go your way through the rest of your life believing in Jesus, and you will rise to receive your inheritance in the Kingdom of God! God has made you a promise! The prophet Daniel was given visions by God. Amen. Daniel was given what will happen to the world at the end of time on Earth. Amen again! This was approximately 500 years before Jesus was born on Earth! Hallelujah! For God has always sent His plans through His servants to reveal His Will. There is no mystery about what is going to happen to the world, God has revealed it! God has always given us advanced knowledge of what will happen, with the accuracy that only Almighty God can provide, because God has already spoken it! Glory to God! Our Scripture begins with the vision that is revealed to Daniel, that, **"At that time (the end of days) Michael (the Arch Angel), the prince who protects your people (God's people), will arise. There will be a time of distress (The Tribulation), such has not happened from the beginning of nations until then. But at that time, your people (God's people), everyone whose name is found written in the book (of Life), will be delivered."** At the end of time, there will be great distress, and those who are alive will see horrible things, that have never happened before! Amen! It is amazing that Daniel was given the prophecy of the Revelation of Jesus, which was given to the apostle John through visions six hundred years later! There will be a great Tribulation on Earth at the end of times, with several horrific woes coming down on the people of Earth. But hallelujah, those who believe in Jesus will have their names in the Book of Life, and they will be delivered from these woes! The angel of God said it to Daniel, and the angel of Jesus said it to

John! God has made a promise! So if you believe in Jesus as your Lord and Savior, go your way through the rest of your life believing in Jesus, and you will rise to receive your inheritance in the Kingdom of God! Amen.

Today, our Word is speaking to God's people. God is making you a promise! At the end of the time for the flesh of people to walk on this earth, God promises that you will rise to receive your glory, and live with God in His Kingdom forever! This promise is only for God's people. And today, that promise is for all people who have been redeemed to God as His people, through the name of Jesus Christ! Glory Hallelujah! So if you believe in Jesus as your Lord and Savior, you can rest assured knowing that God has made you a promise! And you do not have to worry about what will happen to you at the end of the days, God has made you a promise! Glory! So go your way through the rest of your life believing in Jesus, and you will rise to receive your inheritance in the Kingdom of God! God has made you a promise! The prophet Daniel was given what will happen to the world at the end of time on Earth. Amen! This was 500 years before Jesus was born on earth! Hallelujah! For God has always sent His plans through His servants to reveal His Will. Glory to God! There is no mystery about what is going to happen to the world, God has revealed it! God has always given us advanced knowledge of what will happen, with the accuracy that only Almighty God can provide, because God has already spoken it! So God reveals to us what will happen at the end of time on earth. And God tells us that at the end of time, there will be great distress, and those who are alive will see horrible things, that have never happened before! Amen! Our Word tells us that at the end of time, **"Multitudes who sleep in the dust (the dead) will arise; some (God's people) to everlasting life (in the Kingdom of God), others to shame and everlasting contempt (in Hell). Those who are wise will shine like the brightness of the heavens, and those (servants) who lead many to righteousness, (are) like the stars forever and ever."** At the end of time, all who have lived and died, will arise to be judged for the life that they have lived. For all will be judged, and sentenced to their eternity! Amen again! God gives each person free choice, and you can choose to accept Jesus and live your life according to God's Word, or you can choose not to. But no matter what you choose, there are consequences! You will be judged! If you are judged to be without Jesus, you are going to everlasting condemnation in Hell! That is the truth! And the righteous in God's eyes are the ones that have accepted Jesus, and you will receive everlasting life with God! Glory! And if you choose to serve Jesus and do the Will of God, you will be like stars in Heaven! Glory Hallelujah! That is also the truth! God has made a promise! So if you believe in Jesus as your Lord and Savior, go your way through the rest of your life believing in Jesus, and you will rise to receive your inheritance in the Kingdom of God! Amen.

Today, the Word of God is speaking to God's people. God is making you a promise! At the end of the time for the flesh of people to walk on this earth, God promises that you will rise to receive your glory, and live with God in His Kingdom forever! This promise is only for God's people. And today, that promise is for all people who have been redeemed to God as His people, through the name of Jesus Christ! Glory Hallelujah! So if you believe in Jesus as your Lord and Savior, you can rest assured knowing that God has made you a promise! And you do not have to worry about what will happen to you at the end of the days, God has made you a promise! Glory! So go your way through the rest of your life believing in Jesus, and you will rise to receive your inheritance in the Kingdom of God! God has made you a promise! God has always sent His plans through His servants to reveal His Will. Glory to God! There is no mystery about what is going to happen to the world, God has revealed it! God reveals to us what will happen at the end of time on earth. At the end of time, there will be great distress, and those who are alive will see horrible things, that have never happened before! Amen! At the end of time all who have lived and died, will arise to be judged for the life that they have lived. For all will be judged, and sentenced to their eternity! Amen again! And the Word of God has a message for God's people, **"As for you, go your way till the end (of life). You will rest (in death), and then at the end of the days, you will rise to receive your allotted inheritance (from God)."** At the end of time, all of God's people have an assurance that God will receive you into His Kingdom, as He has promised you! Glory! And today, that promise is for all people who have been redeemed to God as His people through the name of Jesus Christ! Glory Hallelujah! Continue to live your life with Jesus as Your Lord and Savior, and when you pass from your human life, you will receive rest! And then you will rise to the inheritance that God has for you in His Kingdom! Glory, glory, glory! Hallelujah! God has made a promise! So if you believe in Jesus as your Lord and Savior, go your way through the rest of your life believing in Jesus, and you will rise to receive your inheritance in the Kingdom of God! Amen.

Today, God is making a promise to His people. God's promise is for all people who have been redeemed to God through the name of Jesus Christ! Glory Hallelujah! You can rest assured knowing that God has made you a promise! And you do not have to worry about what will happen to you at the end of the day; God has made you a promise! Glory! So, go your way through the rest of your life believing in Jesus, and you will rise to receive your inheritance in the Kingdom of God! Glory to God! God has made you a promise! Amen.

Day 216

"I know that good itself, does not dwell in me, that is; in my sinful nature (flesh). For I have the desire to do what is good, but I cannot carry it out.

For I do not do the good I want to do, but the evil I do not want to do, this I keep on doing.

Now if I do what I do not want to do, it is no longer I who do it; but it is sin living in me that does its."

What a wretched man (person) I am! Who will rescue me from this body that is subject to death?

Thanks be to God, who delivers me (from eternal death) though Jesus Christ our Lord!"

(Romans 7:18-20 & 24-25)

In today's Scripture, the great servant of Jesus, the apostle Paul, speaks to us about the sinful nature of people. All people are flesh, and flesh desires to sin. Amen! The Laws of God that were given to Moses identified sins; but could not deliver people from sin. In fact, in many ways, the Law created a desire in people to allow the flesh to desire the sins that were identified in the Law! The Law reveals sin, yet, it also stimulates sin! For the natural (flesh) tendency is to want what is forbidden to us! Because the flesh desires sin, and the Spirit to battle sin is not naturally in us. Amen again! So having laws against sin; does not keep the flesh from sinning. And these laws also do not rescue us from the wages of sin. The only way to be rescued from the penalty of sin is to repent your sin and accept Jesus as your Lord and Savior! Hallelujah, that is the Truth! It is then that God gives each Believer the Holy Spirit, and if we rely on the Holy Spirit, the Holy Spirit will fight our natural desire to sin. Amen! We will still have the desire to sin; because we are still in our flesh; however, we also have the Holy Spirit to lean on to keep us from giving into the temptation to sin. Amen again! And Believers have Jesus, and through Jesus, God takes away the eternal punishment for sins! Glory Hallelujah! Our Scripture begins with Paul stating the truth about humans, saying, **"I know that good itself, does not dwell in me, that is; in my sinful nature (flesh). For I have the desire to do what is good, but I cannot carry it out. For I do not do the good I want to do, but the evil I do not want to do, this I keep on doing. Now if I do what I do not want to do, it is no longer I who do it; but it is a sin living in me that does its."** We need to understand that our flesh desires sin! And no matter how much we want to live a life without sinning, we all will sin! Because the desire to sin lives in our flesh! Amen! Our Word continues with this truth about the guilty state of every person, **"What a wretched man (person) I am! Who will rescue me from this body that is subject to death?"** You and I are guilty of sin! And eternal death hangs over us as our sentence for our sins, and we need to confess that! And search for the only Savior there is who can mediate us from our condemnation! Amen again! And the Word of God concludes with the guilty person who has been rescued from their conviction of sin, speaking praise for salvation, proclaiming, **"Thanks be to God, who delivers me (from eternal death) through Jesus Christ our Lord!"** Only God can commute our death sentence for sin, to eternal salvation through His mercy, and only Jesus can represent us to God for His mercy! Glory Hallelujah! Amen.

Today, our Scripture is speaking to everyone. Every person is a sinner! And every sinner deserves eternal death! But glory to God, there is a way that each person can receive salvation from our death sentence. Amen! One Way, and one Way only! The only way to be rescued from the penalty of sin is to repent your sin and accept Jesus as your Lord and Savior! And Jesus will mediate for you to God, to seek His mercy for you! And God promises that He will be faithful to you, and you will be forgiven of your sins, and be awarded everlasting life with God! Jesus is the only way to be forgiven and redeemed by God! Hallelujah, that is the Truth! Glory to God! The apostle Paul speaks to us about the sinful nature of people. All people are flesh, and flesh desires to sin. Amen! The Laws of God reveal sin, yet, it also stimulates sin! For the natural (flesh) tendency is to want what is forbidden to us! Because the flesh desires sin, and the Spirit to battle sin is not naturally in us. Amen again! So having laws against sin; does not keep the flesh from sinning. And these laws also do not rescue us from the wages of sin. The only way to be rescued from the penalty of sin is to repent your sin and accept Jesus as your Lord and Savior! Hallelujah, that is the Truth! God gives each Believer the Holy

Spirit, and if we rely on the Holy Spirit, the Holy Spirit will fight our natural desire to sin. Amen! And Believers have Jesus, and through Jesus, God takes away the eternal punishment for sins! Glory Hallelujah! Our Scripture begins with Paul stating the truth about humans, saying, **"I know that good itself, does not dwell in me, that is, in my sinful nature (flesh). For I have the desire to do what is good, but I cannot carry it out. For I do not do the good I want to do, but the evil I do not want to do, this I keep on doing. Now if I do what I do not want to do, it is no longer I who do it; but it is sin living in me that does its."** We need to understand that our flesh desires sin! And no matter how much we want to live a life without sinning, we all will sin! Because the desire to sin lives in our flesh! Amen! Without Jesus as your Lord and Savior, you are not strong enough to resist sins; your flesh craves sin too much! You may not want to keep sinning, but you will! Because sin lives in your flesh, and without Jesus, you do not have the Holy Spirit of God in you to battle for you! So even though you may have the mind to want to live good, you do not have the Spirit to help you live good. You will sin, and sin separates you from God and brings you the sentence of everlasting condemnation! For sin is living in you! And you are on your way to Hell without Jesus! Jesus is the only way to be forgiven and redeemed by God! Hallelujah, that is the Truth! Amen.

Today, our Word is speaking to everyone. Every person is a sinner! And every sinner deserves eternal death! But glory to God, there is a way that each person can receive salvation from our death sentence. Amen! One Way, and one Way only! The only way to be rescued from the penalty of sin is to repent your sin and accept Jesus as your Lord and Savior! And Jesus will mediate for you to God, to seek His mercy for you! And God promises that He will be faithful to you, and you will be forgiven of your sins, and be awarded everlasting life with God! Jesus is the only way to be forgiven and redeemed by God! Hallelujah, that is the Truth! Glory to God! All people are flesh, and flesh desires to sin. Amen! The Laws of God reveal sin, yet, the natural (flesh) tendency is to want what is forbidden to us! So having laws against sin; does not keep the flesh from sinning, and laws do not rescue us from the wages of sin. The only way to be rescued from the penalty of sin is to repent your sin and accept Jesus as your Lord and Savior! Hallelujah, that is the Truth! God gives each Believer the Holy Spirit, and if we rely on the Holy Spirit, the Holy Spirit will fight our natural desire to sin. Amen! And Believers have Jesus, and through Jesus, God takes away the eternal punishment for sins! Glory Hallelujah! We all must understand that our flesh desires sin! And no matter how much we want to live a life without sinning, we all will sin! Because the desire to sin lives in our flesh! Amen! Our Word continues with this truth about the guilty state of every person, **"What a wretched man (person) I am! Who will rescue me from this body that is subject to death?"** You and I are guilty of sin! And eternal death hangs over us as our sentence for our sins, and we need to confess that! And we need to turn to the only Savior there is who can mediate us from our condemnation! Amen again! You and I are sinners, and we are justifiably on a path to condemnation! Every single person who wants to be saved from eternal death; must first recognize that we are wretched sinners! Amen! We must acknowledge that we are on the way to Hell; and that we alone cannot stop it or rescue ourselves! Then we will understand that we need to seek the only One who can rescue us, and that person is Jesus, the Son of God, who put His blood on the altar of God as a sacrifice for your sins! Jesus is the only One that can rescue you! Amen again! Jesus is the only way to be forgiven and redeemed by God! Hallelujah, that is the Truth! Amen.

Today, the Word of God is speaking to everyone. Every person is a sinner! And every sinner deserves eternal death! But glory to God, there is a way that each person can receive salvation from our death sentence. Amen! One Way, and one Way only! The only way to be rescued from the penalty of sin is to repent your sin and accept Jesus as your Lord and Savior! And Jesus will mediate for you to God, to seek His mercy for you! And God promises that He will be faithful to you, and you will be forgiven of your sins, and be awarded everlasting life with God! Jesus is the only way to be forgiven and redeemed by God! Hallelujah, that is the Truth! Glory to God! All people are flesh, and flesh desires to sin. Amen! The only way to be rescued from the penalty of sin is to repent your sin and accept Jesus as your Lord and Savior! Hallelujah, that is the Truth! God gives each Believer the Holy Spirit, and if we rely on the Holy Spirit, the Holy Spirit will fight our natural desire to sin. Amen! And Believers have Jesus, and through Jesus, God takes away the eternal punishment for sins! Glory Hallelujah! We all must understand that our flesh desires sin! And no matter how much we want to live a life without sinning, we all will sin! Because the desire to sin lives in our flesh! Amen! You and I are guilty of sin! And eternal death hangs over us as our sentence for our sins, and we need to confess that! And search for the only Savior there is who can mediate us from our condemnation! Amen again! And the Word of God concludes with the guilty person who has been rescued from their conviction of sin, speaking praise for salvation, proclaiming, **"Thanks be to God, who delivers me (from eternal death) through Jesus Christ our Lord!"** Only God can commute our death sentence for sin, to eternal salvation through His mercy, and only Jesus can represent us to God for His mercy! Glory Hallelujah! And every Believer should consistently thank God for His mercy! And every single Believer should thank Jesus for sacrificing His human life; to put His perfect blood on the altar of God, so that you and I could be forgiven for our sins! Thank you, Father God! Thank you, my Lord and Savior Jesus! Praise Him! For Jesus is the only way to be forgiven and redeemed by God! Hallelujah, that is the Truth! Amen.

Today, every single person is a sinner. And every sinner deserves eternal death! But glory to God, there is a way that each person can receive salvation from our death sentence. Amen! One Way, and one Way only! The only way to be rescued from the penalty of sin is to repent your sin and accept Jesus as your Lord and Savior! And Jesus will mediate for you to God, to seek His mercy for you! And God promises that He will be faithful to you, and you will be forgiven of your sins, and be awarded everlasting life with God! Jesus is the only way to be forgiven and redeemed by God! Hallelujah, that is the Truth! Amen.

Day 217

The apostles and elders met to consider this question (of whether or not the Gentiles should be circumcised to keep the Law of Moses).

After much discussion, Peter got up and addressed them: "Brothers, you know that some time ago God made a choice among you that the Gentiles might hear from my lips the message of the Gospel (of Jesus) and believe.

God, who knows the heart, showed that He accepted them (Gentiles who believed in Jesus) by giving the Holy Spirit to them, just as He did to us.

He did not discriminate between us and them, for He purified their hearts by faith.

Now then, why do you try to test God by putting on the Gentiles a yoke that we could not bear?

No! We believe it is through the grace of our Lord Jesus that we are saved, just as they are."

(Acts 15:6-11)

In today's Scripture, the great servant of Jesus, Luke, shares with us the acts of Jesus servants, to show us how the Gospel of Jesus spread rapidly from Jerusalem to other places throughout the territories of the Roman Empire. Amen! These acts of missionary travel and teaching took the message of Jesus, and the Gospel of Jesus from the Jewish people, to the Gentile (non-Jewish) world. Amen again! These acts by Jesus's servants established Believers, and churches, that focused on Jesus, and ministered to people about the saving power of Jesus. Glory! These acts by these servants of Jesus... began growing the Kingdom of God through the name of Jesus! Glory Hallelujah! These acts, by these servants! Glory to God! In our particular Scripture passage, many of the Jewish Believers in Jesus Christ wanted the Gentiles who came to believe in Jesus; to also be loyal to the Laws of Moses to be admitted into the church of Jesus. We must remember that until these "acts" of missionary ministry, only Jewish people knew about, and had accepted Jesus as the Messiah and Son of God. These same Jewish Believers, also had grown up and lived according to the Laws of Moses, and that included circumcision for men. It is not that these Jewish Believers did not want the Gentiles to be part of the church, they just wanted to add circumcision as a part of becoming eligible to receive Jesus, and be part of this "new" Gospel. Amen! In fact, these Jewish Believers had told the Gentiles that had come to believe in Jesus as their Savior; that they could not be saved unless they became circumcised first **(Acts 15:1)**. Our Scripture begins with, **The apostles and elders met to consider this question (of whether or not the Gentiles should be circumcised to keep the Law of Moses).** When there are questions within the church, let the servants appointed by Jesus know about it, so they can utilize their roles as leaders of the church to consult and seek answers through the Word of God and prayer. Amen! Our Word tells us that the servants of Jesus responded to the church, **After much discussion, Peter got up and addressed them: "Brothers, you know that some time ago God made a choice among you that the Gentiles might hear from my lips the message of the Gospel (of Jesus) and believe. God, who knows the heart, showed that He accepted them (Gentiles who believed in Jesus) by giving the Holy Spirit to them, just as He did to us. He did not discriminate between us and them, for He purified their hearts by faith. Now then, why do you try to test God by putting on the Gentiles a yoke that we (Jews) could not bear?"** After meeting and consulting the Word of God, and seeking the spiritual answer from God; then the appointed servant of Jesus should address the issue, utilizing guidance from the Word of God! Amen again! And after that, the appointed servant of God must render a decision to the church, as the servant of Jesus; the apostle Peter did, saying to the church about whether Gentiles should be circumcised to become saved by Jesus, saying, **"No! We believe it is through the grace of our Lord Jesus that we are saved, just as they are."** The answer to church issues should always be based on the Word of God! Not opinion, on the Word of God! Hallelujah! Amen.

Today, our Scripture is speaking to Believers. There will always be issues that come up in the church that require decisions that affect the church body. Amen! At the time of our Scripture

254

passage, the church of Jesus had begun to be spread across the Roman Empire, and many Gentiles began to accept Jesus as their Lord and Savior. Hallelujah! However, since Jesus taught the Gospel to the Jewish people, many of the Jewish Believers in Jesus Christ wanted the Gentiles who came to believe in Jesus; to also be loyal to the Laws of Moses to be saved. We must remember that until these "acts" of missionary ministry, only Jewish people knew about, and had accepted Jesus as the Messiah and Son of God. These same Jewish Believers, also had grown up and lived according to the Laws of Moses, and that included circumcision for men. And these Jewish Believers wanted the Gentiles to add circumcision as a part of becoming eligible to receive Jesus, and be part of this "new" Gospel. Amen! In fact, these Jewish Believers had told the Gentiles that had come to believe in Jesus as their Savior; that they could not be saved unless they became circumcised first. Our Scripture begins with, **The apostles and elders met to consider this question (of whether or not the Gentiles should be circumcised to keep the Law of Moses).** When there are questions within the church, let the servants appointed by Jesus know about it, so they can utilize their roles as leaders of the church to consult and seek answers through the Word of God and prayer. Amen! God has created the servants of Jesus that lead the church, and God has given these servants of Jesus gifts to lead the church. And Jesus has appointed these servants of His to lead the church! Take the issues and disputes to the servants of Jesus that lead the church; so they can do what God has created them to do; and what Jesus has appointed them to do, to lead the church! Amen.

Today, our Word is speaking to Believers. There will always be issues that come up in the church that require decisions that affect the church body. Amen! The church of Jesus had just begun to be spread across the Roman Empire, and many Gentiles began to accept Jesus as their Lord and Savior. Hallelujah! However, many of the Jewish Believers in Jesus Christ wanted the Gentiles to also be loyal to the Laws of Moses to be saved. We must remember that until these "acts" of missionary ministry, only Jewish people had accepted Jesus as the Messiah and Son of God. And these Jewish Believers wanted the Gentiles to add circumcision as a part of becoming eligible to receive Jesus, and be part of this "new" Gospel. Amen! In fact, these Jewish Believers had told the Gentiles that had come to believe in Jesus as their Savior; that they could not be saved unless they became circumcised first. So there were questions in the church that was leading to division. And when there are questions within the church, always let the servants appointed by Jesus know about it, so they can utilize their roles as leaders of the church to consult and seek answers through the Word of God and prayer. Amen! Our Word tells us that the servants of Jesus responded to the church. After much discussion, Peter got up and addressed them: **"Brothers, you know that some time ago God made a choice among you that the Gentiles might hear from my lips the message of the Gospel (of Jesus) and believe. God, who knows**

the heart, showed that He accepted them (Gentiles who believed in Jesus) by giving the Holy Spirit to them, just as He did to us. He did not discriminate between us and them, for He purified their hearts by faith. Now then, why do you try to test God by putting on the Gentiles a yoke that we (Jews) could not bear?" After meeting and consulting the Word of God, and seeking the spiritual answer from God; then the appointed servant of Jesus should address the issue, utilizing guidance from the Word of God! Amen again! Jesus has appointed His servants to lead your church, and they will be guided by the Holy Spirit of God to seek the answers to church issues through prayer to God, and the Word of God! For the answer is a spiritual answer; because leading and deciding issues in the church takes a spiritual process! Amen.

Today, the Word of God is speaking to Believers. There will always be issues that come up in the church that require decisions that affect the church body. Amen! These issues and questions can cause division within the church. Amen again! So when there are questions within the church, always let the servants appointed by Jesus know about it, so they can utilize their roles as leaders of the church to consult and seek answers through the Word of God and prayer. Amen! Then, after meeting and consulting the Word of God; and seeking the spiritual answer from God; then the appointed servant of Jesus should address the issue, utilizing guidance from the Word of God! Amen again! And after that, the appointed servant of God must render a decision to the church, as the servant of Jesus; the apostle Peter did, saying to the church about whether Gentiles should be circumcised to become saved by Jesus, saying, **"No! We believe it is through the grace of our Lord Jesus that we are saved, just as they are."** The answer to church issues should always be based on the Word of God! Not opinion, on the Word of God! Hallelujah! And once the answer to the church issue is delivered to the servant of Jesus through the Word of God or the Holy Spirit, the servant of Jesus must address the issue with strength and truth! Amen.

Today, our Scripture Guidance is for Believers. There will always be issues that come up in the church that require decisions that affect the church body. Amen! These issues and questions can cause division within the church. Amen again! So when there are questions within the church, always let the servants appointed by Jesus know about it, so they can utilize their roles as leaders of the church to consult and seek answers through the Word of God and prayer. Amen! The servants of Jesus that lead your church; have been given the responsibility of utilizing prayer and the Word of God to manage the church body, which includes answering questions and handling disputes. We need to trust them to do that! Then, after meeting and consulting the Word of God; and seeking the spiritual answer from God; then the appointed servant of Jesus should address the issue, utilizing guidance from the Word of God! And finally, the answer to church issues should always be based on the Word of God! Not opinion, on the Word of God! Hallelujah! Amen.

Day 218

"The words of the prophets are in agreement with this (the answers from the servants of Jesus), as it is written:

'After this I will return and rebuild David's fallen tent. Its ruins I will rebuild, and I will restore it,

that the rest of mankind may seek the Lord (God), even all the Gentiles who bear My Name, says the Lord (God), who does these things,

things known from long ago.'

"It is my (the leading servant of Jesus) judgment, therefore, that we should not make it difficult for the Gentiles who are turning to God (through the name of Jesus.)"

(Acts 15:15-19)

In today's Scripture, the great servant of Jesus, Luke, shares with us the acts of Jesus servants, to show us how the Gospel of Jesus spread rapidly from Jerusalem to other places throughout the territories of the Roman Empire. Amen! These acts of missionary travel and teaching took the message of Jesus, and the Gospel of Jesus from the Jewish people, to the Gentile (non-Jewish) world. Amen again! These acts by Jesus servants established Believers, and churches, that focused on Jesus, and ministered to people about the saving power of Jesus. Glory! These acts by these servants of Jesus, began growing the Kingdom of God through the name of Jesus! Glory Hallelujah! These acts, by these servants! Glory to God! Many of the Jewish Believers in Jesus Christ wanted the Gentiles who came to believe in Jesus; to also be loyal to the Laws of Moses to be admitted into the church of Jesus. These same Jewish Believers, also had grown up and lived according to the Laws of Moses, and that included circumcision for men. It is not that these Jewish Believers did not want the Gentiles to be part of the church; they just wanted to add circumcision as a part of becoming eligible to receive Jesus, and be part of this "new" Gospel. Amen! In fact, these Jewish Believers had told the Gentiles that that they could not be saved unless they became circumcised first **(Acts 15:1).** When the servants of Jesus arrived, those who had been given authority to spread the Gospel; and lead the church of Jesus, the Jewish Believers took the issue to them. After praying and searching the Word of God, Peter told the Jewish Believers that there would be no requirement for circumcision, since God did not put that requirement on anyone to be saved by Jesus and redeemed by Him. Hallelujah! And to clarify and support the fact that their decision was based on the Word of God, James (the brother of Jesus) quoted the Old Testament scripture from the prophet Amos, which quoted God. Glory Hallelujah! Our Scripture begins with the authorized leading servant of Jesus saying, **"The words of the prophets are in agreement with this (the answers from the servants of Jesus), as it is written:"** Whenever a difficult decision, or clarifying guidance is given, always utilize the Word of God that supports the decision. Amen! Our Word tells us that the servant of Jesus quoted the words of God that were given in the Old Testament about the coming Messiah, **'After this, I will return and rebuild David's fallen tent. Its ruins I will rebuild, and I will restore it, that the rest of mankind may seek the Lord (God), even all the Gentiles who bear My Name, says the Lord (God), who does these things, things known from long ago.'** There is nothing that supports a spiritual decision more than words spoken by God! Amen again! And the Word of God confirms that the appointed servant of God stood on the decision that was supported by the Word of God, saying, **"It is my (the leading servant of Jesus) judgment, therefore, that we should not make it difficult for the Gentiles who are turning to God (through the name of Jesus)."** The answer to church issues should always be based on the Word of God! Not opinion, on the Word of God! Hallelujah! Amen.

Today, our Scripture is speaking to Believers. There will always be issues that come up in the church that require decisions that affect the church body. Amen! These issues and questions can cause division within the church. Amen again! At the time of our Scripture passage, the church of Jesus had begun to be spread across the Roman Empire, and many Gentiles began to accept Jesus as their Lord and Savior. Hallelujah! However, many of the Jewish Believers in Jesus Christ wanted the Gentiles to also be loyal to the Laws of Moses to be saved; and to prove their loyalty by becoming circumcised before the Jewish Believers would accept them in the church. Jewish Believers had accepted Jesus as their Messiah and Son of God; however, they had also lived according to the Laws of Moses...and that included circumcision for men. And these Jewish Believers wanted the Gentiles to add circumcision as a part of becoming eligible to receive Jesus, and be part of this "new" Gospel. Amen! Peter told the Jewish Believers that there would be no requirement for circumcision, since God did not put that requirement on anyone to be saved by Jesus or redeemed by Him. Hallelujah! And to clarify and support the fact that their decision was based on the Word of God, James (the brother of Jesus) quoted the Old Testament scripture from the prophet Amos, which quoted God. Glory Hallelujah! Our Scripture begins with the authorized leading servant of Jesus saying, **"The words of the prophets are in agreement with this (the answers from the servants of Jesus), as it is written:"** Whenever a difficult decision, or clarifying guidance is given, always utilize the Word of God that supports the decision. Amen! Jesus has appointed these servants of His to lead the church! And to take the issues and disputes of the church, and utilize prayer and the Word of God to receive spiritual direction; so they can do what God has created them to do; and what Jesus has appointed them to do, to lead the church! Amen.

Today, our Word is speaking to Believers. There will always be issues that come up in the church that require decisions that affect the church body. Amen! These issues and questions can cause division within the church. Amen again! So when there are questions within the church, always let the servants appointed by Jesus know about it, so they can utilize their roles as leaders of the church to consult and seek answers through the Word of God and prayer. Amen! And whenever the leading servant of Jesus renders a difficult decision, or gives clarifying guidance, always utilize the Word of God that supports the decision. Amen! Jesus has appointed these servants of His to lead the church! And to take the issues and disputes of the church, and utilize prayer and the Word of God to receive spiritual direction; so they can do what God has created them to do; and what Jesus has appointed them to do, to lead the church! Amen. Our Word tells us that the servant of Jesus quoted the words of God that were given in the Old Testament about the coming Messiah, **'After this, I will return and rebuild David's fallen tent. Its ruins I will rebuild, and I will restore it, that the rest of mankind may seek the Lord (God), even all the Gentiles who bear My Name, says the Lord (God), who does these things, things known from long ago.'** There is nothing that supports a spiritual decision more than words spoken by God! Amen again! So the servant of Jesus quoted the Scripture **(Amos 9:11-12).** For God spoke His words to the prophet, Amos, 750 years before the birth of Jesus! And God's Word never changes! So quoting God reveals that the decision is accurate and spiritual! Hallelujah! Jesus has appointed His servants to lead your church, and they will be guided by the Holy Spirit of God to seek the answers to church issues through prayer to God, and the Word of God! For the answer is a spiritual answer; because leading and deciding issues in the church takes a spiritual process! And as much as possible, utilize the words spoken by God, or spoken by Jesus, or spoken in the Word of God! Amen.

Today, the Word of God is speaking to Believers. There will always be issues that come up in the church that require decisions that affect the church body. Amen! These issues and questions can cause division within the church. Amen again! So when there are questions within the church, always let the servants appointed by Jesus know about it, so they can utilize their roles as leaders of the church to consult and seek answers through the Word of God and prayer. And whenever the leading servant of Jesus renders a difficult decision or gives clarifying guidance, always utilize the Word of God that supports the decision. Amen! There is nothing that supports a spiritual decision more than words spoken by God! Amen again! And the Word of God confirms that the appointed servant of God stood on the decision that was supported by the Word of God, saying, **"It is my (the leading servant of Jesus) judgment, therefore, that we should not make it difficult for the Gentiles who are turning to God (through the name of Jesus)."** Whenever a difficult decision or clarifying guidance is given, always utilize the Word of God that supports the decision. Hallelujah! Jesus has appointed these servants of His to lead the church! And to take the issues and disputes of the church, and utilize prayer and the Word of God to receive spiritual direction; so they can do what God has created them to do; and what Jesus has appointed them to do, to lead the church! Amen.

Today, our Scripture Guidance is for Believers. There will always be issues that come up in the church that require decisions that affect the church body. Amen! These issues and questions can cause division within the church. Amen again! So when there are questions within the church, always let the servants appointed by Jesus know about it, so they can utilize their roles as leaders of the church to consult and seek answers through the Word of God and prayer. And whenever a difficult decision or clarifying guidance is given, always utilize the Word of God that supports the decision. There is nothing that supports a spiritual decision more than words spoken by God! Amen again! Today and always, the answer to church issues should always be based on the Word of God! Not opinion, on the Word of God! Hallelujah! Amen.

Day 219

"The Spirit of the Sovereign Lord (Almighty God) is on me, because the Lord has anointed me to proclaim good news to the poor; He has sent me to bind up the brokenhearted, to proclaim freedom for the captives and release from darkness for the prisoners,

to proclaim the year of the Lord's favor and the day of vengeance of our God, to comfort all who mourn."

(Isaiah 61:1-2)

In today's Scripture, the great servant of God, the prophet Isaiah, shares the plan that God has for His people of imminent judgment, but also their eventual restoration. Amen! For God has a plan for His people! Hallelujah! God has always had a plan for His people, and God has always shared His plans through His servants. Amen again! God wants us to know His plans. Before Jesus, God told His plans through His servants that a Messiah would come to redeem them to God. Then God had Jesus, His Servant, tell people about God's plan of forgiveness, redemption, and salvation. And after Jesus, God told His plans through the servants of Jesus! Glory Hallelujah! God has always had a plan, and God has always shared His plan. Glory to God! In today's Scripture passage, Isaiah speaks of a servant that has been assigned a mission. Isaiah is speaking of himself, yet he is also speaking of Jesus! Amen! For Jesus read this Scripture in the

Synagogue at Nazareth, and after reading it, He told the people there that, "Today this Scripture is fulfilled in your hearing **(Luke 4:17-22)."** Hallelujah! God has always had a plan for His people! Our Scripture begins with the servant of God saying that, **"The Spirit of the Sovereign Lord (Almighty God) is on me, because the Lord has anointed me to proclaim good news to the poor;"** God chooses the servants that spread His Word! Amen! Our Word continues with the servant speaking to the assignment that God has given, **"He has sent me to bind up the brokenhearted, to proclaim freedom for the captives and release from darkness for the prisoners,"** God assigns the servant to utilize His Word to teach and heal with the Word, and to meet every human need with God's Word. Amen again! And the Word of God proclaims that God also sends the servant, **"to proclaim the year of the Lord's favor and the day of vengeance of our God, to comfort all who mourn."** The servant is to teach that there will be a day of judgment, and God will send sinners to damnation, while giving salvation to those who are His people! Glory! God has plans for His people! Amen.

Today, our Scripture is speaking to God's people. If you have accepted Jesus as your Lord and Savior, you are one of God's people! Hallelujah! And God wants you to know what His plans are; for God has always shared His plans for His people! Glory Hallelujah! The prophet Isaiah shares the plan that God has for His people of imminent judgment, but also their eventual restoration. Amen! For God has always had a plan for His people, and God has always shared His plans through His servants. Amen again! God wants us to know His plans. Before Jesus, God told His plans through His servants that a Messiah would come to redeem them to God. Then God had Jesus, His Servant, tell people about God's plan of forgiveness, redemption, and salvation. And after Jesus, God told His plans through the servants of Jesus! Glory Hallelujah! God has always had a plan, and God has always shared His plan. Glory to God! Isaiah speaks of a servant that has been assigned a mission. Isaiah is speaking of himself, yet he is also speaking of Jesus! Amen! For Jesus read this Scripture in the Synagogue at Nazareth, and after reading it, He told the people there, "Today this Scripture is fulfilled in your hearing." Hallelujah! God has always had a plan for His people! Our Scripture begins with the servant of God saying that, **"The Spirit of the Sovereign Lord (Almighty God) is on me, because the Lord has anointed me to proclaim good news to the poor;"** God chooses the servants that spread His Word! Amen! The Spirit of God was on Isaiah! God chose Isaiah, and gave Isaiah visions to give to His people of what would come. Isaiah was not born a prophet, but He was created and gifted to be a servant of God! Hallelujah! The same is true today of the servants of Jesus. The Spirit of God is on each servant of Jesus! You were not born a servant, but God created you and gifted you to be a servant of Jesus! Hallelujah! And you became Jesus's servant when you accepted His call to serve Him! Glory, Hallelujah! The Spirit of God is on you, and you have been anointed by God to serve Jesus!

You have been chosen by God to spread the good news to sinners; so that they can realize that God has chosen them to be His people, through the name of Jesus! Glory! God has plans for His people! Amen.

Today, our Word is speaking to God's people. If you have accepted Jesus as your Lord and Savior, you are one of God's people! Hallelujah! And God wants you to know what His plans are; for God has always shared His plans for His people! Glory Hallelujah! Isaiah shares the plan that God has for His people of imminent judgment, but also their eventual restoration. Amen! For God has always shared His plans through His servants. Amen again! Before Jesus, God told His plans through His servants that a Messiah would come to redeem them to God. Then God had Jesus, His Servant, tell people about God's plan of forgiveness, redemption and salvation. After Jesus, God told His plans through the servants of Jesus! Glory Hallelujah! God has always had a plan, and God has always shared His plan. Glory to God! Hallelujah! God has always had a plan for His people! God chooses the servants that spread His Word! Amen! Our Word continues with the servant speaking to the assignment that God has given, **"He has sent me to bind up the brokenhearted, to proclaim freedom for the captives and release from darkness for the prisoners,"** God assigns the servant to utilize His Word to teach and heal with the Word, and to meet every human need with God's Word. Amen again! The servant of Jesus is given a ministry by God. It may not be a church, but it is a ministry! If

Jesus has called you to teach the Word of God in any fashion, you are part of Jesus's ministry! And God has sent, or will send, you to heal people through your ministry. The healing may be in the form of encouragement; it may be in the form of utilizing the Word of God to educate, rebuke, or guide people to righteousness. But your ministry is there to heal the Spirit of people; so that they may be free from the sickness of sin, and healed by the blood of Jesus! That is your purpose that God has created you to do, and Jesus has assigned you to do. To heal people through His Word, and to utilize the Word of God to help people understand that the Word of God meets every human need! Hallelujah! God has plans for His people! Amen.

Today, the Word of God is speaking to God's people. If you have accepted Jesus as your Lord and Savior, you are one of God's people! Hallelujah! And God wants you to know what His plans are; for God has always shared His plans for His people! Glory Hallelujah! And God plans for His people's imminent judgment, but also their eventual restoration. Amen! For God has always shared His plans through His servants. Amen again! God has always had a plan, and God has always shared His plan. Glory to God! Hallelujah! God has always had a plan for His people! God chooses the servants that spread His Word! Amen! And God assigns the servant to utilize His Word to teach and heal with the Word, and to meet every human need with God's Word. Amen again! And the Word of God proclaims that God also sends the servant, **"to proclaim the year of the Lord's favor and the day**

of vengeance of our God, to comfort all who mourn." The servant is to teach that there will be a day of judgment, and God will send sinners to damnation, while giving salvation to those who are His people! Glory! God has always told His people that there would be a day of reckoning. God tells us to warn us, that we need to seek Him so that we do not receive the punishment that our sins have earned! Sin separates us from God; so God has always told us His plan that there is a Messiah who can mediate for us to God; and save us from damnation. That Messiah is Jesus! Amen! God has always had a plan for Jesus to offer us a way back to God! A way of forgiveness and salvation! Jesus is that Way! Amen again! And the servant of Jesus is to tell people that good news; so that they will have hope that leads to comfort, so that they no longer mourn death! Hallelujah! God has plans for His people! Amen!

Today, our Scripture Guidance is for God's people. To be one of God's people, you must accept Jesus as your Lord and Savior! Amen! Jesus is the only way for anyone today to be God's people. Amen again! God has always had a plan, and God has always shared His plan. Glory to God! Hallelujah! And God has always utilized servants to tell people of His plans through His Word. God chooses the servants that spread His Word! Amen! And God assigns the servant to utilize His Word to teach and heal with the Word, and to meet every human need with God's Word. Amen again! The servant is to teach that there will be a day of judgment, and God will send sinners to damnation, while giving salvation to those who are His people! Glory! God has always had a plan for Jesus to offer us a way back to God! A way of forgiveness and salvation! Jesus is that Way! Amen again! And the servant of Jesus is to tell people that good news; so that they will have hope that leads to comfort, so that they no longer mourn death! Hallelujah! God has plans for His people! Now serve Jesus, and go and tell people about God's plans for them! Amen!

Day 220

"After these things, Jesus walked in Galilee, for He did not want to walk in Judea, because the Jews sought to kill Him.

Now the Jewish Feast of Tabernacles was at hand.

Jesus' brothers therefore said to Him, 'Depart from here and go to Judea, that Your disciples also may see the works that You are doing.

For no one does anything in secret while he himself seeks to be known openly. If You do these things, show Yourself to the world.'

For even His brothers did not believe in Him."

(John 7:1-5)

In today's Scripture, the great servant of Jesus, the apostle John, shares the strong opposition that Jesus faced while serving God and delivering the good news of the Word of God, the New Covenant of God for salvation. Amen! Jesus had the greatest news possible, that God will forgive people of their sins, if they repent and accept the Messiah that God has sent. And that Messiah is Jesus! Hallelujah! However, at that time, Jesus was also a servant! And like every servant of Jesus, Jesus had already lived on this earth for many years, before He started serving. Amen! On top of that, Jesus good news, was about Himself! Amen again! So you can imagine that most people did not want to hear from Jesus, that

He is the Messiah that God has sent to save us! In fact, Jesus own family, His own brothers, did not initially believe that Jesus was the Messiah. Tell the truth! Jesus, the greatest Servant, our Savior, the Son of God, was not even believed to be who He said He is by His own family! Amen! But, hallelujah, Jesus just kept on serving God! Amen again! Even though it must have hurt Him to be rejected by those closest to Him, Jesus kept serving God, and spreading the good news of forgiveness and redemption to God through eternity, by accepting Him as their Messiah that God sent to save them. Glory Hallelujah! And Jesus's example of perseverance through personal rejection, is a lesson for those who serve Jesus. For when you serve Jesus, there will be some people that you are very close to, who will reject you as a servant of Jesus! They will not accept that you serve Jesus, because they knew you before you began to serve Jesus. And that will hurt you, it will! But do like Jesus, and just keep on serving Him and giving glory to God! Hallelujah! Our Scripture begins with, **"After these things, Jesus walked in Galilee, for He did not want to walk in Judea, because the Jews sought to kill Him. Now the Jewish Feast of Tabernacles was at hand."** The servant has an opportunity to serve! Amen! Our Word tells us that, **Jesus' brothers therefore said to Him, 'Depart from here and go to Judea, that Your disciples also may see the works that You are doing. For no one does anything in secret while he himself seeks to be known openly.'** There will be people that will encourage the servant to go serve, but destinations to serve are only ordained by God! Always seek God, and listen for His guidance! Amen again! And the Word of God concludes with Jesus' brothers saying to Him, **'If You do these things, show Yourself to the world.' For even His brothers did not believe in Him."** The people closest to you will reveal that they do not believe that you are a servant of Jesus! And it will hurt you, but keep on serving Jesus! For just like Jesus, you were chosen by God to serve Him! So keep on serving Jesus, and let the Light that is Jesus shine through you! You are a servant of Jesus, so serve Him! For serving Jesus is not about who accepts you! Serving Jesus is about spreading the good news of the New Covenant of God, the Gospel of Jesus, so that others can accept Jesus and receive salvation from God! Amen.

Today, our Scripture is speaking to the servants of Jesus. There will be some who you are very close to, that will initially, and maybe permanently, reject you as a servant that has been created by God to serve Jesus. Amen! After all, people closest to you knew you when you were focused on the world, before you were called to serve. So for them, it is hard to accept you as a servant of Jesus. And the same thing happened to Jesus! Amen again! The apostle John shares the strong opposition that Jesus faced while serving God and delivering the good news of the Word of God, the New Covenant of God, for salvation. Amen! Jesus had the greatest news possible, that God will forgive people of their sins, if they repent and accept the Messiah that God has sent. And that Messiah is Jesus! Hallelujah! However, at that time, Jesus was also a servant! And Jesus had already lived on this earth for many years, before He started serving. Amen! On top of that, Jesus's good news, was about Himself! Amen again! Most people, did not want to hear from Jesus, that He is the Messiah that God has sent to save us! Jesus's own brothers did not initially believe that Jesus was the Messiah. Tell the truth! Jesus, our Savior, the Son of God, was not even believed by His own family! Amen! But Jesus just kept on serving God! Amen again! Even though it must have hurt Him to be rejected by those closest to Him, Jesus kept serving God. Glory Hallelujah! And Jesus's example of perseverance through personal rejection, is a lesson for those who serve Jesus. For when you serve Jesus, there will be people that you are very close to, who will reject you! They will not accept that you serve Jesus, because they knew you before you began to serve Jesus. But do like Jesus, and just keep on serving Him and giving glory to God! Hallelujah! Our Scripture begins with, **"After these things, Jesus walked in Galilee, for He did not want to walk in Judea, because the Jews sought to kill Him. Now the Jewish Feast of Tabernacles was at hand."** The servant has an opportunity to serve! Amen! There will always be opportunities to serve Jesus. And sometimes, these opportunities may be in places that the servant may not want to go to. But rest assured, if Jesus tells you to go, it is the Will of God that you go. And always know that if you are doing the Will of God, all things will work to the good for you, for there is nothing better for you than the Will of God. So keep on serving Jesus, and let the Light that is Jesus shine through you! You are a servant of

Jesus, so serve Him! For serving Jesus is not about who accepts you! Serving Jesus is about spreading the good news of the New Covenant of God, the Gospel of Jesus, so that others can accept Jesus and receive salvation from God! Amen.

Today, our Word is speaking to the servants of Jesus. There will be some who you are very close to, that will reject you as a servant of Jesus. Amen! After all, people closest to you knew you, before you were called to serve! So for them, it is hard to accept you as a servant of Jesus. And the same thing happened to Jesus! Amen again! John shares the strong opposition that Jesus faced while serving God and delivering the good news of the Word of God, the New Covenant of God, for salvation. Amen! Jesus had the greatest news possible, that God will forgive people of their sins, if they repent and accept the Messiah that God has sent. And that Messiah is Jesus! Hallelujah! Jesus had already lived on this earth for many years, before He started serving. Amen! On top of that, Jesus's good news, was about Himself! Amen again! Most people, did not want to hear from Jesus, that He is the Messiah! Jesus's own brothers did not initially believe that Jesus was the Messiah. Tell the truth! Jesus was not even believed by His own family! Amen! But Jesus just kept on serving God! Amen again! Even though it must have hurt Him to be rejected by those closest to Him, Jesus kept serving God. Glory Hallelujah! And Jesus's perseverance through personal rejection, is a lesson for those who serve Him. For when you serve Jesus, there will be people that you are very close to, who will reject you! They will not accept that you serve Jesus, because they knew you before you began to serve Jesus. But do like Jesus, and just keep on serving Him and giving glory to God! Hallelujah! For The servant will have opportunities to serve! Amen! Our Word tells us that, **Jesus' brothers therefore said to Him, 'Depart from here and go to Judea, that Your disciples also may see the works that You are doing. For no one does anything in secret while he himself seeks to be known openly.'** There will be people that will encourage the servant to go serve, but destinations to serve are only ordained by God! Always seek God, and listen for His guidance! Amen again! People may encourage you to go somewhere, but you do not know their motives! And they do not know the Will of God for you. Be careful, and before you go anywhere to serve Jesus, seek God! God will speak to you through His Holy Spirit! Seek Jesus, for Jesus is your Master! Seek God through Jesus and the Holy Spirit! For they are all the same, and you will receive guidance! Amen! So keep on serving Jesus, and let the Light that is Jesus shine through you! You are a servant of Jesus, so serve Him! For serving Jesus is not about who accepts you! Serving Jesus is about spreading the good news of the New Covenant of God, the Gospel of Jesus, so that others can accept Jesus and receive salvation from God! Amen.

Today, the Word of God is speaking to the servants of Jesus. There will be some who you are very close to, that will reject you as a servant of Jesus. Amen! After all, people closest to you knew you, before you were called to serve! So for them, it is hard to accept you as a servant of Jesus. And the same thing happened to Jesus! Amen again! Jesus faced strong opposition while serving God and delivering the good news of the New Covenant of God for salvation. Amen! Jesus had the greatest news possible, that God will forgive people of their sins, if they repent and accept the Messiah that God has sent. And that Messiah is Jesus! Hallelujah! Jesus had already lived on this earth for many years, before He started serving. Amen! Most people, did not want to hear from Jesus, that He is the Messiah! Jesus's own brothers did not initially believe that Jesus was the Messiah. Tell the truth! Jesus was not even believed by His own family! Amen! But Jesus just kept on serving God! Amen again! And Jesus's perseverance through personal rejection, is a lesson for those who serve Him. For when you serve Jesus, there will be people that you are very close to who will reject you! They will not accept that you serve Jesus, because they knew you before you began to serve Jesus. But do like Jesus, and just keep on serving Him and giving glory to God! Hallelujah! For the servant will have opportunities to serve! Amen! And there will be people that will encourage you to go serve, but be careful, for your destinations to serve Jesus are only ordained by God! Always seek God, and listen for His guidance! Amen again! And the Word of God concludes with Jesus' brothers saying to Him, **'If You do these things, show Yourself to the world.' For even His brothers did not believe in Him."** The people closest to you will reveal that they do not believe that you are a servant of Jesus! And it will hurt you, but keep on serving

Jesus! For just like Jesus, you were chosen by God to serve Him! Although we all seek approval from those we love, seek approval from Jesus, who loves you more! Seek approval from God, who loves you more! Do not focus on the approval of others, even those you love, for your service is not about them, and not about you! Your service is about Jesus and doing the Will of God, to the glory of God! Hallelujah! Give glory to God! So keep on serving Jesus, and let the Light that is Jesus shine through you! You are a servant of Jesus, so serve Him! For serving Jesus is not about who accepts you! Serving Jesus is about spreading the good news of the New Covenant of God, the Gospel of Jesus, so that others can accept Jesus and receive salvation from God! Amen.

Day 221

The Lord (Almighty God) says: "These people come to Me with their mouth and honor Me with their lips, but their hearts are far from Me. Their worship of Me is merely human rules they have been taught."

Jesus says, "Isaiah was right when he prophesied about you hypocrites, as it is written: 'These people honor Me with their lips, but their hearts are far from Me.

They worship Me in vain, their teachings are merely human rules.'

You have let go of the commands of God and are holding on to human traditions."

(Isaiah 29:13 & Mark 6-8)

In today's Scripture, the great servant of God, the prophet Isaiah, and the great servant of Jesus, the writer Mark, both write about the hypocrisy of the people of God. Amen! Many people who claim to be God's people live as hypocrites in the face of God! Amen again! This was true before Jesus came to this earth, this was true while Jesus was on this earth, and this is true today! And the people of God are being called out to stop living as hypocrites! You are not fooling God! You are not fooling Jesus! And you are not even fooling the people around you! For your actions are controlled by your heart, while your lies are coming out of your mouth! Tell the truth! It does not matter how much you go to church, or how much you pray, if you are not doing both because of your heart! Hallelujah! God sees your heart! Jesus sees your heart! And the people see your actions! If this is you, confess that you have not been living for Jesus, and ask Him to rule in your heart. Stop being a hypocrite! You are not fooling anyone! Give your heart to Jesus, and live your life the way that serves Jesus and does the Will of God. Glory Hallelujah! Our Scripture begins with the servant of God speaking these words from God, **The Lord (Almighty God) says: "These people come to Me with their mouth and honor Me with their lips, but their hearts are far from Me. Their worship of Me is merely human rules they have been taught."** God knows when His people truly honor Him. It is with their actions, not just their mouths! God sees what you do, and knows why you do it! You cannot fool God with your words! Amen! The Word continues seven hundred years later with the servant of Jesus writing these words from Jesus, **Jesus says, "Isaiah was right when he prophesied about you hypocrites, as it is written: 'These people honor Me with their lips, but their hearts are far from Me. They worship Me in vain, their teachings are merely human rules.'** Jesus also knows when God's people truly honor Him! Jesus sees what you do, and knows why you do it! You cannot fool Jesus with your words! Amen again! And the Word of God concludes with Jesus saying this to God's people who are hypocrites, **"You have let go of the commands of God and are holding on to human traditions."**

God's commands to His people are binding! And God demands that His people do what He has commanded! While human rules have been taught by humans, and have nothing to do with worshiping and obeying God! Hallelujah! Stop being a hypocrite! You are not fooling anyone! Give your heart to Jesus, and live your life the way that serves Jesus and does the Will of God. Amen.

Today, our Scripture is speaking to God's people, who are living their lives by doing human traditions, instead of truly living their life to glorify God. Amen! If this is you, you are a hypocrite! Both the great servant of God, the prophet Isaiah, and the great servant of Jesus, the writer Mark, write about the hypocrisy of the people of God. Amen! Many people who claim to be God's people live as hypocrites in the face of God! Amen again! This was true before Jesus came to this earth, this was true while Jesus was on this earth, and this is true today! And if this is you, stop living as hypocrites! You are not fooling God! You are not fooling Jesus! And you are not even fooling the people around you! For your actions are controlled by your heart, while your lies are coming out of your mouth! Tell the truth! It does not matter how much you go to church, or how much you pray, if you are not doing both because of your heart! Hallelujah! God sees your heart! Jesus sees your heart! And the people see your actions! If this is you, confess that you have not been living for Jesus, and ask Him to rule in your heart. Give your heart to Jesus, and live your life the way that serves Jesus and does the Will of God. Glory Hallelujah! Our

Scripture begins with the servant of God speaking these words from God, **The Lord (Almighty God) says: "These people come to Me with their mouth and honor Me with their lips, but their hearts are far from Me. Their worship of Me is merely human rules they have been taught."** God knows when His people truly honor Him. It is with their actions, not just their mouths! God sees what you do, and knows why you do it! You cannot fool God with your words! Amen! Many of us Believers know to worship God. We know to go to church. We know to tithe or give offerings. We know to pray. All of these things are good things, if we do them from our heart! These things become human rules, or traditions, when we do them just because we think we are supposed to. That makes them human rules! If you are only doing these things, but you are not living your life to glorify God and lift up the name of Jesus, you are following human rules! You are doing these things so people will see you. Or hear you, not because you love God! God sees your heart! Stop being a hypocrite! You are not fooling anyone! Give your heart to Jesus, and live your life the way that serves Jesus and does the Will of God. Amen.

Today, our Word is speaking to God's people who are living their lives by doing human traditions, instead of truly living their life to glorify God. Amen! If this is you, you are a hypocrite! Both the prophet Isaiah, and the writer Mark, write about the hypocrisy of the people of God. Amen! Many people who claim to be God's people live as hypocrites in the face of God! Amen again! And if this is you, stop living as a hypocrite! You are not fooling God! You are not fooling Jesus! For your actions are controlled by your heart, while your lies are coming out of your mouth! Tell the truth! It does not matter how much you go to church, or how much you pray, if you are not doing both because of your heart! Hallelujah! God sees your heart! Jesus sees your heart! If this is you, confess that you have not been living for Jesus, and ask Him to rule in your heart. Give your heart to Jesus, and live your life the way that serves Jesus and does the Will of God. Glory Hallelujah! God knows when His people truly honor Him. It is with their actions, not just their mouths! God sees what you do, and knows why you do it! You cannot fool God with your words! Amen! The Word continues seven hundred years later with the servant of Jesus writing these words from Jesus, **Jesus says, "Isaiah was right when he prophesied about you hypocrites, as it is written: 'These people honor Me with their lips, but their hearts are far from Me. They worship Me in vain, their teachings are merely human rules.'** Jesus also knows when God's people truly honor Him! Jesus sees what you do, and knows why you do it! You cannot fool Jesus with your words! Amen again! Jesus sees your heart! Jesus sees your actions! Jesus knows that He has called you to serve, and you have not served Him yet! When you turn away from serving Jesus when He calls you, you are a hypocrite! You are not honoring Jesus by sitting in a pew every Sunday, while refusing to serve Him! Stop being a hypocrite! You are not fooling anyone! Give your heart to Jesus, and live your life the way that serves Jesus and does the Will of God. Amen.

Today, the Word of God is speaking to God's people who are living their lives by doing human traditions, instead of truly living their life to glorify God. Amen! If this is you, you are a hypocrite! Isaiah and Mark write about the hypocrisy of the people of God. Amen! Many people who claim to be God's people live as hypocrites in the face of God! Amen again! If this is you, stop living as a hypocrite! You are not fooling God! You are not fooling Jesus! For your actions are controlled by your heart, while your lies are coming out of your mouth! Tell the truth! It does not matter how much you go to church, or how much you pray, if you are not doing both because of your heart! Hallelujah! God sees your heart! Jesus sees your heart! If this is you, confess that you have not been living for Jesus, and ask Him to rule in your heart. Give your heart to Jesus, and live your life the way that serves Jesus and does the Will of God. Glory Hallelujah! God knows when His people truly honor Him. It is with their actions, not just their mouths! God sees what you do, and knows why you do it! You cannot fool God with your words! Amen! Jesus also knows when God's people truly honor Him! Jesus sees what you do, and knows why you do it! You cannot fool Jesus with your words! Amen again! And the Word of God concludes with Jesus saying this to God's people who are hypocrites, **"You have let go of the commands of God and are holding on to human traditions."** God's commands to His people are binding! And God demands that His people do what He has commanded! While human rules have been taught by humans, and have nothing to do with worshiping and obeying God! Hallelujah! You cannot turn away from what God commands you to do, and think that because you go to church, God will forgive you. God knows the difference between His commands to you, and what people expect you to do! It does not matter how many "hallelujah" shouts you give in church, if you continue to turn away from what God commands you to do! God cannot be fooled! Stop being a hypocrite! You are not fooling anyone! Give your heart to Jesus, and live your life the way that serves Jesus and does the Will of God. Amen.

Today, our Scripture Guidance is trying to help someone who thinks that they are fooling God by worshiping Him with their mouths and not their hearts. You are doing things that people have taught you, and you are talking like one of God's people, but God does not recognize you! You are a hypocrite! And Jesus also does not recognize you! Stop living as a hypocrite! You are not fooling God! You are not fooling Jesus! And you are not even fooling the people around you! For your actions are controlled by your heart, while your lies are coming out of your mouth! Tell the truth! Stop being a hypocrite! You are not fooling anyone! Give your heart to Jesus, and live your life the way that serves Jesus and does the Will of God. Amen.

Day 222

"For (Jesus) Christ also suffered once for sins, the righteous for the unrighteous, to bring you to God. He was put to death in the body, but made alive in the Spirit."

"Therefore, since Christ suffered in His body, arm yourselves also with the same attitude, because whoever suffers in the body is done with sin.

As a result, they do not live the rest of their earthly lives for evil human desires, but rather for the Will of God.

For you have spent enough time in the past doing what pagans (evil and sinful people), living in debauchery, lust, drunkenness, orgies, carousing and detestable idolatry."

(1 Peter 3:18 & 4:1-3)

In today's Scripture, the great servant of Jesus, the apostle Peter, speaks to Believers about suffering to live good lives in the eyes of God. Amen! Peter makes the point to us that because we are flesh, we desire to sin, so to live a good life in the eyes of God, our flesh must suffer! Because when you deny yourself from sinning, your flesh suffers, but your spirit lives! Amen again! Every single person that was ever born on earth, was born into flesh! This means every single person, not matter how righteous they are, has flesh that desires sin. Tell the truth! And Peter also points out to us that Jesus's flesh suffered because Jesus denied the sinful temptations of this world. So Jesus's body suffered, because the flesh of the body had no sin. However, the Spirit inside of Jesus was stronger than the flesh. Hallelujah! Jesus turned to the Spirit whenever His flesh was tempted. And that is the truth! You and I are being encouraged to suffer today! Our body of flesh needs to suffer, you and I need to deny our flesh, sin! For to live a good life in the eyes of God, we must keep denying our flesh the lust of sin. When our flesh suffers, our Spirit grows! And God is well pleased with us, just as He was when Jesus's own body suffered because the flesh was denied sin. Glory to God! Our Scripture begins with the fact that Jesus suffered to live good in the eyes of God, saying, **"For (Jesus) Christ also suffered once for sins, the righteous for the unrighteous, to bring you to God. He was put to death in the body, but made alive in the Spirit."** Jesus made a decision to live life righteously in the eyes of God, so His flesh suffered because Jesus did not feed His flesh sin. And eventually, His flesh would be put to death, but His Spirit was made alive! Amen! Our Word continues with this encouragement to each Believer, **"Therefore, since Christ suffered in His body, arm yourselves also with the same attitude, because whoever suffers in the body is done with sin. As a result, they do not live the rest of their earthly lives for evil human desires, but rather for the Will of God."** Believers, who are followers of Jesus, must strive to live life with the same attitude as Jesus, and allow our flesh to suffer by denying it the lusts of sin! By denying sin, our focus changes from the need to succumb to evil temptations, to focusing on doing the Will of God! So we must also turn to the Holy Spirit inside of us so that we can deny the flesh, and cause it to suffer! Amen again! And the Word of God concludes by rebuking each of us who still desire sin, proclaiming this truth about each of us, **"For you have spent enough time in the past doing what pagans (evil and sinful people), living in debauchery, lust, drunkenness, orgies, carousing and detestable idolatry."** You have lived enough of your life focused on sin, for before you knew Jesus, your flesh controlled your life! But now you know Jesus, and you have been redeemed to God, so turn your desires to spiritual things. You have been born again to God through the Spirit, so do not live your life focused on the flesh! Because when you deny yourself from sinning, your flesh suffers, but your spirit lives! Amen.

Today, our Scripture is speaking to Believers. The apostle Peter speaks to Believers about suffering to live good lives in the eyes of God. Amen! Peter makes the point to us that because we are flesh, we desire to sin, so to live a good life in the eyes of God, our flesh must suffer! Because when you deny yourself from sinning, your flesh suffers, but your spirit lives! Amen again! Every single person that was ever born on earth, was born into flesh, and that includes you! No matter how righteous you are, you are still flesh, and flesh that desires sin. Tell the truth! And Peter also points out that even Jesus's flesh suffered because Jesus denied His flesh the sinful temptations of this world. So Jesus's body suffered, because the flesh of the body had no sin. Because the Spirit inside of Jesus was stronger than the flesh! Hallelujah! And Jesus turned to the Spirit whenever His flesh was tempted. And that is the truth! Your body of flesh needs to suffer, and my body of flesh needs to suffer, for you and I need to deny our flesh of sin! For when our flesh suffers, our Spirit grows! And God is well pleased with us, just as He was when Jesus's own body suffered because the flesh was denied sin. Glory to God! Our Scripture begins with the fact that Jesus suffered to live good in the eyes of God, saying, **"For (Jesus) Christ also suffered once for sins, the righteous for the unrighteous, to bring you to God. He was put to death in the body, but made alive in the Spirit."** Jesus made a decision to live life righteously in the eyes of God, so His flesh suffered because Jesus did not feed His flesh sin. And eventually, His flesh would be put to death, but His Spirit was made alive! Amen! Often times we forget that Jesus truly suffered on earth. We think that because Jesus is the Son of God, His flesh did not suffer because He denied its sin. But that is not true! Jesus also had to find the strength to deny sinful temptations, which means His body also desired sin! Jesus was human while on earth, and denying sin was also difficult for Him. Jesus did not sin because He knew to turn to God, or the Holy Spirit of God, whenever He was tempted. And Jesus knew by turning away from sin, He was living His life in a way that pleased God! Hallelujah! But do not be fooled, Jesus's flesh suffered while He was on earth. Because when you deny yourself from sinning, your flesh suffers, but your spirit lives! Amen.

Today, our Word is speaking to Believers. Each and every Believer must suffer in the flesh, to live good lives in the eyes of God. Amen! Peter makes the point to us that because we are flesh, we desire to sin, so to live a good life in the eyes of God, our flesh must suffer! Because when you deny yourself from sinning, your flesh suffers, but your spirit lives! Amen again! All of us are flesh, and all of us naturally desire sin! No matter how righteous you are, you are still flesh. Tell the truth! Even Jesus's flesh suffered because He denied His flesh the sinful temptations of this world. So Jesus's body suffered, because the flesh of the body had no sin. The Spirit inside of Jesus was stronger than the flesh. Hallelujah! And Jesus turned to the Spirit whenever His flesh was tempted. And that is the truth! Your body of flesh needs to suffer, and my body of flesh needs to suffer, for you and I need to deny our flesh of sin! For when our flesh suffers, our Spirit grows! And God is well pleased with us, just as He was when Jesus's own body suffered because the flesh was denied sin. Glory to God! Jesus made a decision to live life righteously in the eyes of God, so His flesh suffered because Jesus did not feed His flesh sin. And eventually, His flesh would be put to death, but His Spirit was made alive! Amen! Our Word continues with this encouragement to each Believer, **"Therefore, since Christ suffered in His body, arm yourselves also with the same attitude, because whoever suffers in the body is done with sin. As a result, they do not live the rest of their earthly lives for evil human desires, but rather for the Will of God."** Believers, who are followers of

Jesus, must strive to live life with the same attitude as Jesus, and allow our flesh to suffer by denying it the lusts of sin! By denying sin, our focus changes from the need to succumb to evil temptations, to focusing on doing the Will of God! So we must also turn to the Holy Spirit inside of us so that we can deny the flesh, and cause it to suffer! Amen again! And because Jesus is with us, as well as the Holy Spirit of God, we can have the same attitude that Jesus had when He was tempted to sin on earth. But you must want to deny sin! You must admit that you are weak in your flesh, and seek the spiritual power of God to deny sin! Because when you deny yourself from sinning, your flesh suffers, but your spirit lives! Amen.

Today, the Word of God is speaking to Believers. The Word of God is speaking to you! Each and every Believer must suffer in the flesh, to live good lives in the eyes of God. Amen! Because we are flesh, we desire to sin, so to live a good life in the eyes of God, our flesh must suffer! For when you deny yourself from sinning, your flesh suffers, but your spirit lives! Amen again! All of us are flesh, and all of us naturally desire sin! Tell the truth! Even Jesus's flesh suffered because He denied His flesh the sinful temptations of this world. The Spirit inside of Jesus was stronger than the flesh. Hallelujah! And Jesus turned to the Spirit whenever His flesh was tempted. And that is the truth! Your body of flesh needs to suffer, for you deny your flesh of sin! For when your flesh suffers, your Spirit grows! And God is well pleased with you, just as He was when Jesus's own body suffered because His flesh was denied sin.

Glory to God! Jesus made a decision to live life righteously in the eyes of God, so His flesh suffered because Jesus did not feed His flesh sin. And eventually, His flesh would be put to death, but His Spirit was made alive! Amen! And you must strive to live life with the same attitude as Jesus and allow your flesh to suffer by denying it the lusts of sin! By denying sin, your focus changes from the need to succumb to evil temptations, to focusing on doing the Will of God! So you must also turn to the Holy Spirit inside of you so that you can deny the flesh, and cause it to suffer! Amen again! And the Word of God concludes by rebuking each of us who still desire sin, proclaiming this truth about each of us, **"For you have spent enough time in the past doing what pagans (evil and sinful people), living in debauchery, lust, drunkenness, orgies, carousing and detestable idolatry."** You have lived enough of your life focused on sin, for before you knew Jesus, your flesh controlled your life! But now you know Jesus, and you have been redeemed to God, so turn your desires to spiritual things. You have been born again to God through the Spirit, so do not live your life focused on the flesh! This was always a challenge for me, to turn away from the flesh, because I did not turn to the Holy Spirit! So for many years, I kept living as I did to the desires of the flesh, just as I did before! I did sin as much, but I sinned in the same way! I still allowed my flesh to control my life! That is hard to admit, but it is true! Now I am focusing on spiritual things, and asking the Holy Spirit to fulfill my spiritual desires. For like you, I have been born again, and redeemed to God through Jesus

Christ! And the Holy Spirit is inside of me and you, to help us deny the flesh sin! Glory Hallelujah! Because when you deny yourself from sinning, your flesh suffers, but your spirit lives! Amen.

You are being challenged today! You need to deny sin, and let your flesh suffer, so that you live a good life in the eyes of God! Hallelujah! Jesus made a decision to live life righteously in the eyes of God, so His flesh suffered because Jesus did not feed His flesh sin. Eventually, His flesh would be put to death, but His Spirit was made alive! Amen! And you must strive to live life with the same attitude as Jesus, and allow your flesh to suffer by denying it the lusts of sin! By denying sin, your focus changes from the need to succumb to evil temptations, to focusing on doing the Will of God! So you must also turn to the Holy Spirit inside of you so that you can deny the flesh, and cause it to suffer! Amen again! For you have already lived enough of your life focused on sin, for before you knew Jesus, your flesh controlled you! But now you know Jesus, and you have been redeemed to God, so turn your desires to spiritual things. You have been born again to God through the Spirit, so do not live your life focused on the flesh! Because when you deny yourself from sinning, your flesh suffers, but your spirit lives! Amen.

Day 223

(Caleb said to Joshua) "I was forty years old when Moses the servant of God sent me to explore the (Promised) land.

And I brought Moses back a report according to my conviction (trust in God),

but my fellow Israelites who went up with me, made the hearts of the people melt in fear (based on what they told them). I, however, trusted the Lord my God wholeheartedly.

So on that day Moses swore to me, 'The land on which your feet have walked will be you inheritance, and that of your children forever, because you have trusted the Lord my God wholeheartedly."

"Then Joshua blessed Caleb and gave him (the land) Hebron as his inheritance."

(Joshua 14:7-10 & 13)

In today's Scripture, the unknown writer, possibly Joshua, records the time that Joshua began to divide the Promised Land west of the Jordan River to the tribes of Israel. And as Joshua was doing this, Caleb, who Moses had sent to spy on the Promised Land, while the people of Israel were still in the Wilderness **(Numbers 13:1-30)**, came to speak to Joshua. For God made a promise through Moses to Caleb (Numbers 14:24) that because Caleb had followed God wholeheartedly, trusting that God would have His people defeat the inhabitants of the Promised Land, and take over the land. So even though it was years later, and Moses had died, God had made Caleb a promise. Amen! And when God makes a promise, that promise will happen! Amen again! Our Scripture begins with Caleb speaking to Joshua about what he had done, that was good in the eyes of God, **(Caleb said to Joshua) "I was forty years old when Moses the servant of God sent me to explore the (Promised) land. And I brought Moses back a report according to my conviction (trust in God), but my fellow Israelites who went up with me, made the hearts of the people melt in fear (based on what they told them). I, however, trusted the Lord my God wholeheartedly."** The servant does what God told him to do, and also shows others that He trusted God, regardless that others did not! And God was pleased! Amen! Our Word speaks to the promise that God made through His lead servant, proclaiming, **So on that day Moses swore to me, 'The land on which your feet have walked will be you inheritance, and that of your children forever, because you have trusted the Lord my God wholeheartedly.'** God spoke a promise, and that promise was shared with His servant! God was pleased, and God made a promise of a blessing to the servant! Amen again! And the Word of God concludes with, **"Then Joshua blessed Caleb and gave him (the land) Hebron as his inheritance."** When God makes a promise to you, His promise will be fulfilled! For once He speaks it, it is done! You may have to wait, because God's time is not the same as your time, but His promise to you will be done! Hallelujah! When God makes a promise to you, you will receive what God has promised you! Glory to God! Amen.

Today, our Scripture is speaking to all people. When God makes you a promise, you will receive what God has promised you! Amen! It does not matter how long it may take, you will receive God's promise. Amen again! The great servant of God, Joshua, had begun to divide the Promised Land among the tribes of Israel. And as Joshua was doing this, Caleb, who Moses had sent to spy on the Promised Land, came to speak to Joshua. For God made a promise through Moses to Caleb because Caleb had followed God wholeheartedly, trusting that God would have His people defeat the inhabitants of the Promised Land, and take over the land. This had pleased God! And God made a promise to Caleb. Hallelujah! Even though it was forty-five years later, and Moses had died, God had made Caleb a promise! Amen! And when God makes a promise, that promise will happen! Amen again! Our Scripture begins with Caleb speaking to Joshua about what he had done, that was good in the eyes of God, **(Caleb said to Joshua) "I was forty years old when Moses the servant of God sent me to explore the (Promised) land. And I brought Moses back a report according to my conviction (trust in God), but my fellow Israelites who went up with me, made the hearts of the people melt in fear (based on what they told them). I, however, trusted the Lord my God wholeheartedly."** The servant does what God told him to do, and also showed others that He trusted God, regardless that others did not! And God was pleased! Amen! Imagine what Caleb must have felt as he watched others receive their rightful inheritance of land, and the only human that knew about God's promise to him, Moses, had died! And this was 45 years later! God's promise to Caleb had been made when he was 40 years old, and he is now 85! Yet, hallelujah, God had made a promise! And when God makes a promise to you, you will receive what God has promised you! Give glory to God! Amen.

Today, our Word is speaking to all people. When God makes you a promise, you will receive what God has promised you! Amen! It does not matter how long it may take, you will receive God's promise. Amen again! Joshua had begun to divide the Promised Land among the tribes of Israel. And as Joshua was doing this, Caleb came to speak to Joshua. For God made a promise through Moses to Caleb because Caleb trusted that God would have His people defeat the inhabitants of the Promised Land, and take over the land. This had pleased God, and God made a promise to Caleb. Hallelujah! Even though it was forty-five years later, and Moses had died, God had made Caleb a promise! Amen! And when God makes a promise, that promise will happen! Amen again! For the servant did what God told him to do, and also showed others that He trusted God, even when others did not! And God was pleased! Amen! Our Word speaks to the promise that God made through His lead servant, proclaiming, **"So on that day Moses swore to me, 'The land on which your feet have walked will be you inheritance, and that of your**

children forever, because you have trusted the Lord my God wholeheartedly.'" God spoke a promise, and that promise was shared with His servant! God was pleased, and God made a promise of a blessing to the servant! Amen again! So even though the human who knew about the promise was dead, God is alive! And it is God who makes the promises, not the human! So keep your faith in God, no matter how long it's been, or who knows, or does not know, about the promise. For God knows He made you a promise! Glory Hallelujah! And when God makes a promise to you, you will receive what God has promised you! Give glory to God! Amen.

Today, the Word of God is speaking to all people. When God makes you a promise, you will receive what God has promised you! Amen! It does not matter how long it may take, you will receive God's promise. Amen again! Joshua had begun to divide the Promised Land to the tribes of Israel, when Caleb came to speak to Joshua. For God made a promise through Moses to Caleb, because Caleb trusted that God would have His people defeat the inhabitants of the Promised Land, and take over the land, just as God said He would! This pleased God, and God made a promise to Caleb. Hallelujah! Even though it was forty-five years later, God had made Caleb a promise! Amen! And when God makes a promise, that promise will happen! Amen again! For the servant did what God told him to do, and showed others that He trusted God, even when others did not! And God was pleased! Amen! So God spoke a promise, and that promise was shared with His servant! God was pleased, and God made a promise of a blessing to the servant! Amen again! And the Word of God concludes with, **"Then Joshua blessed Caleb and gave him (the land) Hebron as his inheritance."** When God makes a promise to you, His promise will be fulfilled! For once He speaks it, it is done! You may have to wait, because God's time is not the same as your time, but His promise to you will be done! Hallelujah! If God has made you a promise, you are being encouraged to be patient, and keep your faith in God! God is not the one waiting, you are! God set the date of His promise to you when He spoke it, He just did not give you the date! God wants to see you continue to trust Him, and God knows the best time for you to receive His blessed promise! So wait, and stand on the promise of God! Hallelujah! For when God makes a promise to you, you will receive what God has promised you! Glory to God! Amen.

Today, our Scripture Guidance is trying to encourage someone. God has made you a promise, but it seems like it may never happen, because to you, is taking too long to actually happen! Well, trust God! When God makes you a promise, you will receive what God has promised you! Amen! It does not matter how long it may take, you will receive God's promise. Amen again! And God is always on time, so stop looking at your calendar! Trust God, for it is God Almighty who makes all things happen, that made you a promise! Be encouraged today! For if God made you a promise, whatever He promised you is on its way! Hallelujah!

When God makes a promise to you, you will receive what God has promised you! Give glory to God! Amen.

Day 224

Then Jesus told them (the large crowd of people) many things in parables (a short story to teach Christian principles), saying, "A farmer went out to sow his seed."

(After the story was told) Jesus disciples came to Him and asked, 'Why do you speak to the people in parables?'

Jesus replied, "Because the knowledge of the secrets of the Kingdom of Heaven has been given to you (Jesus servants), but not to them.

Whoever has (this knowledge) will be given more, and they will have an abundance (of this knowledge). Whoever does not have (truly receive this knowledge), even what they have will be taken from them.

This is why I speak to them in parables: Though seeing, they do not see, though hearing, they do not hear or understand."

(Matthew 13:3 & 10-13)

In today's Scripture, the great servant of Jesus, the apostle Matthew, tells us of the time that Jesus utilized parables, or short stories, to teach people that many people will hear the Word of God, but not everyone who hears the Word will receive the Word of God in their heart. Amen! After speaking the parable, Jesus's disciples (His servants) wanted to know why He utilized these short stories. And Jesus gave an answer to His servants that is still the answer to His servants today. Amen again! In fact, the entire Scripture Chapter is Jesus teaching His servants about ministering the Gospel of Jesus, and helping His servants to understand that not all people will truly accept Jesus, and very few will believe in Jesus enough to become His servants, and truly bear fruit for the Kingdom of God! Hallelujah! Jesus is speaking to His servants today, just as He spoke to His servants then! Glory Hallelujah! And as Jesus said in **Matthew 11:15**, and other parts of the Gospel, "He who has ears to hear, let him hear." Glory to God! Our Scripture begins with Jesus speaking to the crowd, saying, **Then Jesus told them (the large crowd of people) many things in parables (a short story to teach Christian principles), saying, "A farmer went out to sow his seed."** Jesus is a Servant, and as a Servant, Jesus recognized that He knew the Gospel of Jesus completely, while the people that He wanted to receive the Word, did not. So Jesus told them a story that they could relate to so that He could then relate the Gospel of Jesus to that story. Amen! Our Word continues with Jesus teaching His servants to realize that they know the mystery of the Word of God, while others do not, for, **(After the story was told) Jesus's disciples came to Him and asked, 'Why do you speak to the people in parables?' Jesus replied, "Because the knowledge of the secrets of the Kingdom of Heaven has been given to you (Jesus's servants), but not to them. Whoever has (this knowledge) will be given more, and they will have an abundance (of this knowledge)."** Jesus reminds His servants that as a servant of Jesus, God has revealed knowledge of His Word to you. In fact, today, that knowledge is revealed to you through the Holy Spirit! Jesus's servants have much more knowledge of the Word than the audience that Jesus will send you to. Amen again! And the Word of God concludes with Jesus teaching His servants that, **"Whoever does not have (truly receive this knowledge), even what they have will be taken from them. This is why I speak to them in parables: Though seeing, they do not see, though hearing, they do not hear or understand."** For the audience that Jesus sends you too, will not truly understand the Word, and what little they may understand, will be taken from them if they do not receive the teaching in a manner that they could understand. So humble yourself and the way you teach! Today, Jesus is speaking to His servants! He who has ears to hear, let them hear! Amen.

Today, our Scripture is speaking to the servants of Jesus Christ. Jesus, Himself, is teaching us that we serve Him so that others will come to understand the Gospel of Jesus, so that they can be forgiven for their sins, redeemed to God, and receive salvation from God! Amen! As a servant, we must understand that our service is about getting those who do not understand the Word, to understand the Gospel of Jesus, so that they can be saved! Hallelujah! Jesus is a Servant, and Jesus is also the first Teacher of the Gospel of Jesus! Glory Hallelujah! So Jesus obviously knew the Gospel of Jesus better than any person that has ever walked the earth. Yet He did not teach the Gospel at a level where others would not be able to understand it. The apostle Matthew tells us of the time that Jesus utilized parables, or short stories, to teach people that many people will hear the Word of God, but not everyone who hears the Word, will receive the Word of God in their heart. Amen! Jesus's disciples (His servants) wanted to know why He utilized these short stories. And Jesus gave an answer to His servants that is still the answer to His servants today. Amen again! Jesus is teaching His servants about ministering the Gospel of Jesus, and helping His servants to understand that not all people will truly accept Jesus, and very few will believe in Jesus enough to become His servants, and truly bear fruit for the Kingdom of God! Hallelujah! Jesus is speaking to His servants today, just as He spoke to His servants then! Glory Hallelujah! Glory to God! Our Scripture begins with Jesus speaking to the crowd, saying, **Then Jesus told them (the large crowd of people) many things in parables (a short story to teach Christian principles), saying, "A farmer went out to sow his seed."** Jesus is a Servant, and as a Servant, Jesus recognized that He knew the Gospel of Jesus completely, while the people that He wanted to receive the Word, did not. So Jesus told them a story that they could relate to, so that He could then relate the Gospel of Jesus to that story. Amen! Teaching the Gospel of Jesus is not about the servant showing off their knowledge. It is about getting others to understand the Word of God! Each servant of Jesus was selected by God, and given knowledge of His Word, by God! So humble yourself, and the way you teach! Today, Jesus is speaking to His servants! He who has ears to hear, let them hear! Amen.

Today, our Word is speaking to the servants of Jesus Christ. Jesus is teaching us that we serve Him, so that others will come to understand the Gospel of Jesus, and that they can be forgiven for their sins, redeemed to God, and receive salvation from God! Amen! As a servant, we must understand that our service is about getting those who do not understand the Word, to understand the Gospel of Jesus, so that they can be saved! Hallelujah! As a Servant of God, Jesus is also the first Teacher of the Gospel of Jesus! Glory Hallelujah! So Jesus obviously, Jesus knew the Gospel of Jesus! Yet He did not teach the Gospel at a level where others would not be able to understand it. Jesus utilized parables to teach people. Amen! Jesus disciples (His servants) wanted to know why He utilized these short stories. And Jesus gave an answer to His servants that is still the answer to His servants today. Amen again! Jesus is teaching His servants, and helping His servants to understand that not all people will truly accept Jesus, and very few will believe in Jesus enough to truly bear fruit for the Kingdom of God! Hallelujah! Jesus is speaking to His servants today, just as He spoke to His servants then! Glory Hallelujah! Glory to God! Jesus is a Servant, and as a Servant, Jesus recognized that He knew the Gospel of Jesus completely, while the people that He wanted to receive the Word, did not. So Jesus told them a story that they could relate to so that He could then relate the Gospel of Jesus to that story. Amen! Our Word continues with Jesus teaching His servants to realize that they know the mystery of the Word of God, while others do not, for, **(After the story was told) Jesus's disciples came to Him and asked, 'Why do you speak to the people in parables?' Jesus replied, "Because the knowledge of the secrets of the Kingdom of Heaven has been given to you (Jesus's servants), but not to them. Whoever has (this knowledge) will be given more, and they will have an abundance (of this knowledge)."** Jesus reminds His servants that as a servant of Jesus, God has revealed knowledge of His Word to you. In fact, that knowledge is revealed to you through the Holy Spirit! And as you continue to serve Jesus, God will give you more and more knowledge of His Word! Hallelujah! But you must understand that even though your knowledge has gone up, most people will not understand your level of knowledge, unless you translate that knowledge into a way that others can truly understand it. Jesus's servants have much more knowledge of the Word than the audience that Jesus will send you to. Amen again! So humble yourself and the way you teach! Today, Jesus is speaking to His servants! He who has ears to hear, let them hear! Amen.

Today, the Word of God is speaking to the servants of Jesus Christ. Jesus is teaching us that we serve Him, so that others will come to understand the Gospel of Jesus, and that they can be forgiven for their sins, redeemed to God, and receive salvation from God! Amen! As a servant of Jesus, your service is to help people understand the Word, to understand the Gospel of Jesus, so that they can be saved! Hallelujah! Jesus obviously knew the Gospel of Jesus! Yet He taught the Gospel at a level where others would be able to understand it. Jesus utilized parables to teach people. Amen! And Jesus is teaching His servants, and helping you to understand that not all people will truly accept Jesus, and very few will believe in Jesus enough to truly bear fruit for the Kingdom of God! Hallelujah! But it is up to you to teach the Gospel of Jesus in a way that others will understand it. Glory Hallelujah! "He who has ears to hear, let him hear." Glory to God! Jesus is a Servant, and as a Servant, Jesus recognized that He knew the Gospel of Jesus completely, while the people that He wanted to receive the Word, did not. So Jesus told them a story that they could relate to, so that He could then relate the Gospel of Jesus to that story. Amen! And Jesus reminds us that as a servant of Jesus, God has revealed knowledge of His Word to you. That knowledge is revealed to you through the Holy Spirit! So you have much more knowledge of the Word than the audience that Jesus sends you to. Amen again! And the Word of God concludes with Jesus teaching His servants, that, **"Whoever does not have (truly receive this knowledge), even what they have will be taken from them. This is why I speak to them in parables: Though seeing, they do not see, though hearing, they do not hear or understand."** For the audience that Jesus sends you to, will not truly understand the Word, and what little they may understand, will be taken from them if they do not receive the teaching in a manner that they could understand. So humble yourself! You do not serve Jesus to impress people with your knowledge! Your knowledge was given to you by God, and your knowledge will continue to increase, because of God! Humble yourself, and the way you teach! Today, Jesus is speaking to His servants! He who has ears to hear, let them hear! Amen.

Jesus is teaching His servants that it is not about the knowledge of the servants, who have already received and understand the Word, and are saved! As a servant, we must understand that our service is about getting those who do not understand the Word, to understand the Gospel of Jesus, so that they can be saved! Hallelujah! Humble yourself, and the way you teach! Today, Jesus is speaking to His servants! He who has ears to hear, let them hear! Amen.

Day 225

Then Jesus told them (the large crowd of people) many things in parables (a short story to teach Christian principles), saying, "A farmer went out to sow his seed.

As he was scattering the seed, some fell along the path, and the birds came and ate it up."

"Listen then to what the parable of the sower means:

When anyone hears the message about the Kingdom (of God) and does not understand it, the evil one (Satan) comes and snatches away what was sown in their heart."

(Matthew 13:3-4 & 18-19)

In today's Scripture, the great servant of Jesus, the apostle Matthew, tells us of the time that Jesus utilized parables to teach people about the Word of God. Amen! After speaking the parable, Jesus's disciples (His servants) wanted to know why He utilized these short stories. And Jesus began teaching His servants about ministering the Gospel of Jesus, and helping His servants to understand that not all people will truly accept Jesus, and very few will believe in Jesus enough to become His servants, and truly bear fruit for the Kingdom of God! Hallelujah! Jesus is speaking to His servants today, just as He spoke to His servants then! Glory Hallelujah! The parable that Jesus spoke is not only about those who hear the Word, it is also a lesson for the servant of Jesus that teaches the Word! Amen! In fact, the sower in the parable, represents the servant of Jesus! Amen again! Jesus is teaching His servants with this parable! For His servants are the ones who have ears, for Jesus is only explaining the meaning of the parable to His servants! And Jesus is saying to His servants, "He who has ears to hear, let him hear!" Glory to God! Jesus's servants have ears (knowledge), so let them hear (gain wisdom). Thank you, Jesus, for teaching us today! Our Scripture begins with Jesus speaking to the crowd, saying, **Then Jesus told them (the large crowd of people) many things in parables (a short story to teach Christian principles), saying, "A farmer went out to sow his seed."** As a servant of Jesus, you are the working farmer, and your work is to sow seeds to bear fruit for the Kingdom of God! Amen! Our Word continues with Jesus teaching His servants to realize that each person they sow the seed of the Gospel of Jesus to reacts differently to the seed, saying, **"As he was scattering the seed, some fell along the path, and the birds came and ate it up."** Jesus is speaking to His servants! Not all of your seeds will bear fruit. Some of your seeds will go to some, and be quickly taken away from them. Amen again! And the Word of God concludes with Jesus teaching His servants to, **"Listen then to what the parable of the sower means: When anyone hears the message about the Kingdom (of God) and does not understand it, the evil one (Satan) comes and snatches away what was sown in their heart."** The sower (servant of Jesus) must understand that when we teach the Gospel of Jesus, and the listener does not quite understand it, Satan sees that, and quickly attacks the listener with temptations of the earth to turn them completely from the seed that was given to them. Tell the truth! Yet, the sower must keep on sowing! Hallelujah! He who has ears to hear, let them hear! Amen.

Today, Our Scripture is speaking to, and teaching the servants of Jesus Christ. The apostle Matthew tells us that Jesus utilized parables to teach people about the Word of God. Amen! Jesus's disciples (His servants) wanted to know why He utilized these short stories. And Jesus began teaching His servants about ministering the Gospel of Jesus, and helping His servants to understand that not all people will truly accept Jesus, and very few will believe in Jesus enough to become His servants, and truly bear fruit for the Kingdom of God! Hallelujah! Jesus is teaching His servants today, just as He taught His servants then! Glory Hallelujah! The parable that Jesus spoke is also a lesson for the servant of Jesus that teaches the Word! Amen! In fact, the sower in the parable, represents the servant of Jesus! Amen again! Jesus is teaching His servants with this parable! For His servants are the ones who have ears, for Jesus is only explaining the meaning of the parable to His servants! And Jesus is saying to His servants, "He who has ears to hear, let him hear!" Glory to God! Jesus's servants have ears (knowledge), so let them hear (gain wisdom). Hallelujah! Our Scripture begins with Jesus speaking to the crowd, saying, **Then Jesus told them (the large crowd of people) many things in parables (a short story to teach Christian principles), saying, "A farmer went out to sow his seed."** As a servant of

Jesus, you are the working farmer, and your work is to sow seeds to bear fruit for the Kingdom of God! Amen! Wherever Jesus sends us to, as His servant, we are to sow seeds! That is the work that Jesus calls us to do, no matter what the exact assignment is. You are His servant, a farmer of His land, and you are to sow seeds! And the servants of Jesus must utilize methods that allow the seed to be understood by those the servant is sowing to. Hallelujah! Jesus is speaking to His servants! The sower must find ways that allow the seed of Jesus to be sowed! He who has ears to hear, let them hear! Amen.

Today, our Word is speaking to the servants of Jesus Christ. Jesus is teaching us that we serve Him, so that others will come to understand the Gospel of Jesus, and that they can be forgiven for their sins, redeemed to God, and receive salvation from God! Amen! As a servant, we must understand that our service is about getting those who do not understand the Word, to understand the Gospel of Jesus, so that they can be saved! Hallelujah! Jesus is the first Teacher of the Gospel of Jesus! Glory Hallelujah! And Jesus utilized parables to teach people. Amen! Jesus's disciples (His servants) wanted to know why He utilized these short stories. And Jesus began teaching His servants about ministering the Gospel of Jesus! Hallelujah! The parable that Jesus spoke is a guide for the servant of Jesus that teaches the Word! Amen! In fact, the sower in the parable, represents the servant of Jesus! Amen again! Jesus is teaching His servants with this parable! And Jesus is saying to His servants, "He who has ears to hear, let him hear!" Glory to

God! Jesus's servants have ears (knowledge), so let them hear (gain wisdom). Hallelujah! As a servant of Jesus, you are the working farmer, and your work is to sow seeds to bear fruit for the Kingdom of God! Amen! Our Word continues with Jesus teaching His servants to realize that each person they sow the seed of the Gospel of Jesus, reacts differently to the seed, saying, **"As he was scattering the seed, some fell along the path, and the birds came and ate it up."** Jesus is speaking to His servants! Not all of your seeds will bear fruit. Some of your seeds will go to some and be quickly taken away from them. Amen again! As a servant of Jesus, our job is to sow seeds! And as we sow seeds, some will fall on people, but they will not receive the seed into their heart, because they do not truly understand what you have given them. And the enemy, Satan, is watching you sow seeds, so that when you pass by, he can steal the seed away! Satan wants to get to where you have sowed the seed, before you can put water and fertilizer on it! For that is his best chance to take the seed away, before the servant can continue to teach and guide utilizing the Word of God, which is to water and fertilize! Yet, the sower must keep on sowing! He who has ears to hear, let them hear! Amen.

Today, the Word of God is speaking to the servants of Jesus Christ. Jesus is teaching us that we serve Him, so that others will come to understand the Gospel of Jesus, and that they can be forgiven for their sins, redeemed to God, and receive salvation from God! Amen! As a servant, we must understand that our service is about getting those who do not understand the Word, to understand the Gospel of Jesus, so that they can be saved! Hallelujah! Jesus is the first Teacher of the Gospel of Jesus! Glory Hallelujah! And Jesus utilized parables to teach people. Amen! Jesus's disciples (His servants) wanted to know why He utilized these short stories. And Jesus began teaching His servants about ministering the Gospel of Jesus! Hallelujah! The parable that Jesus spoke is a guide for the servant of Jesus that teaches the Word! Amen! In fact, the sower in the parable, represents the servant of Jesus! Amen again! Jesus is teaching His servants with this parable! And Jesus is saying to His servants, "He who has ears to hear, let him hear!" Glory to God! Jesus's servants have ears (knowledge), so let them hear (gain wisdom). Hallelujah! As a servant of Jesus, you are the working farmer, and your work is to sow seeds to bear fruit for the Kingdom of God! Amen! Jesus is speaking to His servants! Not all of your seeds will bear fruit. Some of your seeds will go to some, and be quickly taken away from them. Amen again! And the Word of God concludes with Jesus teaching His servants, to, **"Listen then to what the parable of the sower means: When anyone hears the message about the Kingdom (of God) and does not understand it, the evil one (Satan) comes and snatches away what was sown in their heart."** The sower (servant of Jesus) must understand that when we teach the Gospel of Jesus, and the listener does not quite understand it, Satan sees that, and quickly attacks the listener with temptations of the earth to turn them completely from the seed that was given to them. Satan knows that if he can distract the sinner who recently heard the Word, right away, before they understand the Word, he can keep the sinner from receiving Jesus! So Satan is able to do that with some who have heard the Word of God. And sower must know this, and not be disheartened. For not every seed that is sowed will bear fruit, because God gives each person a free choice, and Satan will utilize lies and evil to snatch the seed before it can begin to root. Tell the truth! Yet the sower must keep on sowing! Hallelujah! Jesus is speaking to His servants! He who has ears to hear, let them hear! Amen.

Today, Jesus is teaching His servants that our job is to sow the seeds of the Gospel of Jesus Christ to as many people as we can, and to do it in a way that they will understand it. Yet, not everyone who the seed lands on will receive, and hold on to the seed. Amen! For some of the seeds you sow will land on people who do not quite understand the Gospel of Jesus, and they will be quickly distracted by Satan's lies, and their interest in the Gospel of Jesus will leave them. But you are still the sower of seeds, so keep on sowing the seeds! Today, Jesus is speaking to His servants! He who has ears to hear, let them hear! Amen.

Day 226

Then Jesus told them (the large crowd of people) many things in parables (a short story to teach Christian principles), saying, "A farmer went out to sow his seed."

"Some fell on rocky places, where it did not have much soil. It sprang up quickly, because the soil was shallow.

But when the sun came up, the plants were scorched and withered because they had no root."

"Listen then to what the parable of the sower means:"

"The seed falling on rocky ground, refers to someone who hears the Word and at once receives it with joy.

But since they have no root, they last only a short time. When trouble or persecution comes because of the Word, they quickly fall away."

(Matthew 13:3, 5-6, 18 & 20-21)

In today's Scripture, the great servant of Jesus, the apostle Matthew, continues telling us of the time that Jesus utilized parables to teach people about the Word of God. Amen! Jesus's disciples (His servants) wanted to know why He utilized these short stories. And Jesus began teaching His servants about ministering the Gospel of Jesus, and helping His servants to understand that not all people will truly accept Jesus, and very few will believe in Jesus enough to become His servants, and truly bear fruit for the Kingdom of God! Hallelujah! And now, Jesus continues His teaching to His servants today, just as He taught His servants then! Glory Hallelujah! For the parable that Jesus spoke serves as guidance for the servant of Jesus that teaches the Word! Amen! In fact, the sower in the parable represents the servant of Jesus! Amen again! Jesus is teaching His servants with this parable! Jesus's servants are the ones who have ears, and Jesus is only explaining the meaning of the parable to His servants! And Jesus is saying to His servants, "He who has ears to hear, let him hear!" Glory to God! Jesus's servants have ears (knowledge), so let them hear (gain wisdom). So Jesus is speaking to and teaching, His servants! Hallelujah! Our Scripture begins with Jesus speaking to the crowd, saying, **Then Jesus told them (the large crowd of people) many things in parables (a short story to teach Christian principles), saying, "A farmer went out to sow his seed."** As a servant of Jesus, you are the working farmer, and your work is to sow seeds to bear fruit for the Kingdom of God! Amen! Our Word continues with Jesus teaching His servants to realize that each person that they sow the seed of the Gospel of Jesus to, reacts differently to the seed, saying, **"Some fell on rocky places, where it did not have much soil. It sprang up quickly, because the soil was shallow. But when the sun came up, the plants were scorched and withered because they had no root."** Jesus is speaking to His servants! Not all of your seeds will bear fruit. Some of your seed will go to some, who will spring up with joy when they first receive the seed, but the ground that the seed lands on is too difficult for the plant to continue to grow on its own, and the plant's joy dries up and is gone. Amen again! And the Word of God concludes with Jesus teaching His servants to, **"Listen then to what the parable of the sower means: The seed falling on rocky ground, refers to someone who hears the Word and at once receives it with joy. But since they have no roots, they last only a short time. When trouble or persecution comes because of the Word, they quickly fall away."** The sower (servant of Jesus) must understand that when we teach the Gospel of Jesus, the seed has been sowed, but the ground (person) the seed landed on has not yet been fertilized! Hallelujah! Tell the truth! For just sowing the seed will not be enough for it to grow on the rocky ground! Hallelujah! Jesus is speaking to, and teaching His servants! He who has ears to hear, let them hear! Amen.

Today, our Scripture is speaking to, and teaching the servants of Jesus Christ. The apostle Matthew continues telling us that Jesus utilized parables to teach people about the Word of God. Amen! Jesus's disciples (His servants) wanted to know why He utilized these short stories. And Jesus began teaching His servants about ministering the Gospel of Jesus, and helping His servants to understand that not all people will truly accept Jesus, and very few will believe in Jesus enough to become His servants, and truly bear fruit for the Kingdom of God! Hallelujah! And now, Jesus continues His teaching to His servants today, just as He taught His servants then! Glory Hallelujah! For the parable that Jesus spoke serves as guidance for the servant of Jesus that teaches the Word! Amen! In fact, the sower in the parable represents the servant of Jesus! Amen again! Jesus is teaching His servants with this parable! Jesus's servants are the ones who have ears, and Jesus is only explaining the meaning of the parable to His servants! And Jesus is saying to His servants, "He who has ears to hear, let him hear!" Glory to God! Jesus's servants have ears (knowledge), so let them hear (gain wisdom). So Jesus is speaking to, and teaching, His servants! Hallelujah! Our Scripture begins with Jesus speaking to the crowd, saying, **Then Jesus told them (the large crowd of people) many things in parables (a short story to teach Christian principles), saying, "A farmer went out to sow his seed."** As a servant of Jesus, you are the working farmer, and your work is to sow seeds to bear fruit for the Kingdom of God! Amen! Wherever Jesus sends us to, as His servant, we are to sow seeds! That is the work that Jesus calls us to do, no matter what the exact assignment is. You are His servant, a farmer of His land...and you are to sow seeds! Jesus is speaking to His servants! For just sowing the seed will not be enough for it to grow on the rocky ground! Hallelujah! Jesus is speaking to, and teaching His servants! He who has ears to hear, let them hear! Amen.

Today, our Word is speaking to the servants of Jesus Christ. Jesus is teaching us that we serve Him, so that others will come to understand the Gospel of Jesus, and that they can be forgiven for their sins, redeemed to God, and receive salvation from God! Amen! As a servant, we must understand that our service is about getting those who do not understand the Word, to understand the Gospel of Jesus, so that they can be saved! Hallelujah! Jesus is the first Teacher of the Gospel of Jesus! Glory Hallelujah! Jesus utilized parables to teach people. Amen! Now Jesus continues teaching His servants about ministering the Gospel of Jesus! Hallelujah! The parable that Jesus spoke is a guide for the servant of Jesus that teaches the Word! Amen! For the parable that Jesus spoke serves as guidance for the servant of Jesus that teaches the Word! Amen! In fact, the sower in the parable represents the servant of Jesus! Amen again! Jesus is teaching His servants with this parable! Glory to God! So Jesus is speaking to, and teaching, His servants! Hallelujah! Jesus is teaching His servants with this parable! And Jesus is saying to His servants, "He who has ears to hear, let him hear!" Glory to God! As a servant of Jesus, you are the working farmer, and your work is to sow seeds to bear fruit for the Kingdom of God! Amen! Our Word continues with Jesus teaching His servants to realize that each person that they sow the seed of the Gospel of Jesus, reacts differently to the seed, saying, **"Some fell on rocky places, where it did not have much soil. It sprang up quickly, because the soil was shallow. But when the sun came up, the plants were scorched and withered because they had no root."** Jesus is speaking to His servants! Not all of your seeds will bear fruit. Some of your seed will go to some, who will spring up with joy when they first receive the seed, but the ground that the seed lands on is too difficult for the plant to continue to grow on its own, and the plant's joy dries up and is gone. Amen again! As a servant of Jesus, your job is to sow seeds! And as we sow seeds, some will fall on people, whose ground (where and how they live) is too rocky for the seed to grow! There is not enough support in their life for the seed to take hold in their heart, so when difficulties and temptations come up, their joy for the Word quickly goes away. For just sowing the seed will not be enough for it to grow on the rocky ground! Hallelujah! Jesus is speaking to, and teaching His servants! He who has ears to hear, let them hear! Amen.

Today, the Word of God is speaking to the servants of Jesus Christ. Jesus is teaching us that we serve Him, so that others will come to understand the Gospel of Jesus, and that they can be forgiven for their sins, redeemed to God, and receive salvation from God! Amen! As a servant, we must understand that our service is about getting those who do not understand the Word, to understand the Gospel of Jesus, so that they can be saved! Hallelujah! Jesus is the first Teacher of the Gospel of Jesus! Glory Hallelujah! And Jesus utilized parables to teach people. Amen! Jesus's disciples (His servants) wanted to know why He utilized these short stories. And Jesus began teaching His servants about ministering the Gospel of Jesus! Hallelujah! For the sower in the parable, represents the servant of Jesus! Amen again! Jesus is teaching His servants with this parable! And Jesus is saying to His servants, "He who has ears to hear, let him hear!" Glory to God! Hallelujah! As a servant of Jesus, you are the working farmer, and your work is to sow seeds to bear fruit for the Kingdom of God!

Amen! Jesus is speaking to His servants! Not all of your seeds will bear fruit. Some of your seed will go to some, who will spring up with joy when they first receive the seed, but the ground that the seed lands on is too difficult for the plant to continue to grow on its own, and the plant's joy dries up and is gone. Amen again! And the Word of God concludes with Jesus teaching His servants to, **"Listen then to what the parable of the sower means: The seed falling on rocky ground, refers to someone who hears the Word and at once receives it with joy. But since they have no root, they last only a short time. When trouble or persecution comes because of the Word, they quickly fall away."** The sower (servant of Jesus) must understand that when we teach the Gospel of Jesus, the seed has been sowed, but the ground (person) the seed landed on has not yet been prepared or fertilized! Hallelujah! The seed has been sowed, and landed, but the ground is hard! For the listener will oftentimes hear the Word, and will find great joy! But still, that person lives in a sinful world, and there will be difficult things that happen to them, or people that attack them to steal the joy that they had from hearing the Word! For although they had joy when they heard the Word, their knowledge and faith of the Word has not grown in them to where their heart truly has received the Word. Tell the truth! The sower must also know that once the seed lands, the ground may need to be tilled! The sower (servant of Jesus) must be aware when the ground that the seed falls on is hard; there is a chance that the seed will quickly fall away. So if you are the sower, also be ready to till the ground, and fertilize the ground! For just sowing the seed will not be enough for it to grow on the rocky ground! Hallelujah! Jesus is speaking to, and teaching His servants! He who has ears to hear, let them hear! Amen.

Today, Jesus is teaching His servants that our job is to sow the seeds of the Gospel of Jesus Christ to as many people as we can, and to do it in a way that they will understand it. Yet, not everyone who the seed lands on will receive, and hold on to the seed. Amen! And even though there will be some people who hear the Word who will receive joy and express commitment to the Word, the seed does not go any deeper into their hearts. For the land (their heart) is still too hard, and once the difficulties of life (the sun) come up, they burn and fall away from the Word! For just sowing the seed will not be enough for it to grow on the rocky ground! Hallelujah! Jesus is speaking to, and teaching His servants! He who has ears to hear, let them hear! Amen.

Day 227

"Jesus answered them, "It is not the healthy who need a doctor, but the sick.

I have not come to call the righteous, but sinners to repentance."

"Early on the first day of the week (after the crucifixion of Jesus), while it was still dark (in the early morning), Mary Magdalene, (whom Jesus had driven seven evil spirits out of), went to the tomb of Jesus and saw that the stone had been removed from the entrance.

So she went running to Simon Peter and the other Disciple, the one that Jesus loved (John), and said, 'They have taken the Lord out of the tomb, and we don't know where they have put Him.'

So Peter and the other Disciple started for the tomb."

(Luke 5:31-32 & John 20:1-35)

In today's Scripture, Luke and the Apostle John utilize two different times to illustrate to all people that Jesus came to this earth to heal and save sinners. Amen! Jesus taught and encouraged those who had come to believe in Him and therefore recognized God, but His mission was to seek those who did not know the righteousness of God. Amen again! In fact, Jesus was criticized for being with those who the people saw as sinful. Yet, Jesus knew that all people were sinful, and in need of healing. Hallelujah, tell the truth! And Jesus often utilized the most sinful people to show

His love to and for others to see these reformed sinners serving Jesus. Hallelujah again! Jesus spoke to His mission when the "self-appointed righteous" Pharisees and teachers of the Law of Moses, complained to His Disciples that Jesus ate and drank with tax collectors and sinners. Our Scripture begins with, **"Jesus answered them, "It is not the healthy who need a doctor, but the sick. I have not come to call the righteous, but sinners to repentance."** Each person must recognize they are "sick in sin" before Jesus will heal them! Amen! Our Word moves forward, saying, **"Early on the first day of the week (after the crucifixion of Jesus), while it was still dark (in the early morning), Mary Magdalene, (whom Jesus had driven seven evil spirits out of), went to the tomb of Jesus and saw that the stone had been removed from the entrance."** Jesus will use the people who were most sinful and sick to serve Him and glorify God! Amen again! And the Word of God proclaims, **"So she went running to Simon Peter and the other Disciple, the one that Jesus loved (John), and said, 'They have taken the Lord out of the tomb, and we don't know where they have put Him.' So Peter and the other Disciple started for the tomb."** Jesus sent the one that was once seen as the "most sinful and sick" to move the most righteous of His followers to Him! Hallelujah! Jesus will use the "most unworthy" sinner, who He heals, to serve Him, and send others to Him. Glory Hallelujah! Jesus is speaking to those sinners who He has sought and healed, but others see as unworthy! Jesus came to this earth seeking you! Amen! You admitted you were sick in sin, and Jesus, your Doctor, has healed you! Amen again! Now go forward and do what Jesus has chosen you to do! Hallelujah! For Jesus came to this earth to heal the sick in sin, and to give everlasting "health" from God! Glory Hallelujah! Glory to God! Amen.

Today, our Scripture is speaking to all people. Jesus came to this earth from Heaven, to heal and save sinners! Amen! For all people are sinners! Amen again! And no one is forgiven of their sins, until they come to Jesus and repent, and ask Jesus to save them! Hallelujah! Jesus's mission was to seek those who did not know the righteousness of God, and to show them God's plan for their salvation. Amen again! And that plan is there for every single person, because every single person is a sinner! Hallelujah, tell the truth! Yet, Jesus was criticized for being with those who the people saw as sinful. And Jesus often utilized the most sinful people to show His love to, and for others to see these reformed sinners serving Jesus. Hallelujah again! Jesus spoke to His mission when the "self-appointed righteous" Pharisees and teachers of the Law of Moses, complained to His Disciples that Jesus ate and drank with tax collectors and sinners. Our Scripture begins with, **"Jesus answered them, "It is not the healthy who need a doctor, but the sick. I have not come to call the righteous, but sinners to repentance."** Each person must recognize they are "sick in sin" before Jesus will heal them! Amen! When Jesus answered the Pharisees, He was not implying that the Pharisees were healthy. What He was saying is that all people must recognize themselves as sinners... that need Jesus! And that Jesus is the only One that can heal them! Hallelujah! No one can spiritually heal themselves; only Jesus can heal the Spirit through mediating forgiveness from God for each person's spiritual sickness of sin. You must realize and admit that you are sick, and you must admit that sickness to Jesus! And that is the truth! For Jesus came to this earth to heal the sick in sin, and to give everlasting "health" from God! Glory Hallelujah! Glory to God! Amen.

Today, our Word is speaking to all people. Jesus came to this earth from Heaven, to heal and save sinners! Amen! For all people are sinners! Amen again! And no one is forgiven of their sins, until they come to Jesus and repent, and ask Jesus to save them! Hallelujah! Jesus's mission was to seek those who did not know the righteousness of God, and to show them God's plan for their salvation. Amen again! Yet, Jesus was criticized for being with those who the people saw as sinful. And Jesus often utilized the most sinful people to show His love to, and for others to see these reformed sinners serving Jesus. Hallelujah again! However, each person must recognize they are "sick in sin" before Jesus will heal them! Amen! Our Word moves forward, saying, **"Early on the first day of the week (after the crucifixion of Jesus), while it was still dark (in the early morning), Mary Magdalene, (whom Jesus had driven seven evil spirits out of), went to the tomb of Jesus and saw that the stone had been removed from the entrance."** Jesus will use the people were most sinful and sick to serve Him and glorify God! Amen again! Mary Magdalene was so sick, that Jesus had to remove seven demons from her before she could follow Him! Seven demons! Yet it was Mary Magdalene who Jesus allowed to see that the stone that locked down the tomb that Jesus's physical body was in, had been removed! Not one of the twelve Disciples, twelve of the most righteous men on earth. No! In fact, Jesus utilized this woman, who once had seven of Satan's demons inside her body, to be the first to see that the tomb was now prepared for Jesus to rise and walk through! Hallelujah, hallelujah, hallelujah! Jesus will utilize the sinner to serve Him and glorify God! For Jesus came to this earth to heal the sick in sin, and to give everlasting "health" from God! Glory Hallelujah! Glory to God! Amen.

Today, the Word of God is speaking to all people. Jesus came to this earth from Heaven, to heal and save sinners! Amen! For all people are sinners! Amen again! And no one is forgiven of their sins, until they come to Jesus and repent, and ask Jesus to save them! Hallelujah! Jesus's mission was to seek those who did not know the righteousness of God, and to show them God's plan for their salvation. Amen again! Yet, Jesus was criticized for being with those who the people saw as sinful. And Jesus often utilized the most sinful people to show His love to, and for others to see these reformed sinners serving Jesus. Hallelujah again! However, each person must recognize they are "sick in sin" before Jesus will heal them! Amen! And Jesus will use the people who were once the most sinful and sick to serve Him and glorify God! Amen again! And the Word of God proclaims, **"So she went running to Simon Peter and the other Disciple, the one that Jesus loved (John), and said, 'They have taken the Lord out of the tomb, and we don't know where they have put Him.' So Peter and the other Disciple started for the tomb."** Jesus sent the one that was once seen as the "most sinful and sick" to move the most righteous of His followers to Him! Hallelujah! Jesus sent Mary to notify the Apostle Peter, who was seen as the leading figure among the twelve Disciples, that the tomb that held Jesus had been opened! Amen! Jesus will use the "most unworthy" sinner, who He heals, to serve Him, and send others to Him. Glory Hallelujah! For Jesus came to this earth to heal the sick in sin, and to give everlasting "health" from God! Glory Hallelujah! Glory to God! Amen.

Today, our Scripture Guidance is for all people. Jesus came to this earth from Heaven, to heal and save sinners! Amen! For all people are sinners! Amen again! And no one is forgiven of their sins, until they come to Jesus and repent, and ask Jesus to save them! Hallelujah! Jesus's mission was to seek those who did not know the righteousness of God, and to show them God's plan for their salvation. Jesus is speaking to those sinners who He has sought and healed, but others see as unworthy! Do not listen to others that judge your righteousness with their own "self-appointed righteousness" and complain that Jesus has chosen you to be with and serve Him! Jesus came to this earth seeking you! Amen again! Jesus often utilized the most sinful people to show

His love to, and for others to see these reformed sinners serving Jesus. Hallelujah again! Each person must recognize they are "sick in sin" before Jesus will heal them! Amen! And Jesus will use the "most unworthy" sinner, who He heals, to serve Him, and send others to Him. Glory Hallelujah! Jesus is speaking to you! Jesus came to heal and save the sinner, and to be healed and saved; you must admit you need Him! You must admit you are sick in sin, and call Him to save you! Amen! And once Jesus has healed you, He will call on you to serve Him, no matter how sick you once were! Thank you, Jesus! So do not listen or worry about the judgment of others, of whether or not you are worthy, for no one is worthy! But hallelujah, Jesus is worthy to be served! Amen again! Now go forward and do what Jesus has chosen you to do, so that others may see a reformed sinner serves Jesus, so that they too can repent and be healed! Hallelujah! For Jesus came to this earth to heal the sick in sin, and to give everlasting "health" from God"! Glory Hallelujah! Glory to God! Amen.

Day 228

Jesus answered them, "It is not the healthy who need a doctor, but the sick.

I have not come to call the righteous, but sinners to repentance."

"Both were running (to Jesus' tomb) but John outran Peter and reached the tomb first."

"Then Peter came and went straight into the tomb. He saw the strips of linen lying there."

"Finally John, who had reached the tomb first, also went inside. He saw and believed (that Jesus was no longer in the tomb)."

"Then the Disciples went back to where they were staying.

But Mary stood outside the tomb weeping, and as she wept, she stooped down and looked into the tomb."

(Luke 5:31-32 & John 20:4, 6, 8, & 10-11)

In today's Scripture, Luke, and the Apostle John utilize two different times to illustrate to all people that Jesus came to this earth to heal and save sinners. Amen! Jesus taught and encouraged those who had come to believe in Him, and therefore recognized God, but His mission was to seek those who did not know the righteousness of God. Amen again! Many people criticized Jesus for being with those who they saw as sinful. Yet, Jesus knew that all people were sinful, and in need of healing. Hallelujah, tell the truth! Jesus spoke to His mission when the "self-appointed righteous" Pharisees and teachers of the Law of Moses, complained to His Disciples that Jesus ate and drank with tax collectors and sinners. In fact, there are many cases where Jesus often utilized the most sinful people to show His love to, and for others to see these reformed sinners serving Jesus in magnificent ways. Hallelujah again! Mary Magdalene was one of those people. Our Scripture begins with, **Jesus answered them, "It is not the healthy who need a doctor, but the sick. I have not come to call the righteous, but sinners to repentance."** Each person must recognize they are "sick in sin" before Jesus will heal them! Amen! Our Word moves forward, saying that after Mary Magdalene told the Disciples that Jesus was no longer in the tomb, that, **"Both were running (to Jesus' tomb), but John outran Peter and reached the tomb first. Then Peter came and went straight into the tomb. He saw the strips of linen lying there. Finally, John, who had reached the tomb first, also went inside. He saw and believed (that Jesus was no longer in the tomb)."** The righteous run to Jesus, and believe! They know that Jesus is risen! Amen again! And the Word of God proclaims, **"Then the Disciples went back to where they were staying. But Mary stood outside the tomb weeping, and as she wept, she stooped down and looked into the tomb."** Jesus will often keep the most "unworthy" of His followers near Him, so that He can use them to glorify Him! Hallelujah! Jesus will use the "most unworthy" sinner, who He heals, to serve Him, and send others to

Him. Glory Hallelujah! Our Scriptures are talking to someone today! Jesus is speaking to those sinners who He has sought and healed, but others see as unworthy! Jesus came to this earth seeking you! Amen! Jesus is calling on you to serve Him, but you can't believe He would use you because of your sinful past. Well, all of Jesus's servants have sinful pasts! Amen again! But glory to God, you have admitted you were sick in sin, and Jesus, your Doctor, has healed you! Amen again! Now go forward and do what Jesus has chosen you to do! Hallelujah! Jesus has chosen you to glorify His Father by lifting the name of Jesus! Jesus is calling you to stay, and look for Him! Glory! For Jesus came to this earth to heal the sick in sin, and to give everlasting "health" from God! Glory Hallelujah! Glory to God! Amen.

Today, our Scripture is speaking to all people. Jesus came to this earth from Heaven, to heal and save sinners! Amen! For all people are sinners! Amen again! And no one is forgiven of their sins, until they come to Jesus and repent, and ask Jesus to save them! Hallelujah! Jesus's mission was to seek those who did not know the righteousness of God, and to show them God's plan for their salvation. Amen again! And that plan is there for every single person, because every single person is a sinner! Hallelujah, tell the truth! Jesus often utilized the most sinful people to show His love to, and for others to see these reformed sinners serving Jesus. Hallelujah again! Jesus spoke to His mission when the "self-appointed righteous" Pharisees and teachers of the Law of Moses, complained to His Disciples that Jesus ate and drank with tax collectors and sinners. Our Scripture begins with, **Jesus answered them, "It is not the healthy who need a doctor, but the sick. I have not come to call the righteous, but sinners to repentance."** Each person must recognize they are "sick in sin" before Jesus will heal them! Amen! When Jesus answered the Pharisees, He was not implying that the Pharisees were health. What He was saying is that all people must recognize themselves as sinners, that need Jesus! And that Jesus is the only One that can heal them! Hallelujah! No one can spiritually heal themselves, only Jesus can heal the Spirit through mediating forgiveness from God for each person's spiritual sickness of sin. You must realize and admit that you are sick, and you must admit that sickness to Jesus! And that is the truth! For Jesus came to this earth to heal the sick in sin, and to give everlasting "health" from God! Glory Hallelujah! Glory to God! Amen.

Today, our Word is speaking to all people. Jesus came to this earth from Heaven, to heal and save sinners! Amen! For all people are sinners! Amen again! And no one is forgiven of their sins, until they come to Jesus and repent, and ask Jesus to save them! Hallelujah! Jesus's mission was to seek those who did not know the righteousness of God, and to show them God's plan for their salvation. Amen again! Yet, Jesus was criticized for being with those who the people saw as sinful. But Jesus often will utilize the most sinful people to show His love to, and for others to see these reformed sinners serving Jesus. Hallelujah again! However, each person must recognize they are "sick in sin" before Jesus will heal them! Amen! Mary Magdalene was so sick, that Jesus had to remove seven demons from her before she could follow Him! Seven demons! Yet it was Mary Magdalene who Jesus allowed to see that the stone that locked down the tomb that Jesus's physical body was in, had been removed! Not one of the twelve Disciples, twelve of the most righteous men on earth. No! In fact, Jesus utilized this woman, who once had seven of Satan's demons inside her body, to be the first to see that the tomb was now prepared for Jesus to rise and walk through! Hallelujah, hallelujah, hallelujah! And it is Mary Magdalene who ran to tell the Disciples that the stone had been removed from Jesus's tomb! Glory to God! Our Word moves forward, saying that after Mary Magdalene told the Disciples that Jesus was no longer in the tomb, that, **"Both were running (to Jesus' tomb), but John outran Peter and reached the tomb first. Then Peter came and went straight into the tomb. He saw the strips of linen lying there. Finally, John, who had reached the tomb first, also went inside. He saw and believed (that Jesus was no longer in the tomb)."** The righteous run to Jesus, and believe! They know that Jesus is risen! Amen again! Yet, Jesus loves to have servants that are not always seen as righteous by others, so that the work that they do is seen more miraculous than those that are already seen by others as righteous. For the greater the turnaround is of a sinner that serves Jesus doing great work, the greater that others see the power of Jesus in them! Hallelujah! The world sees the righteous as righteous, and they will always do the work of Jesus. Amen! For Jesus came to this earth to heal the sick in sin, and to give everlasting "health" from God! Glory Hallelujah! Glory to God! Amen.

Today, the Word of God is speaking to all people. Jesus came to this earth from Heaven, to heal and save sinners! Amen! For all people are sinners! Amen again! And no one is forgiven of their sins, until they come to Jesus and repent, and ask Jesus to save them! Hallelujah! Jesus's mission was to seek those who did not know the righteousness of God, and to show them God's plan for their salvation. Amen again! And Jesus often utilized the most sinful people to show His love to, and for others to see these reformed sinners serving Jesus. Hallelujah again! Mary Magdalene was so sick, that Jesus had to remove seven demons from her before she could follow Him! Seven demons! Yet it was Mary Magdalene who Jesus allowed to see that the stone that locked down the tomb that Jesus's physical body was in, had been removed! Not one of the twelve Disciples, twelve of the most righteous men on earth. No! Jesus utilized this woman, the "sinful sinner" who had repented, to be the first to see that the tomb was now prepared for Jesus to rise and walk through! Hallelujah! And it is Mary Magdalene who ran to tell the Disciples that the stone had been removed from Jesus's tomb! Glory to God! Amen! Jesus will use the people who were once the most sinful and sick to serve Him and glorify God! Amen again! And the Word of God proclaims, **"Then the Disciples went back to where they were staying. But Mary stood outside the tomb weeping, and as she wept, she stooped down and looked into the tomb."** Jesus will often keep the most "unworthy" of His followers near Him, so that He can use them to glorify Him! Hallelujah! Jesus will use the "most unworthy" sinner, who He heals, to serve Him, and send others to Him. Glory Hallelujah! But glory to God, you have admitted you were sick in sin, and Jesus, your Doctor, has healed you! Amen again! Now go forward and do what Jesus has chosen you to do! Hallelujah! Jesus has chosen you to glorify His Father by lifting the name of Jesus! Jesus is calling you to stay, and look for Him! Jesus wants you to serve Him! And when the "greater sinner" serves Jesus, they shine a greater light on the forgiving mercy of God, and the healing power of Jesus! Because people will remember that Jesus drove Satan's demons out of them! Glory! Glory! For Jesus came to this earth to heal the sick in sin, and to give everlasting "health" from God! Glory Hallelujah! Glory to God! Amen.

Today, our Scripture Guidance is for all people. Jesus came to this earth from Heaven, to heal and save sinners! Amen! For all people are sinners! Amen again! And no one is forgiven of their sins, until they come to Jesus and repent, and ask Jesus to save them! Hallelujah! Jesus's mission was to seek those who did not know the righteousness of God, and to show them God's plan for their salvation. Jesus came to this earth seeking you! Amen again! And Jesus will use the "most unworthy" sinner, who He heals, to serve Him, and send others to Him. Glory Hallelujah! Jesus is speaking to you! Jesus came to heal and save the sinner, and to be healed and saved; you must admit you need Him! You must admit you are sick in sin, and call Him to save you! Amen! And once Jesus has healed you, He will call on you to serve Him, no matter how sick you once were! Thank you, Jesus! Our Scriptures are talking to someone today! Jesus is speaking to those sinners who He has sought and healed, but others see as unworthy! Jesus came to this earth seeking you! Amen! Jesus is calling on you to serve Him, but you can't believe He would use you because of your sinful past. Well, all of Jesus's servants have sinful pasts! Amen again! And Jesus will utilize the "greater sinner" that has repented, to serve Him and glorify God! Because that "greater sinner" is now righteous in the eyes of God! And when the "greater sinner" serves Jesus, they shine a greater light on the forgiving mercy of God, and the healing power of Jesus! Because people will remember that Jesus drove Satan's demons out of them! Glory! Now go forward and do what Jesus has chosen you to do, so that others may see a reformed sinner serving Jesus, so that they too can repent and be healed! Hallelujah! For Jesus came to this earth to heal the sick in sin, and to give everlasting "health" from God"! Glory Hallelujah! Glory to God! Amen.

Day 229

Jesus answered them, "It is not the healthy who need a doctor, but the sick.

I have not come to call the righteous, but sinners to repentance."

"And Mary (Magdalene) saw two Angels in white sitting, one at the head and the other at the feet, where Jesus had lain.

Then they said to her, 'Woman, why are you weeping?' She said to them, 'Because they have taken away my Lord (Jesus), and I do not know where they have laid Him.'

Now when she had said this, she turned around and saw Jesus standing there, but did not know that it was Jesus."

(Luke 5:31-32 & John 20:12, 13 & 14)

In today's Scripture, Luke and the Apostle John utilize two different times to illustrate to all people that Jesus came to this earth to heal and save sinners. Amen! Jesus taught and encouraged those who had come to believe in Him, and therefore recognized God, but His mission was to seek those who did not know the righteousness of God. Amen again! Many people criticized Jesus for being with those who they saw as sinful. Yet, Jesus knew that all people were sinful, and in need of healing. Hallelujah, tell the truth! Jesus spoke to His mission when the "self-appointed righteous" Pharisees and teachers of the Law of Moses, complained to His Disciples that Jesus ate and drank with tax collectors and sinners. In fact, there are many cases where Jesus often utilized the most sinful people to show His love to, and for others to see these reformed sinners serving Jesus in magnificent ways. Hallelujah again! Mary Magdalene was one of those people. Our Scripture begins with, **"Jesus answered them, "It is not the healthy who need a doctor, but the sick. I have not come to call the righteous, but sinners to repentance."** Each person must recognize they are "sick in sin" before Jesus will heal them! Amen! Our Word moves forward, saying that after the Disciples saw that Jesus was no longer in the tomb, they left, but Mary Magdalene stayed at the tomb of Jesus, and looked in the tomb of Jesus, **"And Mary (Magdalene) saw two Angels in white sitting, one at the head and the other at the feet, where Jesus had lain. Then they said to her, 'Woman, why are you weeping?' She said to them, 'Because they have taken away my Lord (Jesus), and I do not know where they have laid Him.'"** Jesus kept Mary Magdalene at the tomb, because Jesus had a plan to utilize her! This redeemed "sinful" woman in the eyes of many people, a woman that had seven of Satan's demons inside of her! This woman stayed at the tomb of Jesus, weeping! Because she loved her Lord! She cried because she thought that the people had taken Him away from her! And Jesus sent His Angels to her! Amen again! And the Word of God proclaims, **"Now when she had said this, she turned around and saw Jesus standing there, but did not know that it was Jesus."** Jesus will always be with those who love Him, no matter how much you have sinned! Hallelujah! And Jesus will use the "most unworthy" sinner, who He heals, to serve Him, and send others to Him. Glory Hallelujah! Our Scriptures are talking to someone today! Jesus is speaking to those sinners who He has sought and healed, but others see as unworthy! Jesus came to this earth seeking you! Amen! Jesus is calling on you to serve Him, but you can't believe He would use you because of your sinful past. Well, all of Jesus's servants have sinful pasts! Amen again! But glory to God, you have admitted you were sick in sin, and Jesus, your Doctor, has healed you! Amen again! And even in your worst possible times, the times that you think Jesus is no longer with you, Jesus is right there! Jesus is always there for those who love Him! And Jesus has His Angels around you, all the time! They will be there to see about you, and guide you! And that is the truth! Trust Him! Man cannot stop Jesus from being with you, and man cannot stop you from being with Jesus! Jesus is with you, because Jesus loves those who love Him! Now go forward and do what Jesus has chosen you to do! Hallelujah! Jesus has chosen you to glorify His Father by lifting the name of Jesus! Jesus is calling you to stay, and look for Him! Glory! For Jesus came to this earth to heal the sick in sin, and to give everlasting "health" from God! Glory Hallelujah! Now Jesus is keeping you in His presence, because He has a special plan for you! Glory to God! Amen.

Today, our Scripture is speaking to all people. Jesus came to this earth from Heaven, to heal and save sinners! Amen! For all people are sinners! Amen again! And no one is forgiven of their sins, until they come to Jesus and repent, and ask Jesus to save them! Hallelujah! Jesus's mission was to seek those who did not know the righteousness of God, and to show them God's plan for their salvation. Amen again! And that plan is there for every single person, because every single person is a sinner! Hallelujah, tell the truth! Jesus often utilized the most sinful people to show His love to, and for others to see these reformed sinners serving Jesus. Hallelujah again! Jesus spoke to His mission when the "self-appointed righteous" Pharisees and teachers of the Law of Moses, complained to His Disciples that Jesus ate and drank with tax collectors and sinners. Our Scripture begins with, **"Jesus answered them, "It is not the healthy who need a doctor, but the sick. I have not come to call the righteous, but sinners to repentance."** Each person must recognize they are "sick in sin" before Jesus will heal them! Amen! All people must recognize themselves as sinners... that need Jesus! And that Jesus is the only One that can heal them! Hallelujah! No one can spiritually heal themselves; only Jesus can heal the Spirit through mediating forgiveness from God for each person's spiritual sickness of sin. You must realize and admit that you are sick, and you must admit that sickness to Jesus! That is the truth! And Jesus will utilize those who were sick in sin, no matter what their sins were! The sinners that were the "sickest" in the eyes of people, that are redeemed by Jesus, and serve Jesus, show the world that Jesus can save anyone, and will love and utilize anyone! It does not matter how "sick in sin" you were; Jesus is looking for you, and will utilize you to give glory to God! For Jesus came to this earth to heal the sick in sin, and to give everlasting "health" from God! Glory Hallelujah! Now Jesus is keeping you in His presence, because He has a special plan for you! Glory to God! Amen.

Today, our Word is speaking to all people. Jesus came to this earth from Heaven, to heal and save sinners! Amen! For all people are sinners! Amen again! And no one is forgiven of their sins, until they come to Jesus and repent, and ask Jesus to save them! Hallelujah! Jesus's mission was to seek those who did not know the righteousness of God, and to show them God's plan for their salvation. Amen again! And Jesus often will utilize the most sinful people to show His love to, and for others to see these reformed sinners serving Jesus. Hallelujah again! Mary Magdalene had been sick in sin. Mary Magdalene was so sick, that Jesus had to remove seven demons from her before she could follow Him! Seven demons! Yet it was Mary Magdalene who Jesus allowed to see that the stone that locked down the tomb that Jesus's physical body was in had been removed! Not one of the twelve Disciples, twelve of the most righteous men on earth. No! In fact, Jesus, this woman, who once had seven of Satan's demons inside her body, was the first human being to see that the tomb was now prepared for Jesus to rise and walk through! Hallelujah, hallelujah, hallelujah! And it is Mary Magdalene who ran to tell the Disciples that the stone had been removed from Jesus's tomb! Glory to God! Our Word moves forward, saying that after the Disciples saw that Jesus was no longer in the tomb, they left, but Mary Magdalene stayed at the tomb of Jesus and looked in the tomb of Jesus, **"And Mary (Magdalene) saw two Angels in white sitting, one at the head and the other at the feet, where Jesus had lain. Then they said to her, 'Woman, why are you weeping?' She said to them, 'Because they have taken away my Lord (Jesus), and I do not know where they have laid Him.'"** Jesus kept Mary Magdalene at the tomb, because Jesus had a plan to utilize her! This redeemed "sinful" woman in the eyes of many people, a woman that had seven of Satan's demons inside of her! This woman stayed at the tomb of Jesus, weeping! Because she loved her Lord! She cried because she thought that the people had taken Him away from her! And Jesus sent His Angels to her! Amen again! Jesus loves to have servants that are not always seen as righteous by others, so that the work that they do is seen as more miraculous than those that are already seen by others as righteous. For the greater the turnaround is of a sinner that serves Jesus doing great work, the greater that others see the power of Jesus in them! Hallelujah! Mary Magdalene was saved by Jesus, and loved Jesus! And that is who Jesus is looking for, to do great things! Jesus is not looking for those who proclaim to be righteous! Amen! Jesus wants to utilize Believers that know how sinful they once were, and absolutely love Jesus because Jesus has saved them from Hell! Jesus is looking for servants who knew they were sick, and Jesus healed them! Jesus has a plan to utilize you! Mary Magdalene had been sick, and Jesus healed her, and she loved Him for that! You were sick in sin, and Jesus found you, and healed you! Amen again!

Jesus came looking for you! For Jesus came to this earth to heal the sick in sin, and to give everlasting "health" from God! Glory Hallelujah! Now Jesus is keeping you in His presence, because He has a special plan for you! Glory to God! Amen.

Today, the Word of God is speaking to all people. Jesus came to this earth from Heaven, to heal and save sinners! Amen! For all people are sinners! Amen again! And no one is forgiven of their sins, until they come to Jesus and repent, and ask Jesus to save them! Hallelujah! Jesus's mission was to seek those who did not know the righteousness of God, and to show them God's plan for their salvation. Amen again! And Jesus often will utilize the most sinful people to show His love to, and for others to see these reformed sinners serving Jesus. Hallelujah again! Mary Magdalene had been sick in sin. Jesus had to remove seven demons from her before she could follow Him! Yet it was Mary Magdalene who Jesus allowed to see that the stone that locked down His tomb, had been removed! Hallelujah! And it is Mary Magdalene who ran to tell the Disciples that the stone had been removed from Jesus's tomb! Glory to God! Amen! Jesus kept Mary Magdalene at the tomb, because Jesus had a plan to utilize her! This redeemed "sinful" woman in the eyes of many people, a woman that had seven of Satan's demons inside of her! This woman stayed at the tomb of Jesus, weeping! Because she loved her Lord! Amen again! And the Word of God proclaims, **"Now when she had said this, she turned around and saw Jesus standing there, but did not know that it was Jesus."** Jesus will always be with those who love Him, no matter how much you have sinned! Hallelujah! And Jesus will use the "most unworthy" sinner, who He heals, to serve Him, and send others to Him. Glory Hallelujah! For Jesus came to this earth to heal the sick in sin, and to give everlasting "health" from God! Glory Hallelujah! Now Jesus is keeping you in His presence, because He has a special plan for you! Glory to God! Amen.

Today, our Scripture Guidance is for all people. Jesus came to this earth from Heaven, to heal and save sinners! Amen! For all people are sinners! Amen again! And no one is forgiven of their sins, until they come to Jesus and repent, and ask Jesus to save them! Hallelujah! Jesus came to this earth seeking you! Amen again! And Jesus will use the "most unworthy" sinner, who He heals, to serve Him, and send others to Him. Glory Hallelujah! Jesus is speaking to you! Our Scriptures are talking to someone today! Jesus is speaking to those sinners who He has sought and healed, but others see as unworthy! Jesus came to this earth seeking you! Amen! Jesus is calling on you to serve Him, but you can't believe He would use you because of your sinful past. Well, all of Jesus's servants have sinful pasts! Amen again! And even in your worst possible times, the times that you think Jesus is no longer with you, Jesus is right there! Jesus is always there for those who love Him! And Jesus has His Angels around you, all the time! They will be there to see about you, and guide you! And that is the truth! Trust Him! Man cannot stop Jesus from being with you, and man cannot stop you from being with Jesus! Jesus is with you, because Jesus loves those who love Him! Now go forward and do what Jesus has chosen you to do! Hallelujah! Jesus has chosen you to glorify His Father by lifting the name of Jesus! Jesus is calling you to stay, and look for Him, just like He did with Mary Magdalene! The righteous Disciples came to the tomb, and left! But Jesus kept Mary there, for He had a special plan for her! And Jesus has a special plan for you! Glory! For Jesus came to this earth to heal the sick in sin, and to give everlasting "health" from God! Glory Hallelujah! Now Jesus is keeping you in His presence, because He has a special plan for you! Glory to God! Amen.

Day 230

"Jesus answered them, "It is not the healthy who need a doctor, but the sick.

I have not come to call the righteous, but sinners to repentance."

"Jesus asked her (Mary), 'Woman, why are you crying? Who is it you are looking for?'

Thinking that He was the gardener, Mary said (to Jesus), 'Sir, if you have carried Him away, tell me where you have put Him, and I will get Him.'

Jesus said to her, 'Mary.' She turned toward Him and cried out , 'Rabboni!' (Teacher).

Jesus said, 'Do not hold on to Me, for I have not yet ascended to the Father. Go instead to My brothers and tell them, I am ascending to My Father and your Father, to My God and your God.'

Mary Magdalene went to the Disciples with the news: 'I have seen the Lord! And she told them that He had said these things to her."

(Luke 5:31-32 & John 20:15-18)

In today's Scripture, Luke and the Apostle John utilize two different times to illustrate to all people that Jesus came to this earth to heal and save sinners. Amen! Jesus taught and encouraged those who had come to believe in Him, and therefore recognized God, but His mission was to seek those who did not know the righteousness of God. Amen again! Many people criticized Jesus for being with those who they saw as sinful. Yet, Jesus knew that all people were sinful, and in need of healing. Hallelujah, tell the truth! Jesus spoke to His mission when the "self-appointed righteous" Pharisees and teachers of the Law of Moses, complained to His Disciples that Jesus ate and drank with tax collectors and sinners. In fact, there are many cases where Jesus often utilized the most sinful people to show His love to, and for others to see these reformed sinners serving Jesus in magnificent ways. Hallelujah again! Mary Magdalene was one of those people. Our Scripture begins with, **"Jesus answered them, "It is not the healthy who need a doctor, but the sick. I have not come to call the righteous, but sinners to repentance."** Each person must recognize they are "sick in sin" before Jesus will heal them! Amen! Mary Magdalene had been "very sick", and Jesus healed her! And she loved Jesus! Hallelujah! Our Word moves forward, saying that after the Disciples saw that Jesus was no longer in the tomb, they left, but Mary Magdalene stayed at the tomb of Jesus, and looked in the tomb of Jesus, and Jesus came to her, **"Jesus asked her (Mary), 'Woman, why are you crying? Who is it you are looking for?' Thinking that He was the gardener, Mary said (to Jesus), 'Sir, if you have carried Him away, tell me where you have put Him, and I will get Him.' Jesus said to her, 'Mary.' She turned toward Him and cried out, 'Rabboni!'**

(Teacher).'" Jesus came to Mary, not only because she sought Him, but she also loved Him enough to serve Him! Amen again! And the Word of God proclaims, **"Jesus said, 'Do not hold on to Me, for I have not yet ascended to the Father. Go instead to My brothers and tell them, I am ascending to My Father and your Father, to My God and your God.' Mary Magdalene went to the Disciples with the news: 'I have seen the Lord! And she told them that He had said these things to her."** Jesus will always be with those who love Him, no matter how much you have sinned! Hallelujah! And Jesus will use the "most unworthy" sinner, who He heals, to serve Him, and send others to Him. Jesus revealed Himself to Mary, and then gave her the task that would serve Him! Hallelujah! Jesus sent the one that others had seen as "very sick in sin" at the time that He saved her, to be he first person to know that He had risen! And then Jesus sent her to tell the ones that most people saw as the "most righteous", His Disciples, that he had risen from the tomb, and that He was on His way to glory to be with His Father! Glory Hallelujah! Our Scriptures are talking to someone today! Jesus is speaking to those sinners who He has sought and healed, but others see as unworthy! Jesus came to this earth seeking you! Amen! Jesus is calling on you to serve Him, but you can't believe He would use you because of your sinful past. Well, all of Jesus's servants have sinful pasts! Amen again! Now Jesus is speaking to you, because He has a special plan for you! Just like He had a special plan for Mary! Jesus wants you to tell someone, "I have seen the Lord!" Glory to God! Amen.

Today, our Scripture is speaking to all people. Jesus came to this earth from Heaven, to heal and save sinners! Amen! For all people are sinners! Amen again! And no one is forgiven of their sins, until they come to Jesus and repent, and ask Jesus to save them! Hallelujah! Jesus's mission was to seek those who did not know the righteousness of God, and to show them God's plan for their salvation. Amen again! And that plan is there for every single person, because every single person is a sinner! Hallelujah, tell the truth! Jesus often utilizes the most sinful people to show His love to, and for others to see these reformed sinners serving Jesus. Hallelujah again! Jesus spoke to His mission when the "self-appointed righteous" Pharisees and teachers of the Law of Moses, complained to His Disciples that Jesus ate and drank with tax collectors and sinners. Our Scripture begins with, **"Jesus answered them, "It is not the healthy who need a doctor, but the sick. I have not come to call the righteous, but sinners to repentance."** Each person must recognize they are "sick in sin" before Jesus will heal them! Amen! All people must recognize themselves as sinners, that need Jesus! And that Jesus is the only One that can heal them! Hallelujah! No one can spiritually heal themselves; only Jesus can heal the Spirit through mediating forgiveness from God for each person's spiritual sickness of sin. And once Jesus saves you from everlasting death, Jesus wants you to love Him! That is the truth! And Jesus will utilize those who were sick in sin, no matter what their sins were! The sinners that were the "sickest" in the eyes of people, that are redeemed by

Jesus, and serve Jesus, show the world that Jesus can save anyone, and will love and utilize anyone! It does not matter how "sick in sin" you were, Jesus is looking for you, and will utilize you to give glory to God! No one was more sick in sin than Mary Magdalene. Just imagine having seven demons living inside of you! That is sick, yet Jesus healed her! And Jesus healed you from the wages of your sin, for your sins have been forgiven, and you are healed! Hallelujah! For Jesus came to this earth to heal the sick in sin, and to give everlasting "health" from God! Glory Hallelujah! Now Jesus is speaking to you, because He has a special plan for you! Just like He had a special plan for Mary! Jesus wants you to tell someone, "I have seen the Lord! " Glory to God! Amen.

Today, our Word is speaking to all people. Jesus came to this earth from Heaven, to heal and save sinners! Amen! For all people are sinners! Amen again! And no one is forgiven of their sins, until they come to Jesus and repent, and ask Jesus to save them! Hallelujah! Jesus's mission was to seek those who did not know the righteousness of God, and to show them God's plan for their salvation. Amen again! And Jesus often will utilize the most sinful people to show His love to, and for others to see these reformed sinners serving Jesus. Hallelujah again! Mary Magdalene had been sick in sin. Mary Magdalene was so sick, that Jesus had to remove seven demons from her before she could follow Him! Seven demons! Yet it was Mary Magdalene who Jesus allowed to see that the stone that locked down the tomb that Jesus's physical body was in had been removed! Not one of the twelve Disciples, twelve of the most righteous men on earth. No! In fact, Jesus, this woman, who once had seven of Satan's demons inside her body, was the first human being to see that the tomb was now prepared for Jesus to rise and walk through! Hallelujah, hallelujah, hallelujah! And it is Mary Magdalene who ran to tell the Disciples that stone had been removed from Jesus's tomb! Glory to God! Our Word moves forward, saying that after the Disciples saw that Jesus was no longer in the tomb, they left, but Mary Magdalene stayed at the tomb of Jesus, and looked in the tomb of Jesus, **"Jesus asked her (Mary), 'Woman, why are you crying? Who is it you are looking for?' Thinking that He was the gardener, Mary said (to Jesus), 'Sir, if you have carried Him away, tell me where you have put Him, and I will get Him.' Jesus said to her, 'Mary.' She turned toward Him and cried out, 'Rabboni!' (Teacher).'"** Jesus came to Mary, not only because she sought Him, but she also loved Him enough to serve Him! Amen again! Mary loved Jesus, because Jesus healed her! Hallelujah! Mary Magdalene was saved by Jesus, and loved Jesus! And that is who Jesus is looking for, to do great things! Jesus is not looking for those who proclaim to be righteous! Amen! Jesus will come to you, if you truly love Him! For Jesus has the plan to utilize you! Mary Magdalene had been sick, and Jesus healed her, and she loved Him for that! And although Mary did not recognize Jesus at first, when she heard His voice, she knew it was her Master! You were sick in sin, and Jesus found you, and healed you! Amen again! Jesus is looking for you! For Jesus came to this earth to heal the sick in sin, and to give everlasting "health" from God! Glory Hallelujah! Now Jesus is speaking to you, because He has a special plan for you! But are you hearing His voice? Just like He had a special plan for Mary! But you have to hear His voice! Jesus wants you to tell someone, "I have seen the Lord!" Glory to God! Amen.

Today, the Word of God is speaking to all people. Jesus came to this earth from Heaven, to heal and save sinners! Amen! For all people are sinners! Amen again! And no one is forgiven of their sins, until they come to Jesus and repent, and ask Jesus to save them! Hallelujah! Jesus's mission was to seek those who did not know the righteousness of God, and to show them God's plan for their salvation. Amen again! And Jesus often will utilize the most sinful people to show His love to, and for others to see these reformed sinners serving Jesus. Hallelujah again! Mary Magdalene had been sick in sin. Jesus had to remove seven demons from her before she could follow Him! Yet it was Mary Magdalene who Jesus allowed to see that the stone that locked down His tomb, had been removed! Hallelujah! And it is Mary Magdalene who ran to tell the Disciples that stone had been removed from Jesus's tomb! Glory to God! Amen! Jesus kept Mary Magdalene at the tomb, because Jesus had a plan to utilize her! This redeemed "sinful" woman in the eyes of many people, a woman that had seven of Satan's demons inside of her! This woman stayed at the tomb of Jesus, weeping! Because she loved her Lord! Amen again! And the Word of God proclaims, **"Jesus**

said, 'Do not hold on to Me, for I have not yet ascended to the Father. Go instead to My brothers and tell them, I am ascending to My Father and your Father, to My God and your God.' Mary Magdalene went to the Disciples with the news: 'I have seen the Lord! And she told them that He had said these things to her." Jesus will always be with those who love Him, no matter how much you have sinned! Hallelujah! And Jesus wants to utilize you, to serve Him, and send others to Him. Glory Hallelujah! For Jesus came to this earth to heal the sick in sin, and to give everlasting "health" from God! Glory Hallelujah! Now Jesus is speaking to you, because He has a special plan for you! Just like He had a special plan for Mary! Jesus does not care how much you have sinned, because your sins are forgiven! Jesus wants to utilize the "redeemed" you! Jesus wants you to tell someone, "I have seen the Lord!" Glory to God! Amen.

Today, our Scripture Guidance is for all people. Jesus came to this earth from Heaven, to heal and save sinners! Amen! For all people are sinners! Amen again! Jesus came to this earth seeking you! Amen again! And Jesus will use the "most unworthy" sinner, who He heals, to serve Him, and send others to Him. Glory Hallelujah! Jesus is speaking to you! Hallelujah! Jesus is revealing Himself to you just like He did to Mary Magdalene! Jesus is speaking to you just like He spoke to Mary!! Amen! Jesus is calling on you to serve Him, but you can't believe He would use you because of your sinful past. Well, all of Jesus's servants have sinful pasts! Tell the truth! Jesus came to Mary, not only because she sought Him, but she also loved Him enough to serve Him! Amen again! Mary loved Jesus, because Jesus healed her! Hallelujah! Jesus will always be with those who love Him, no matter how much you have sinned! Hallelujah! And that is the truth! Trust Him! But glory to God, you have admitted you were sick in sin, and Jesus, your Doctor, has healed you! Jesus chose Mary to see Him risen and in His glorious body, not His Disciples! Now Jesus is speaking to you, because He has a special plan for you! Just like He had a special plan for Mary! Jesus does not care how much you have sinned, because your sins are forgiven! Jesus wants to utilize the "redeemed" you! Jesus wants you to tell someone, "I have seen the Lord!" Glory to God! Amen.

Day 231

"Be wise (servants of Jesus) in the way you act toward outsiders (those who do not know Jesus), make the most of every opportunity (that God gives you).

Let your conversations be always full of grace (humble), seasoned with salt (wisdom of the Word of God), so that you may know how to answer everyone."

(Colossians 4:5-6)

In today's Scripture, the Apostle Paul is giving instructions for Christian living. Amen! For once you accept Jesus, God has expectations for His children. If you have truly accepted Jesus as your Lord and Savior, you can tell someone who does not know Jesus, about the good news of Jesus! Amen again! Yet, there is a way that God wants you to treat those who do not know Jesus, when God gives you the opportunity to do so. That is right; God will give you opportunities to speak to Non-Believers about Jesus! Hallelujah! And this opportunity could be the only chance, or the last chance, for this person to gain an understanding about Jesus, and God's plan for salvation! Glory Hallelujah! That is why the Word of God gives instructions to us. Each Believer must understand that there will be opportunities that God will give you to teach, or help, someone, to understand that Jesus is available to save them from eternal damnation! Amen! You must understand that if you are a Believer, the moment you accepted Jesus, you became available to serve Him! Amen again! And God will give you opportunities to do so! Hallelujah, glory to God! Our Scripture begins with instructions to each person that speaks about Jesus to anyone that has not yet accepted Jesus, say that you should, **"Be wise (servants of Jesus) in the way you act toward outsiders (those who do not know Jesus), make the most of every opportunity (that God gives you)."** Non-Believers will watch how you act, before they will ever trust what you say about Jesus! And it is God that placed you in front of that Non-Believer! God is giving you an opportunity! Amen! Our Word continues with instructions on how to speak to Non-Believers, telling Believers, **"Let your conversations be always full of grace (humble), seasoned with salt (wisdom of the Word of God),"** When you have the opportunity to serve Jesus, you must be humble! And you must speak with what you know about Jesus through the Word of God! So be prepared; study the Word of God! Amen again! And finally, the Word of God tells us why this is important as you speak to the Non-Believer, **"so that you may know how to answer everyone."** If you are humble and speak with knowledge and wisdom about Jesus and the Word of God, you can do that with anyone, and everyone! Hallelujah! Amen.

Today, our Scripture is speaking to all Believers. You will get an opportunity from God to serve Jesus. Amen! For once you accept Jesus, God has expectations for His children. If you have truly accepted Jesus as your Lord and Savior, you can tell someone who does not know Jesus, about the good news of Jesus! Amen again! Yet, there is a way that God wants you to treat those who do not know Jesus, when God gives you the opportunity to do so. That is why the Word of God gives instructions to us. Each Believer must understand that there will be opportunities that God will give you to teach, or help, someone, to understand that Jesus is available to save them from eternal damnation! Amen! You must understand that if you are a Believer, the moment you accepted Jesus, you became available to serve Him! Amen again! And God will give you opportunities to do so! Hallelujah, glory to God! Our Scripture begins with instructions to each person that speaks about Jesus to anyone that has not yet accepted Jesus, say that you should, **"Be wise (servants of Jesus) in the way you act toward outsiders (those who do not know Jesus), make the most of every opportunity (that God gives you)."** Non-Believers will watch how you act, before they will ever trust what you say about Jesus! And it is God that placed you in front of that Non-Believer! God is giving you an opportunity! Amen! So focus on living your life in a way that others see Jesus in you. For it is the Light of Jesus in you that may attract others to you, and/or as God gives you an opportunity to witness, the Non-Believer will see you as a person that is "different" from someone in the world that does not have the Light of Jesus in them. Hallelujah! For Non-Believers are watching you, and God will give you an opportunity to serve Jesus! Amen.

Today, our Word is speaking to all Believers. You will get an opportunity from God to serve Jesus. Amen! If you have truly accepted Jesus as your Lord and Savior, you can tell someone who does not know Jesus, about the good news of Jesus! Amen again! That is why the Word of God gives instructions to us. Each Believer must understand that there will be opportunities that God will give you to teach, or help, someone, to understand that Jesus is available to save them from eternal damnation! Amen! You will have a role in growing the Kingdom of God and sharing with someone the love of Jesus! Amen again! And God will give you opportunities to do so! Hallelujah, glory to God! However, before you have the opportunity to speak to a Non-Believer, you must understand, that Non-Believers will watch how you act, before they will ever trust what you say about Jesus! And it is God that placed you in front of that Non-Believer! God is giving you an opportunity! So be wise in how you act toward them! Amen! Our Word continues with instructions on how to speak to Non-Believers, telling Believers, **"Let your conversations be always full of grace (humble), seasoned with salt (wisdom of the Word of God),"** When you have the opportunity to serve Jesus, you must be humble! And you must speak with what you know about Jesus through the Word of God! So be prepared, study the Word of God! Amen again! It is so important that Believers read and study the Word of God. God does not require you to be a Bible scholar. However, He wants you to be in His Word to equip yourself to serve Jesus! In fact, (which truly means in the Word of God), in **2 Timothy 3:16-17** states this truth, "All Scripture is given by the inspiration of God, and is useful for teaching, rebuking, correcting and training in righteousness, so that the servant of God may be well equipped for every good work." Amen! The Word of God will well equip you! And our instructions tell us to be humble and let our conversations by full of salt, the Word of God! So that Non-Believers will listen to you, when God gives you an opportunity to serve Jesus! Amen.

Today, the Word of God is speaking to all Believers. The Word of God is speaking to you! Hallelujah! You will get an opportunity from God to serve Jesus. Amen! You will have an opportunity to tell someone who does not know Jesus, about the good news of Jesus! Amen again! That is why the Word of God gives instructions to us. Each Believer must understand that there will be opportunities that God will give you to teach, or help, someone, to understand that Jesus is available to save them from eternal damnation! Amen! You will have a role in growing the Kingdom of God and sharing with someone the love of Jesus! Amen again! Almighty God will give you opportunities to do so! Hallelujah, glory to God! However, before you have the opportunity to speak to a Non-Believer, you must understand, that Non-Believers will watch how you act, before they will ever trust what you say about Jesus! And it is God that placed you in front of that Non-Believer! God is giving you an opportunity! So be wise in how you act toward them! Amen! And when you have the opportunity to serve Jesus, you must be humble! And you must speak with what you know about Jesus through the Word of God! So be prepared, study the Word of God! Amen again! And finally, the Word of God tells us why this is important as you speak to the Non-Believer, **"so that you may know how to answer everyone."** If you are humble and speak with knowledge and wisdom about Jesus and the Word of God, you can do that with anyone, and everyone! Hallelujah! When God gives you an opportunity to speak about Jesus to a Non-Believer, that Non-Believer may ask you many questions. And each Non-Believer may ask different questions! A Non-Believer may start out just to challenge your belief in Jesus. Amen! That is why our instruction tells you to be prepared, so that you can speak the Word of God, and answer the questions that will come to you! Amen again! For each opportunity God gives you to serve Jesus, and speak to a Non-Believer, will be different each time! And our instructions are to be prepared, each time so that you will know how to answer every one, when God gives you an opportunity to serve Jesus! Amen.

Today, our Scripture Guidance is for each Believer. Our Scripture Guidance is for you! For you will get an opportunity from God to serve Jesus! Amen! It will happen, because God had already designed it, before you even accepted Jesus! Amen again! That is why God put gifts inside of you, when He created you! Hallelujah! And you will have an opportunity to tell someone who does not know Jesus, about the good news of Jesus! Amen! You will have a role in growing the Kingdom of God! Amen again! Almighty God will give you opportunities to do so! Hallelujah, glory to God! However, before you have the opportunity to speak to a Non-Believer, you must understand, that Non-Believers will watch how you act, before they will ever trust what you say about Jesus! And it is God that placed you in front of that Non-Believer! God is giving you an opportunity! So be wise in how you act toward them! Amen! And when you have the opportunity to serve Jesus, you must be humble! And you must speak with what you know about Jesus through the Word of God! So be prepared, study the Word of God! Amen again! If you are humble and speak with knowledge and wisdom about Jesus and the Word of God, you can do that with anyone, and everyone! Hallelujah! And your instructions are to be prepared, each time so that you will do the Will of God, when God gives you an opportunity to serve Jesus! Amen.

Day 232

"See to it brothers and sisters (Believers), that none of you has a sinful, unbelieving heart that turns away from the living God.

But encourage one another daily, as long as it is called "Today", so that none of you may be hardened by sin's deceitfulness.

We (all Believers in Jesus Christ) have come to share in Christ, if indeed we hold our original conviction firmly to the very end (of our human life)."

(Hebrews 3:12-14)

In today's Scripture, the author, possibly Apollos or Barnabas, has written to Believers to warn us about allowing the sinful world to change our belief in Jesus, to unbelief. Amen! For the evil in the world who work (unknowingly, or knowingly) for Satan, will try to question your faith, and utilize sinful desires to change you! Amen again! And it is not enough to have accepted Jesus at some point in your life, if you do not believe in Jesus at the end of your life. Tell the truth! This warning is not about sin, it is about sin overwhelming you to the point that you no longer believe in Jesus! We must remember that Satan is here to steal your faith in Jesus, so that you will be dead in sin, and will not have eternal life with God! And that is the truth! So all Believers are being warned today! Hallelujah! Our Scripture begins with, **"See to it, brothers and sisters (Believers), that none of you has a sinful,**

unbelieving heart that turns away from the living God." Satan utilizes sin to lure you away from your faith! Amen! Our Word tells each Believer to not only be careful against an unbelieving heart, the Word tells us, **"But encourage one another daily, as long as it is called "Today", so that none of you may be hardened by sin's deceitfulness."** Each of us has a responsibility to each other, each and every day! To help each of us from becoming hardened to Jesus by sin! Amen again! And finally, the Word of God says to each Believer, **"We (all Believers in Jesus Christ) have come to share in Christ, if indeed we hold our original conviction firmly to the very end (of our human life)."** As a Believer, if we hold onto our faith to the end of our life, we will share with Jesus all the benefits of being God's eternal child! Glory! But to receive eternal benefits from God, you must believe in Jesus through the end of your life! So do not be misled by sin to a state of unbelief in Jesus! Encourage yourself, and encourage others each day, to keep their faith in Jesus! For God has a Will that shares all His gifts with you and Jesus, for eternity! Glory to God! Amen.

Today, our Scripture is speaking to Believers! You must continue to hold your faith to the end of your human life, to reap the eternal gifts that God has for you! Glory! Yet, you are being warned about allowing the sinful world to change your belief in Jesus, to unbelief. Amen! For the evil in the world who work (unknowingly, or knowingly) for Satan, will try to question your faith, and utilize sinful desires to change you! Amen again! This warning is not about sin, it is about sin overwhelming you to the point that you no longer believe in Jesus! Satan is here to steal your faith in Jesus, so that you will be dead in sin, and will not have eternal life with God! And that is the truth! His demons are all around you! So all Believers are being warned today! Hallelujah! Our Scripture begins with, **"See to it brothers ad sisters (Believers), that none of you has a sinful, unbelieving heart that turns away from the living God."** Satan utilizes sin to lure you away from your faith! Amen! Stay in prayer daily and constantly, to receive strength from God! That is how you see to it that you do not have an unbelieving heart! Stay in the Word, so that you may receive guidance from the Holy Spirit! That is how you see to it that you do not have an unbelieving heart!! So do not be misled by sin to a state of unbelief in Jesus! Encourage yourself, and encourage others each day, to keep their faith in Jesus! For God has a Will that shares all His gifts with you and Jesus, for eternity! Glory to God! Amen.

Today, our Word is speaking to Believers! You must continue to hold your faith to the end of your human life, to reap the eternal gifts that God has for you! Glory! You are being warned about allowing the sinful world to change your belief in Jesus, to unbelief. Amen! For the evil in the world will try to question your faith, and utilize sinful desires to change you! Amen again! This warning is not about sin; it is about sin overwhelming you to the point that you no longer believe in Jesus! Satan is here to steal your faith in Jesus, so that you will be dead in sin, and will not have eternal life with God! And that is the truth! His demons are all around you! That is why it is important to stay in prayer, and stay in the Word, so that you may receive guidance from the Holy Spirit, and strength through prayer! Hallelujah! All Believers are being warned today! Satan utilizes sin to lure you away from your faith! Amen! Our Word tells each Believer to not only be careful against an unbelieving heart, the Word tells us, **"But encourage one another daily, as long as it is called "Today", so that none of you may be hardened by sin's deceitfulness."** Each of us has a responsibility to each other, each and every day! To help each of us from becoming hardened to Jesus by sin! Amen again! That is why fellowship with other Believers is so important, so that you may be encouraged, and can encourage others! That is why Bible teaching classes are so important! That is why singing songs of praise to Jesus, and to our Father God, is so important! So that you may be encouraged! Glory Hallelujah! So do not be misled by sin to a state of unbelief in Jesus! Encourage yourself, and encourage others each day, to keep their faith in Jesus! For God has a Will that shares all His gifts with you and Jesus, for eternity! Glory to God! Amen.

Today, the Word of God is speaking to Believers! The Word of God is speaking to you! You must continue to hold your faith to the end of your human life, to reap the eternal gifts that God has for you! Glory! You are being warned about allowing the sinful world to change your belief in Jesus, to unbelief. Amen! For the evil in the world will utilize sinful desires to change you! Amen again! This warning is not about sin, for each of us will continue to sin, because our flesh desires it! However, it is about sin overwhelming you to the point that you no longer believe in Jesus! Satan is here to steal your faith in Jesus, so that you will not have eternal life with God! Satan wants you in Hell with him! And that is the truth! His demons are all around you! That is why it is important to stay in prayer, and stay in the Word, so that you may receive guidance from the Holy Spirit, and strength through prayer! Hallelujah! All Believers are being warned today! Satan utilizes sin to lure you away from your faith! Amen! And each of us also has a responsibility to each other, each and every day! To help each of us from becoming hardened to Jesus by sin! Amen again! That is why fellowship with other Believers is so important, so that you may be encouraged, and can encourage others! And finally, the Word of God says to each Believer, **"We (all Believers in Jesus Christ) have come to share in Christ, if indeed we hold our original conviction firmly to the very end (of our human life)."** As a Believer, if we hold onto our faith to the end of our life, we will share with Jesus all the benefits of being God's eternal child! Glory! Unfortunately, there are many who have accepted Jesus, but because of life, and the overwhelming dependence on sin, they have become non-Believers! They have now rejected Christ, but still may believe that they are safe because they once accepted Jesus. But they are wrong! Satan is a liar! For to receive eternal benefits from God, you must believe in Jesus through the end of your life! So do not be misled by sin to a state of unbelief in Jesus! Hold on to your faith to the end of your human life! Encourage yourself, and encourage others each day, to keep their faith in Jesus! For God has a Will that shares all His gifts with you and Jesus, for eternity! Glory to God! Amen.

Today, our Scripture Guidance is for Believers! Our Scripture Guidance is speaking to you! You must continue to hold your faith to the end of your human life, to reap the eternal gifts that God has for you! Glory! You are being warned about allowing the sinful world to change your belief in Jesus, to unbelief. Amen! So do not be misled by sin to a state of unbelief in Jesus! Hold on to your faith to the end of your human life! Encourage yourself, and encourage others each day, to keep their faith in Jesus! For God has a Will that shares all His gifts with you and Jesus, for eternity! Glory to God! Amen.

Day 233

"The people walking in darkness have seen a great light, on those living in the land of darkness (in the shadow of death), upon them a light has shined."

"For to us a child is born, to us a Son is given, and the government (people) will be on His shoulders. And He will be called Wonderful Counselor, Might God, Everlasting Father, Prince of Peace.

Of the greatness of His government (Kingdom) and peace, there will be no end. He will reign on David's throne and over his kingdom, establishing and upholding it with justice and righteousness from that time on and forever. The zeal (love) of the Lord (God) Almighty will accomplish this."

(Isaiah 9:2 & 6-7)

In today's Scripture, the great servant of, the prophet Isaiah, gives the prophecy of God that darkness (despair/death) will turn to light (light/living). Amen! God wanted His people to know that no matter how bad it can be on earth, He would bring them a Ruler that would bring them out of the darkness of death, and that Ruler would be a Son! Amen again! This Ruler will bring peace forever to His Kingdom. Hallelujah! And this will be accomplished because God loves His people! Glory Hallelujah, glory to God! Of course, we know today that the Ruler that God spoke about through Isaiah, is Jesus! And that the Son that God spoke about through Isaiah, is His Son! Amen! Jesus is that great Light that will rule God's Kingdom and bring everlasting peace to God's people. Amen again! God gave this prophecy to Isaiah 700 years before the human birth of Jesus. And the Light of Jesus is still bringing people out of the darkness of eternal death, over 2,000 years later! Glory! Our Scripture begins with, **"The people walking in darkness have seen a great light, on those living in the land of darkness (in the shadow of death), upon them a light has shined."** God has sent a Light to shine on people to lead them out of the darkness! Amen! Our Word continues with a promise from God, saying... **"For to us a child is born, to us a Son is given, and the government (people) will be on His shoulders. And He will be called Wonderful Counselor, Mighty God, Everlasting Father, Prince of Peace."** God gives us His Son! He shall put us on His shoulders! He will guide us with the wonderful plan of God, our everlasting Father, and He will bring us salvation and peace from God! Amen again! And the Word of God proclaims to us that this truth about our Light, **"Of the greatness of His government (Kingdom) and peace, there will be no end. He will reign on David's throne and over his kingdom, establishing and upholding it with justice and righteousness from that time on and forever. The zeal (love) of the Lord (God) Almighty will accomplish this."** There will be no end to the peace of His Kingdom, and He will reign with the righteousness of God! And God is giving us this gift of a Savior, because He loves us! Hallelujah! God gave us this Light, His Son, because He loves us! Glory Hallelujah! Glory to God! Amen.

Today, our Scripture is speaking to God's people. For God's people have been given a great Light! God gave us this great Light, so that we could be saved from the darkness of the sin that each and every one of us have walked in! Amen! God gave us a great Light, and upon each Believer, that Light has shined! Amen again! And that great Light is God's Son! Hallelujah! That great Light is Jesus! Glory Hallelujah! God gave us His Son, our Great Light and Savior Jesus, because God loves us! Glory to God! The prophet Isaiah, gives the prophecy of God that darkness (despair/death) will turn to light (light/living). Amen! God wanted His people to know that no matter how bad it can be on earth, He would bring them a Ruler that would bring them out of the darkness of death, and that Ruler would be a Son! Amen again! This Ruler will bring peace forever to His Kingdom. Hallelujah! And this will be accomplished because God loves His people! Glory Hallelujah, glory to God! Of course, we know today that the Ruler that God spoke about through Isaiah, is Jesus! And that the Son that God spoke about through Isaiah, is His Son! Amen! Jesus is that great Light that will rule God's Kingdom and bring everlasting peace to God's people. Amen again! God gave this prophecy to Isaiah 700 years before the human birth of Jesus. And the Light of Jesus is still bringing people out of the darkness of eternal death, over 2,000 years later! Glory! Our Scripture begins with, **"The people walking in darkness have seen a great light,**

on those living in the land of darkness (in the shadow of death), upon them a light has shined." God has sent a Light to shine on people to lead them out of the darkness! Amen! We need to understand, and we need to tell others that without the Light of Jesus, our walk in sinful darkness will lead to eternal damnation! We have all sinned, and our sin is punishable by death, and we cannot escape on our own! That is the truth! But hallelujah... God has sent us a great Light that can save us! And God is giving us this gift of a Savior, because He loves us! Hallelujah! God gave us this Light, His Son, because He loves us! Glory Hallelujah! Glory to God! Amen.

Today, our Word is speaking to God's people. For God's people have been given a great Light! God gave us this great Light, so that we could be saved from the darkness of the sin that each and every one of us have walked in! Amen! God gave us a great Light, and upon each Believer, that Light has shined! Amen again! And that great Light is God's Son! Hallelujah! That great Light is Jesus! Glory Hallelujah! God gave us His Son, our Great Light and Savior Jesus, because God loves us! Glory to God! Isaiah spoke the prophecy of God that darkness (despair/death) will turn to light (light/living). Amen! God wanted His people to know that He would bring them a Ruler that would bring them out of the darkness of death, and that Ruler would be a Son! Amen again! This Ruler will bring peace forever to His Kingdom. Hallelujah! And this will be accomplished because God loves His people! Glory Hallelujah, glory to God! And that the Son that God spoke about through Isaiah, is His Son! Amen! Jesus is that great Light that will rule God's Kingdom and bring everlasting peace to God's people. Amen again! And the Light of Jesus is still bringing people out of the darkness of eternal death! Glory! God has sent a Light to shine on people to lead them out of the darkness! Amen! Our Word continues with a promise from God, saying... **"For to us a child is born, to us a Son is given, and the government (people) will be on His shoulders. And He will be called Wonderful Counselor, Mighty God, Everlasting Father, Prince of Peace."** God gives us His Son! He shall put us on His shoulders! He will guide us with the wonderful plan of God, our everlasting Father, and He will bring us salvation and peace from God! Amen again! God sent us His own Son, Jesus! Jesus will put our sins on His shoulders, for He paid the "perfect blood" price for our sins! That is the truth! And God is giving us this gift of a Savior, because He loves us! Hallelujah! God gave us this Light, His Son, because He loves us! Glory Hallelujah! Glory to God! Amen.

Today, the Word of God is speaking to God's people. The Word of God is speaking to you! For you have been given a great Light! God gave you this great Light, so that you could be saved from the darkness of the sin that you have walked in! Amen! If you believe in Jesus as your Lord and Savior, that great Light has shined on you! Amen again! That great Light is Jesus! Glory Hallelujah! God gave us His Son, our Great Light and Savior Jesus, because God loves us! And God sent you to Jesus to accept Him, because God loves you! Glory to God! Isaiah spoke the prophecy of God that darkness (despair/death) will turn to light (light/living). Amen! For God wanted His people to know that He would bring them a Ruler that would bring them out of the darkness of death, and that Ruler would be a Son! Amen again! And that Son that God spoke about through Isaiah, is His Son! Amen! Jesus is that great Light that will rule God's Kingdom and bring everlasting peace to God's people. Amen again! And the Light of Jesus is still bringing people out of the darkness of eternal death! Glory! God has sent a Light to shine on people to lead them out of the darkness! Amen! God gives us His Son! He shall put us on His shoulders! He will guide us with the wonderful plan of God, our everlasting Father, and He will bring us salvation and peace from God! Amen again! And the Word of God proclaims to us that this truth about our Light, **"Of the greatness of His government (Kingdom) and peace, there will be no end. He will reign on David's throne and over his kingdom, establishing and upholding it with justice and righteousness from that time on and forever. The zeal (love) of the Lord (God) Almighty will accomplish this."** There will be no end to the peace of His Kingdom, and He will reign with the righteousness of God! And God is giving us this gift of a Savior, because He loves us! Hallelujah! God gave us this Light, His Son, because He loves us! Glory Hallelujah! Glory to God! Amen.

Today, the great Light that God sent to save us, and rule over us in His Kingdom with peace forever, is still available to give peace. Amen! That great Light is Jesus! God sent a Light that will bring sinners out of the darkness of death, and that Ruler is God's own Son! Amen again! And that Son is Jesus! Amen! Jesus is that great Light that will rule God's Kingdom and bring everlasting peace to God's people. Amen again! And the Light of Jesus is still bringing people out of the darkness of eternal death! Glory! God gave us His Son! And His Son, Jesus, has put us on His shoulders! Only Jesus can guide sinners to the wonderful plan of God, our everlasting Father, and He will bring us salvation and peace from God! Amen again! And just like Isaiah did, you and I need to tell people about Jesus! The only Way out of the darkness of sin to everlasting peace, is the light that only Jesus can provide! And there will be no end to the peace of His Kingdom, and He will rein His Kingdom with the righteousness of God! And God gave us this gift of a Savior, because He loves us! Hallelujah! God gave us this Light, His Son, because He loves us! Glory Hallelujah! Glory to God! Amen.

Day 234

"Dear friends, although I was very eager to write to you about the salvation we share, I felt compelled to write and urge you to contend for the faith that was once for all entrusted to God's holy people.

For certain individuals, whose condemnation was written about long ago, have secretly slipped in among you. They are ungodly people, who pervert the grace of our God into a license for immorality and deny Jesus Christ our only Sovereign and Lord."

"But you, dear friends, by building yourselves up in your most holy faith and praying in the Holy Spirit,
keep yourselves in God's love as you wait for the mercy of our Lord Jesus Christ to bring you to eternal life."

(Jude:3-4 & 20-21)

In today's Scripture, the great servant of Jesus, Jude (who was most likely Jesus's brother), is warning Believers about false teachers in our midst, that try to convince Believers that once they are saved by the grace of God, they have a license to sin. Amen! These false teachers want Believers to think that since they were saved, their continuing sins would no longer receive punishment. Well, just like Satan, these false teachers are liars! Amen again! It is true that the blood of Jesus will keep true Believers from eternal damnation for their sins. Hallelujah! However, Believers must repent to God and ask for His forgiveness in the name of Jesus as they continue to sin. Glory Hallelujah! And continued sin by Believers, will be punished on this earth, based on the righteous judgment of God! Glory to God! For even though a Believer is saved by Jesus, God still hates sin, and wants each Believer to live as closely to His righteousness as each of us can. Amen! So we must beware of false teachers, and some may even be leading your church, or family, that teach that it is acceptable to sin constantly without fear of God's punishment. For that is not God's Will for you! Amen again! Our Scripture begins with the servant of Jesus saying to Believers, **"Dear friends, although I was very eager to write to you about the salvation we share, I felt compelled to write and urge you to contend for the faith that was once for all entrusted to God's holy people."** The servant of Jesus may only want to talk about salvation, but when the Holy Spirit compels you to challenge Believers, that servant must challenge Believers! Amen! Our Word continues with the servant of Jesus warning us, **"For certain individuals whose condemnation was written about long ago, have secretly slipped in among you. They are ungodly people, who pervert the grace of our God into a license for immorality and deny Jesus Christ our only Sovereign and Lord."** The Holy Spirit is warning us about false teachers who are around us, leading us down an unrighteous path! They may look like servants of Jesus, but they are ungodly soldiers of Satan! Amen again! And the Word of God gives us guidance that will keep us from being influenced by false teachers, saying to Believers, **"But you, dear friends, by building yourselves up in your most holy faith and praying in the Holy Spirit, keep yourselves in God's love as you wait for the mercy of our Lord Jesus Christ to bring you to eternal life."** Keep strengthening your faith through prayer in the Spirit, and by reading and studying the Word of God! This will protect you from Satan and his false teachers, for God will keep you in His love as you wait for the return of Jesus, to take you to the Kingdom of God! Glory! Not every person in the church who speaks as if they are servants of Jesus Christ, speaks the truth of the Word of God! There are false teachers around you, who want you to commit to sin, instead of committing to the Will of God! Don't be fooled, for Satan is a liar! Stay in prayer and know the Word of God, and God will keep you on this earth in His love, until Jesus returns to take you to your glory in Heaven with God! Amen.

Today, our Scripture is speaking to Believers. Jude is warning Believers about false teachers in our midst, that try to convince Believers that once they are saved by the grace of God, they have a license to sin. Amen! These false teachers want Believers to think that their continuing sins will no longer receive punishment. These false teachers are liars! Amen again! Believers must repent to God and ask for His forgiveness in the name of Jesus as they continue to sin. Glory Hallelujah! And continued sin by Believers, will be punished on this earth, based on the righteous judgment of God! Glory to God! God still hates sin, and wants each Believer to live as closely to His righteousness as each of us can. For when a Believer chooses to sin, that Believer has chosen sin over the righteousness of God's Will for us! Amen! So we must beware of false teachers that teach that it is acceptable to sin constantly without fear of God's punishment. For that is not God's Will for you! And God will punish His children for constant sin! Amen again! Our Scripture begins with the servant of Jesus saying to Believers, **"Dear friends, although I was very eager to write to you about the salvation we share, I felt compelled to write and urge you to contend for the faith that was once for all entrusted to God's holy people."** The servant of Jesus may only want to talk about salvation, but when the Holy Spirit compels you to challenge Believers, that servant must challenge Believers! Amen! Jude wanted to write a letter to Believers about salvation, but the Holy Spirit told him to speak about false teachers, to warn Believers about their lies! Today, we are being warned! Not every person in the church who speaks as if they are servants of Jesus Christ, speaks the truth of the Word of God! There are false teachers around you, who want you to commit to sin, instead of committing to the Will of God! Don't be fooled, for Satan is a liar! Stay in prayer and know the Word of God, and God will keep you on this earth in His love, until Jesus returns to take you to your glory in Heaven with God! Amen.

Today, our Word is speaking to Believers. There are false teachers in our midst, that try to convince us that once you are saved by the grace of God through repentance and acceptance of Jesus, you have a license to sin. Amen! These false teachers want

Believers to think that their continuing sins will no longer receive punishment. These false teachers are liars! Amen again! Believers must repent to God and ask for His forgiveness in the name of Jesus as they continue to sin, and continued sin by Believers will be punished on this earth, based on the righteous judgment of God! Glory to God! God wants each Believer to live as closely to His righteousness as he can. And when we can't, God wants us to seek forgiveness from Him in the name of Jesus. For when a Believer chooses to sin, that Believer has chosen sin over the righteousness of God's Will for us! Amen! So we must beware of false teachers that teach that it is acceptable to sin constantly without fear of God's punishment. For that is not God's Will for you! And God will punish His children for constant sin! Amen again! And even though the servant of Jesus may only want to talk about salvation, when the Holy Spirit compels you to challenge Believers, that servant must challenge Believers! Amen! Our Word continues with the servant of Jesus warning us, **"For certain individuals whose condemnation was written about long ago, have secretly slipped in among you. They are ungodly people, who pervert the grace of our God into a license for immorality and deny Jesus Christ, our only Sovereign and Lord."** The Holy Spirit is warning us about false teachers who are around us, leading us down an unrighteous path! They may look like servants of Jesus, but they are ungodly soldiers of Satan! Amen again! These false teachers are slick, and sound like they know the Word of God, but by their very actions and guidance, they deny Jesus as their Lord and Savior! And God has already condemned them! But you have to understand, they have slipped in with you, and they are out to change your faith in Jesus so that you give away the eternal grace that God has given you. Amen! Today, we are being warned! Not every person in the church who speaks as if they are servants of Jesus Christ, speaks the truth of the Word of God! There are false teachers around you, who want you to commit to sin, instead of committing to the Will of God! Don't be fooled, for Satan is a liar! Stay in prayer and know the Word of God, and God will keep you on this earth in His love, until Jesus returns to take you to your glory in Heaven with God! Amen.

Today, the Word of God is speaking to you. There are false teachers in your midst, that want to convince you that once you are saved by the grace of God through repentance and acceptance of Jesus, you have a license to sin. Amen! These false teachers want you to think that your continuing sins will no longer receive punishment. These false teachers are liars! Amen again! You must repent to God and ask for His forgiveness in the name of Jesus as you continue to sin, for continued sin by Believers will be punished on this earth, based on the righteous judgment of God! Glory to God! Although knows you will continue to sin, because you are still in the flesh, and your flesh desires sin. Yet, God wants each Believer to live as closely to His righteousness as we can. And when you can't, God wants you to seek forgiveness from Him in the name of Jesus. You must understand that when you choose to sin, you have chosen sin over the righteousness of God's Will for us! Amen! So you must beware of false teachers that teach that it is alright to sin constantly without fear of God's punishment. For that is a lie! And God will punish His children for constant sin! Amen again! And even though the servant of Jesus may only want to talk about salvation, the Holy Spirit compels the servant of Jesus to challenge Believers; that servant must challenge Believers! Amen! And through the servant of Jesus, the Holy Spirit is warning you about false teachers who are around you, attempting to lead you down an unrighteous path! They may look like servants of Jesus, but they are ungodly soldiers of Satan! Amen again! And the Word of God gives us guidance that will keep us from being influenced by false teachers, saying to Believers, **"But you, dear friends, by building yourselves up in your most holy faith and praying in the Holy Spirit, keep yourselves in God's love as you wait for the mercy of our Lord Jesus Christ to bring you to eternal life."** Keep strengthening your faith through prayer in the Spirit, and by reading and studying the Word of God! This will protect you from Satan and his false teachers, for God will keep you in His love as you wait for the return of Jesus, to take you to the Kingdom of God! Glory! The Word of God gives you strength, and the Holy Spirit has been given to you by Jesus to be with you and help you. Amen! Today, we are being warned! Not every person in the church who speaks as if they are servants of Jesus Christ, speaks the truth of the Word of God! There are false teachers around you, who want you to commit to sin, instead of committing to the Will of God! Don't be fooled, for Satan is a liar! Stay in prayer and know the Word of God, and God will keep you on this earth in His love, until Jesus returns to take you to your glory in Heaven with God! Amen.

Today, our Scripture Guidance is for Believers. Not every person in the church who speaks as if they are servants of Jesus Christ, speaks the truth of the Word of God! There are false teachers around you, who want you to commit to sin, instead of committing to the Will of God! Do not be fooled by false teachers! God will punish His children for constant sin! So stay in prayer and know the Word of God, and God will keep you on this earth in His love, until Jesus returns to take you to your glory in Heaven with God! Amen.

Day 235

Jesus said to two of His disciples, "Go into the village opposite you, and as soon as you have entered it, you will find a colt tied, on which no one has sat. Loose it and bring it.

And if anyone says to you, 'Why are you doing this?" say, 'The Lord has need of it,' and immediate he will send it here."

So they went their way, and found the colt tied by the door outside on the street, and they loosed it.

But some of those who stood there said to them, "What are you doing, loosing the colt?"

And they spoke to them just as Jesus had commanded. So they let them go.

(Mark 11:2-6)

In today's Scripture, the great servant of Jesus, the author Mark, re-tells us of the time that Jesus told two of His Disciples (whose names are not mentioned in the Scriptures), to go to another town and serve Him. Amen! And these two servants of Jesus did not question Him, they just went! Amen again! Jesus gave them specific instructions, and these two servants of Jesus did not question Him, they just did what He told them to do! Hallelujah! And when people questioned what they were doing, they told them just what He told them to tell them! Glory Hallelujah! Jesus is speaking to someone today! Jesus is calling you to serve Him! Jesus is telling you to go! Jesus is telling you exactly what He wants you to do! And when people question you, just tell them what Jesus told you to tell them! Amen! These are the things that Jesus's servants must do. Serve Him! Go, do, and speak! That is what Jesus is calling you to do! Hallelujah! That is serving Jesus! Glory to God! So be obedient to Jesus! Glory Hallelujah! Our Scripture begins with Jesus speaking to His servants, **Jesus said to two of His disciples, "Go into the village opposite you, and as soon as you have entered it, you will find a colt tied, on which no one has sat. Lose it and bring it."** Jesus will call you to serve Him, be obedient and go! And Jesus will give you instructions! Amen! Our Word tells us, **Then Jesus said to His servants, "And if anyone says to you, 'Why are you doing this?' say, 'The Lord has need of it,' and immediate he will send it here."** Jesus will call you to serve Him, be obedient, and Jesus will tell you what to say! Amen again! **And the Word of God proclaims that Jesus's servants were obedient to Jesus, telling us, "So they went their way, and found the colt tied by the door outside on the street, and they loosed it. But some of those who stood there said to them, "What are you doing, losing the colt?" And they spoke to them just as Jesus had commanded. So they let them go.** Hallelujah! Jesus will call you to serve Him, be obedient and do what Jesus has told you to do, and say what Jesus has told you to say! Amen! And you will serve Jesus, and you will give glory to God! Glory Hallelujah! Jesus is speaking to someone today! Serve Him! Go, do, and speak! That is what Jesus is calling you to do! Amen.

Today, our Scripture is speaking to Believers. Jesus is calling you to serve Him. Amen! Jesus is speaking to you today! Amen again! Mark re-tells us of the time that Jesus told two of His Disciples (whose names are not mentioned in the Scriptures), to go to another town and serve Him. Amen! And these two servants of Jesus did not question Him; they just went! Amen again! Jesus gave them specific instructions, and these two servants of Jesus did not question Him, they just did what He told them to do! Hallelujah! And when people questioned what they were doing, they told them just what He told them to tell them! Glory Hallelujah! And today, Jesus is calling you to serve Him! Jesus is telling you to go! Jesus is telling you exactly what He wants you to do! And when people question you, just tell them what Jesus told you to tell them! Amen! These are the things that Jesus's servants must do. Go, do, and speak! That is what Jesus is calling you to do! Hallelujah! That is serving Jesus! Glory to God! So be obedient to Jesus! Glory Hallelujah! Our Scripture begins with Jesus speaking to His servants, **Jesus said to two of His disciples, "Go into the village opposite you, and as soon as you have entered it, you will find a colt tied, on which no one has sat. Lose it and bring it."** Jesus will call you to serve Him, be obedient and go! And Jesus will give you instructions! Amen! Serving Jesus starts with His commandment for you to go! Serving Jesus is active, and to start, you must go where Jesus tells you to go. You do not get to decide! You must accept that He is calling you, and go! You show commitment to Jesus, when you go! And Jesus will give you instructions! Hallelujah! Jesus is speaking to someone today! Jesus is calling you to serve Him! Will you be obedient to Jesus? These are the things that Jesus's servants must do. Serve Him! Go! That is what Jesus is calling you to do! Amen.

Today, our Word is speaking to Believers. Jesus is calling you to serve Him. Amen! Jesus is speaking to you today! Amen again! In our Word, Jesus told two of His Disciples (whose names are not mentioned in the Scriptures), to go to another town and serve Him. Amen! And these two servants of Jesus did not question Him; they just went! Amen again! Jesus gave them specific instructions, and these two servants of Jesus did not question Him; they just did what He told them to do! Hallelujah! And when people questioned what they were doing, they told them just what He told them to tell them! Glory Hallelujah! Today, Jesus is calling you to serve Him! Jesus is telling you to go! Jesus is telling you exactly what He wants you to do! And when people question you, just tell them what Jesus told you to tell them! Amen! These are the things that Jesus's servants must do. Go, do, and speak! That is what Jesus is calling you to do! Hallelujah! That is serving Jesus! Glory to God! So be obedient to Jesus! Glory Hallelujah! Jesus has called you to serve Him, be obedient and go! And Jesus will give you instructions! Amen! Our Word tells us, **Then Jesus said to His servants, "And if anyone says to you, 'Why are you doing this?' say, 'The Lord has need of it,' and immediate he will send it here."** Jesus will call you to serve Him, be obedient, and Jesus will tell you what to say! Amen again! When you accept the call to serve Him, Jesus will always tell you what to say! If you are truly serving Jesus, Jesus will be with you in Spirit! You will not be alone, and you do not have to figure out what to say! You will receive the guidance of Jesus, through the Holy Spirit in you! Hallelujah! Jesus is speaking to someone today! Jesus is calling you to serve Him! Will you be obedient to Jesus? These are the things that Jesus's servants must do. Serve Him! Go, and do! That is what Jesus is calling you to do! Amen.

Today, the Word of God is speaking to you. Jesus is calling you to serve Him. Amen! Jesus is speaking to you today! Amen again! Jesus told two of His Disciples to go to another town and serve Him. Amen! And these two servants of Jesus did not question Him, they just went! Amen again! Jesus gave them specific instructions, and these two servants of Jesus did not question Him, they just did what He told them to do! Hallelujah! And when people questioned what they were doing, they told them just what He told them to tell them! Glory Hallelujah! Today, Jesus is calling you to serve Him! Jesus is telling you to go! Jesus is telling you exactly what He wants you to do! And when people question you, just tell them what Jesus told you to tell them! Amen! These are the things that Jesus's servants must do. Go, do, and speak! That is what Jesus is calling you to do! Hallelujah! That is serving Jesus! Glory to God! So be obedient to Jesus! Glory Hallelujah! Jesus has called you to serve Him, be obedient and go! And Jesus will give you instructions! Amen! Jesus has called you to serve Him, be obedient, and Jesus will tell you what to say! Amen again! And the Word of God proclaims that Jesus's servants were obedient to Jesus, telling us, **"So they went**

their way, and found the colt tied by the door outside on the street, and they loosed it. But some of those who stood there said to them, "What are you doing, losing the colt?" And they spoke to them just as Jesus had commanded. So they let them go. Hallelujah! Jesus will call you to serve Him, be obedient and do what Jesus has told you to do, and say what Jesus has told you to say! Amen! And you will serve Jesus, and you will give glory to God! Glory Hallelujah! Jesus will tell you what to say, so just say it, and Jesus will take care of the rest! Amen! Just trust Jesus! Amen again! Jesus is speaking to someone today! Jesus is calling you to serve Him! Will you be obedient to Jesus? These are the things that Jesus's servants must do. Serve Him! Go, do, and speak! That is what Jesus is calling you to do! Amen.

Today, Jesus is calling you to serve Him. Amen! Jesus is speaking to you! Jesus is telling you to go! Jesus is telling you exactly what He wants you to do! And when people question you, just tell them what Jesus told you to tell them! Amen again! These are the things that Jesus's servants must do. Go, do, and speak! That is what Jesus is calling you to do! Hallelujah! That is serving Jesus! Glory to God! So be obedient to Jesus! Serve Jesus! Go, do, and speak! Amen!

Day 236

"Without weakening in his faith (in God), Abraham faced the fact that his body was as good as dead, since he was about 100 years old, and that Sarah's womb was also dead.

Yet Abraham did not waver through unbelief regarding the promise of God, but was strengthened in his faith, and gave glory to God (before the promise had been fulfilled),

being fully persuaded that God had the power to do what He had promised.

This is why it was credited to Abraham (by God) as righteousness."

(Romans 4:19-22)

In today's Scripture, the great servant of Jesus, the Apostle Paul, writes about Abraham, and how he was justified by God for his faith in God. Amen! For justification comes through faith in God. Amen again! And faith is belief that God can do what He says He will do, no matter how impossible it may seem to man. The Bible proclaims to all people... "And without faith, it is impossible to please God, because anyone who comes to him must believe that he exists and that he rewards those who earnestly seek him." **(Hebrews 11:6).** Paul utilizes Abraham as a great example of faith in God. Abraham was old, and his wife Sarah was old, and they had never had a child. Yet, God came to Abraham and told him that he would have a child with his wife. Hallelujah! Our Scripture begins with the servant of Jesus that, **"Without weakening in his faith (in God), Abraham faced the fact that his body was as good as dead, since he was about 100 years old, and that Sarah's womb was also dead."** God will make promises to His people that seem impossible, yet it is important that we keep our faith in what God says He will do! Never let the magnitude of the promise, weaken your faith in God! Amen! Our Word tells us that even though Abraham had never imagined at this point that his body, and Sarah's body, could conceive a child at this point in his life, **"Yet Abraham did not waver through unbelief regarding the promise of God, but was strengthened in his faith, and gave glory to God (before the promise had been fulfilled), being fully persuaded that God had the power to do what He had promised."** Faith is glorifying and praising God for what He has promised, even if you do not know how it could happen! Keep your faith, and show God that you know that He will do what He says He will do! For God, is Almighty God! If He said it, so know that He has the power to do it! Amen again! The Word of God proclaims that it was because of Abraham's faith in God, **"This is why it was credited to Abraham (by God) as righteousness."** You can only be credited righteousness from God, by having faith in the promises of God! Glory! And today, righteousness is credited to those that have faith in the promises of God, through Jesus, that God will forgive you and grant you everlasting life in His Kingdom! Glory Hallelujah! Now that is crediting you with righteousness! Amen.

Today, our Scripture is speaking to all people. You can only receive righteousness from God, by having faith in the promises of God. Amen! There is no other way that God will credit you with righteousness. Amen again! Paul writes about Abraham, and how he was justified by God for his faith in God. Amen! For justification comes through faith in God. Amen again! And faith is the belief that God can do what He says He will do, no matter how impossible it may seem to man. And Paul utilizes Abraham as a great example of faith in God. Abraham and his wife Sarah were old, and they had never had a child. And they were both now past the age when people can physically conceive a child. Abraham was nearly 100 years old! Sarah was 90 years old! Yet, God came to Abraham and told him that he would have a child with his wife. Hallelujah! Our Scripture begins with the servant of Jesus that, **"Without weakening in his faith (in God), Abraham faced the fact that his body was as good as dead, since he was about 100 years old, and that Sarah's womb was also dead."** God will make promises to His people that seem impossible, yet it is important that we keep our faith in what God says He will do! Never let the magnitude of the promise, weaken your faith in God! Amen! Today, righteousness is credited to those that have faith in the promises of God, through Jesus, that God will forgive you and grant you everlasting life in His Kingdom! Glory Hallelujah! Now that is crediting you with righteousness! Amen.

Today, our Scripture is speaking to all people. You can only receive righteousness from God, by having faith in the promises of God. Amen! There is no other way that God will credit you with righteousness. Amen again! Abraham was justified by God for his faith in God. Amen! For justification comes through faith in God. Amen again! And faith is the belief that God can do what He says He will do, no matter how impossible it may seem to man. Abraham and his wife Sarah were old, and they had never had a child. And they were both now past the age when people can physically conceive a child. Abraham was nearly 100 years old! Sarah was 90 years old! Just imagine a 100-year-old man, and a 90-year-old woman telling you that they were going to have their first child together! You would say it is impossible! Yet, God came to Abraham and told him that he would have a child with his wife. Hallelujah! God will make promises to His people that seem impossible, yet it is important that we keep our faith in what God says He will do! Never let the magnitude of the promise, weaken your faith in God! Amen! Our Word tells us that even though Abraham had never imagined at this point that his body, and Sarah's body, could conceive a child at this point in his life, **"Yet Abraham did not waver through unbelief regarding the promise of God, but was strengthened in his faith, and gave glory to God (before the promise had been fulfilled), being fully persuaded that God had the power to do what He had promised."** Faith is glorifying and praising God for what He has promised, even if you do not know how it could happen! Keep your faith, and show God that you know that He will do what He says He will do! For God, is Almighty God! If He said it, so know that He has the power to do it! Amen again! Today, righteousness is credited to those that have faith in the promises of God, through Jesus, that God will forgive you and grant you everlasting life in His Kingdom! Glory Hallelujah! Now that is crediting you with righteousness! Amen.

Today, the Word of God is speaking to you. You can only receive righteousness from God, by having faith in the promises of God. Amen! There is no other way that God will credit you with righteousness. Amen again! For justification comes through faith in God. Amen again! And faith is the belief that God can do what He says He will do, no matter how impossible it may seem to man. Just imagine a 100-year-old man, and a 90-year-old woman telling you that they were going to have their first child together! You would say it is impossible! Yet, God came to Abraham and told him that he would have a child with his wife. Hallelujah! God will make promises to His people that seem impossible, yet it is important that we keep our faith in what God says He will do! Never let the magnitude of the promise, weaken your faith in God! Amen! And faith is glorifying and praising God for what He has promised, even if you do not know how it could happen! Keep your faith, and show God that you know that He will do what He says He will do! For God, is Almighty God! If He said it, so know that He has the power to do it! Amen again! The Word of God proclaims that it was because of Abraham's faith in God, **"This is**

why it was credited to Abraham (by God) as righteousness."
You can only be credited righteousness from God, by having faith in the promises of God! Glory! And today, righteousness is credited to those that have faith in the promises of God, through Jesus, that God will forgive you and grant you everlasting life in His Kingdom! Glory Hallelujah! Now that is crediting you with righteousness! Amen.

Day 237

"Anyone who claims to be in the Light (of Jesus), but hates a brother or sister, is still in the darkness.

Anyone who loves their brother and sister lives in the Light, and there is nothing in them to make them stumble (away from Jesus).

But anyone who hates a brother or sister is in the darkness and walks around in the darkness. They do not know where they are going, because the darkness has blinded them."

(1 John 2:9-11)

In today's Scripture, the great servant of Jesus, the Apostle John, writes to Believers in the church, about love and hatred for fellow Believers. Amen! John refers to fellow Believers in Jesus Christ as brothers and sisters, because once we accept Jesus, we are in the family of God! Amen again! And as family members, we must love our brothers and sisters! Hallelujah! If you hate your brother or sister, you cannot truly fellowship with the family! And because of that hate, you are not truly in fellowship with the Father (God) and the Son (Jesus)! Tell the truth! And John writes to Believers to put forth several key tests of authentic Christian faith and fellowship, and one of those tests was love for brothers and sisters in Christ. Amen! Loving your brothers and sisters in Christ is a hallmark of true Believers. Amen again! And it is still a hallmark, and an expectation of Believers today! To love your brothers and sisters in Christ! And that is the truth! Glory to God! Our Scripture begins with this proclamation to Believers, **"Anyone who claims to be in the Light (of Jesus), but hates a brother or sister, is still in the darkness."** You are not living in the Light of Jesus, if you cannot show love to all brothers and sisters in Christ! Amen! Our Word tells us this truth, **"Anyone who loves their brother and sister lives in the Light, and there is nothing in them to make them stumble (away from Jesus)."** When you show love to your brothers and sisters in Christ, you are walking in the Light of Jesus! Amen again! And the Word of God says this about those who claim to be Believers, **"But anyone who hates a brother or sister is in the darkness and walks around in the darkness. They do not know where they are going, because the darkness has blinded them."** If you hate a brother or sister in Christ, then you yourself are not walking in the Light of Jesus. For your hatred has you walking in the darkness of Satan! So, therefore, you are lost! Amen! Today, we are being challenged! We are being given a test! Amen.

Today, our Scripture is speaking to Believers. As a Believer in Jesus Christ, you are now a part of the family of God! Hallelujah! And God our Father wants his family to fellowship with each other. But to do that, you must show love to all of your brothers and sisters, as well as to the Father, and the Son! John writes to Believers in the church, about love and hatred for fellow Believers. Amen! John refers to fellow Believers in Jesus Christ as brothers and sisters, because once we accept Jesus, we are in the family of God! Amen again! And as family members, we must love our brothers and sisters! Hallelujah! If you hate your brother or sister, you cannot truly fellowship with the family! And because of that hate, you are not truly in fellowship with the Father (God) and the Son (Jesus)! Tell the truth! John writes to Believers to put forth several key tests of authentic Christian faith and fellowship, and one of those tests is love for brothers and sisters in Christ. Amen! Loving your brothers and sisters in Christ is a hallmark of true Believers, and an expectation of God for fellowship. Amen again! To love your brothers and sisters in Christ! And that is the truth! Glory to God! Our Scripture begins with this proclamation to Believers, **"Anyone who claims to be in the Light (of Jesus), but hates a brother or sister, is still in the darkness."** You are not living in the Light of Jesus, if you cannot show love to all brothers and sisters in Christ! Amen! How can you claim to be in the Light of Jesus, and fellowship with God's family, when you hate members of God's family? That is not love, and hate does not allow true fellowship! Amen! Today, we are being challenged! We are being given a test! Amen.

Today, our Word is speaking to Believers. You are a part of the family of God! Hallelujah! And God our Father wants his family to fellowship with each other. But to do that, you must show love to all of your brothers and sisters, as well as to the Father, and the Son! Amen! John refers to fellow Believers in Jesus Christ as brothers and sisters, because once we accept Jesus, we are in the family of God! Amen again! And as family members, we are expected to love our brothers and sisters! Hallelujah! If you hate your brother or sister, you cannot truly fellowship with the family! And you are not truly in fellowship with the Father (God) and the Son (Jesus)! Tell the truth! John writes to Believers to put forth a test of authentic Christian faith and fellowship, which is to love all your brothers and sisters in Christ. Amen! Loving your brothers and sisters in Christ is an expectation of God for fellowship. Amen again! To love your brothers and sisters in Christ! And that is the truth! Glory to God! You are not living in the Light of Jesus, if you cannot show love to all brothers and sisters in Christ! Amen! Our Word tells us this truth, **"Anyone who loves their brother and sister lives in the Light, and there is nothing in them to make them stumble (away from Jesus)."** When you show love to your brothers and sisters in Christ, you are walking in the Light of Jesus! Amen again! Showing love does not mean you agree with everyone who is in God's family. Families have disagreements! It also does not mean loving that person in a way that compels you to be with them all the time. I have family members I love, but I do not want to be with them all the time! This love is one of respect, of caring, of helping, of educating, of empathy. When you can love your brothers and sisters in ways that show them you love them, you are living in the Light of Jesus! Glory! Today, we are being challenged! We are being given a test! Amen.

Today, the Word of God is speaking to you. You are a part of the family of God! Hallelujah! And God our Father wants his family to fellowship with each other. But to do that, you must show love to all of your brothers and sisters, as well as to the Father, and the Son! Amen! For once you accept Jesus, you are in the family of God, with every other person that has accepted Jesus as the Lord and Savior! Amen again! And you are expected to love your brothers and sisters! Hallelujah! If you hate your brother or sister, you cannot truly fellowship with the family! And you are not truly in fellowship with the Father (God) and the Son (Jesus)! Tell the truth! Amen! Loving your brothers and sisters in Christ is an expectation of God for fellowship. Amen again! To love your brothers and sisters in Christ! And that is the truth! Glory to God! You are not living in the Light of Jesus, if you cannot show love to all brothers and sisters in Christ! Amen! But when you show love to your brothers and sisters in Christ, you are walking in the Light of Jesus! Amen again! And the Word of God says this about those who claim to be Believers, **"But anyone who hates a brother or sister is in the darkness and walks around in the darkness. They do not know where they are going, because the darkness has blinded them."** If you hate a brother or sister in Christ, then you yourself are not walking in the Light of Jesus. For your hatred has you walking in the darkness of Satan! Love is from Jesus, hate is from Satan! And Jesus does not fellowship with Satan! So, therefore, you are lost! Amen!

Today, you are being given a test! You are a part of the family of God! Hallelujah! And God our Father wants his family to fellowship with each other. But to do that, you must show love to all of your brothers and sisters, as well as to the Father, and the Son! Amen! Loving your brothers and sisters in Christ is an expectation of God for fellowship. Amen again! To love your brothers and sisters in Christ! And that is the truth! Glory to God! You are not living in the Light of Jesus, if you cannot show love to all brothers and sisters in Christ! Amen! But when you show love to your brothers and sisters in Christ, you are walking in the Light of Jesus! Amen again! However, if you hate a brother or sister in Christ, then you yourself are not walking in the Light of Jesus. For your hatred has you walking in the darkness of Satan! So, therefore, you are lost! Amen! Today, you are being challenged! You are being given a test! And that test is, do you love all of your brothers and sisters in Christ? If you show love to all brothers and sisters in Christ, you are walking in the Light of Jesus! Hallelujah! But if you are showing hate to some, or any, brother or sister in Christ, you have stepped into the darkness! And you are not truly in fellowship with the Father (God) and the Son (Jesus). Amen.

Day 238

"For you are all sons of God through faith in Christ Jesus."

(Galatians 3:26)

In today's Scripture, the great servant of Jesus Christ, the Apostle Paul, is speaking to all Believers, reminding Believers that we are children of God. For Paul knew then, as we know today, that there are too many divisions within the church, and too many Believers that favor people who are like them, and choose not to fellowship with people who are not like them. Amen! And that is a problem that hurts the One True Church, the body of Christ! Amen again! Paul wrote to guide the people in the church to unity, for as Believers, we are all the same in the name of Jesus! Glory Hallelujah! That was the truth at the time of Paul, and that is the same truth today! All Believers are all the same in the eyes of God, and we are being challenged today to see that all Believers are the same, in our own eyes! Glory to God! Our Scripture begins by speaking to Believers, **"For you are all."** All Believers! And the Word continues by identifying all Believers as, **"Sons of God."** Hallelujah! And the Word proclaims that we are all the same, **"Through faith in Christ Jesus."** Hallelujah! All Believers are all sons and daughters of God! There is no difference! Thank you, Jesus! Thank you, Father God! Amen.

Today, our Scripture is profound and forever true. And the

Scripture is challenging us to remember who we are, for all Believers are a part of one family. The family of God! If you believe in Jesus Christ as your Lord and Savior, you are part of one family. God's family! It does not matter what church denomination you worship in, or what color or ethnic identity you have. You, and every Believer in the world alive today, and those who are Believers and have passed away, we are all part of one family! God's family! There is no difference in God's family! And the Word is challenging all Believers to accept all Believers as a family! Amen. Our Scripture begins with this identification of Believers, **"For you are all."** All Believers! Our Scripture is speaking to all Believers! All of us are more comfortable around Believers who look like us, or act like us, and sometimes we are less accepting of Believers who do not look like us, or act like us. Our Scripture is challenging us today to get rid of anything that divides the family. God's family! All Believers are with God! Hallelujah! Our Scripture is challenging us to see all Believers, as Believers in the same family. God's family! All Believers! All Believers are all sons and daughters of God! There is no difference! Thank you, Jesus! Thank you, Father God! Amen.

Today, our Word is challenging us to see all Believers as part of the same family. The family of God! If you believe in Jesus Christ as your Lord and Savior, you are part of one family. God's family! It does not matter what church, or what color, or ethnic identity you have. You, and every Believer in the world alive today, and those who are Believers and have passed away, we are all part of one family! All Believers! Our Word is speaking to all Believers! God's family! There is no difference in God's family! And the Word is challenging all Believers to accept all Believers as a family! Amen! The Word says for you are all, **"Sons of God."** Hallelujah! Sons of God! You and I, and all Believers, are sons of God! Amen again! God's family! When we became Believers, we became sons of God! God adopted us as His sons! His daughters! And by this adoption, we became God's children! God's family! All Believers became God's children. And every Believer is now an heir in God's family, with all the rights and privileges that God grants all His children! Believers are sons of God! All Believers are all sons and daughters of God! There is no difference! Thank you, Jesus! Thank you, Father God! Amen.

Today, the Word of God is speaking to you! The Word of God wants you to know that all Believers are sons of God! We are all family! If you believe in Jesus Christ as your Lord and Savior, you are part of one family. We are all in the same family, God's family! We are all children of God. Hallelujah! There is no difference in God's family! And the Word is challenging all Believers to accept all Believers as a family! Amen! Hallelujah! Sons of God! You and I, and all Believers, are sons of God! Amen again! And the Word of God proclaims that Believers are sons of God, **"Through faith in Christ Jesus."** Thank you, Jesus! Only through faith in Christ Jesus can we become sons of God! Through our faith in Jesus, God has adopted each and every Believer. Thank you,

Father God! We are all part of one family, God's family! This happened the moment we accepted Jesus Christ! The very moment! All Believers are part of the same family. There is no difference, and we should see, nor make any difference. For when we falsely see or make a difference, we cause division within the family of God! Tell the truth! And there is no difference! That is what the Word of God is telling us! Amen! There is no difference between Believers! Amen again! We were all adopted by God through our faith in Christ Jesus. All Believers are all sons and daughters of God! There is no difference! Thank you, Jesus! Thank you, Father God! Amen.

Today, our Scripture Guidance is reminding each of us of who we are today. Each and all Believers are all sons of God through faith in Christ Jesus. Hallelujah! We are all part of the same family. There is no difference! We are all sons and daughters of God! We are all part of the same family. So today, go spend time with your family! And love each one of your brothers and sisters in God's family, for there is no difference! We are all part of one family! God's family! Thank you, Jesus! Thank you, Father God! Glory to God! Amen!

Day 239

Paul arrived at Ephesus. There he found some disciples (Believers) and asked them, "Did you receive the Holy Spirit when you believed?"

The answered, "No, we have not heard that there is a Holy Spirit."

So Paul asked, "Then what baptism did you receive?" They replied, "Johns baptism."

Paul told them, "John's baptism was a baptism of repentance. He told the people to believe in the One coming after him, that is, in Jesus."

On hearing this, they were baptized in the name of the Lord Jesus.

When Paul placed his hands on them, the Holy Spirit came on them, and they spoke in tongues, and prophesied.

(Acts 19:1-6)

In today's Scripture, the great servant of Jesus Christ, the Apostle Paul, is speaking to all Believers, speaks to a time that he came upon a group that identified themselves as Believers in Jesus Christ. Amen! But like many people today, these people were not saved, but had accepted an understanding of the Gospel, but had not truly accepted Jesus as their Lord and Savior. Amen again!

And through our Scriptures, we are being challenged, both as Believers, and as servants of Jesus! Hallelujah! For Believers, have you truly accepted Jesus, or do you have an understanding of the Gospel? Tell the truth! And for servants of Jesus, your role is to help people understand the Gospel of Jesus, and to make it clear that they have to truly accept Jesus as their Lord and Savior. And that is the truth! Too many Believers are in church, and claim to be Believers, when in truth, they have only accepted an understanding of the Gospel of Jesus! And too many servants of Jesus, assume people are saved because they say they are Believers! This is a difficult, but necessary discussion that we need to have today! There are too many "church folks" that are going to miss everlasting life, because they accepted Jesus with knowledge in their head, but not with the commitment of their heart! Amen! Paul ensured that the Believers in our text understood that they had not yet received Jesus. In fact, they had received John! But once the servant of Jesus helped them to understand that they were not yet saved, they accepted Jesus! Hallelujah! And too many Believers today, have not yet received Jesus; they have received an understanding! Well, as a servant of Jesus, we need to help them understand that they are not yet saved! Because if they never understand the difference, they will not be saved! Amen! Our Scripture begins with, **Paul arrived at Ephesus. There he found some disciples (Believers) and asked them, "Did you receive the Holy Spirit when you believed?" They answered, "No, we have not heard that there is a Holy**

Spirit." It is up to the servant of Jesus to inquire of their flock! Do not assume that people that are in church, are saved! Amen! Our Word tells us that once the servant of Jesus knew that they were not saved, the servant began to serve Jesus, telling us that, **So Paul asked, "Then what baptism did you receive?" They replied, "John's baptism." Paul told them, "John's baptism was a baptism of repentance. He told the people to believe in the One coming after him, that is, in Jesus."** When the servant of Jesus finds out that someone has a misunderstanding that they are saved, the servant must immediately teach the true way to be saved! Amen again! And the Word of God proclaims that, **"On hearing this, they were baptized in the name of the Lord Jesus. When Paul placed his hands on them, the Holy Spirit came on them, and they spoke in tongues, and prophesied."** Glory! For when people are truly saved, they are changed! Glory Hallelujah! God is trying to save someone! Someone is thinking they are saved, but they are not! And the servants of Jesus need to help them understand that! For those people will miss heaven by 18 inches, which is the difference between the head, and the heart! Amen.

Today, our Scripture is addressing a big problem in the church, and in the world. Too many people believe they are saved, when in fact, they are not! Amen! Many people, and many are church people, have accepted an understanding of the Gospel, but have not truly accepted Jesus as their Lord and Savior. Amen again! Through our Scriptures, we are being challenged, both as

Believers, and as servants of Jesus! Hallelujah! For Believers, have you truly accepted Jesus, or do you have an understanding of the Gospel? Tell the truth! And for servants of Jesus, your role is to help people understand the Gospel of Jesus, and to make it clear that they have to truly accept Jesus as their Lord and Savior. And that is the truth! Too many Believers are in church, and claim to be Believers, when in truth, they have only accepted an understanding of the Gospel of Jesus! And too many servants of Jesus, assume people are saved because they say they are Believers! This is a difficult, but necessary discussion that we need to have today! There are too many "church folks" that are going to miss everlasting life, because they accepted Jesus with knowledge in their head, but not with the commitment of their heart! Amen! Too many Believers have not yet received Jesus; they have received an understanding! And servants of Jesus need to help them understand that they are not yet saved! Because if they never understand the difference, they will not be saved! Amen! Our Scripture begins with, **Paul arrived at Ephesus. There he found some disciples (Believers) and asked them, "Did you receive the Holy Spirit when you believed?" They answered, "No, we have not heard that there is a Holy Spirit."** It is up to the servant of Jesus to inquire of their flock! Do not assume that people that are in church, are saved! Amen! This is a difficult, but necessary discussion that we need to have today! There are too many "church folks" that are going to miss everlasting life, because they accepted Jesus with knowledge in their head, but not with the commitment of their heart! And those people will miss heaven by 18 inches, which is the difference between the head, and the heart! Amen.

Today, our Word is addressing a big problem in the church, and in the world. Too many people believe they are saved, when in fact, they are not! Amen! Many people have accepted an understanding of the Gospel, but have not truly accepted Jesus as their Lord and Savior. Amen again! And we are being challenged, both as Believers, and as servants of Jesus! Hallelujah! For Believers, have you truly accepted Jesus, or do you have an understanding of the Gospel? And for servants of Jesus, your role is to help people understand the Gospel of Jesus, and to make it clear that they have to truly accept Jesus as their Lord and Savior. Too many Believers are in church, and claim to be Believers, when in truth, they have only accepted an understanding of the Gospel of Jesus! And too many servants of Jesus, assume people are saved because they say they are Believers! This is a difficult, but necessary discussion that we need to have today! There are too many people that are going to miss everlasting life, because they accepted Jesus with knowledge in their heads, but not with the commitment of their hearts! Amen! Too many Believers have not yet received Jesus, they have received an understanding! And servants of Jesus need to help them understand that they are not yet saved! Because if they never understand the difference, they will not be saved! Amen! It is up to the servant of Jesus not to assume that people in church, are saved! Amen! Our Word tells us that once the servant of Jesus knew that they were not saved, the servant began to serve Jesus, telling us that, **So Paul asked, "Then what baptism did you receive?" They replied, "John's baptism." Paul told them, "John's baptism was a baptism of repentance. He told the people to believe in the One coming after him, that is, in Jesus."** When the servant of Jesus finds out that someone has a misunderstanding that they are saved, the servant must immediately teach the true way to be saved! Amen again! This is a difficult, but necessary discussion, that we need to have today! There are too many "church folks" that are going to miss everlasting life, because they accepted Jesus with knowledge in their head, but not with the commitment of their heart! And those people will miss heaven by 18 inches,, which is the difference between the head, and the heart! Amen.

Today, the Word of God is addressing a big problem in the church, and in the world. Too many people believe they are saved, when in fact, they are not! Amen! Many people have accepted an understanding of the Gospel, but have not truly accepted Jesus as their Lord and Savior. Amen again! The Word of God is speaking to you! And you are being challenged, whether you are a Believer, or a servant of Jesus! Hallelujah! Have you truly accepted Jesus, or do you have an understanding of the Gospel? And if you are a servant of Jesus, your role is to make it clear that people have to truly accept Jesus as their Lord and Savior. Too many Believers are in church, and claim to be Believers, when in truth, they have only accepted an understanding of the Gospel of Jesus! Do not assume people are saved because they say they are Believers! There are too many people that are going to miss everlasting life, because they accepted Jesus with knowledge in their heads, but not with the commitment of their heart! Amen! And servants of Jesus need to help them understand that they are not yet saved! Because if they never understand the difference, they will not be saved! Amen! It is up to the servant of Jesus not to assume that people in the church, are saved! Amen! And as a servant of Jesus, when you find out that someone has a misunderstanding that they are saved, but they have not truly accepted Jesus, the servant must immediately teach the true way to be saved! Amen again! And the Word of God proclaims that, **"On hearing this, they were baptized in the name of the Lord Jesus. When Paul placed his hands on them, the Holy Spirit came on them, and they spoke in tongues, and prophesied."** Glory! For when people are truly saved, they are changed! Glory Hallelujah! God is trying to save someone! Someone is thinking they are saved, but they are not! And the servants of Jesus need to help them understand that! This is a difficult, but necessary discussion, that we need to have today! There are too many "church folks" that are going to miss everlasting life, because they accepted Jesus with knowledge in their head, but not with the commitment of their heart! And those people will miss heaven by 18 inches, which is the difference between the head, and the heart! Amen.

Today, our Scripture Guidance is addressing a big problem in the church, and in the world. Too many people believe they are saved, when in fact, they are not! Amen! And yes, this is a difficult discussion, but it is necessary! You are not going to be saved, because your Mother taught you about Jesus! You are not going to be saved because you go to church! You are not going to be saved because, as a child, you knew who Jesus was, and answered the question in church! Amen! And you will not be saved because someone sprinkled your face, because your Mother took you to church, or because a Minister dumped you in a tub of water! Do not let Satan deceive you! It is not about your knowledge! It is about your heart accepting Jesus as your Lord and Savior! Amen again! God is asking you the same question that John asked over 2000 years ago. "Did you receive the Holy Spirit when you believed? Then what baptism did you receive?" Hallelujah! You need to tell the truth today! Please! Accept Jesus in your heart, and let the Holy Spirit into your soul! Please, do not miss heaven by 18 inches! Amen!

Day 240

"Then he (the Angel of the Lord) showed me (in the 4th vision given to Zechariah that night) Joshua (the people of Israel, God's chosen people), the high priest, standing before the Angel of the Lord, and Satan standing at his right side to accuse him (the people of Israel).

The Lord God said to Satan, 'The Lord rebuke you, Satan! The Lord God who has chosen Jerusalem, rebuke you! Is not this man a burning stick, snatched from the fire?'

Now Joshua (Israel) was dressed in filthy clothes as he stood before the Angel.

The Angel said to those who were standing before him (other Angels), 'Take off his (the people of Israel) filthy clothes.'"

(Zechariah 3:1-4)

In today's Scripture, the great servant of God, the Prophet Zechariah, had been given eight visions in one night, by the Angel of the Lord. Our Scriptures cover the fourth vision. Amen! In this particular vision, Zechariah is shown that the High Priest (which is Israel, God's chosen people), would have their filthy garments (sinful bodies) replaced by clean garments (forgiven and glorious bodies). Amen again! And the same is true for God's chosen people today, those that have accepted Jesus as their Lord and Savior! Glory! For every single Believer, there will be a day when your filthy garments (your sinful body) will be replaced by clean garments, your glorious eternal body! Glory Hallelujah! That is the vision that Believers must hold on to, as we live in a filthy and sinful world. Glory to God! Our Scripture begins with, **"Then he (the Angel of the Lord) showed me (in the 4th vision given to Zechariah that night) Joshua (the people of Israel, God's chosen people), the high priest, standing before the Angel of the Lord, and Satan standing at his right side to accuse him (the people of Israel). The Lord God said to Satan, 'The Lord rebuke you, Satan! The Lord God who has chosen Jerusalem, rebuke you! Is not this man a burning stick, snatched from the fire?'** Satan will utilize sin to keep Believers from the Kingdom of God, but through our faith in Jesus, God will protect you from burning in Hell! For you are His chosen people! And you have been snatched from the fire by Jesus, to be set aside for the Will of God! Amen. Our Word continues with, **"Now Joshua (Israel) was dressed in filthy clothes as he stood before the Angel."** Each Believer must stand in front of Jesus while we are still sinners, and in our filthy clothes, and ask Jesus to forgive us of our sins. And we will still be in our filthy clothes (sinful bodies), until Jesus returns. Amen again! And the Word of God proclaims the vision of hope that all Believers must cling to in faith, saying that when we stand before the Angel, that, **The Angel said to those who were standing before him (other Angels), 'Take off his (the people of Israel) filthy clothes.'"** Hallelujah! That is what each Believer must hold on to! That we will stand with Jesus and hear Almighty God tell His Angels, "Take off his filthy clothes!" Glory! And you will never be dirty from sin again! For you are one of God's people! Glory Hallelujah! Amen.

Today, our Scripture is speaking to God's people. If you believe in Jesus Christ as your Lord and Savior, you are one of God's people! Amen! This vision of promise is for you! Amen again! The Prophet, Zechariah, had been given eight visions in one night, by the Angel of the Lord. Amen! In this particular vision, Zechariah is shown that the High Priest (which is Israel, God's chosen people) would have their filthy garments (sinful bodies) replaced by clean garments (forgiven and glorious bodies). Amen again! And the same is true for God's chosen people who have accepted Jesus as their Lord and Savior! Glory! For that is the only way that you can become one of God's people! Hallelujah! And for every single Believer, there will be a day when your filthy garments (your sinful body), will be replaced by clean garments, your glorious eternal body! Glory Hallelujah! That is the vision that Believers must hold on to, as we live in a filthy and sinful world. Glory to God! Our Scripture begins with, **"Then he (the Angel of the Lord) showed me (in the 4th vision given to Zechariah that night) Joshua (the people of Israel, God's chosen people), the high priest, standing before the Angel of the Lord, and Satan standing at his right side to accuse him (the people of Israel). The Lord God said to Satan, 'The Lord rebuke you, Satan! The Lord God who has chosen Jerusalem, rebuke you! Is not this man a burning stick, snatched from the**

fire?' Satan will utilize sin to keep Believers from the Kingdom of God, but through our faith in Jesus, God will protect you from burning in Hell! For you are His chosen people! And you have been snatched from the fire by Jesus, to be set aside for the Will of God! Amen! For you are one of God's people! Glory Hallelujah! Amen.

Today, our Word is speaking to God's people. If you believe in Jesus Christ as your Lord and Savior, you are one of God's people! Amen! This vision of promise is for you! Amen again! Zechariah had been given eight visions in one night by the Angel of the Lord. Amen! Zechariah is shown that the High Priest (which is Israel, God's chosen people), would have their filthy garments (sinful bodies) replaced by clean garments (forgiven and glorious bodies). Amen again! And the same is true for God's chosen people who have accepted Jesus as their Lord and Savior! Glory! For that is the only way that you can become one of God's people! Hallelujah! And for every single Believer, there will be a day when your filthy garments (your sinful body), will be replaced by clean garments, your glorious eternal body! Glory Hallelujah! That is the vision that Believers must hold on to, as we live in a filthy and sinful world. Glory to God! Satan will utilize sin to keep Believers from the Kingdom of God, but through our faith in Jesus, God will protect you from burning in Hell! For you are His chosen people! And you have been snatched from the fire by Jesus, to be set aside for the Will of God! Amen! Our Word continues with, **"Now Joshua (Israel) was dressed in filthy**

clothes as he stood before the Angel." Each Believer must stand in front of Jesus while we are still sinners, and in our filthy clothes, and ask Jesus to forgive us of our sins. And we will still be in our filthy clothes (sinful bodies), until Jesus returns to give us our glorious body! Amen again! For you are one of God's people! Glory Hallelujah! Amen.

Today, the Word of God is speaking to God's people. If you believe in Jesus Christ as your Lord and Savior, the Word of God is speaking to you! Amen! This vision of promise is for you! Amen again! Zechariah had been given eight visions in one night by the Angel of the Lord. Amen! Zechariah is shown that the High Priest (which is Israel, God's chosen people), would have their filthy garments (sinful bodies) replaced by clean garments (forgiven and glorious bodies). Amen again! And the same is true for you! Glory! For through your faith, you have become one of God's people! Hallelujah! And there will be a day when your filthy garments, will be replaced the clean garments, which will be your glorious eternal body! Glory Hallelujah! That is the vision you must hold on to, as you live in a filthy and sinful world. Glory to God! Satan will utilize sin to turn you away from the Kingdom of God, but through your faith in Jesus, God will protect you from burning in Hell! For you are His chosen people! And you have been snatched from the fire by Jesus, to be set aside for the Will of God! Because you stood in front of Jesus while you were still a sinner, and in your filthy clothes, and asked Jesus to forgive you of our sins. Amen! And we will still be in our filthy clothes (sinful bodies), until Jesus returns! Amen again! And the Word of God proclaims the vision of hope that all Believers must cling to in faith, saying that when we stand before the Angel, that, **The Angel said to those who were standing before him (other Angels), 'Take off his (the people of Israel) filthy clothes.'"** Hallelujah! That is what each Believer must hold on to! For you are one of God's people! Glory Hallelujah! Amen.

Today, God's people are being given a vision. And if you believe in Jesus Christ, you are one of God's people, and this vision is a promise for you to hold on to. Amen! For through your faith, you have become one of God's people! Hallelujah! And there will be a day when your filthy garments, will be replaced the clean garments, which will be your glorious eternal body! Glory Hallelujah! That is the vision you must hold on to, as you live in a filthy and sinful world. Glory to God! And that is what each Believer must hold on to! For you are one of God's people! Glory Hallelujah! Amen.

Day 241

Then I (Zechariah) said, "Put a clean turban on His (Joshua, the symbol of Israel, as God's chosen people) head." So they (God's Angels) put a clean turban on his head and clothed him; while the Angel of the Lord stood by.

The Angel of the Lord gave this charge to Joshua (Israel): "This is what the Lord Almighty says: 'If you will walk in obedience to Me and keep My requirements,

then you will govern My house and have charge of My courts, and I will give you a place among these (Angels) standing here.

(Zechariah: 5-7)

In today's Scripture, the great servant of God, the Prophet Zechariah, had been given eight visions in one night by the Angel of the Lord. Amen! In this vision, Zechariah has already shown us that Joshua (which is Israel, God's chosen people); will have their filthy garments (sinful bodies) replaced by clean garments (forgiven and glorious bodies) when they stand before the Angel of God. Amen again! And that God would rebuke Satan as His people stand before the Angel of the Lord. Hallelujah! Zechariah now continues to tell us what else he saw in the fourth vision. And this vision is also true for God's chosen people today; those that have accepted Jesus as their Lord and Savior! Glory! For every single Believer, there will be a day when your filthy garments (your sinful body); will be replaced by clean garments, your glorious eternal body! Glory Hallelujah! That is the vision that Believers must hold on to, as we live in a filthy and sinful world. Glory to God! In addition to that, our Scripture says that this happened next in the fourth vision, **Then I (Zechariah) said, "Put a clean turban on His (Joshua, the symbol of Israel, as God's chosen people) head." So they (God's Angels) put a clean turban on his head and clothed him; while the Angel of the Lord stood by.** God's people will receive a glorious body, and a clean turban on our heads, that grants us the divine High Priest. Jesus! Amen! Our Word continues with, **The Angel of the Lord gave this charge to Joshua (Israel): "This is what the Lord Almighty says: 'If you will walk in obedience to Me and keep My requirements,"** And now God is challenging each of His people. God is proclaiming to us, that once we are clean from sin, "if" we do as he states! This is the start of a promise from God! "If" we do as he states! Amen again! And the Word of God proclaims what God will do for each of His people; if you do what He states, **"then you will govern My house and have charge of My courts, and I will give you a place among these (Angels) standing here."** Hallelujah! That is a promise from God to those that walk in obedience to God's Will! "If" you do the requirements that God gives to you, "then" you be given a place among the Angels! Glory! For you are one of God's people! Hallelujah! And you did what God required you to do! Glory Hallelujah! Amen.

Today, our Scripture is speaking to God's people. If you believe in Jesus Christ as your Lord and Savior, you are one of God's people! Amen! This vision of promise is for you! Amen again! The Prophet Zechariah; had been given eight visions in one night, by the Angel of the Lord. Amen! In this vision, Zechariah has already shown us that Joshua (which is Israel, God's chosen people); will have their filthy garments (sinful bodies) replaced by clean garments (forgiven and glorious bodies), when they stand before the Angel of God. Amen again! And that God would rebuke Satan as His people stand before the Angel of the Lord. Hallelujah! Zechariah now continues to tell us what else he saw in the fourth vision. And this vision is also true for God's chosen people today; those that have accepted Jesus as their Lord and Savior! Glory! For every single Believer, there will be a day when your filthy garments (your sinful body); will be replaced by clean garments, your glorious eternal body! Glory Hallelujah! That is the vision that Believers must hold on to, as we live in a filthy and sinful world. Glory to God! In addition to that, our Scripture says that this happened next in the fourth vision, **Then I (Zechariah) said, "Put a clean turban on His (Joshua, the symbol of Israel, as God's chosen people) head." So they (God's Angels) put a clean turban on his head and clothed him; while the Angel of the Lord stood by.** God's people will receive a glorious body, and a clean turban on our heads, that grants us the divine High Priest. Jesus! Amen! For you are one of God's people! Glory Hallelujah! Amen.

Today, our Word is speaking to God's people. If you believe in Jesus Christ as your Lord and Savior, you are one of God's people! Amen! This vision of promise is for you! Amen again! Zechariah had been given eight visions in one night by the Angel of the Lord. Amen! Zechariah now continues to tell us what else he saw in the fourth vision. And this vision is also true for God's chosen people today; those that have accepted Jesus as their Lord and Savior! Glory! For every single Believer, there will be a day when your filthy garments (your sinful body); will be replaced by clean garments, your glorious eternal body! Glory Hallelujah! That is the vision that Believers must hold on to, as we live in a filthy and sinful world. Glory to God! God's people will receive a glorious body, and a clean turban on our heads, that grants us the divine High Priest. Jesus! Amen! For you are one of God's people! Glory Hallelujah! Amen. Our Word continues with, **The Angel of the Lord gave this charge to Joshua (Israel): "This is what the Lord Almighty says: 'If you will walk in obedience to Me and keep My requirements,"** And now God is challenging each of His people. God is proclaiming to us, that once we are clean from sin, "if" we do as he states! This is the start of a promise from God! "If" we do as he states! Amen again! For you are one of God's people! Glory Hallelujah! Amen.

Today, the Word of God is speaking to God's people. If you believe in Jesus Christ as your Lord and Savior, the Word of God is speaking to you! Amen! This vision of promise is for you! Amen again! For through your faith, you have become one of

God's people! Hallelujah! And there will be a day when your filthy garments; will be replaced the clean garments, which will be your glorious eternal body! Glory! That is the vision you must hold on to, as you live in a filthy and sinful world. Glory to God! God's people will receive a glorious body, and a clean turban on our heads, that grants us the divine High Priest. Jesus! Amen! For you are one of God's people! Glory Hallelujah! And now God is challenging each of His people. God is proclaiming to us, that once we are clean from sin, "if" we do as he states! This is the start of a promise from God! "If" we do as he states! Amen again! And the Word of God proclaims what God will do for each of His people; if you do what He states, **"then you will govern My house and have charge of My courts, and I will give you a place among these (Angels) standing here."** Hallelujah! That is a promise from God to those that walk in obedience to God's Will! "If" you do the requirements that God gives to you, "then" you be given a place among the Angels! Glory! And you did what God required you to do! Glory Hallelujah! Amen. That is what each Believer must hold on to! That once you are "clean", God has an "if/then" promise for you! For you are one of God's people! Glory Hallelujah! Amen.

Today, God's people are being given a vision. And if you believe in Jesus Christ, you are one of God's people, and this vision is a promise for you to hold on to. Amen! For through your faith, you have become one of God's people! Hallelujah! And there will be a day when your filthy garments; will be replaced the clean garments, which will be your glorious eternal body! Glory Hallelujah! God's people will receive a glorious body, and a clean turban on our heads, that grants us the divine High Priest. Jesus! Amen! For you are one of God's people! Glory Hallelujah! And now God is challenging each of His people. God is proclaiming to you, that once you are clean from sin, "if" you walk in obedience to God's Will, "then" you be given a place among the Angels! Glory! Glory from God! Amen. That is what each Believer must hold on to! That now that you are "clean", God has an "if/then" promise for you! For you are one of God's people! Glory Hallelujah! Amen.

Day 242

"Now both Jesus and His disciples were invited to a wedding.

And when they (the host of the wedding) ran out of wine, the mother of Jesus said to Him, 'they have no wine.'"

His mother said to the servants, "Whatever He (Jesus) says to you, do it."

Jesus said to them, "Fill the water pots with water." And they filled them up to the brim.

And Jesus said, "Draw some out now, and take it to the master of the feast." And they took it. (For Jesus had changed the water to wine)

"This (was) the beginning of signs Jesus did in Galilee, and (these) signs manifested His glory; and His disciples believed in Him."

(John 2:2-3, 5, 7-8 & 11)

In today's Scripture, the great servant of Jesus, the Apostle John, tells us about the first recorded miracle that Jesus did on earth! Amen! And the Apostle John, and other servants of Jesus, were there to see it! Amen again! What is important in our story is not the miracle itself, but that Jesus's servants would truly begin to believe in Him because of the miracles they witnessed. Hallelujah! For it is one thing to hear the Gospel of Jesus, but it is quite another thing, to see the power of Jesus! Glory Hallelujah! Jesus Believers believe when they hear the Gospel of Jesus, but Jesus servants begin to serve Him, when they see the power of Jesus! That is when you truly, truly believe in Jesus; when you see, and recognize the miracles that His power has created! Whether in your own life, or witness to the miracles in the lives of others, you begin to truly serve Jesus when you realize His power! Glory to God! For when you see or feel the power of Jesus, you are compelled to serve Him! The disciples had already been following Jesus, but the miracles glorified Him, and that is when the disciples truly believed in Him! And after that, they began to serve Him! Our Scripture begins with, **"Now both Jesus and His disciples were invited to a wedding. And when they (the host of the wedding) ran out of wine, the mother of Jesus said to Him, 'they have no wine.' His mother said to the servants, "Whatever He (Jesus) says to you, do it."** Jesus is always around, and if you seek Him, He will be there for you! But you must seek Him and be prepared to do whatever He says to do. Amen! Our Word tells us that, **Jesus said to them, "Fill the water pots with water." And they filled them up to the brim. And Jesus said, "Draw some out now, and take it to the master of the feast." And they took it. (For Jesus had changed the water to wine)** If you are obedient to Jesus; and have faith in Him, Jesus will create miracles in your life! Amen again! And the Word of God proclaims, **"This (was) the beginning of signs Jesus did in Galilee, and (these) signs manifested His glory; and His**

disciples believed in Him." Look at the miracles that Jesus has done in your life! These miracles manifest His glory to you! Believe in Him, and serve Him! Hallelujah! Amen.

Today, our Scripture is speaking to Believers; who have not yet served Jesus. John tells us about the first recorded miracle that Jesus did on earth! Amen! And the Apostle John and other servants of Jesus were there to see it! Amen again! Jesus's servants would truly begin to believe in Him because of the miracles they witnessed. Hallelujah! For it is one thing to hear the Gospel of Jesus, but it is quite another thing, to see the power of Jesus! Glory Hallelujah! Jesus Believers believe when they hear the Gospel of Jesus, but Jesus servants begin to serve Him, when they see the power of Jesus! That is when you truly, truly believe in Jesus; when you see, and recognize the miracles that His power has created! When will you truly believe in the power of Jesus, and serve Him? Whether in your own life, or witness to the miracles in the lives of others, you begin to truly serve Jesus when you realize His power! Glory to God! Look at your own life, have you seen the power of Jesus? For when you see or feel the power of Jesus, you are compelled to serve Him! The disciples had already been following Jesus, but the miracles glorified Him, and that is when the disciples truly believed in Him! And after that, they began to serve Him! Our Scripture begins with, **"Now both Jesus and His disciples were invited to a wedding. And when they (the host of the wedding) ran out of wine, the mother of Jesus said to Him, 'they have no wine.' His mother said to the**

servants, "Whatever He (Jesus) says to you, do it." Jesus is always around, and if you seek Him, He will be there for you! But you must seek Him and be prepared to do whatever He says to do. Amen! Mary sought Jesus for the miracle! Mary believed that Jesus could do the miracle! And the servants obeyed Jesus for the miracle! When you seek Jesus for the impossible, you must believe that He can do the impossible! Then trust in whatever He tells you to do, and be obedient, for that shows Jesus that you have faith in Him! Amen! Believe in Him, and serve Him! Hallelujah! Amen.

Today, our Word is speaking to Believers; who have not yet served Jesus. John tells us about the first recorded miracle that Jesus did on earth! Amen! Jesus Believers believe when they hear the Gospel of Jesus, but Jesus servants begin to serve Him, when they see the power of Jesus! That is when you truly, truly believe in Jesus; when you see, and recognize the miracles that His power has created! When will you truly believe in the power of Jesus, and serve Him? Glory to God! Look at your own life, have you seen the power of Jesus? For when you see or feel the power of Jesus, you are compelled to serve Him! The disciples had already been following Jesus, but the miracles glorified Him, and that is when the disciples truly believed in Him! And after that, they began to serve Him! Jesus is always around, and if you seek Him, He will be there for you! But you must seek Him and be prepared to do whatever He says to do. Amen! Our Word tells us that, **Jesus said to them, "Fill the water pots with water." And they filled**

them up to the brim. And Jesus said, "Draw some out now, and take it to the master of the feast." And they took it. (For Jesus had changed the water to wine) If you are obedient to Jesus; and have faith in Him, Jesus will create miracles in your life! Amen again! Jesus has done more for you than making wine out of water! Jesus has made you clean from the dirt of sin, and has saved you from eternal damnation for sin! Glory! Jesus has even led you to be adopted by Almighty God! Glory Hallelujah! Believe in Him, and serve Him! Amen.

Today, the Word of God is speaking to Believers; who have not yet served Jesus. The Word of God may be speaking to you! Are you serving Jesus? John tells us about the first recorded miracle that Jesus did on earth! Amen! Jesus Believers believe when they hear the Gospel of Jesus, but Jesus servants begin to serve Him, when they see the power of Jesus! That is when you truly, truly believe in Jesus; when you see, and recognize the miracles that His power has created! Glory to God! Look at your own life, have you seen the power of Jesus? For when you understand that the power of Jesus has given you miracles in your life, you will be compelled to serve Him! The disciples had already been following Jesus, but the miracles glorified Him, and that is when the disciples truly believed in Him! And after that, they began to serve Him! Jesus is always around, and if you seek Him, He will be there for you! But you must seek Him and be prepared to do whatever He says to do. Amen! And if you are obedient to Jesus; and have faith in Him, Jesus will create miracles in your life! Amen again!

And the Word of God proclaims, **"This (was) the beginning of signs Jesus did in Galilee, and (these) signs manifested His glory; and His disciples believed in Him."** Look at the miracles that Jesus has done in your life! These miracles manifest His glory to you! Jesus has always been there for you, and He has given you miracles, even when you did not understand them at the time. Jesus has shown you His power, and has protected you with His power, because He loves you! When you look at the miracles that Jesus has already done in your life, those are just the beginning of the signs that manifest His glory to you! Glory! Believe in Him, and serve Him! Hallelujah! Amen.

Today, our Scripture Guidance is for Believers who have not yet begun to serve Jesus. Amen! Jesus Believers believe when they hear the Gospel of Jesus, but Jesus servants begin to serve Him, when they see the power of Jesus! That is when you truly, truly believe in Jesus; when you see, and recognize the miracles that His power has created! Glory to God! Look at your own life, have you seen the power of Jesus? Jesus has given you miracles, and you know that! Jesus is always around, and if you seek Him, He will continue to be there for you! But you must seek Him and be prepared to do whatever He says to do. Amen! And if you are obedient to Jesus; and have faith in Him, Jesus will continue to create miracles in your life! Amen again! Look at the miracles that Jesus has done in your life! These miracles manifest His glory to you! Believe in Him, and serve Him! Hallelujah! Amen.

Day 243

Then there was a great uproar, and some of the teachers of The Law (of Moses) who were Pharisees, stood up and argued vigorously, "We find nothing wrong with this man (Apostle Paul)", they said. "What if a Spirit or an Angel has spoken to him?"

The dispute (between the people in the crowd) became so violent that the commander was afraid Paul would be torn to pieces by them. He ordered the troops to go down and take Paul away from them by force, and bring into the barracks (prison).

The following night, the Lord (Jesus) stood near Paul and said, "Take courage! As you have testified about Me in Jerusalem, so you must also testify in Rome."

(Acts 23:9-11)

In today's Scripture, the great servant of Jesus, the author Luke, writes Acts to show us how the Gospel of Jesus spread rapidly from Jerusalem to the whole Roman empire. Amen! Thus moving from the origin of the Gospel in its Jewish roots, to the entire Gentile (non-Jewish) world. Amen again! This was always God's plan for hope and salvation for the entire world of people. Hallelujah! And Acts covers many of the initial "acts" by the servants of Jesus that spread the good news of Jesus to the Gentiles. Glory Hallelujah! The author Luke, was himself, a

Gentile! He was a physician who traveled with Paul on many of Paul's missionary journeys. Therefore, Acts speaks to Paul's missionary journeys; and provides a selective account of the first 30 years of the church of Jesus. Glory Hallelujah! Luke provided a basic outline of the Book of Acts in **Chapter 1:8 of Acts** when Jesus said to His chosen Disciples, "You will receive power when the Holy Spirit comes on you, and you will be My witnesses in Jerusalem, and in all Judea and Samaria, and to the ends of the earth." Amen! And the Book of Acts serves as a witness; to the activities of Jesus's witnesses, who witnessed to the ends of the earth. Amen again! In our particular Scripture passage, one of Jesus's witnesses, Paul, has been arrested in Jerusalem for witnessing about Jesus and accused by some Jews of "teaching everyone everywhere against our people and our Law, and this place (Jerusalem)." **(Acts 21:28)** Paul then had a chance to address those accusations to the crowd, and to testify about his spiritual transition from a persecutor or those who followed Jesus; to one who served Jesus. Hallelujah! Our Scripture begins after Paul has spoken to the crowd, telling us that, **Then there was a great uproar, and some of the teachers of The Law (of Moses) who were Pharisees, stood up and argued vigorously, "We find nothing wrong with this man (Apostle Paul)", they said. "What if a Spirit or an Angel has spoken to him?"** When the servant of Jesus gives an account of why they serve Jesus, people can really find nothing wrong with them! Amen! Our Word continues, saying that, **"The dispute (between the people in the**

crowd) became so violent that the commander was afraid Paul would be torn to pieces by them. He ordered the troops to go down and take Paul away from them by force, and bring into the barracks (prison)." Jesus's servants may still be persecuted by the evil in the world! Amen again! Yet the Word of God proclaims that, **The following night, the Lord (Jesus) stood near Paul and said, "Take courage! As you have testified about Me in Jerusalem, so you must also testify in Rome."** Servants of Jesus must stay strong and be of courage; no matter what man does to you, you will be able to serve Jesus as He has called you! Hallelujah! For man is not in control, God is! Jesus called you to do the Will of God! And God's Will, will be done; on Earth, as it is in Heaven! Glory to God! Amen.

Today, our Scripture is speaking to Believers that Jesus has called to serve Him. Stay strong and be of courage; no matter what man does to you, you will be able to serve Jesus as He has called you! Hallelujah! For man is not in control, God is! Jesus is encouraging His servants today! Do not let the hate of man discourage you from serving Jesus as He has called you! Amen! Jesus called you to do the Will of God! Amen again! Luke wrote the Book of Acts as a witness to the activities of Jesus's witnesses, who witnessed to the ends of the earth. Amen again! One of Jesus's witnesses, Paul, has been arrested in Jerusalem for witnessing about Jesus. Paul then had a chance to address those accusations to the crowd, and to testify about his spiritual transition from a persecutor or those who followed Jesus; to one who served Jesus.

Hallelujah! Our Scripture begins after Paul has spoken to the crowd, telling us that, **Then there was a great uproar, and some of the teachers of The Law (of Moses) who were Pharisees, stood up and argued vigorously, "We find nothing wrong with this man (Apostle Paul)", they said. "What if a Spirit or an Angel has spoken to him?"** When the servant of Jesus gives an account of why they serve Jesus, people can really find nothing wrong with them! Amen! For if you speak what the Holy Spirit of God gives you to speak, you speak the truth! And people with a good heart, will find nothing wrong with you! Hallelujah! So be encouraged and speak the truth, as Jesus has called you to do. Glory Hallelujah! Jesus called you to do the Will of God! And God's Will, will be done; on Earth, as it is in Heaven! Glory to God! Amen.

Today, our Word is speaking to Believers that Jesus has called to serve Him. Stay strong and be of courage; no matter what man does to you, you will be able to serve Jesus as He has called you! Hallelujah! Always remember; man is not in control, God is! Jesus is encouraging His servants today! Do not let the hate of man discourage you from serving Jesus as He has called you! Amen! Jesus called you to do the Will of God! Amen again! Luke was a witness to the activities of Jesus witnesses to one of Jesus witnesses, Paul, has been arrested in Jerusalem for witnessing about Jesus. Paul then had a chance to testify to a crowd of people about his spiritual transition from a persecutor or those who followed Jesus; to one who served Jesus. Hallelujah! When the servant of Jesus gives an account of why they serve Jesus, people can really find nothing wrong with them! Amen! Our Word continues, saying that, **"The dispute (between the people in the crowd) became so violent that the commander was afraid Paul would be torn to pieces by them. He ordered the troops to go down and take Paul away from them by force, and bring into the barracks (prison)."** Jesus's servants may still be persecuted by the evil in the world! Amen again! Even though you speak the truth, evil people will not care, and will still persecute you! But stand in the truth, and stand with courage! For Jesus called you to do the Will of God! And God's Will, will be done; on Earth, as it is in Heaven! Glory to God! Amen.

Today, the Word of God is speaking to Believers that Jesus has called to serve Him. The Word of God is speaking to you! Jesus is speaking to you! Stay strong and be of courage; no matter what man does to you, you will be able to serve Jesus as He has called you! Hallelujah! Man is not in control, God is! Jesus is encouraging you today! Do not let the hate of man discourage you from serving Jesus as He has called you! Amen! Jesus called you to do the Will of God! Amen again! One of the greatest servants of Jesus, the Apostle Paul, had been arrested in Jerusalem for witnessing about Jesus. Paul testified to the crowd of people about his spiritual transition from a persecutor or those who followed Jesus; to one who served Jesus. Hallelujah! When the servant of Jesus gives an account of why they serve Jesus, people can really find nothing wrong with them! Amen! However, Jesus's servants may still be persecuted by the evil in the world! Amen again! Yet the Word of God proclaims that, **The following night, the Lord (Jesus) stood near Paul and said, "Take courage! As you have testified about Me in Jerusalem, so you must also testify in Rome."** Servants of Jesus must stay strong and be of courage; no matter what man does to you, you will be able to serve Jesus as He has called you! Hallelujah! For man is not in control, God is! And Jesus called you to do the Will of God! And God's Will, will be done; on Earth, as it is in Heaven! Glory to God! Amen.

Today, our Scripture Guidance is for the servants of Jesus Christ. You will be persecuted by the evil people in the world, who are being used by Satan to put hurdles in your way, and make it difficult for you to serve Jesus! They may even find a way to lock you up, or lock you down! Well, Jesus is speaking to you today! Amen! Stay strong and be of courage; no matter what man does to you, you will be able to serve Jesus as He has called you! Hallelujah! Man is not in control, God is! Jesus is encouraging you today! Do not let the hate of man discourage you from serving Jesus as He has called you! Amen! Jesus called you to do the Will of God! Amen again! Jesus called you to do the Will of God! And God's Will, will be done; on Earth, as it is in Heaven! Glory to God! Amen.

Day 244

"When Joseph's master (in Egypt) heard the story his wife told him (about Joseph), 'This is how your slave treated me,' he burned with anger.

Joseph's master took him and put him in prison, the place where the king's prisoners were contained. But while Joseph was there in the prison,

the Lord (God) was with him.; He showed him kindness, and granter him favor in the eyes of the prison warden.

So the warden put Joseph in charge of all those held in the prison, and he was made responsible for all that was done there.

The warden paid no attention to anything under Joseph's care, because the Lord God was with Joseph, and gave him success in whatever he did."

(Genesis 39:19-23)

In today's Scripture, the great servant of God, Moses, writes to tell us the history of Joseph, and the time that Joseph was put into a jail in Egypt. Amen! And although Joseph was mistreated by man, accused and sentenced for something that he did not do, it was God's plan for him to be in prison! Amen again! For God had a plan! God had a plan for Joseph to serve Him, but it took this miscarriage of justice to have Joseph in a position to move forward in God's plan! Hallelujah! Of course, Joseph did not know God's plan, but God knew God's plan! For God's plan was in place before Joseph was born! Glory Hallelujah! And God has a plan for you! Just like Joseph, you may not know what it is, and just like Joseph, your life may take a turn for the worse. But hallelujah, God has a plan for you! Glory to God! Joseph was lied upon and accused of attempting to be with his master's wife. And her lie put Joseph on a path that he did not understand. Our Scripture begins with, **"When Joseph's master (in Egypt) heard the story his wife told him (about Joseph), 'This is how your slave treated me,' he burned with anger. Joseph's master took him and put him in prison, the place where the king's prisoners were contained."** God will use the evil in others, to put His people in a position to do great things! God will put you in the right place at the right time! Amen! Our Word continues to tell us, **"But while Joseph was there in the prison, the Lord (God) was with him.; He showed him kindness, and granter him favor in the eyes of the prison warden. So the warden put Joseph in charge of all those held in the prison, and he was made responsible for all that was done there."** When God puts you on the path to do His Will, He will show you favor! And good things will happen for you, even though you are in "bad places"! Amen again! And the Word of God proclaims that, **"The warden paid no attention to anything under Joseph's care, because the Lord God was with Joseph, and gave him success in whatever he did."** God will give you success, and other people will notice that even in hard times, God is with you! Hallelujah! God is putting you in the perfect position; to give you an opportunity to shine in His plan for you! Glory Hallelujah! God is just setting you up, to do great things! All according to His plan for you! Glory to God! God has a plan for you! Amen.

Today, our Scripture is speaking to God's people. God has a plan for you! Amen! You may not know what it is, and you may be in a terrible place right now; but God may have you in that place as part of His plan for you to do His Will, and bring Him glory! Amen again! Moses writes to tell us the history of Joseph, and the time that Joseph was put into a jail in Egypt. Amen! And although Joseph was mistreated by man, accused and sentenced for something that he did not do, it was God's plan for him to be in prison! Amen again! For God had a plan! But it took this miscarriage of justice to have Joseph in a position to move forward in God's plan! Hallelujah! Joseph did not know God's plan, but God knew God's plan! For God's plan was in place before Joseph was born! Glory Hallelujah! And God has a plan for you! You may not know what it is, and just like Joseph, your life may take a turn for the worse. But hallelujah, God has a plan for you! Glory to God! Joseph was lied upon by his master's wife. But her lie, put Joseph on a path that would lead him to do great things according to God's plan for him. For God had a plan! Glory! Our Scripture begins with, **"When Joseph's master (in Egypt) heard the story his wife told him (about Joseph), 'This is how your slave treated me,' he burned with anger. Joseph's master took him and put him in prison, the place where the king's prisoners**

were contained." God will use the evil in others, to put His people in a position to do great things! God will put you in the right place at the right time! Amen! God is putting you in the perfect position; to give you an opportunity to shine in His plan for you! Hallelujah! Man may think that they are truly punishing you, but man is not in control of you! Glory Hallelujah! God is just setting you up, to do great things! All according to His plan for you! Glory to God! God has a plan for you! Amen.

Today, our Word is speaking to God's people. God has a plan for you! Amen! You may not know what it is, and you may be in a terrible place right now; but God may have you in that place as part of His plan for you to do His Will, and bring Him glory! Amen again! Joseph was put into a jail in Egypt. Amen! Joseph was mistreated by man, accused and sentenced for something that he did not do, but it was God's plan for him to be in prison! Amen again! God had a plan! Hallelujah! Joseph did not know God's plan, but God knew God's plan! For God's plan was in place before Joseph was born! Glory Hallelujah! And God has a plan for you! You may not know what it is, and your life may take a turn for the worse. But hallelujah, God has a plan for you! Glory to God! Joseph was lied upon by his master's wife, but that lie put Joseph on a path that would lead him to do great things according to God's plan for him. For God had a plan! Glory! God will use the evil in others, to put His people in a position to do great things! God will put you in the right place at the right time! Amen! Our Word continues to tell us, **"But while Joseph was there in the prison,**

the Lord (God) was with him.; He showed him kindness, and granter him favor in the eyes of the prison warden. So the warden put Joseph in charge of all those held in the prison, and he was made responsible for all that was done there." When God puts you on the path to do His Will, He will show you favor! And good things will happen for you, even though you are in "bad places"! Amen again! For what is a bad place to man, or even a bad place for you, may end up being the greatest place to give you an opportunity to shine in God's plan for you! Hallelujah! God is putting you in the perfect position; to give you an opportunity to shine in His plan for you! Glory Hallelujah! God is just setting you up to do great things! All according to His plan for you! Glory to God! God has a plan for you! Amen.

Today, the Word of God is speaking to God's people. The Word of God is speaking to you! God has a plan for you! Amen! You may not know what it is, and you may be in a terrible place right now; but God may have you in that place as part of His plan for you to do His Will and bring Him glory! Amen again! Joseph was put into a jail in Egypt. Amen! And it was God's plan for him to be in prison! Amen again! God had a plan! Hallelujah! Joseph did not know God's plan, but God knew God's plan! Glory Hallelujah! And God has a plan for you! You may not know what it is, and your life may take a turn for the worse. But hallelujah, God has a plan for you! Glory to God! God will use the evil in others to put you in a position to do great things! God will put you in the right place at the right time! Amen! And when God puts you on the path to do His Will, He will show you favor! Good things will happen for you, even though you are in "bad places"! Amen again! And the Word of God proclaims that, **"The warden paid no attention to anything under Joseph's care, because the Lord God was with Joseph, and gave him success in whatever he did."** God will give you success, and other people will notice that even in hard times, God is with you! Hallelujah! And when God is with you, you will shine so bright in the darkest places, that others will see the glory of God in you! Hallelujah! So even in your worst situations, trust God! For God is putting you in the perfect position, to give you an opportunity to shine in His plan for you! Glory Hallelujah! God is just setting you up to do great things! All according to His plan for you! Glory to God! God has a plan for you! Amen.

Today, our Scripture Guidance is encouraging you! When you are on the path that God has for you, what you think is a terrible thing that has happened to you, is really God putting you in a place where you can shine and move forward to do His plan for you! Amen! God has a plan for you! And the evil in man, will not stop you from doing God's plan for you. Amen again! God has a plan for you! God will use the evil in others, to put you in a position to do great things! God will put you in the right place at the right time! Amen! And when God puts you on the path to do His Will, He will show you favor! Good things will happen for you, even though you are in "bad places"! Amen again! God will give you success, and other people will notice that even in hard times, God is with you! Hallelujah! So when bad things happen to you, trust that God has a plan for you, and He will use this to move you forward on His plan. God is putting you in the perfect position; to give you an opportunity to shine in His plan for you! Glory Hallelujah! God is just setting you up, to do great things! All according to His plan, for you! Glory to God! God has a plan for you! Amen.

Day 245

"Sometime later, the cupbearer and the baker of the king of Egypt; offended their master, the king of Egypt.

Pharaoh was angry with his two officials, the chief cupbearer and the chief baker,

and put them in custody in the house of the captain of the guard, in the same prison where Joseph was confined.

The captain of the guard assigned them to Joseph, and he attended them."

(Genesis 40:1-4)

In today's Scripture, the great servant of God, Moses, continuous to tell us about the great servant of God, Joseph, and the time that Joseph was put into a jail in Egypt. Amen! And although Joseph was mistreated by man, accused and sentenced for something that he did not do, it was God's plan for him to be in prison! Amen again! For God had a plan! God had a plan for Joseph to serve Him, and Joseph would become a great servant of God, but it took this miscarriage of justice to have Joseph in a position to move forward in God's plan! Hallelujah! Of course, Joseph did not know God's plan, but God knew God's plan! Glory Hallelujah! And God has a plan for you! Your life may take an unexpected turn for the worse. But hallelujah, it is not an unexpected turn to God. For God has a plan for you! Glory to God!

Joseph was lied upon, and put in jail, and that lie put Joseph on a path that he did not understand. But God kept Joseph in His favor, and inside the jail, Joseph became a trusted leader of other men. Amen! This was part of God's plan to put Joseph in a position to serve Him! Amen again! Joseph may have thought he was in the wrong place, but God knew that Joseph was in the right place! Hallelujah! God is speaking to someone today! You think you are in the wrong place; because you do not know God's plan for you, but God knows His plan for you! You are in the right place, right now! And God will continue to move you along His path for you! Glory to God! Our Scripture begins with, **"Sometime later, the cupbearer and the baker of the king of Egypt; offended their master, the king of Egypt. Pharaoh was angry with his two officials, the chief cupbearer and the chief baker, and put them in custody in the house of the captain of the guard,"** God will always have His servants in the right place, and at the right time! Even though you may still think that you are in the wrong place! Amen! Our Word continues to tell us that God put these people, **"in the same prison where Joseph was confined. The captain of the guard assigned them to Joseph,"** When God puts you on the path to do His Will, He will create opportunities for you to serve Him! He will put people in your life to keep you moving along the path He has for you. For that is all according to His plan! And you will have the opportunity to do good things, even though you are in "bad places"! Amen again! And the Word of God proclaims that, **"and he attended them."** God will put people in your life, and you will be able to impact their lives! For God sends people to you to minister too! God has a plan for you, and God is with you! Hallelujah! God has put you in the perfect position; to give you an opportunity to shine in His plan for you! Glory Hallelujah! God has set you up, to do great things! All according to His plan, for you! Glory to God! God has a plan for you! Amen.

Today, our Scripture is speaking to God's people. God has a plan for you! Amen! You may not know what it is, and you may be in a terrible place right now; but God may have you in that place as part of His plan for you to do His Will, and bring Him glory! Amen again! Moses writes to tell us the history of Joseph, and the time that Joseph was put into a jail in Egypt. Amen! And although Joseph was mistreated by man, accused and sentenced for something that he did not do, it was God's plan for him to be in prison! Amen again! For God had a plan! But it took this miscarriage of justice to have Joseph in a position to move forward in God's plan! Hallelujah! Joseph did not know God's plan, but God knew God's plan! For God's plan was in place before Joseph was born! Glory Hallelujah! And God has a plan for you! You may not know what it is, and just like Joseph, your life may take a turn for the worse. But hallelujah, God has a plan for you! Glory to God! Joseph was lied upon by his master's wife. But her lie, put Joseph on a path that would lead him to do great things according to God's plan for him. For God had a plan! Glory! Our Scripture begins with, **"Sometime later, the cupbearer and the baker of the king of Egypt; offended their master, the king of Egypt.**

Pharaoh was angry with his two officials, the chief cupbearer and the chief baker, and put them in custody in the house of the captain of the guard," God will always have His servants in the right place, and at the right time! Even though you may still think that you are in the wrong place! Hallelujah! Joseph did not know these men were coming to Him, but God knew! And these men did not know Joseph; or that Joseph would be there to take care of them, but God knew! For God had a plan for Joseph, and God has a plan for you! Hallelujah! God has put you in the perfect position; to give you an opportunity to shine in His plan for you! Glory Hallelujah! God has set you up, to do great things! All according to His plan, for you! Glory to God! God has a plan for you! Amen.

Today, our Word is speaking to God's people. God has a plan for you! Amen! You may not know what it is, and you may be in a terrible place right now; but God may have you in that place as part of His plan for you to do His Will and bring Him glory! Amen again! Joseph was put into a jail in Egypt. Amen! Joseph was mistreated by man, accused and sentenced for something that he did not do, but it was God's plan for him to be in prison! Amen again! God had a plan! Hallelujah! Joseph did not know God's plan, but God knew God's plan! For God's plan was in place before Joseph was born! Glory Hallelujah! And God has a plan for you! You may not know what it is, and your life may take a turn for the worse. But hallelujah, God has a plan for you! Glory to God! God will always have His servants in the right place, and at the right time! Even though you may still think that you are in the wrong place! Amen! Our Word continues to tell us, **"in the same prison where Joseph was confined. The captain of the guard assigned them to Joseph,"** When God puts you on the path to do His Will, He will create opportunities for you to serve Him! He will put people in your life to keep you moving along the path He has for you. For that is all according to His plan! And you will have the opportunity to do good things, even though you are in "bad places"! Amen again! For what is a bad place to man, or even a bad place for you, may give you an opportunity to shine in God's plan for you! Hallelujah! God has put you in the perfect position; to give you an opportunity to shine in His plan for you! Glory Hallelujah! God has set you up, to do great things! All according to His plan, for you! Glory to God! God has a plan for you! Amen.

Today, the Word of God is speaking to God's people. The Word of God is speaking to you! God has a plan for you! Amen! You may not know what it is, and you may be in a terrible place right now; but God may have you in that place as part of His plan for you to do His Will, and bring Him glory! Amen again! Joseph was put into a jail in Egypt. Amen! And it was God's plan for him to be in prison! Amen again! God had a plan! Hallelujah! Joseph did not know God's plan, but God knew God's plan! Glory Hallelujah! And God has a plan for you! You may not know what it is, and your life may take a turn for the worse. But hallelujah, God has a plan for you! Glory to God! God will always have His servants in the right place, and at the right time! Even though you may still think that you are in the wrong place! Amen! God puts you on the path to do His Will; He will create opportunities for you to serve Him! He will put people in your life to keep you moving along the path He has for you. For that is all according to His plan! And you will have the opportunity to do good things, even though you are in "bad places"! Amen again! And the Word of God proclaims that, **"and he attended them."** God will put people in your life, and you will be able to impact their lives! For God sends people to you to minister too! God has a plan for you, and God is with you! Hallelujah! God Has put you in the perfect position; to give you an opportunity to shine in His plan for you! Glory Hallelujah! God will put people in your life, and you will be able to impact their lives! For God sends people to you to minister too! God has a plan for you, and God is with you! Hallelujah! God has set you up, to do great things! All according to His plan, for you! Glory to God! God has a plan for you! Amen.

Today, our Scripture Guidance is encouraging you! When you are on the path that God has for you, what you think is a terrible thing that has happened to you, is really God putting you in a place where you can shine and move forward to do His plan for you! Amen! God has a plan for you! God will always have His servants in the right place, and at the right time! Even though you may still think that you are in the wrong place! Amen! God puts you on the path to do His Will; He will create opportunities for you to serve Him! He will put people in your life to keep you moving along the path He has for you. For that is all according to His plan! And you will have the opportunity to do good things, even though you are in "bad places"! Amen again! God has a plan for you, and God is with you! Hallelujah! God has set you up, to do great things! All according to His plan, for you! Glory to God! God has a plan for you! Amen.

Day 246

"After they (the king's cupbearer and baker) had been in custody for some time, each of the two men, who were being held in the same prison (as Joseph), had a dream the same night, and each dream had a meaning of its own.

When Joseph came to them the next morning, he saw that they were dejected.

So he asked (these two) Pharaoh's officials who were in custody with him in his master's house, 'Why do you look so sad today?'

'We both had dreams,' they answered, 'but there is no one to interpret them.' Then Joseph said to them, 'Do not interpretations belong to God? Tell me your dreams.'"

(Genesis 40:5-8)

In today's Scripture, the great servant of God, Moses, continuous to tell us about the servant of God, Joseph, and the time that Joseph was put into a jail in Egypt. Amen! Joseph was mistreated by man, accused and sentenced for something that he did not do, but it was God's plan for him to be in prison! Amen again! For God had a plan! God had a plan for Joseph to serve Him, but it took this miscarriage of justice to have Joseph in a position to move forward in God's plan! Hallelujah! Joseph did not know God's plan, but God knew God's plan! Glory Hallelujah! And God has a plan for you! Your life may take an unexpected turn for the worse, but hallelujah, it is not an unexpected turn to God. And although you may think it is the worse, you are there for the better! For God has a plan for you! Glory to God! Joseph was put in jail, and that was part of God's plan! Glory Hallelujah! And God kept Joseph in His favor, and inside the jail, Joseph became a trusted leader of other men. Amen! This was part of God's plan to put Joseph in a position to serve Him! Amen again! Joseph thought he was in the wrong place, but God put Joseph in the right place! Hallelujah! God is speaking to someone today! You think you are in the wrong place; because you do not know God's plan for you, but God knows His plan for you! God will always have His servants in the right place, and at the right time! Amen! You are in the right place, right now! Amen again! And when God puts you on the path to do His Will, He will put people in your life, and you will be able to impact their lives! For God sends people to you so that you can do His Will! Hallelujah! God has a plan for you, and God is with you! Glory Hallelujah! For these things are all according to His plan! And God will continue to move you along His path for you, creating opportunities for you to serve Him! Glory to God! Our Scripture begins with, **"After they (the king's cupbearer and baker) had been in custody for some time, each of the two men, who were being held in the same prison (as Joseph), had a dream the same night, and each dream had a meaning of its own. When Joseph came to them the next morning, he saw that they were dejected."** God creates an opportunity for His servant! Amen! Our Word continues to tell us that the servant of God reached out to the people that God had sent him, telling us, **"So he asked (these two) Pharaoh's officials who were in custody with him in his master's house, 'Why do you look so sad today?' 'We both had dreams,' they answered, 'but there is no one to interpret them.'"** When God gives you an opportunity to serve Him, you still must seek knowledge of what the opportunity is! You must speak to the people that God has sent to you. For that is all according to His plan! Amen again! And the Word of God proclaims that, **"Then Joseph said to them, 'Do not interpretations belong to God? Tell me your dreams.'"** And today, when you begin to serve God, in the name of Jesus, and that you will seek His guidance to serve the people. Hallelujah! God will give His servants the opportunity to serve; but His servants serve His Will! So when God presents you with people to serve; seek Him, and give Him the glory, in the name of Jesus! For today, if you are serving the Will of God, you have been called by Jesus to be His servant. Glory Hallelujah! And as a servant of Jesus; God has set you up, to do great things! All according to His plan for you! Now seek God; serve Jesus, and give all the glory to God! God has a plan for you! Amen.

Today, our Scripture is speaking to God's people. God has a plan for you! Amen! You may not know what it is, and you may be in a terrible place right now; but God may have you in that place as part of His plan for you to do His Will, and bring Him glory! Amen again! Joseph was put in jail; and that was part of God's plan! Glory Hallelujah! And through the favor of God,

Joseph became a trusted leader of other men. Amen! This was part of God's plan! Amen again! Joseph thought he was in the wrong place, but God put Joseph in the right place! Hallelujah! God is trying to help someone! You think you are in the wrong place; because you do not know God's plan for you, but God knows His plan for you! God will always have His servants in the right place, and at the right time! Amen! You are in the right place, right now! Amen again! And when God puts you on the path to do His Will; He will put people in your life; and you will be able to impact their lives! For God sends people to you so that you can do His Will! Hallelujah! God has a plan for you, and God is with you! Glory Hallelujah! Whatever you are going through; is all according to His plan! And God will continue to move you along His path for you; creating opportunities for you to serve Him! Glory to God! Our Scripture begins with, **"After they (the king's cupbearer and baker) had been in custody for some time, each of the two men, who were being held in the same prison (as Joseph), had a dream the same night, and each dream had a meaning of its own. When Joseph came to them the next morning, he saw that they were dejected."** God creates an opportunity for His servant! Amen! God has put you in the perfect position; to give you an opportunity to shine in His plan for you! Glory Hallelujah! Today, if you are serving the Will of God, you have been called by Jesus to be His servant. Glory Hallelujah! And as a servant of Jesus; God has set you up, to do great things! All according to His plan for you! Now seek God; serve Jesus, and give all the glory to

God! God has a plan for you! Amen. Today, our Word is speaking to God's people. God has a plan for you! Amen! You may not know what it is, and you may be in a terrible place right now; but God may have you in that place as part of His plan for you to do His Will, and bring Him glory! Amen again! Joseph thought he was in the wrong place, but God put Joseph in the right place! Hallelujah! God is trying to help someone! You think you are in the wrong place; because you do not know God's plan for you, but God knows His plan for you! God will always have His servants in the right place, and at the right time! Amen! You are in the right place, right now! Amen again! And when God puts you on the path to do His Will; He will put people in your life; and you will be able to impact their lives! For that is His Will! Hallelujah! God has a plan for you! Glory Hallelujah! Whatever you are going through; is all according to His plan! And God will continue to move you along His path for you; and God creates opportunities for His servants! Amen! Glory to God! Our Word continues to tell us, **"So he asked (these two) Pharaoh's officials who were in custody with him in his master's house, 'Why do you look so sad today?' 'We both had dreams,' they answered, 'but there is no one to interpret them.'"** When God gives you an opportunity to serve Him, you still must seek knowledge of what the opportunity is! You must speak to the people that God has sent to you. For that is all according to His plan! Amen again! You will have opportunities to do good things, even though you are in "bad places"! But God still requires you to understand what the opportunity is. Amen! Today, if you are serving the Will of God, you have been called by Jesus to be His servant. Glory Hallelujah! And as a servant of Jesus; God has set you up, to do great things! All according to His plan for you! Now seek God; serve Jesus, and give all the glory to God! God has a plan for you! Amen.

Today, the Word of God is speaking to God's people. The Word of God is speaking to you! God has a plan for you! Amen! You may not know what it is, and you may be in a terrible place right now; but God may have you in that place as part of His plan for you to do His Will, and bring Him glory! Amen again! God is trying to help you! You think you are in the wrong place; because you do not know God's plan for you, but God knows His plan for you! God will always have His servants in the right place, and at the right time! Amen! You are in the right place, right now! Amen again! And when God puts you on the path to do His Will; He will put people in your life; and you will be able to impact their lives! For that is His Will! Hallelujah! God has a plan for you! Glory Hallelujah! Whatever you are going through; is all according to His plan! And God will continue to move you along His path for you; and God creates opportunities for His servants! Amen! Glory to God! But when God gives you an opportunity to serve Him, you still must seek knowledge of what the opportunity is! You must speak to the people that God has sent to you. For that is all according to His plan! Amen again! And the Word of God proclaims that, **"Then Joseph said to them, 'Do not interpretations belong to God? Tell me your dreams.'"** And today, when you begin to serve God, in the name of Jesus; you must give honor to God, and represent yourself His servant, in the name of Jesus; and that you will seek His guidance to serve the people. Hallelujah! Today, if you are serving the Will of God, you have been called by Jesus to be His servant. Glory Hallelujah! And as a servant of Jesus; God has set you up, to do great things! When you are on the path that God has for you; what you think is a terrible thing that has happened to you, is really God putting you a place where you can shine and move forward to do His plan for you! Amen! God has a plan for you! And Jesus will call you to be His servant, which is also part of God's plan for you. Amen again! God will always have Jesus servants in the right place, and at the right time! Even though you may still think that you are in the wrong place! Amen! God puts you on the path to do His Will; And God will continue to move you along His path for you; and God creates opportunities for Jesus servants! Amen! Glory to God! But when God gives you an opportunity to serve Him, you still must seek knowledge of what the opportunity is! You must speak to the people that God has sent to you. For that is all according to His plan! Amen again! And when you begin to serve Jesus; you must give honor to God, and represent yourself as a servant of Jesus; and that you will seek His guidance to serve the people. Hallelujah! God will give Jesus servants the opportunity to serve; but His servants serve His Will! So when God presents you with people to serve; seek Him, and give Him the glory! Glory Hallelujah! And today, when you begin to serve God, in the name of Jesus; seek His guidance to serve the people. Hallelujah! And when God presents you with people to serve; seek Him, and give Him the glory, in the name of Jesus! For today, if you are serving the Will of God, you have been called by Jesus to be His servant. Glory Hallelujah! And as a servant of Jesus; God has set you up, to do great things! All according to His plan for you! Now seek God; serve Jesus, and give all the glory to God! God has a plan for you! Amen.

Day 247

"This is what it (the dream of the Cupbearer) means," Joseph said to him. "The three branches are three days.

Within those three days, Pharaoh will lift up your head and restore you to your position, and you will put Pharaoh's cup in his hand, just as you used to do when you were his Cupbearer.

But when all goes well with you, remember me and show me kindness; mention me to Pharaoh and get me out of this prison."

(Genesis 40:12-14)

In today's Scripture, the great servant of God, Moses; continuous to tell us about the servant of God, Joseph, and the time that Joseph was put into a jail in Egypt. Amen! Joseph was mistreated by man, accused and sentenced to prison for something that he did not do, but it was God's plan for him to be in prison! Amen again! For God had a plan! God had a plan for Joseph to serve Him; but it took this miscarriage of justice to have Joseph in a position to move forward in God's plan! Hallelujah! Joseph did not know God's plan, but God knew God's plan! Glory Hallelujah! And God has a plan for you! Your life may take an unexpected turn for the worse, but hallelujah, it is not an unexpected turn to God. And although you may think it is the worse; you are there for the better! For God has a plan for you! Glory to God! Joseph was put in jail; and that was part of God's plan! Glory Hallelujah! And

God kept Joseph in His favor; and inside the jail, Joseph became a trusted leader of other men. Amen! This was part of God's plan to put Joseph in a position to serve Him! Amen again! Joseph thought he was in the wrong place, but God put Joseph in the right place! Hallelujah! God is speaking to someone today! You think you are in the wrong place; because you do not know God's plan for you, but God knows His plan for you! God will always have His servants in the right place, and at the right time! Amen! You are in the right place, right now! Amen again! And when God puts you on the path to do His Will; He will put people in your life; and you will be able to impact their lives! For God sends people to you so that you can do His Will! Hallelujah! God creates opportunities for His servants! Amen! When God gives you an opportunity to serve Him, you still must seek knowledge of what the opportunity is! You must speak to the people that God has sent to you. For that is all according to His plan! Amen again! And when you begin to serve God, in the name of Jesus; you must seek His guidance to serve the people that God has chosen. Hallelujah! God has a plan for you, and God is with you! Glory Hallelujah! For all of these things are according to His plan! Glory Hallelujah! And God will continue to move you along His path for you; creating opportunities for you to serve Him! Glory to God! Our Scripture begins with, **"This is what it (the dream of the cup bearer) means," Joseph said to him. "The three branches are three days. Within those three days, Pharaoh will lift up your head and restore you to your position, and you will put Pharaoh's**

cup in his hand, just as you used to do when you were his cup bearer." God will give His servants wisdom through the Holy Spirit; so that the servant will know what to say to those that God has sent! Amen! Our Word continues to tell us that once the servant of God shared the message from God to the people, the servant said, **"But when all goes well with you, remember me and show me kindness;"** When you serve God through one opportunity, God will begin to set your path for the next opportunity to serve Him. Amen again! For that is all according to His plan! Amen again! And the Word of God proclaims that, **"mention me to Pharaoh and get me out of this prison."** God will utilize other people to spread the word that you are a servant, with gifts from God! Hallelujah! The more you serve God's Will, the more opportunities you will receive to serve God's Will! Amen! And those opportunities will come because God will utilize "witnesses" of your gifts, to tell other people about you! Amen again! All according to His plan for you! Now seek God; serve Jesus, and give all the glory to God! God has a plan for you! Amen.

Today, our Scripture is speaking to God's people. God has a plan for you! Amen! You may not know what it is, and you may be in a terrible place right now; but God may have you in that place as part of His plan for you to do His Will, and bring Him glory! Amen again! Joseph was put in jail; and that was part of God's plan! Glory Hallelujah! And through the favor of God, Joseph became a trusted leader of other men. Amen! This was part of God's plan! Amen again! Joseph thought he was in the wrong place, but God put Joseph in the right place! Hallelujah! God is trying to help someone! You think you are in the wrong place; because you do not know God's plan for you, but God knows His plan for you! God will always have His servants in the right place, and at the right time! Amen! You are in the right place, right now! Amen again! And when God puts you on the path to do His Will; He will put people in your life; and you will be able to impact their lives! For God sends people to you so that you can do His Will! Hallelujah! God has a plan for you, and God is with you! Glory Hallelujah! Whatever you are going through; is all according to His plan! And God will continue to move you along His path for you; creating opportunities for you to serve Him! Glory to God! Our Scripture begins with, **"This is what it (the dream of the cup bearer) means," Joseph said to him. "The three branches are three days. Within those three days, Pharaoh will lift up your head and restore you to your position, and you will put Pharaoh's cup in his hand, just as you used to do when you were his cup bearer."** God will give His servants wisdom through the Holy Spirit; so that the servant will know what to say to those that God has sent! Amen! God has put you in the perfect position; to give you an opportunity to shine in His plan for you! Glory Hallelujah! Today, if you are serving the Will of God, you have been called by Jesus to be His servant. Glory Hallelujah! God has set you up, to do great things! All according to His plan for you! Now seek Him; serve Him, and give all the glory to God! God has a plan for you! Amen.

Today, our Word is speaking to God's people. God has a plan for you! Amen! You may not know what it is, and you may be in a terrible place right now; but God may have you in that place as part of His plan for you to do His Will, and bring Him glory! Amen again! Joseph thought he was in the wrong place, but God put Joseph in the right place! Hallelujah! God is trying to help someone! You think you are in the wrong place; because you do not know God's plan for you, but God knows His plan for you! God will always have His servants in the right place, and at the right time! Amen! You are in the right place, right now! Amen again! And when God puts you on the path to do His Will; He will put people in your life; and you will be able to impact their lives! For that is His Will! Hallelujah! God has a plan for you! Glory Hallelujah! Whatever you are going through; is all according to His plan! God will give His servants wisdom through the Holy Spirit; so that the servant will know what to say to those that God has sent! Amen! Glory to God! Our Word continues to tell us, **"But when all goes well with you, remember me and show me kindness;"** When you serve God through one opportunity, God will begin to set your path for the next opportunity to serve Him. Amen again! You will have opportunities to do good things, even though you are in "bad places"! But God still requires you to understand what the opportunity is. Amen! Today, if you are serving the Will of God, you have been called by Jesus to be His servant. Glory Hallelujah! God has set you up, to do great things! All according to His plan for you! Now seek Him; serve Him, and give all the glory to God! God has a plan for you! Amen.

Today, the Word of God is speaking to God's people. The Word of God is speaking to you! God has a plan for you! Amen! You may not know what it is, and you may be in a terrible place right now; but God may have you in that place as part of His plan for you to do His Will, and bring Him glory! Amen again! God is trying to help you! You think you are in the wrong place; because you do not know God's plan for you, but God knows His plan for you! God will always have His servants in the right place, and at the right time! Amen! You are in the right place, right now! Amen again! And when God puts you on the path to do His Will; He will put people in your life; and you will be able to impact their lives! For that is His Will! Hallelujah! God has a plan for you! Glory Hallelujah! Whatever you are going through; is all according to His plan! And God will continue to move you along His path for you; and God will give His servants wisdom through the Holy Spirit, so that the servant will know what to say to those that God has sent! Amen! Glory to God! After you serve God through one opportunity, God will begin to set your path for the next opportunity to serve Him. Amen again! And the Word of God proclaims that, **"mention me to Pharaoh and get me out of this prison."** God will utilize other people to spread the word that you are a servant, with gifts from God! Hallelujah! Today, know that the more you serve Jesus and do the Will of God; the more opportunities you will receive to serve God's Will! All according to His plan for you! Now seek God; serve Jesus, and give all the glory to God! God has a plan for you! Amen.

Today, our Scripture Guidance is encouraging you! If you are serving the Will of God, you have been called by Jesus to be His servant. And God has already written your path; you just have to serve Him, utilizing the guidance of the Holy Spirit to serve the people God sends to you. Glory Hallelujah! As a servant of Jesus; God has set you up to do great things! And God will continue to move you along His path for you, so that you can continue to do great things! God creates opportunities for Jesus servants! Amen! Glory to God! And when you serve Jesus; you must give honor to God, and represent yourself as a servant of Jesus; and seek God's guidance to serve the people. Hallelujah! So when God presents you with people to serve; seek God, and God will give you wisdom through the Holy Spirit, so that you will know what to say to those that God has sent! Amen! After you serve God through one opportunity, God will begin to set your path for the next opportunity to serve Him. Amen again! God will utilize other people to spread the word that you are a servant, with gifts from God! Hallelujah! And as a servant of Jesus; God has set you up, to do great things! Now seek God; serve Jesus, and give all the glory to God! God has a plan for you! God has set you up, to do great things! Today, know that the more you serve Jesus and do the Will of God; the more opportunities you will receive to serve God's Will! All according to His plan for you! Now seek God;

serve Jesus, and give all the glory to God! God has a plan for you! Amen.

Day 248

"The chief cup bearer, however, did not remember Joseph; he forgot him.

When two full years had passed (and Joseph was still in jail) Pharaoh had a dream. (In this dream) He was standing by the Nile."

"In the morning Pharaoh's mind was troubled, so he sent for all the magicians and wise men of Egypt. Pharaoh told them his dreams, but no once could interpret them.

Then the chief cup bearer said to Pharaoh, 'Today I am reminded of my shortcomings.'"

"Now a young Hebrew (Joseph) was there with us, a servant of the captain of the guard. We told him our dreams, and he interpreted them for us, giving each man the meaning them.

And things turned out exactly as he interpreted them to us: I was restored to my position and the other man was hanged."

(Genesis 40:23 & 41:1, 8-9 &12-13)

In today's Scripture, the great servant of God, Moses; continuous to tell us about the servant of God, Joseph, and the time that Joseph was put into a jail in Egypt. Amen! Joseph was mistreated by man, accused and sentenced to prison for something that he did not do, but it was God's plan for him to be in prison!

Amen again! For God had a plan! God had a plan for Joseph to serve Him; but Joseph had to be in jail, to be on the path to serve God! Hallelujah! Joseph did not know God's plan, but God knew God's plan! Glory Hallelujah! And God has a plan for you! Your life may take an unexpected turn for the worse, but hallelujah, it is not an unexpected turn to God. And although you may think it is the worse; you are there for the better! God has a plan for you! Glory to God! Joseph was put in jail; and that was part of God's plan! Glory Hallelujah! Joseph thought he was in the wrong place, but God put Joseph in the right place! Hallelujah! God is speaking to someone today! You think you are in the wrong place; because you do not know God's plan for you, but God knows His plan for you! God will always have His servants in the right place, and at the right time! Amen! You are in the right place, right now! Amen again! And will put people in your life; and you will be able to impact their lives! Hallelujah! God creates opportunities for His servants! Amen! When God gives you an opportunity to serve Him, you must speak to the people that God has sent to you. For that is all according to His plan! Amen again! And when you begin to serve God, in the name of Jesus; you must seek His guidance to serve the people that God has chosen. Hallelujah! For all of these things are according to His plan! Glory Hallelujah! Seek Him and God will give you wisdom through the Holy Spirit, so that you will know what to say to those that God has sent! Amen! And after you serve God through one opportunity, God will begin to set your path for the next opportunity to serve Him. Amen again! God will utilize other people to spread the word that you are a servant, with gifts from God! Hallelujah! And as a servant of Jesus; God has set you up, to do great things! All according to His plan for you! And God will continue to move you along His path for you; using other people to create opportunities for you to serve Him! For God has a plan for you! Glory to God! Our Scripture begins with, **"The chief cup bearer, however, did not remember Joseph; he forgot him."** God's plan for you is on His timeline, not yours! So be patient! When you think the plan is not moving; it is because you do not know the timeline of God! Amen! Our Word continues to tell us that once the servant of God shared the message from God to the people, the servant said, **"When two full years had passed (and Joseph was still in jail) Pharaoh had a dream. (In this dream) He was standing by the Nile. In the morning Pharaoh's mind was troubled, so he sent for all the magicians and wise men of Egypt. Pharaoh told them his dreams, but no one could interpret them. Then the chief cup bearer said to Pharaoh, 'Today I am reminded of my shortcomings.'"** God knows the path He has for you, it is already spoken! And He is moving you along His path, even when you think you are not moving! God is in control! Amen again! For that is all according to His plan! Amen again! And the Word of God proclaims that, **"Now a young Hebrew (Joseph) was there with us, a servant of the captain of the guard. We told him our dreams, and he interpreted them for us, giving each man the meaning them. And things turned out exactly as he interpreted them to us: I**

was restored to my position and the other man was hanged." God will utilize other people to spread the word that you are a servant, with gifts from God! But all will happen according to His plan,not your plan! Hallelujah! Today, if you are a servant of Jesus; God is continuing to move you along the His path, so that you will have more opportunities to serve Jesus and give glory to God! All according to His plan for you! Now seek God; serve Jesus, and give all the glory to God! God has a plan for you! Amen.

Today, our Scripture is speaking to God's people. God has a plan for you! Amen! You may not know what it is, and you may be in a terrible place right now; but God may have you in that place as part of His plan for you to do His Will, and bring Him glory! Amen again! God is trying to help someone! You think you are in the wrong place; because you do not know God's plan for you, but God knows His plan for you! God will always have His servants in the right place, and at the right time! Amen! You are in the right place, right now! Amen again! God has a plan for you, and God is with you! Glory Hallelujah! Whatever you are going through; is all according to His plan! And God will continue to move you along His path for you; creating opportunities for you to serve Him! Glory to God! Our Scripture begins with, **"The chief cup bearer, however, did not remember Joseph; he forgot him."** God's plan for you is on His timeline, not yours! So be patient! When you think the plan is not moving; it is because you do not know the timeline of God! Amen! The cup bearer did not know he was part of God's plan for Joseph, so once he was out of jail, he forgot about Joseph. But God never forgot about Joseph! and the cup bearer was still on time, the time that God had planned! Hallelujah! Today, if you are a servant of Jesus; God is continuing to move you along the His path, so that you will have more opportunities to serve Jesus and give glory to God! All according to His plan for you! Now seek God; serve Jesus, and give all the glory to God! God has a plan for you! Amen.

Today, our Word is speaking to God's people. God has a plan for you! Amen! You may be in a terrible place right now; but God may have you in that place as part of His plan for you to do His Will, and bring Him glory! Amen again! God is trying to help someone! You think you are in the wrong place; because you do not know God's plan for you, but God knows His plan for you! God will always have His servants in the right place, and at the right time! Amen! You are in the right place, right now! Amen again! Whatever you are going through; is all according to His plan! And God will continue to move you along His the path He has for you; creating opportunities for you to serve Him! God has a plan for you! Glory Hallelujah! And God's plan for you is on His timeline, not yours! So be patient! When you think the plan is not moving; it is because you do not know the timeline of God! Amen! Glory to God! Our Word continues to tell us, **"When two full years had passed (and Joseph was still in jail) Pharaoh had a dream. (In this dream) He was standing by the Nile. In the morning Pharaoh's mind was troubled, so he sent for all the**

magicians and wise men of Egypt. Pharaoh told them his dreams, but no one could interpret them. Then the chief cup bearer said to Pharaoh, 'Today I am reminded of my shortcomings.'" God knows the path He has for you, it is already spoken! And He is moving you along His path, even when you think you are not moving! God is in control! Amen again! The Pharaoh's dream, and the cup bearer being reminded of his time in jail, was all right on time! The time of God! Glory Hallelujah! Today, if you are a servant of Jesus; God is continuing to move you along the His path, so that you will have more opportunities to serve Jesus and give glory to God! All according to His plan for you! Now seek God; serve Jesus, and give all the glory to God! God has a plan for you! Amen.

Today, the Word of God is speaking to God's people. The Word of God is speaking to you! God has a plan for you! Amen! You may not know what it is, and you may be in a terrible place right now; but God may have you in that place as part of His plan for you to do His Will, and bring Him glory! Amen again! God is trying to help you! You think you are in the wrong place; because you do not know God's plan for you, but God knows His plan for you! God will always have His servants in the right place, and at the right time! Amen! You are in the right place, right now! Amen again! God has a plan for you! Whatever you are going through; is all according to His plan! God's plan for you is on His timeline, not yours! So be patient! When you think the plan is not moving; it is because you do not know the timeline of God! Amen! God knows the path He has for you, it is already spoken! And He is moving you along His path, even when you think you are not moving! God is in control! Amen again! And the Word of God proclaims that, **"Now a young Hebrew (Joseph) was there with us, a servant of the captain of the guard. We told him our dreams, and he interpreted them for us, giving each man the meaning them. And things turned out exactly as he interpreted them to us: I was restored to my position and the other man was hanged."** God will utilize other people to spread the word that you are a servant, with gifts from God! But all will happen according to His plan,not your plan! Hallelujah! God has a plan for you; and it is running along right on time! God's time, not yours! And Almighty God is never late! Glory to God! Today, if you are a servant of Jesus; God is continuing to move you along the His path, so that you will have more opportunities to serve Jesus and give glory to God! All according to His plan for you! Now seek God; serve Jesus, and give all the glory to God! God has a plan for you! Amen.

Today, our Scripture Guidance is encouraging you! You have been called by Jesus to be His servant. And God has already written your path; you just have to serve Him, utilizing the guidance of the Holy Spirit to serve the people God sends to you. Glory Hallelujah! As a servant of Jesus; God has set you up to do great things! And God will continue to move you along His path for you, so that you can continue to do great things! God creates opportunities for Jesus servants! Amen! Glory to God! And when you serve Jesus; you must give honor to God, and represent yourself as a servant of Jesus; and seek God's guidance to serve the people. Hallelujah! So when God presents you with people to serve; seek God, and God will give you wisdom through the Holy Spirit, so that you will know what to say to those that God has sent! Amen! After you serve God through one opportunity, God will begin to set your path for the next opportunity to serve Him. Amen again! But be patient! God knows that you want to serve Jesus; for once you experience serving Jesus, your joy drives a hunger to serve Him more. However, God's plan for you is on His timeline, not yours! When you think the plan is not moving; it is because you do not know the timeline of God! Amen! God knows the path He has for you, it is already spoken! And He is moving you along His path, even when you think you are not moving! God is in control! Amen again! Yes, God will utilize other people to spread the word that you are a servant with gifts from God! But all will happen according to His plan,not your plan! Hallelujah! Today, if you are a servant of Jesus; God is continuing to move you along the His path, so that you will have more opportunities to serve Jesus and give glory to God! All according to His plan for you! Now seek God; serve Jesus, and give all the glory to God! God has a plan for you! Amen.

Day 249

"So Pharaoh sent for Joseph, and he was quickly brought from the dungeon (jail). When he had shaved and changed his clothes, he came before Pharaoh.

Pharaoh said to Joseph, 'I had a dream, and no one can interpret it. But I have heard it said of you that when you hear a dream, you can interpret it.'

'I cannot do it,' Joseph replied to Pharaoh, 'but God will give Pharaoh the answer he desires.'"

"(After Pharaoh had told Joseph his dreams) Then Joseph said to Pharaoh, 'The dreams of Pharaoh are one: God has shown Pharaoh what He is about to do.'"

(Genesis 41:14-16 & 25)

In today's Scripture, the great servant of God, Moses; continuous to tell us about the servant of God, Joseph, and the time that Joseph was put into a jail in Egypt. Amen! But God had a plan for Joseph to serve Him; but Joseph had to be in jail, to be on the path to serve God! Hallelujah! Joseph did not know God's plan, but God knew God's plan! Glory Hallelujah! And God has a plan for you! Your life may take an unexpected turn for the worse, but hallelujah, God has put you in the right place, to do great things! For God has a plan for you! Glory to God! Joseph thought he was in the wrong place, but God put Joseph in the right place!

Hallelujah! God is speaking to someone today! You do not know God's plan for you, but God knows His plan for you! God will always have His servants in the right place, and at the right time! Amen! You are in the right place, right now! Amen again! And when you begin to serve God, in the name of Jesus; you must seek His guidance to serve the people that God has chosen. Hallelujah! For all of these things are according to His plan! Glory Hallelujah! Seek Him and God will give you wisdom through the Holy Spirit, so that you will know what to say to those that God has sent! Amen! And as a servant of Jesus; God will continue to move you along His path for you; using other people to create opportunities for you to serve Him! Amen again! God had a plan for Joseph, and God has a plan for you! Glory to God! Our Scripture begins with, **"So Pharaoh sent for Joseph, and he was quickly brought from the dungeon (jail). When he had shaved and changed his clothes, he came before Pharaoh."** God will continue to bring different people to you; with different opportunities for you to serve the Will of God! But you must prepare yourself; and be ready to speak to the people God sends you. Amen! Our Word continues to tell us that once the servant of God was prepared and in the right place, **"Pharaoh said to Joseph, 'I had a dream, and no one can interpret it. But I have heard it said of you that when you hear a dream, you can interpret it.' 'I cannot do it,' Joseph replied to Pharaoh, 'but God will give Pharaoh the answer he desires.'"** When God puts people in front of you looking for guidance; be humble! Give all the glory for serving

Jesus to God! For what you will tell the people, must come from the Holy Spirit of God! Amen again! And the Word of God proclaims that, **"(After Pharaoh had told Joseph his dreams) Then Joseph said to Pharaoh, 'The dreams of Pharaoh are one: God has shown Pharaoh what He is about to do.'"** The servant of Jesus must completely acknowledge to the people; that the guidance and help comes from God! Always; always, give the glory to God! Hallelujah! Today, God is continuing to move you along the His path, so that you will have more opportunities to serve Jesus and give glory to God! All according to His plan for you! Now seek God; serve Jesus, and give all the glory to God! God has a plan for you! Amen.

Today, our Scripture is speaking to God's people. God has a plan for you! Amen! You may not know what it is, and you may be in a terrible place right now; but God may have you in that place as part of His plan for you to do His Will, and bring Him glory! Amen again! God is trying to help someone! God had a plan for Joseph to serve Him; but Joseph had to be in jail, to be on the path to serve God! Hallelujah! And God has a plan for you! God has put you in the right place, to do great things! Glory to God! Joseph thought he was in the wrong place, but God put Joseph in the right place! Hallelujah! God is speaking to someone today! You do not know God's plan for you, but God knows His plan for you! God will always have His servants in the right place, and at the right time! Amen! You are in the right place, right now! Amen again! And when you serve God in the name of Jesus; you must seek His guidance to serve the people that God has chosen. Hallelujah! For all of these things are according to His plan! Glory Hallelujah! Seek Him and God will give you wisdom through the Holy Spirit, so that you will know what to say to those that God has sent! Amen! And as a servant of Jesus; God will continue to move you along His path for you; using other people to create opportunities for you to serve Him! Amen again! God had a plan for Joseph, and God has a plan for you! Glory to God! Our Scripture begins with, **"So Pharaoh sent for Joseph, and he was quickly brought from the dungeon (jail). When he had shaved and changed his clothes, he came before Pharaoh."** God will continue to bring different people to you; with different opportunities for you to serve the Will of God! But you must prepare yourself; and be ready to speak to the people God sends you. Amen! The cup bearer did not know he was part of God's plan for Joseph, so once he was out of jail, he forgot about Joseph. But God never forgot about Joseph! and the cup bearer was still on time, the time that God had planned! Hallelujah! Today, God is continuing to move you along the His path, so that you will have more opportunities to serve Jesus and give glory to God! All according to His plan for you! Now seek God; serve Jesus, and give all the glory to God! God has a plan for you! Amen.

Today, our Word is speaking to God's people. God has a plan for you! Amen! You may not know what it is, and you may be in a terrible place right now; but God may have you in that place as part of His plan for you to do His Will, and bring Him glory!

Amen again! God is trying to help someone! God has a plan for you! God has put you in the right place, to do great things! Glory to God! You do not know God's plan for you, but God knows His plan for you! God will always have His servants in the right place, and at the right time! Amen! You are in the right place, right now! Amen again! And you must seek His guidance to serve the people that God has chosen. Hallelujah! For all of these things are according to His plan! Glory Hallelujah! Jesus calls you, to do the Will of God that God planned for you! So seek Him and God will give you wisdom through the Holy Spirit, so that you will know what to say to those that God has sent! God had a plan for Joseph, and God has a plan for you! Glory to God! And God will continue to bring different people to you; with different opportunities for you to serve the Will of God! But you must prepare yourself; and be ready to speak to the people God sends you. Amen! Our Word continues to tell us, **"Pharaoh said to Joseph, 'I had a dream, and no one can interpret it. But I have heard it said of you that when you hear a dream, you can interpret it.' 'I cannot do it,' Joseph replied to Pharaoh, 'but God will give Pharaoh the answer he desires.'"** When God puts people in front of you looking for guidance; be humble! Give all the glory for serving Jesus to God! For what you will tell the people, must come from the Holy Spirit of God! Amen again! You are a servant of Jesus; so be humble, just as your Master Jesus was humble! Hallelujah! Today, God is continuing to move you along the His path, so that you will have more opportunities to serve Jesus and give glory to

God! All according to His plan for you! Now seek God; serve Jesus, and give all the glory to God! God has a plan for you! Amen.

Today, the Word of God is speaking to God's people. The Word of God is speaking to you! God has a plan for you! Amen! You may not know what it is, and you may be in a terrible place right now; but God may have you in that place as part of His plan for you to do His Will, and bring Him glory! Amen again! God is trying to help you! You think you are in the wrong place; because you do not know God's plan for you, but God knows His plan for you! God will always have His servants in the right place, and at the right time! Amen! You are in the right place, right now! Amen again! God has a plan for you! Whatever you are going through; is all according to His plan! God's plan for you is on His timeline, not yours! God will continue to bring different people to you; with different opportunities for you to serve the Will of God! But you must prepare yourself; and be ready to speak to the people God sends you. Amen! When God puts people in front of you looking for guidance; be humble! Give all the glory for serving Jesus to God! For what you will tell the people, must come from the Holy Spirit of God! Amen again! And the Word of God proclaims that, **"(After Pharaoh had told Joseph his dreams) Then Joseph said to Pharaoh, 'The dreams of Pharaoh are one: God has shown Pharaoh what He is about to do.'"** The servant of Jesus must completely acknowledge to the people; that the guidance and help comes from God! Always; always, give the glory to God!

Hallelujah! You serve Jesus to do the Will of God, not the will of you! And if you are truly serving Jesus, your guidance comes from the Holy Spirit of God! Today, God is continuing to move you along the His path, so that you will have more opportunities to serve Jesus and give glory to God! All according to His plan for you! Now seek God; serve Jesus, and give all the glory to God! God has a plan for you! Amen.

Today, our Scripture Guidance is encouraging you! You have been called by Jesus to be His servant. And God has already written your path; you just have to serve Him, utilizing the guidance of the Holy Spirit to serve the people God sends to you. Glory Hallelujah! As a servant of Jesus; God has set you up to do great things! God will continue to move you along His path for you, so that you can continue to do great things! God creates opportunities for Jesus servants! Amen! Glory to God! And God will continue to bring different people to you; with different opportunities for you to serve the Will of God! But you must prepare yourself; and be ready to speak to the people God sends you. Amen! When God puts people in front of you looking for guidance; be humble! Give all the glory for serving Jesus to God! For what you will tell the people, must come from the Holy Spirit of God! Amen again! And always, the servant of Jesus must completely acknowledge to the people; that the guidance and help comes from God! Always; always, give the glory to God! Hallelujah! Today, God is continuing to move you along the His path, so that you will have more opportunities to serve Jesus and give glory to God! All according to His plan for you! Now seek God; serve Jesus, and give all the glory to God! God has a plan for you! Amen.

Day 250

"Now therefore," Joseph said to Pharaoh, "let Pharaoh select a discerning and wise man, and set him over the land of Egypt.

Let Pharaoh do this, and let him appoint officers over the land, to collect one fifth of the produce of the land of Egypt in the seven plentiful years (according to Pharaoh's dream).

And let them gather all the food of those good years under the authority of Pharaoh,

Then that food shall be as a reserve for the land for the seven years of famine which shall be in the land of Egypt (according Pharaoh's dream), that the land may not perish during the famine."

So the advice was good to Pharaoh and in the eyes of all his servants.

And Pharaoh said to his servants, "Can we find such a one as this, a man in whom is the Spirit of God?"

(Genesis 41:33-38)

In today's Scripture, the great servant of God, Moses continuous to tell us about the servant of God, Joseph, and the time that Joseph was put into a jail in Egypt. Amen! But God had a plan for Joseph to serve Him; but Joseph had to be in jail, to be on the path to serve God! Hallelujah! Joseph did not know God's plan, but God knew God's plan! Glory Hallelujah! And God has a plan for you! Your life may take an unexpected turn for the worse, but hallelujah, God has put you in the right place, to do great things! But God has a plan for you! Glory to God! God is speaking to someone today! You do not know God's plan for you, but God knows His plan for you! God will always have His servants in the right place, and at the right time! Amen! You are in the right place, right now! Amen again! For all of these things are according to His plan! Glory Hallelujah! And as a servant of Jesus; God will continue to move you along His path for you; using other people to create opportunities for you to serve Him! Amen again! God had a plan for Joseph, and our Scriptures continue to tell us of the journey that God took Joseph on so that Joseph could do the Will of God by helping the people of God! Hallelujah! Glory to God! Our Scripture begins with, **"Now therefore," Joseph said to Pharaoh, "let Pharaoh select a discerning and wise man, and set him over the land of Egypt. Let Pharaoh do this, and let him appoint officers over the land, to collect one fifth of the produce of the land of Egypt in the seven plentiful years (according to Pharaoh's dream). And let them gather all the food of those good years under the authority of Pharaoh, then that food shall be as a reserve for the land for the seven years of famine which shall be in the land of Egypt** (according Pharaoh's dream**), that the land may not perish during the famine."** God will provide His servants with the exact truth to speak to those He sends them to! Amen! Our Word tells us that once the servant of God told the people the truth that God gave the servant to say, the people accepted the truth, **"So the advice was good to Pharaoh and in the eyes of all his servants." When you tell the truth of God's words to the people that He sent you too, they will recognize that truth, as the truth! Amen again!** When you tell the truth of God's words to the people that He sent you too, they will recognize that truth, as the truth! Amen again! And the Word of God proclaims that, **"And Pharaoh said to his servants, "Can we find such a one as this, a man in whom is the Spirit of God?"** Once the people recognize that the servant is guided by the truth of God, they will want someone with the same access to the truth of God to give them guidance. Hallelujah! Even if they do not know the Holy Spirit, they will be drawn to hearing more of the truth of God! Glory Hallelujah! The people will want more guidance from the truth of God! And that may eventually lead them to God; through His Son, Jesus! Glory to God! Today, God is continuing to move you along the His path, so that you will have more opportunities to serve Jesus and give glory to God! All according to His plan for you! Now seek God; serve Jesus, and give all the glory to God! God has a plan for you! Amen.

Today, our Scripture is speaking to God's people. God has a plan for you! Amen! You may not know what it is, and you may be in a terrible place right now; but God may have you in that place as part of His plan for you to do His Will, and bring Him glory! Amen again! God is trying to help someone! Moses continuous to tell us about the servant of God, Joseph, and the time that Joseph was put into a jail in Egypt. Amen! But God had a plan for Joseph to serve Him; but Joseph had to be in jail, to be on the path to serve God! Hallelujah! Joseph did not know God's plan, but God knew God's plan! Glory Hallelujah! And God has a plan for you! Your life may take an unexpected turn for the worse, but hallelujah, God has put you in the right place, to do great things! But God has a plan for you! Glory to God! God is speaking to someone today! You do not know God's plan for you, but God knows His plan for you! God will always have His servants in the right place, and at the right time! Amen! You are in the right place, right now! Amen again! For all of these things are according to His plan! Glory Hallelujah! And as a servant of Jesus; God will continue to move you along His path for you; using other people to create opportunities for you to serve Him! Amen again! God had a plan for Joseph, and God has a plan for you! Our Scriptures continue to tell us of the journey that God took Joseph on so that Joseph could do the Will of God by helping the people of God! Hallelujah! Glory to God! Our Scripture begins with, **"Now therefore," Joseph said to Pharaoh, "let Pharaoh select a discerning and wise man, and set him over the land of Egypt. Let Pharaoh do this, and let him appoint officers over the land, to collect one fifth of the produce of the land of Egypt in the seven plentiful years (according to Pharaoh's dream). And let them gather all the food of those good years under the authority of Pharaoh, then that food shall be as a reserve for the land for the seven years of famine which shall be in the**

land of Egypt (according to the dream), that the land may not perish during the famine." God will provide you with the exact truth to speak to those He sends them to! Amen! When you serve Jesus, the Holy Spirit of God that is inside of you will provide you with the words to say, to the people that God has sent you! For this is not your plan, and the words you speak will not be yours. It is God's plan for you and the people to be together; at the right place, and the right time! So it will be God's words that you will speak to them! Hallelujah! All according to His plan for you! Now seek God; serve Jesus, and give all the glory to God! God has a plan for you! Amen.

Today, our Word is speaking to God's people. God has a plan for you! Amen! You may not know what it is, but God is trying to help someone! Moses continuous to tell us about the servant of God, Joseph, and the time that Joseph was put into a jail in Egypt. Amen! But God had a plan for Joseph to serve Him; but Joseph had to be in jail, to be on the path to serve God! Hallelujah! Joseph did not know God's plan, but God knew God's plan! Glory Hallelujah! And God has a plan for you! Your life may take an unexpected turn for the worse, but hallelujah, God has put you in the right place, to do great things! But God has a plan for you! Glory to God! God is speaking to someone today! You do not know God's plan for you, but God knows His plan for you! God will always have His servants in the right place, and you are in the right place, right now! Amen again! For all of these things are according to His plan! Glory Hallelujah! And God will continue to move you along His path for you; using other people to create opportunities for you to serve Him! Amen again! God had a plan for Joseph, and God has a plan for you! God will continue to bring different people to you; so that you can do the Will of God! Glory Hallelujah! And God will provide you with the exact truth to speak to those He sends them to! Amen! Our Word tells us that once the servant of God told the people the truth that God gave the servant to say, the people accepted the truth, **"So the advice was good to Pharaoh and in the eyes of all his servants."** When you tell the truth of God's words to the people that He sent you too, they will recognize that truth, as the truth! Amen again! As people hear and understand the words that the Holy Spirit of God sends through your mouth; they will understand that the advice from the servant of Jesus is good! Amen! That is why God has you in the right place at the right time, to give the good advice to the people he sends to you! Hallelujah! All according to His plan for you! Now seek God; serve Jesus, and give all the glory to God! God has a plan for you! Amen.

Today, the Word of God is speaking to God's people. The Word of God is speaking to you! God has a plan for you! Amen! You may not know what it is, but God is trying to help you! God has a plan for you! God has put you in the right place, to do great things! But God has a plan for you! Glory to God! God is speaking to you today! You do not know God's plan for you, but God knows His plan for you! God will always have His servants in the right place, and you are in the right place, right now! Amen again! For all of these things are according to His plan! Glory Hallelujah! And God will continue to move you along His path for you; using other people to create opportunities for you to serve Him! Amen again! God has a plan for you! God kept moving Joseph along His path, and God is moving you along His path! Hallelujah! God will provide you with the exact truth to speak to those He sends them to! Amen! When you tell the truth of God's words to the people that He sent you too, they will recognize that truth, as the truth! Amen again! And the Word of God proclaims that, **"And Pharaoh said to his servants, "Can we find such a one as this, a man in whom is the Spirit of God?"** Once the people recognize that the servant is guided by the truth of God, they will want someone with the same access to the truth of God to give them guidance. Hallelujah! Even if they do not know the Holy Spirit, they will be drawn to hearing more of the truth of God! Glory Hallelujah! The people will want more guidance from the truth of God! And that may eventually lead them to God; through His Son, Jesus! Glory to God! That is why God has you in the right place, and the right time, right now! All according to His plan for you! Now seek God; serve Jesus, and give all the glory to God! God has a plan for you! Amen.

Today, our Scripture Guidance is encouraging you! You have been called by Jesus to be His servant. And God has already written your path; you just have to serve Him, utilizing the guidance of the Holy Spirit to serve the people God sends to you. Glory Hallelujah! As a servant of Jesus; God has set you up to do great things! God will continue to move you along His path for you, so that you can continue to do great things! God creates opportunities for Jesus servants! Amen! Glory to God! And God will continue to bring different people to you; with different opportunities for you to serve the Will of God! God will provide you with the exact truth to speak to those He sends them to! Amen! When you tell the truth of God's words to the people that He sent you too, they will recognize that truth, as the truth! Amen again! And as people hear and understand the words that the Holy Spirit of God sends through your mouth; they will understand that the advice from the servant of Jesus is good! Amen! That is why God has you in the right place at the right time, to give the good advice to the people he sends to you! Amen again! And once the people recognize that the servant is guided by the truth of God, they will want someone with the same access to the truth of God to give them guidance. Hallelujah! Even if they do not know the Holy Spirit, they will be drawn to hearing more of the truth of God! Glory Hallelujah! The people will want more guidance from the truth of God! And that may eventually lead them to God; through His Son, Jesus! Glory to God! Glory! That is why God has you in the right place, and the right time, right now! Today, God is continuing to move you along the His path, so that you will have more opportunities to serve Jesus and give glory to God! All according to His plan for you! Now seek God; serve Jesus, and give all the glory to God! God has a plan for you! Amen.

Day 251

"Then Pharaoh said to Joseph, 'Since God has made all this known to you, there is no one so discerning and wise as you.

You shall be in charge of my palace, and all my people are to submit to your orders. Only with respect to the throne will I be greater than you.'

So Pharaoh said to Joseph, 'I hereby put you in charge of the whole land of Egypt."

(Genesis 41:39-41)

In today's Scripture, Moses continuous to tell us about the servant of God, Joseph, and the time that Joseph was put into a jail in Egypt. Amen! God had a plan for Joseph to serve Him; but Joseph had to be in jail, to be on the path to serve God! Hallelujah! Joseph did not know God's plan, but God knew God's plan! Glory Hallelujah! And God has a plan for you! God is speaking to someone today! You do not know God's plan for you, but God knows His plan for you! God will always have His servants in the right place, and at the right time! Amen! And you are in the right place, right now! Amen again! No matter where you are in life; you are along the path that God has for you! No matter what has happened to you; or what you have gone through, or are going through, you are exactly where God has spoken you to be. For all of these things are according to His plan! Glory Hallelujah! God had a plan for Joseph, and our Scriptures continue to tell us of the journey that God took Joseph on; so that Joseph could do the Will of God! It took many years, throughout his life, for Joseph to be in the exact place and situation to do what God had planned him to do! Hallelujah! But every time; Joseph was in the right place, at the right time! Glory to God! Our Scripture continues to chronicle Joseph's life, and begins with, **Then Pharaoh said to Joseph, "Since God has made all this known to you, there is no one so discerning and wise as you."** People will see the wisdom of God in His servants! And there is no greater wisdom than that! Amen! Our Word tells us that once the servant of God told the people the truth that God gave the servant to say, the people accepted the truth, **"You shall be in charge of my palace, and all my people are to submit to your orders. Only with respect to the throne will I be greater than you."** God will give His servants authority! And God's servants will be leaders! Amen again! And the Word of God proclaims that after the people saw the wisdom of God in His servant, **So Pharaoh said to Joseph, "I hereby put you in charge of the whole land of Egypt."** It does not matter where you begin, God has great plans for you! And you will have influence over the people that God sends to you! Hallelujah! Glory to God! God chose Joseph to be His servant; and God has chosen you to be a servant of Jesus! Hallelujah! All according to His plan for you! Glory Hallelujah! Now seek God; serve Jesus, and give all the glory to God! God has a plan for you! Amen.

Today, our Scripture is speaking to God's people. God has a plan for you! Amen! You may not know what it is, and you may be in a terrible place right now; but God has plan for you to do His Will, and bring Him glory! Amen again! God had a plan for Joseph to serve Him. Hallelujah! Joseph did not know God's plan, but God knew God's plan! Glory Hallelujah! And God has a plan for you! God is speaking to you today! You do not know God's plan for you, but God knows His plan for you! God will always have His servants in the right place, and at the right time! Amen! And you are in the right place, right now! Amen again! No matter where you are in life; and no matter what has happened to you; or what you have gone through, or are going through, you are exactly where God has spoken you to be! For all of these things are according to His plan! Glory Hallelujah! Our Scriptures continue to tell us of the journey that God took Joseph on; so that Joseph could do the Will of God! It took many years of his life, for Joseph to be in the exact place, and situation, to do what God had planned him to do! Hallelujah! But every time; Joseph was in the right place, at the right time! Glory to God! Our Scriptures continue to tell us of the journey that God took Joseph on so that Joseph could do the Will of God by helping the people of God! Hallelujah! Glory to God! Our Scripture continues to chronicle Joseph's life, and begins with, **"Then Pharaoh said to Joseph, 'Since God has made all this known to you, there is no one so discerning and wise as you."** People will see the wisdom of God in His servants! And there is no greater wisdom than that! Amen! When you speak what God gives you to speak, you speak with the wisdom of God! For it is not your words you are speaking; but the Holy Spirit's words! Amen! God chose Joseph to be His servant; and God has chosen you to be a servant of Jesus! Hallelujah! All according to His plan for you! Glory Hallelujah! Now seek God; serve Jesus, and give all the glory to God! God has a plan for you! Amen.

Today, our Word is speaking to God's people. God has a plan for you! Amen! You may not know what it is, and you may be in a terrible place right now; but God has plan for you to do His Will, and bring Him glory! Amen again! God had a plan for Joseph to serve Him. Hallelujah! Joseph did not know God's plan, but God knew God's plan! Glory Hallelujah! And God has a plan for you! God is speaking to you today! You do not know God's plan for you, but God knows His plan for you! God will always have His servants in the right place, and at the right time! Amen! And you are in the right place, right now! Amen again! No matter where you are in life; and no matter what has happened to you; or what you have gone through, or are going through, you are exactly where God has spoken you to be! For all of these things are according to His plan! Glory Hallelujah! Our Scriptures continue to tell us of the journey that God took Joseph on; so that Joseph could do the Will of God! It took many years of his life for Joseph to be in the exact place, and situation, to do what God had planned him to do! Hallelujah! But every time; Joseph was in the right place, at the right time! Glory to God! ,Our Scriptures continue to tell us of the journey that God took Joseph on so that Joseph could do the Will of God by helping the people of God! Hallelujah! Glory to God! And the people will see the wisdom of God in His servants! There is no greater wisdom than that! Amen! Our Word tells us that once the servant of God told the people the truth that God gave the servant to say, the people accepted the truth, **"You shall be in charge of my palace, and all my people are to submit to your orders. Only with respect to the throne will I be greater than you."** God will give His servants authority! And God's servants will be leaders! Amen again! People will see the Light of Jesus in you; and that Light is a beacon that draws people to you, to be guided by you! People will want you to guide them; because they recognize the authority that God has given you as a servant of Jesus! Glory! God chose Joseph to be His servant; and God has chosen you to be a servant of Jesus! Hallelujah! All according to His plan for you! Glory Hallelujah! Now seek God; serve Jesus, and give all the glory to God! God has a plan for you! Amen.

Today, the Word of God is speaking to God's people. The Word of God is speaking to you! God has a plan for you! Amen! You may not know what it is, but God is trying to help you! God has a plan for you! God is speaking to you Amen again!! You do not know God's plan for you, but God knows His plan for you! God will always have His servants in the right place, and at the right time! Amen! And you are in the right place, right now! Amen again! No matter where you are in life; and no matter what has happened to you; or what you have gone through, or are going through, you are exactly where God has spoken you to be! And it is exactly at the right time! For all of these things are according to His plan! Glory Hallelujah! Our Scriptures tell us of the journey that God took Joseph on. It took many years of his life for Joseph to be in the exact place, and situation, to do what God had planned him to do! Hallelujah! But every time; Joseph was in the right place, at the right time! Glory to God! God continually took Joseph on journeys so that Joseph could do the Will of God; and help the people of God! Hallelujah! Glory to God! The people will see the wisdom of God in His servants! There is no greater wisdom than that! Amen! And God will give His servants authority! For God's servants will be leaders! Amen again! And the Word of God proclaims that after the people saw the wisdom of God in His servant, **So Pharaoh said to Joseph, 'I hereby put you in charge of the whole land of Egypt."** It does not matter where you begin, God has great plans for you! And you will have influence over the people that God sends to you! Hallelujah! You have the opportunity to lead others to God, through the name of Jesus! And there is no greater position in the eyes of God; than a servant of Jesus Christ, who therefore, is God's servant! Glory to God! God chose Joseph to be His servant; and God has chosen you to be a servant of Jesus! Hallelujah! All according to His plan for you! Glory Hallelujah! Now seek God; serve Jesus, and give all the glory to God! God has a plan for you! Amen.

Today, our Scripture Guidance is encouraging you! You have been called by Jesus to be His servant. And God has already written your path; you just have to serve Him, utilizing the guidance of the Holy Spirit to serve the people God sends to you. Glory Hallelujah! As a servant of Jesus; God has set you up to do great things! And just like with Joseph, God will continue to move you along His path for you, so that you can continue to do great things! It may take longer than you think it should take; but you do not know the timeline God has for you! It took many years of his life for Joseph to be in the exact place, and situation, to do what God had planned him to do! Hallelujah! But every time; Joseph was in the right place, at the right time! Glory to God! God took Joseph many journeys throughout his life; so that Joseph could do the Will of God at different times, each time helping the people of God! Hallelujah! Glory to God! God is doing that for you! Just speak the Words that God gives you when you are serving Jesus. And the people will see the wisdom of God in you! There is no greater wisdom than that! Amen! And once the people recognize that you guided by the truth of God, they will want someone with the same access to the truth of God to give them guidance. Hallelujah! Even if they do not know the Holy Spirit, they will be drawn to hearing more of the truth of God! Glory Hallelujah! And God will give you authority! For each of the servants of Jesus Christ; are blessed by God to be leaders! Amen again! And God will give His servants authority! For God's servants will be leaders! Amen again! So that you may eventually lead someone to Jesus, this leads them to God! Glory! Glory to God! Today, God is continuing to move you along the His path, so that you will have more opportunities to serve Jesus and give glory to God! God chose Joseph to be His servant; and God has chosen you to be a servant of Jesus! Hallelujah! All according to His plan for you! Glory Hallelujah! Now seek God; serve Jesus, and give all the glory to God! God has a plan for you! Amen.

Day 252

"So then, about eating food sacrificed to idols. We (Believers) know that 'An idol is nothing at all in the world', and that 'There is no God but One.'

For even if there are so-called gods, whether in heaven or on earth (as indeed there are many "gods" and many "lords"),

yet for us (Believers) there is but one God, the Father; from Whom all things came and for Whom we live; and there is but one Lord, Jesus Christ, through Whom all things came and through Whom we live."

(1 Corinthians 8:4-6)

In today's Scripture, the great servant of Jesus, the apostle Paul; addresses Believers at the church in Corinth, regarding their question about whether or not it is right to eat food with others that are sacrificing that food to idols. And although at that time, the context of the question was around eating food that was leftover after pagan sacrifices, on pagan altars; and then given by these pagan worshipers to their Christian friends and even Christian priests. It is important to note that Corinth was a thriving city in Greece, and the Greek people at that time worshiped the Greek god's of Greek mythology. The Romans also worshiped the Roman gods of Roman mythology. So this was an important question for the newly found church of Jesus. Amen! As the

Believers at that time were concerned if they were seen as associating and participating with some parts of pagan worshipers; that they may compromise their testimony for Jesus, in how they lived their life. And this question is relevant today! Amen again! Because our world is a world of inclusion; and rightly so, however, that inclusion brings us in contact with many cultures! These different cultures may also worship the "gods" of their culture. So, we may knowingly; or unknowingly, be participating in some parts with those who are pagan worshipers. Tell the truth! In fact, you and I most likely have eaten food, that may have been part of a sacrifice to the altar of an idol. Well our Scripture provided an answer to the people of God at the time of Paul, and that same answer is for the people of God today! Hallelujah! Our Scripture begins with, **"So then, about eating food sacrificed to idols. We (Believers) know that 'An idol is nothing at all in the world', and that 'There is no God but One.'** As a Believer in Jesus Christ, you know there is only one God! So an idol of any kind, is nothing! Amen! Our Word also tells Believers, **"For even if there are so-called gods, whether in heaven or on earth (as indeed there are many "gods" and many "lords"), yet for us (Believers) there is but one God, the Father; from Whom all things came and for Whom we live;"** It does not matter how many gods the world makes up and worships; there is only one God; that created all things, and the only One God to be worshiped! Amen again! And the Word of God also proclaims this truth, **"and there is but one Lord, Jesus Christ, through Whom**

all things came and through Whom we live." And Jesus is God the Son; the One God in the flesh! And only Jesus, who is God in the flesh, came to offer eternal salvation to those who live their life through Him! Glory! So what you eat, or whether what you ate was sacrificed by someone to a "god or idol". For Satan is a liar! There is but one God! And as long as you believe in that One God; and His Son Jesus who is the One God in the flesh, you are still saved, protected, and loved, by the only God! Amen!

Today, our Scripture is speaking to Believers. Because our world is a world of inclusion; and rightly so, that inclusion brings us in contact with many cultures! These different cultures may also worship the "gods" of their culture. So, we may knowingly; or unknowingly, be participating in some parts with those who are pagan worshipers. Tell the truth! In fact, you and I most likely have eaten food, that may have been part of a sacrifice to the altar of an idol. The apostle Paul addressed Believers at the church in Corinth, regarding their question about whether or not it is right to eat food with others that are sacrificing that food to idols. It is important to note that Corinth was a thriving city in Greece, and the Greek people at that time worshiped the Greek god's of Greek mythology. The Romans also worshiped the Roman gods of Roman mythology. So this was an important question for the newly found church of Jesus. Amen! They were concerned if they were seen as associating and participating with some parts of pagan worshipers; that they may compromise their testimony for Jesus, in how they lived their life. And this question is relevant today! Amen again! Paul provided an answer to the people of God at that time; and that same answer is for the people of God today! Hallelujah! Our Scripture begins with, **"So then, about eating food sacrificed to idols. We (Believers) know that 'An idol is nothing at all in the world', and that 'There is no God but One.'** As a Believer in Jesus Christ, you know there is only one God! So an idol of any kind, is nothing! Amen! And you are set aside to God as holy! Jesus said in **Mark 7:15**, "Nothing outside a person can defile them by going into them. Rather, it is what comes out of a person that defiles them." Hallelujah! So what you eat does not change who you belong to, and what you eat cannot harm you in the eyes of God. As long as you recognize and acknowledge that, there is but one God! Glory to God! And as long as you believe in that One God; and His Son Jesus who is the One God in the flesh, you are still saved, protected, and loved, by the only God! Amen!

Today, our Word is speaking to Believers. Our world is a world of inclusion; and rightly so, but that inclusion brings us in contact with many cultures! Amen! These different cultures may also worship the "gods" of their culture. So, we may be participating in some parts, with those who are pagan worshipers. Amen again! In fact, you and I most likely have eaten food that may have been part of a sacrifice to the altar of an idol. Tell the truth! Paul addresses Believers regarding the question about whether or not it is right, to eat food with others that are sacrificing that food to idols. This was an important question for the newly found church of Jesus. Amen! They were concerned if they were seen as associating and participating with some parts of pagan worshipers; that they may compromise their testimony for Jesus, in how they lived their life. And this question is relevant today! Amen again! Paul provided an answer to the people of God at that time; and that same answer is for the people of God today! Hallelujah! As a Believer in Jesus Christ, you know there is only one God! So an idol of any kind, is nothing! Amen! Our Word also tells Believers, **"For even if there are so-called gods, whether in heaven or on earth (as indeed there are many "gods" and many "lords"), yet for us (Believers) there is but one God, the Father; from Whom all things came and for Whom we live;"** It does not matter how many gods the world makes up and worships; there is only one God; that created all things, and the only One God to be worshiped! Amen again! It is sad that other people do not worship the One God; but instead worship "idols and other gods". But God gives everyone free choice. But as long as you recognize this truth, there is but one God! And as long as you believe in that One God; and His Son Jesus who is the One God in the flesh, you are still saved, protected, and loved, by the only God! Amen!

Today, the Word of God is speaking to Believers. The Word of God is speaking to you! Our world is a world of inclusion; and rightly so, but that inclusion brings you in contact with many cultures! Amen! These different cultures may also worship the "gods" of their culture. So, you may be participating in some parts, with those who are pagan worshipers. Amen again! In fact, you most likely have eaten food that may have been part of a sacrifice to the altar of an idol. Tell the truth! Is it right for you to eat food that may have been sacrificed to idols? This question is relevant today! Amen again! Paul provided an answer to the people of God at that time; and that same answer is for the people of God today! Hallelujah! As a Believer in Jesus Christ, you know there is only one God! So an idol of any kind, is nothing! Amen! It does not matter how many gods the world makes up and worships; there is only one God; that created all things, and the only One God to be worshiped! Amen again! And the Word of God also proclaims this truth, **"and there is but one Lord, Jesus Christ, through Whom all things came and through Whom we live."** And Jesus is God the Son; the One God in the flesh! And only Jesus, who is God in the flesh, came to offer eternal salvation to those who live their life through Him! Glory! That is the only important truth; and you must always rely on this truth! There is but one God! And as long as you believe in that One God; and His Son Jesus who is the One God in the flesh, you are still saved, protected, and loved, by the only God! Amen!

Today, our Scripture Guidance is for Believers. Our world is a world of inclusion; and rightly so, but that inclusion brings you in contact with many cultures! Amen! These different cultures may also worship the "gods" of their culture. So, you most likely have eaten food that may have been part of a sacrifice to the altar of an idol. Tell the truth! Is it right for you to eat food that may have been sacrificed to idols? Amen again! As a Believer in Jesus

Christ, you know there is only one God! So an idol of any kind, is nothing! Amen! It does not matter how many gods the world makes up and worships; there is only one God; that created all things, and the only One God to be worshiped! Amen again! And Jesus is God the Son; the One God in the flesh! And only Jesus, who is God in the flesh, came to offer eternal salvation to those who live their life through Him! Glory! So what you eat, or whether what you ate was sacrificed by someone to a "god or idol". For Satan is a liar! There is but one God! And as long as you believe in that One God; and His Son Jesus who is the One God in the flesh, you are still saved, protected, and loved, by the only God! And that, answers that! Amen!

Day 253

"You foolish person, do you want evidence that faith without works is useless?

Was not our father Abraham considered righteous for what he did when he offered his son Isaac on the altar?

You see that his faith and his actions were working together, and his faith was made complete by what he did."

"You see that a person is considered righteous by what they do and not by faith alone."

"As the body without the Spirit is dead; so faith without works is dead."

(James 2:20-22, 24 & 26)

In today's Scripture, the servant of Jesus (and probably the brother of Jesus), James; writes to Believers to speak about the importance of faith in driving work for the body of Christ. Amen! Your belief and faith in Jesus brings you salvation; hallelujah, but your faith should also compel you to work for Jesus! Amen again! The faith of Believers in Jesus should go together with the work in serving Jesus, to truly be credited with righteous living! Hallelujah! Your faith in Jesus should not only drive your works; your faith in Jesus should change your works! Amen! For your works should be evidence of your faith! Amen again! James was challenging Believers in the church to show their faith, by showing their works! And you are being challenged today! You say that you have faith in Jesus Christ as your Lord and Savior; show it, by showing your works! Hallelujah! Our Scripture begins with, **"You foolish person, do you want evidence that faith without works is useless?"** You are being challenged! Amen! Our Word says to Believers, **"Was not our father Abraham considered righteous for what he did when he offered his son Isaac on the altar? You see that his faith and his actions were working together, and his faith was made complete by what he did. You see that a person is considered righteous by what they do and not by faith alone."** Faith must be accompanied by actions, that live your faith! Amen again! And the Word of God concludes with this summation to Believers, **"As the body without the Spirit is dead; so faith without works is dead."** If your faith does not produce works that show your faith, then your faith is not growing any fruit for Jesus! Therefore, your faith is dead! It just sits there! Hallelujah, tell the truth! You are being challenged! So today, show God your faith, serve Jesus with your works! Amen.

Today, our Scripture is speaking to Believers. You are being challenged to live your life in faith; and your faith should drive you to serve Jesus in works. Amen! James writes to Believers to speak about the importance of faith in driving work for the body of Christ. Amen! Your belief and faith in Jesus brings you salvation; hallelujah, but your faith should also compel you to work for Jesus! Amen again! The faith of Believers in Jesus should go together with the work in serving Jesus, to truly be credited with righteous living! Hallelujah! Your faith in Jesus should not only drive your works; your faith in Jesus should change your works! Amen! For your works should be evidence of your faith! Amen again! James was challenging Believers in the church to show their faith, by showing their works! You say that you have faith in Jesus Christ as your Lord and Savior; show it, by showing your works! Hallelujah! Our Scripture begins with, **"You foolish person, do you want evidence that faith without works is useless?"** You are being challenged! Amen! Too many Believers today, do not do any work serving Jesus! Too many Believers believe that all they need to do is believe in Jesus. And it is true, salvation is gifted to you by God when you accept Jesus as your Lord and Savior. And too many Believers just sit on their faith! Going to church every Sunday is not working for Jesus! It is good that you go, but understand; that is not your faith driving you to works, that is your faith just driving you to church! Tell the truth! Your faith without works is useless! And you are being challenged, right now! Your faith should drive you to live righteously; and to live righteously in the eyes of God, your faith must drive your works! And that is the truth! So today, show God your faith, serve Jesus with your works! Amen.

Today, our Word is speaking to Believers. You are being challenged to live your life in faith; and your faith should drive you to serve Jesus in works. Amen! James writes to Believers to speak about the importance of faith in driving work for the body of Christ. Amen! Your belief and faith in Jesus brings you salvation; hallelujah, but your faith should also compel you to work for Jesus! Amen again! The faith of Believers in Jesus should go together with the work in serving Jesus, to truly be credited with righteous living! Hallelujah! Your faith in Jesus should not only drive your works; your faith in Jesus should change your works! Amen! For your works should be evidence of your faith! Amen again! James was challenging Believers in the church to show their faith, by showing their works! And you are being challenged today! You say that you have faith in Jesus Christ as your Lord and Savior; show it, by showing your works! Hallelujah! You are being challenged! Amen! Our Word says to Believers, **"Was not our father Abraham considered righteous for what he did when he offered his son Isaac on the altar? You see that his faith and his actions were working together, and his faith was made complete by what he did. You see that a person is considered righteous by what they do and not by faith alone."** Faith must be accompanied by actions, that live your faith! Amen again! Too many Believers go to church every Sunday to express their faith, but that faith never drives them to do work! So where is your faith? Why don't you feel compelled to serve Jesus and do the work that He has for you? You have faith, but do you want to be considered righteous? You have faith, but no actions!!! And you are being challenged, right now! Your faith should drive you to live righteously; and to live righteously in the eyes of God, your faith must drive your works! And that is the truth! So today, show God your faith, serve Jesus with your works! Amen.

Today, the Word of God is speaking to Believers. You are being challenged to live your life in faith; and your faith should drive you to serve Jesus in works. Amen! James writes to Believers to speak about the importance of faith in driving work for the body of Christ. Amen! Your belief and faith in Jesus brings you salvation; hallelujah, but your faith should also compel you to work for Jesus! Amen again! The faith of Believers in Jesus should go together with the work in serving Jesus, to truly be credited with righteous living! Hallelujah! Your faith in Jesus should not only drive your works; your faith in Jesus should change your works! Amen! For your works should be evidence of your faith! Amen again! James was challenging Believers in the church to show their faith, by showing their works! And you are being challenged today! You say that you have faith in Jesus Christ as your Lord and Savior; show it, by showing your works! Hallelujah! You are being challenged! Amen! Your faith must be accompanied by actions, that live your faith! Amen again! And the Word of God concludes with this summation to Believers, **"As the body without the Spirit is dead; so faith without works is dead."** If your faith does not produce works that show your faith, then your faith is not growing any fruit for Jesus! Therefore, your faith is dead! It just sits there! Hallelujah, tell the truth! Are you going to church Sunday after Sunday, but just sitting there? If so, your faith is dead! Yes, you may have faith; but if you are not serving Jesus and doing work, your faith is dead! Your faith is not producing anything! Your faith,. is just sitting there! Your faith, is dead! So, you are being challenged, right now! Your faith should drive you to live righteously; and to live righteously in the eyes of God, your faith must drive your works! And that is the truth! So today, show God your faith, serve Jesus with your works! Amen.

Today, our Scripture Guidance is for you. You are being challenged! And you are being challenged with one question. Where are the works that show your faith? You say that you have faith in Jesus Christ as your Lord and Savior; so show it, by showing your works! Hallelujah! You are being challenged! Amen! Your faith must be accompanied by actions, that live your faith! Amen again! You are being challenged! If your faith does not produce works that show your faith, then your faith is not growing any fruit for Jesus! Therefore, your faith is dead! You are being challenged! Your faith should drive you to live righteously; and to live righteously in the eyes of God, your faith must drive your works! And that is the truth! So today, show God your faith, serve Jesus with your works! Amen.

Day 254

*"So Moses, Aaron and the leaders of Israel counted all the
Levites (who were chosen by God to serve as the Ministers of the
Law to His people) by their clans and families.*

*All the men from thirty to fifty years of age who came to do the
work of serving and carrying the Tent of Meeting,*

numbered 8,580.

*At the Lord's (Almighty God) command through Moses, each was
assigned his work and told what to carry."*

*"Now Jesus Himself (who was chosen by God to serve as the
Minister of the Gospel to His people) was about thirty years old
when He began His ministry."*

(Numbers 4:46-49 & Luke 3:23)

In today's Scripture, the great servant of God, Moses; writes to
the chosen people of God, to bring order and responsibility to
God's people as they prepare to depart for the Promised Land.
Amen. It is important to remember, that at the time, there are many
tribes of people that have never lived together in freedom. And
although God has performed so many miracles to enable them to
be on this journey; many of them still do not have faith in God!
Amen again! Yet God is still moving them to the Promised Land,
and thus must organize them as His people who will have different
roles; but all as His people, with the assignment of establishing

His kingdom on earth. Hallelujah! So God works through Moses to organize this vast number of people; into an army, with specific duties for specific people. Our Scriptures today speak to those people that God has chosen to be Ministers to His people. The Levites, and later on His Son, Jesus! Amen! And what is truly amazing, that God had a minimum age requirement for His Ministers; that was established in 1400 BC,and still in place at the time of Jesus! Amen again! God's plans were written before time began! God is not making things up on the fly! Glory to God! Our Scripture begins with, **"So Moses, Aaron and the leaders of Israel counted all the Levites (who were chosen by God to serve as the Ministers of the Law to His people) by their clans and families. All the men from thirty to fifty years of age who came to do the work of serving and carrying the Tent of Meeting, numbered 8,580."** God chooses His Ministers, and God determines the requirements! Amen! Our Word continues with, **"At the Lord's (Almighty God) command through Moses, each was assigned his work and told what to carry."** And God assigns His Ministers with exact duties; for God has preordained their work! Amen again! And the Word of God tells us this fact, **"Now Jesus Himself (who was chosen by God to serve as the Minister of the Gospel to His people) was about thirty years old when He began His ministry."** Even the Son of God had to meet God's requirements! Hallelujah! God set His requirements up; and Jesus met God's requirement! Glory Hallelujah! All part of His plan, all under His requirements! God's plans were written before time began! God is not making things up on the fly! Glory to God! Amen.

Today, our Scripture is speaking to the people of God. God has always had plans for His chosen people. He had plans at the time of Moses; and His plans continued through the time of Jesus on earth, and His plans continue today. And all of God's plans were written before time began! Amen! That is why it is so important for God's people to read and study the Old Testament; for the Old Testament is about learning God's plans for His people, and how these plans are tied to His people today. Amen again! The New Testament is not a standalone history! Hallelujah! The New Testament is a continuation of God's plans, not new plans! Glory Hallelujah! In fact the history in the New Testament validates God's plans that were spoken in the Old Testament! Glory to God! God has a plan that chooses people to be Ministers of His Word, and servants to His people. That has not changed! Amen! And God has requirements for these Ministers. And our Scriptures tie those requirements that were spoken in the Old Testament at the time of Moses, to Jesus! Amen again! Our Scriptures today speak to those people that God has chosen to be Ministers to His people. The Levites, and later on His Son, Jesus! Amen! And what is truly amazing, that God had a minimum age requirement for His Ministers; that was established in 1400 BC,and still in place at the time of Jesus! Amen again! Our Scripture begins with, **"So Moses, Aaron and the leaders of Israel counted all the Levites (who were chosen by God to serve as the Ministers of the Law**

to His people) by their clans and families. All the men from thirty to fifty years of age who came to do the work of serving and carrying the Tent of Meeting, numbered 8,580." God chooses His Ministers, and God determines the requirements! Amen! God determined that the people that He chose to minister; should experience 30 years of life, before they could minister to His people! Amen again! God chooses His Ministers before they are born; but he also determined a minimum age requirement! Hallelujah! All part of His plan, all under His requirements! God's plans were written before time began! God is not making things up on the fly! Glory to God! Amen.

Today, our Word is speaking to God's chosen people. If you believe in Jesus as your Lord and Savior, you are one of God's chosen people. Amen! God has always had plans for His chosen people. He had plans at the time of Moses; and His plans continued through the time of Jesus on earth, and His plans continue today. Amen again! And all of God's plans were written before time began! That is why it is so important for God's people to read and study the Old Testament; for the Old Testament is about learning God's plans for His people, and how these plans are tied to His people today. Hallelujah! The New Testament is a continuation of God's plans, not new plans! Glory Hallelujah! The New Testament validates God's plans that were spoken in the Old Testament! Glory to God! God has a plan that chooses people to be Ministers of His Word, and God has requirements for these Ministers. And our Scriptures tie those requirements that were spoken in the Old

Testament at the time of Moses, to Jesus! Amen! What is truly amazing is that God had a minimum age requirement for His Ministers; that was established in 1400 BC,and still in place at the time of Jesus! Amen again! God is not making things up on the fly! Glory to God! God chooses His Ministers, and God determines the requirements! Amen! Our Word continues with, **"At the Lord's (Almighty God) command through Moses, each was assigned his work and told what to carry."** And God assigns His Ministers with exact duties; for God has preordained their work! Amen again! The true Ministers and servants that God has chosen; are also preassigned by the Will of God. They did not choose what they are doing. They did choose to accept the call to serve Jesus; but each one was given their assignment by Jesus, according to the Will of God! What they are doing was not their choice; it is not random, and it is not by coincidence. That Minister; and that servant of Jesus, has been assigned by God! Hallelujah! All part of His plan, all under His requirements! God's plans were written before time began! God is not making things up on the fly! Glory to God! Amen.

Today, the Word of God is speaking to God's chosen people. The Word of God is speaking to you! Amen! God has always had plans for His chosen people. He had plans at the time of Moses; and His plans continued through the time of Jesus on earth, and His plans continue today. Amen again! The Old Testament is about learning God's plans for His people, and how these plans are tied to His people today. Hallelujah! The New Testament is a continuation of God's plans, not new plans! Glory Hallelujah! God has a plan that chooses people to be Ministers of His Word, and God has requirements for these Ministers. And our Scriptures tie those requirements to Jesus! Amen! God had a minimum age requirement for His Ministers that was established in 1400 BC,and still in place at the time of Jesus! Amen again! God's plans were written before time began! God is not making things up on the fly! Glory to God! God chooses His Ministers, and God determines the requirements! Amen! And God assigns His Ministers with exact duties; for God has preordained their work! Amen again! And the Word of God tells us this fact, **"Now Jesus Himself (who was chosen by God to serve as the Minister of the Gospel to His people) was about thirty years old when He began His ministry."** Even the Son of God had to meet God's requirements! Hallelujah! God set His requirements up; and Jesus met God's requirement! Glory Hallelujah! Jesus! Son of God! God in the flesh! Had to wait until He was 30! Glory! All part of His plan, all under His requirements! God's plans were written before time began! God is not making things up on the fly! Glory to God! Amen.

Today, our Scripture Guidance is for God's people. Our Scripture Guidance is for you! God has always had plans for His chosen people. And that plan included assignments for Ministers; and requirements for Ministers! I have often wondered why Jesus waited until He was 30 to be baptized and to start His Ministry. Surely the Son of God; God in the flesh, had the knowledge and wisdom to begin teaching the Gospel of Himself earlier than that. But now I realize through the Word of God, that Jesus had to meet the minimum age requirement; for God had set that requirement with His chosen people at the time of Moses! Amen! God is an amazing and exact God! God had set the minimum age for Ministers and servants at 30; and God was going to obey God's requirements! Even Jesus, God in the flesh! Amen again! All part of His plan, all under His requirements! God's plans were written before time began! God is not making things up on the fly! Glory to God! Amen.

Day 255

"As God's co-workers (servants of Jesus Christ) we urge you not to receive God's grace in vain.

For He says, 'In the time of My favor I heard you, and in the day of salvation I helped you.'

I tell you (that) now is the time of God's favor, now is the day of salvation."

(2 Corinthians 6:1-2)

In today's Scripture, the great servant of Jesus, the Apostle Paul, is speaking to Believers about the grace of God. Amen! For it is only through the grace of God that any of us have been moved to hear and receive the Gospel of Jesus Christ! Amen again! And it is only through the grace of God that God heard us repent, accept Jesus as our Lord and Savior, and receive the gift of salvation from God! Glory! Hallelujah, it is God's grace toward you that you have received salvation; and that gift of salvation was given to you the very day that you accepted Jesus. Glory Hallelujah! God gave you; and continues to give you, His grace! Glory to God! And Paul is challenging each of us not to receive the grace of God to you in vain; by living your life for yourself, and not for God! Amen! For if you have truly accepted God's gracious gift of salvation on the day that you accepted Jesus, how can you live your life for yourself; and live it focused on the things of the world? That would be accepting God's gracious gift of salvation in vain! Amen again! If you have accepted Jesus and received the gift of salvation from God, that means God heard you in your time of need and gifted you salvation from the eternal death penalty that you rightfully earned by sinning! God has shown you His tremendous grace! Hallelujah! And too many Believers receive the greatest gift of salvation from God; and live their life without God while relying on salvation on the Day of Salvation. Tell the truth! Well, your day of salvation is every day! God's grace has been given to you, and every day, you have God's favor. So why waste God's favor? God is with you right now! You do not have to wait until the end of days; to seek His favor again for salvation! You can have God's favor right now! But to maximize God's favor for you, you have to live a life that pleases God! You have to live a life seeking God! You have to live a life serving Jesus and doing the Will of God! Amen; Amen, Amen! Do not live your life of God's gift of grace to you in vain. God's grace for you will provide you with more gifts according to His favor for you. So do not waste His grace and His favor. Live your life to please Him every day; for every day, is your day of salvation! Glory Hallelujah! Our Scripture begins with a challenge, **"As God's co-workers (servants of Jesus Christ), we urge you not to receive God's grace in vain."** God has given you His grace through your acceptance of Jesus, so do not live your life in vain of God's grace! Amen! Our Word continues with this quote from God, **For He says, 'In the time of My favor I heard you, and in the day of**

salvation I helped you.' It is only through God's favor that He heard you repent your sins in the name of Jesus, and gifted you with salvation! Amen again! And the Word of God concludes with this guidance from the servant of Jesus, **"I tell you (that) now is the time of God's favor, now is the day of salvation."** God's favor is with you every day! For every day is a day of salvation for those, who believe in Jesus Christ! Glory! Are you living your life to please God, and continue to receive His favor and His grace! Do not live your daily gift of salvation by not living in a way that pleases God. If you do that, you have received God's grace in vain! Amen.

Today, our Scripture is speaking to Believers. As a believer in Jesus Christ as your Lord and Savior, you have received God's grace, and the greatest gift of salvation. Amen! The Apostle Paul is speaking to Believers about that grace. For it is only through the grace of God that any of us have been moved to hear and receive the Gospel of Jesus Christ! Amen again! And it is only through the grace of God that God heard us repent, accept Jesus as our Lord and Savior, and receive the gift of salvation from God! Glory! God gave you His grace, and continues to give you His grace! Glory to God! Now Paul is challenging each of us not to receive the grace of God to you in vain; by living your life for yourself, and not for God! Amen! For if you have truly accepted God's gracious gift of salvation on the day that you accepted Jesus, how can you live your life for yourself; and live it focused on the things of the world? That would be accepting God's gracious gift of salvation in vain! Amen again! God has shown you His tremendous grace! Hallelujah! And too many Believers receive the greatest gift of salvation from God; and live their life without God while relying on salvation on the Day of Salvation. Tell the truth! Well, your day of salvation is every day! God's grace has been given to you, and every day, you have God's favor. So why waste God's favor? God is with you right now! You can have God's favor right now! But to maximize God's favor for you, you have to live a life that pleases God! You have to live a life seeking God! You have to live a life serving Jesus and doing the Will of God! Amen; Amen, Amen! God's grace for you will provide you with more gifts according to His favor for you. So do not waste His grace and His favor. Live your life to please Him every day; for every day, is your day of salvation! Glory Hallelujah! Our Scripture begins with a challenge, **"As God's co-workers (servants of Jesus Christ), we urge you not to receive God's grace in vain."** God has given you His grace through your acceptance of Jesus, so do not live your life in vain of God's grace! Amen! Are you living your life to please God, and continue to receive His favor and His grace! Do not live your daily gift of salvation by not living in a way that pleases God. If you do that, you have received God's grace in vain! Amen.

Today, our Word is speaking to Believers. You have received God's grace, and the greatest gift of salvation. Amen! And it is only through the grace of God that any of us have been moved to hear; and receive, the Gospel of Jesus Christ! Amen again! And it is only through the grace of God that you have received the gift of salvation from God! Glory! God gave you His grace then, and continues to give you His grace now! Glory to God! But Paul is challenging each of us not to receive the grace of God to you in vain; by living your life for yourself, and not for God! Amen! For if you have truly accepted God's gracious gift of salvation, how can you live your life for yourself; and live it focused on the things of the world? That would be accepting God's gracious gift of salvation in vain! Amen again! Too many Believers receive the greatest gift of salvation from God; and live their life without God while relying on salvation on the Day of Salvation. Tell the truth! God's grace has been given to you, and every day, you have God's favor. So why waste God's favor? God is with you right now! You can have God's favor right now! But to maximize God's favor for you, you have to live a life that pleases God! You have to live a life seeking God! You have to live a life serving Jesus and doing the Will of God! Amen; Amen, Amen! God's grace for you will provide you with more gifts according to His favor for you. So do not waste His grace and His favor. Live your life to please Him every day; for every day, is your day of salvation! Glory Hallelujah! Almighty God has given you His grace through your acceptance of Jesus, so do not live your life in vain of God's grace! Amen! Our Word continues with this quote from God, For He says, **'In the time of My favor I heard you, and in the day of salvation I helped you.'** It is only through God's favor that He heard you repent your sins in the name of Jesus, and gifted you with salvation! Amen again! Are you living your life to please God, and continue to receive His favor and His grace! Do not live your daily gift of salvation by not living in a way that pleases God. If you do that, you have received God's grace in vain! Amen.

Today, the Word of God is speaking to Believers. The Word of God is speaking to you! You have received God's grace, and the greatest gift of salvation. Amen! And it is only through the grace of God that you have received the gift of salvation from God! Amen again! God gave you His grace then, and continues to give you His grace now! Glory to God! But if you have truly accepted God's gracious gift of salvation, how can you live your life for yourself; and live it focused on the things of the world? For too many Believers receive the greatest gift of salvation from God; and live their life without God while relying on salvation on the Day of Salvation. Tell the truth! God's grace has been given to you, and every day, you have God's favor. So why waste God's favor? God is with you right now! You can have God's favor right now! But to maximize God's favor for you, you have to live a life that pleases God! You have to live a life seeking God! You have to live a life serving Jesus and doing the Will of God! Amen; Amen, Amen! God's grace for you will provide you with more gifts according to His favor for you. So do not waste His grace and His favor. Live your life to please Him every day; for every day, is your day of salvation! Glory Hallelujah! Almighty God has given you His grace through your acceptance of Jesus, so do not live your life in vain of God's grace! Amen! For it is only through

God's favor that He heard you repent your sins in the name of Jesus, and gifted you with salvation! Amen again! And the Word of God concludes with this guidance from the servant of Jesus, **"I tell you (that) now is the time of God's favor, now is the day of salvation."** God's favor is with you every day! For every day is a day of salvation for those, who believe in Jesus Christ! Glory! Are you living your life to please God, and continue to receive His favor and His grace! Do not live your daily gift of salvation by not living in a way that pleases God. If you do that, you have received God's grace in vain! Amen.

Today, our Scripture Guidance is a question to you! Have your received God's grace to you in vain? Almighty God has given you His grace through your acceptance of Jesus, so do not live your life in vain of God's grace! Amen! For it is only through God's favor that He heard you repent your sins in the name of Jesus, and gifted you with salvation! Amen again! God's favor is with you every day! For every day is a day of salvation for those, who believe in Jesus Christ! Glory! So, are you living your life to please God? By living in a way that pleases God; you will continue to receive His favor and His grace! Do not live your daily gift of salvation by not living in a way that pleases God. If you do that, you have received God's grace in vain! Amen.

Day 256

"Paul and his companions traveled throughout the region of Phrygia and Galatia, having been kept by the Holy Spirit from preaching the Word in the province of Asia.

When they came to the border of Mysia, they tried to enter Bithynia; but the Spirit of Jesus would not allow them to.

So they passed by Mysia and went down to Troas.

During the night, Paul had a vision of a man of Macedonia standing and begging Paul, 'Come over to Macedonia and help us.'

After Paul had seen the vision, we got ready at once to leave for Macedonia; concluding that God had called us to preach the Gospel to them."

(Acts 16:6-10)

In today's Scripture, the great servant of Jesus, the author Luke, is speaking to Believers to share with us the history of the beginning of the church of the Gospel of Jesus, and how rapidly the Gospel spread from Jerusalem to the whole Roman empire. Amen! In fact, it is the "acts" of the missionary journeys that these servants of Jesus did; that brought the Gospel of Jesus from it's beginning in Jerusalem, to the Gentile people all over the world. Amen again! Luke chronicles these journeys so that we can understand how God's plan to offer salvation to all people, was initially spread to the Gentiles by these "acts" during these missionary journeys. Glory to God! At this particular time in our Scriptures, Paul and his companions have begun their second missionary journey. It is also important that God wants us to know that these servants of Jesus did not choose where they went to serve Jesus; they went where God told them to go! Amen! For servants of Jesus have never, and do not, serve Jesus based on their own will. Amen again! The servants of Jesus have always, and will always, serve Jesus based on the Will of God! Hallelujah! This was true at the beginning of the church of Jesus; it is true now for the church of Jesus, and it will always be true for the church of Jesus! Glory Hallelujah! The destinations, and the "acts" that the servants of Jesus do, are decided by the Will of God! Glory to God! Our Scripture begins with, **"Paul and his companions traveled throughout the region of Phrygia and Galatia, having been kept by the Holy Spirit from preaching the Word in the province of Asia."** The Holy Spirit of God has the plan for each servant; that is the Will of God! And the Holy Spirit will guide the servants of Jesus! Amen! And the Word tells us that the servants of Jesus continued on their journey to serve Jesus, and, **"When they came to the border of Mysia, they tried to enter Bithynia; but the Spirit of Jesus would not allow them to. So they passed by Mysia and went down to Troas."** The servant of Jesus must continue to move forward on their journey, and the Holy Spirit will continue to keep the servant of Jesus on the righteous path that is the Will of God! The servant of Jesus must keep on moving!

Amen again! Finally, the Word of God proclaims, **"During the night, Paul had a vision of a man of Macedonia standing and begging Paul, 'Come over to Macedonia and help us.' After Paul had seen the vision, we got ready at once to leave for Macedonia; concluding that God had called us to preach the Gospel to them."** The Holy Spirit will tell the servant of Jesus where He will serve! And it will always be spoken to the servant by the Holy Spirit! Hallelujah! When you accept the call of Jesus to serve Him, you will serve Him, but only by the Will of God! Just keep moving; until the Holy Spirit tells you what the Will of God is for you. Jesus has called you to serve, and God has already spoken about your journey and your destination. Just commit to serve, and show your commitment by trusting the Will of God, and keep moving along His path for you! And His Holy Spirit will tell you your destination; and the work that you will do serving Jesus, according to the Will of God! Glory to God! Amen.

Today, our Scripture is speaking to Believers. God's divine plan utilizes Believers who accept the call of Jesus to serve Him; and to do the Will of God! Amen! And to serve Jesus, you must be willing to go on a journey, and to be willing to do the "acts" that are the Will of God for you! That is how the church grows! Amen again! The author Luke is speaking to Believers to share the history of the beginning of the church and how rapidly the Gospel spread from Jerusalem to the whole Roman Empire. Amen! It is the "acts" of the missionary journeys that these servants of Jesus did; that brought the Gospel of Jesus from it's beginning in

Jerusalem, to the Gentile people all over the world. Amen again! God's plan to offer salvation to all people was initially spread to the Gentiles by these "acts" during these missionary journeys. Glory to God! At this particular time, Paul and his companions have begun their second missionary journey. God wants us to know that these servants of Jesus did not choose where they went to serve Jesus; they went where God told them to go! Amen! Servants of Jesus have never, and do not, serve Jesus based on their own will. Amen again! The servants of Jesus have always, and will always, serve Jesus based on the Will of God! Hallelujah! This will always be true for the church of Jesus! Glory Hallelujah! The destinations, and the "acts" that the servants of Jesus do, are decided by the Will of God! Glory to God! Our Scripture begins with, **"Paul and his companions traveled throughout the region of Phrygia and Galatia, having been kept by the Holy Spirit from preaching the Word in the province of Asia."** The Holy Spirit of God has the plan for each servant; that is the Will of God! And the Holy Spirit will guide the servants of Jesus! Amen! Jesus has called you to serve, and God has already spoken your journey and your destination. And the Holy Spirit of God will keep you on the right track! So trust God! And just commit to serve, and show your commitment by trusting the Will of God, and keep moving along His path for you! And His Holy Spirit will tell you your destination; and the work that you will do serving Jesus, according to the Will of God! Glory to God! Amen.

Today, our Word is speaking to Believers. God's divine plan utilizes Believers who accept the call of Jesus to serve Him; and to do the Will of God! Amen! And to serve Jesus, you must be willing to go on a journey, and to be willing to do the "acts" that are the Will of God for you! That is how the church grows! Amen again! The author Luke is speaking to Believers to share the history of the beginning of the church, and how rapidly the Gospel spread from Jerusalem to the whole Roman Empire. Amen! It is the "acts" of the missionary journeys that these servants of Jesus did; that brought the Gospel of Jesus from its beginning in Jerusalem to the Gentile people all over the world. Amen again! God's plan to offer salvation to all people was initially spread to the Gentiles by these "acts" during these missionary journeys. Glory to God! At this particular time, Paul and his companions have begun their second missionary journey. God wants us to know that these servants of Jesus did not choose where they went to serve Jesus; they went where God told them to go! Amen! Servants of Jesus have never, and do not, serve Jesus based on their own will. Amen again! The servants of Jesus have always, and will always, serve Jesus based on the Will of God! Hallelujah! This will always be true for the church of Jesus! Glory Hallelujah! The destinations, and the "acts" that the servants of Jesus do, are decided by the Will of God! Glory to God! The Holy Spirit of God has the plan for each servant; that is the Will of God! And the Holy Spirit will guide the servants of Jesus! Amen! And the Word tells us that the servants of Jesus continued on their journey to serve

Jesus, and, **"When they came to the border of Mysia, they tried to enter Bithynia; but the Spirit of Jesus would not allow them to. So they passed by Mysia and went down to Troas."** The servant of Jesus must continue to move forward on their journey, and the Holy Spirit will continue to keep the servant of Jesus on the righteous path that is the Will of God! The servant of Jesus must keep on moving! Amen again! And do not rely on your own understanding! God will reveal His plan to you at His right time! Hallelujah! Jesus called you, and God has a righteous plan for you to serve Jesus and do the Will of God! So just commit to serve, show your commitment by trusting the Will of God, and keep moving along His path for you! And His Holy Spirit will tell you your destination; and the work that you will do serving Jesus, according to the Will of God! Glory to God! Amen.

Today, the Word of God is speaking to Believers. The Word of God is speaking to you! God's divine plan wants you to accept the call of Jesus to serve Him, and to do the Will of God! Amen! And to serve Jesus, you must be willing to go on a journey, and to be willing to do the "acts" that are the Will of God for you! That is how the church grows! Amen again! It is the "acts" of the servants of Jesus that bring the Gospel of Jesus to people all over the world. Hallelujah! God's plan to offer salvation to all people is spread by these "acts" of serving Jesus. Glory to God! And God wants us to know that the servants of Jesus do not choose where they went to serve Jesus; they must go where God tells them to go! Amen! Servants of Jesus have never, and do not, serve Jesus based on their own will. Amen again! The servants of Jesus have always, and will always, serve Jesus based on the Will of God! Hallelujah! This will always be true for the church of Jesus! Glory Hallelujah! The destinations, and the "acts" that the servants of Jesus do, are decided by the Will of God! Glory to God! The Holy Spirit of God has the plan for each servant; that is the Will of God! And the Holy Spirit will guide the servants of Jesus! Amen! The servant of Jesus must continue to move forward on their journey, and the Holy Spirit will continue to keep the servant of Jesus on the righteous path that is the Will of God! The servant of Jesus must keep on moving! Amen again! Finally, the Word of God proclaims, **"During the night, Paul had a vision of a man of Macedonia standing and begging Paul, 'Come over to Macedonia and help us.' After Paul had seen the vision, we got ready at once to leave for Macedonia; concluding that God had called us to preach the Gospel to them."** The Holy Spirit will tell the servant of Jesus where He will serve! And it will always be spoken to the servant by the Holy Spirit! Hallelujah! Make no mistake about it; God has a destination and "acts" that He wants you to perform as a servant of Jesus. Glory Hallelujah! So keep your faith and wait on the Holy Spirit of God to give you direction! For when you accept the call of Jesus to serve Him, you will serve Him, but only by the Will of God! Just commit to serve, and show your commitment by trusting the Will of God, and keep moving along His path for you! And His Holy Spirit will tell you your destination; and the work that you will do serving Jesus, according to the Will of God! Glory to God! Amen.

Today, our Scripture Guidance is for Believers who Jesus has called to serve Him. When you accept the call of Jesus to serve Him, you will serve Him, but only by the Will of God! The Holy Spirit of God has the plan for each servant; that is the Will of God! And the Holy Spirit will guide the servants of Jesus! Amen! The servant of Jesus must continue to move forward on their journey, and the Holy Spirit will continue to keep the servant of Jesus on the righteous path that is the Will of God! The servant of Jesus must keep on moving! Amen again! The Holy Spirit will tell the servant of Jesus where He will serve! And it will always be spoken to the servant by the Holy Spirit! Hallelujah! So if you have accepted the call of Jesus, and you do not know what your destination is, just keep moving! Keep moving until the Holy Spirit tells you what the Will of God is for you. Jesus has called you to serve, and God has already spoken your journey and your destination. You just commit to serve, and show your commitment by trusting the Will of God, and keep moving along His path for you! And His Holy Spirit will tell you your destination; and the work that you will do serving Jesus, according to the Will of God! Glory to God!

Day 257

*(Jesus says) "To you who are listening I say: Love your enemies,
do good to those who hate you;*

bless those who curse you, pray for those who mistreat you."

*"Give to everyone who asks you, and if anyone takes what
belongs to you, do not demand it back.*

Do to others as you would have them do to you."

(Luke 6:27-28 & 30-31)

In today's Scripture, the great servant of Jesus, Luke, shares with us the words that Jesus spoke on the Sermon on the Mount. Amen! This is right after Jesus has called His first Disciples, the twelve Apostles. And it is the first inaugural address to people to explain what He expects of those who will become His followers and represent His Kingdom. Amen again! Jesus begins the first part of this sermon, by speaking of the declarations of blessings to His followers. These declarations of blessings are often referred to as "The Beatitudes" **(Matthew 5:3-12)**. Hallelujah! And now Jesus begins to teach us about loving our enemies. This is a real challenge to change from the natural reactions of the flesh; to the righteous reactions of the Spirit! Glory Hallelujah! Jesus is teaching us how, as His followers, we must change the way we naturally treat people, to reflect the love that Jesus has when He treats people! Amen! For flesh treats people one way, while the

Spirit treats people another way! Amen again! And Jesus is speaking to us to teach us that difference; and what His expectation is of you, now that you have accepted Jesus and received the Holy Spirit of God! Glory to God! Our Scripture begins with Jesus speaking to people, **(Jesus says) "To you who are listening I say: Love your enemies, do good to those who hate you: bless those who curse you, pray for those who mistreat you."** Jesus is challenging you to leave your flesh, and allow the Spirit to enable you to to love and forgive those who do not love you! For forgiveness is love! Amen! Our Word continues with Jesus saying to us, **"Give to everyone who asks you, and if anyone takes what belongs to you, do not demand it back."** Jesus is challenging us to value giving over receiving! For giving is love! Amen again! And the Word of God concludes with Jesus saying to you, **"Do to others as you would have them do to you."** Treat others with the same love you have for yourself! For loving others the way you love yourself, is love! Hallelujah! Jesus is challenging you to change from the ways of the flesh, to the ways of the Spirit! For the ways of the Spirit, is love! Amen.

Today, our Scripture is for those who follow Jesus. Jesus is teaching you to change, and let your actions toward other people to be driven by the Spirit, not by the flesh! Amen! For the ways of the Spirit, is love! Amen again! And Jesus lived His life driven by the Spirit; Jesus lived His life with actions that showed love. Hallelujah! And Jesus is challenging His followers, teaching us that we must reflect His love for us, even in the way we treat our enemies. Glory Hallelujah! Now that is a challenge! Tell the truth! Luke shares with us the words that Jesus spoke on the Sermon on the Mount. Amen! It is the first inaugural address from Jesus, to people to explain what He expects of those who will become His followers and represent His Kingdom. Jesus begins to teach us about loving our enemies. Jesus is teaching that we must change how we respond to our enemies, from the natural reactions of the flesh, to the righteous reactions of the Spirit! Glory Hallelujah! Jesus is teaching His followers that we must change the way we naturally treat people, to reflect the love that Jesus has when He treats people! Amen! This is not easy for any of us, for we are still in the flesh, and to treat people differently, we must become alive in the Spirit. For flesh treats people one way, while the Spirit treats people another way! Amen again! Jesus is speaking to us to teach us that difference; and what His expectation is of you, now that you have accepted Jesus and received the Holy Spirit of God! Glory to God! Our Scripture begins with Jesus speaking to people, **(Jesus says) "To you who are listening I say: Love your enemies, do good to those who hate you: bless those who curse you, pray for those who mistreat you."** Jesus is challenging you to leave your flesh, and allow the Spirit to enable you to love those who do not love you! For forgiveness is love! Amen! Quite frankly, it is hard enough for us to love, bless, and pray for people we like! But to do it for people who hate us, curse us, and mistreat us? Love our enemies, that truly will take the Spirit of God to help us do that! And that is why we must turn to, and be led by the

Spirit! That is the only way to show that kind of love! Hallelujah, tell the truth! You are being challenged! Jesus is challenging you to change from the ways of the flesh, to the ways of the Spirit! For the ways of the Spirit, is love! Amen.

Today, our Word is for those who follow Jesus. Jesus is teaching you to change, and let your actions toward other people to be driven by the Spirit, not by the flesh! Amen! For the ways of the Spirit, is love! Amen again! And Jesus lived His life driven by the Spirit; Jesus lived His life with actions that showed love. Hallelujah! And Jesus is teaching us that we must reflect His love for us, even in the way we treat our enemies. Glory Hallelujah! Now that is a challenge! Jesus is teaching us to love our enemies. And Jesus is teaching that we must change how we respond to our enemies, from the natural reactions of the flesh, to the righteous reactions of the Spirit! Glory Hallelujah! Jesus is teaching us that we must change the way we naturally treat people, to reflect the love that Jesus has when He treats people! Amen! This is not easy for any of us, for we are still in the flesh, but to treat people differently, we must become alive in the Spirit. For flesh treats people one way, while the Spirit treats people another way! Amen again! Jesus is teaching each of His followers, what His expectation is of you, now that you have accepted Jesus and received the Holy Spirit of God! Glory to God! Jesus is challenging you to change from the ways of the flesh, to the ways of the Spirit! For the ways of the Spirit, is love! Jesus is challenging you to leave your flesh, and allow the Spirit to enable you to love and forgive those who do not love you! For forgiveness is love! Amen! Our Word continues with Jesus saying to us, **"Give to everyone who asks you, and if anyone takes what belongs to you, do not demand it back."** Jesus is challenging us to value giving over receiving! For giving is love! Amen again! It is very difficult for any of us to give something of ours away, and Jesus wants us to give to everyone who asks you! Most of us can give our things away to someone we love, but to give it away to someone you do not love, just because they asked you! That is not easy! We naturally do not do that, and that is why Jesus is challenging you! Jesus is challenging you to change from the ways of the flesh, to the ways of the Spirit! For the ways of the Spirit, is love! Amen.

Today, the Word of God is for those who follow Jesus. The Word of God is for you, and the Word of God is being spoken by Jesus! Jesus is teaching you to change, and let your actions toward other people to be driven by the Spirit, not by the flesh! Amen! For the ways of the Spirit, is love! Amen again! And Jesus lived His life driven by the Spirit; Jesus lived His life with actions that showed love. Hallelujah! And Jesus is teaching us that we must reflect His love for us, even in the way we treat our enemies. Glory Hallelujah! Now that is a challenge! Jesus is teaching us to love our enemies. And Jesus is teaching that we must change how we respond to our enemies, from the natural reactions of the flesh, to the righteous reactions of the Spirit! Glory Hallelujah! Jesus is teaching us that we must change the way we naturally treat people, to reflect the love that Jesus has when He treats people! Amen! This is not easy for any of us, for we are still in the flesh, but to treat people differently, we must become alive in the Spirit. For flesh treats people one way, while the Spirit treats people another way! Amen again! Jesus is challenging you to change from the ways of the flesh, to the ways of the Spirit! For the ways of the Spirit, is love! Jesus is challenging you to leave your flesh, and allow the Spirit to enable you to love and forgive those who do not love you! For forgiveness is love! Amen! Jesus is challenging us to value giving over receiving! For giving is love! Amen again! And the Word of God concludes with Jesus saying to you, **"Do to others as you would have them do to you."** Treat others with the same love you have for yourself! For loving others the way you love yourself, is love! Hallelujah! We have all learned to call this the "golden rule." But many people do not realize how great a challenge that is! Jesus understood it, and lived it! He loved others so much that He gave His life for others! That is love! Do you love others as much as you love your own life, your own self? The level of love that Jesus wants you to show does not come from the flesh! That level of love can only come from the Spirit, not the flesh! And that is the truth! And you are being challenged! Jesus is challenging you to change from the ways of the flesh, to the ways of the Spirit! For the ways of the Spirit, is love! Amen.

Today, Jesus is speaking to you! Jesus is challenging you to change from the ways of the flesh, to the ways of the Spirit! For the ways of the Spirit, is love! Jesus is challenging you to leave your flesh, and allow the Spirit to enable you to love and forgive those who do not love you! For forgiveness, is love! Amen! Jesus is challenging us to value giving over receiving! For giving, is love! Amen again! And Jesus is challenging you to treat others with the same love you have for yourself! For loving others the way you love yourself, is love! Hallelujah! That is love! And that level of love can only come from the Spirit, not the flesh! And that is the truth! You are being challenged! Jesus is challenging you to change from the ways of the flesh, to the ways of the Spirit! For the ways of the Spirit, is love! Amen.

Day 258

(Jesus says) "If you love those who love you, what credit is that to you? Even sinners love those who love them.

And if you do good to those who are good to you, what credit is that to you? Even sinners do that.

If you lend to those from whom you expect repayment, what credit is that to you? Even sinners lend to sinners, expecting to be repaid in full.

But love your enemies; do good to them, and lend to the without expecting to get anything back. Then your reward will be great, and you will be children of the Most High (God), because He is kind to the ungrateful and wicked.

Be merciful, just as your Father (Almighty God) is merciful."

(Luke 6:32-36)

In today's Scripture, the great servant of Jesus, Luke, shares with us the words that Jesus spoke on the Sermon on the Mount. Amen! This is right after Jesus has called His first Disciples, the twelve Apostles. And it is the first inaugural address to people to explain what He expects of those who will become His followers and represent His Kingdom. Amen again! Jesus begins the first part of this sermon, by speaking of the declarations of blessings to His followers. Hallelujah! And now Jesus continues to teach us about loving our enemies. Glory Hallelujah! Jesus is teaching us how, as His followers, we must change the way we naturally treat people. Amen! We must change the way we treat our enemies, and those who we do not know; to reflect the love that Jesus has when He treats people! Amen again! We must change from being led by the flesh, to be led by the Spirit! Hallelujah! For flesh treats people one way, while the Spirit treats people another way! Tell the truth! And God has put His Holy Spirit in each person that has accepted Jesus as their Lord and Savior! Yes, you have the Holy Spirit in you! Glory Hallelujah! So you are being challenged by Jesus to allow the Holy Spirit to lead you; and change you, so that you may treat your enemies with love! This will give glory to God! Our Scripture begins with Jesus speaking to people, **(Jesus says) "If you love those who love you, what credit is that to you? Even sinners love those who love them. And if you do good to those who are good to you, what credit is that to you? Even sinners do that. If you lend to those from whom you expect repayment, what credit is that to you? Even sinners lend to sinners, expecting to be repaid in full."** Jesus is challenging you to be different from those who do not know Him! You should no longer be led by the flesh, nor treat people the same way as those who do not know Jesus! Amen! Our Word continues with Jesus guiding His followers, **"But love your enemies; do good to them, and lend to the without expecting to get anything back. Then your reward will be great, and you will be children of the Most High (God), because He is kind to the ungrateful and wicked."** Jesus is challenging us to love our enemies and treat them better than the world treats them! For great will be your reward; because you have allowed His Holy Spirit to lead you! Amen again! And the Word of God concludes with Jesus saying to you, **"Be merciful, just as your Father (Almighty God) is merciful."** God has shown you great mercy! God has forgiven you of all your sins, and God has given you the greatest gift of all, eternal salvation! Hallelujah! Which you did not earn, nor can you pay it back! Glory Hallelujah! God showed you mercy when you were a friend of Satan in sin, and an enemy of God's righteousness! And that is the truth! God had mercy on you! So show the same kind of mercy toward your enemies! For showing mercy, is love! Hallelujah! Jesus is challenging you to change from the ways of the flesh to the ways of the Spirit! For the ways of the Spirit, is love! Amen.

Today, our Scripture is for those who follow Jesus. Jesus is teaching you to change, and let your actions toward other people to be driven by the Spirit, not by the flesh! Amen! For the ways of the Spirit, is love! Amen again! And Jesus lived His life driven by the Spirit; Jesus lived His life with actions that showed love. Hallelujah! And Jesus is challenging His followers, teaching us that we must reflect His love for us, even in the way we treat our enemies. Glory Hallelujah! Now that is a challenge! Tell the truth! Luke shares with us the words that Jesus spoke on the Sermon on the Mount. Amen! It is the first inaugural address from Jesus, to people to explain what He expects of those who will become His followers and represent His Kingdom. Jesus begins to teach us about loving our enemies. Jesus is teaching that we must change how we respond to our enemies, from the natural reactions of the flesh, to the righteous reactions of the Spirit! Glory Hallelujah! Jesus is teaching His followers that we must change the way we naturally treat people, to reflect the love that Jesus has when He treats people! Amen! This is not easy for any of us, for we are still in the flesh, and to treat people differently, we must become alive in the Spirit. For flesh treats people one way, while the Spirit treats people another way! Amen again! Jesus is speaking to us to teach us that difference; and what His expectation is of you, now that you have accepted Jesus and received the Holy Spirit of God! Glory to God! Our Scripture begins with Jesus speaking to people, **(Jesus says) "If you love those who love you, what credit is that to you? Even sinners love those who love them. And if you do good to those who are good to you, what credit is that to you? Even sinners do that. If you lend to those from whom you expect repayment, what credit is that to you? Even sinners lend to sinners, expecting to be repaid in full."** Jesus is challenging you to be different from those who do not know Him! You should no longer be led by the flesh, nor treat people the same way as those who do not know Jesus! Amen! Everyone loves the ones who love them; that makes you no different than the flesh! Of course, you like doing good to those who do good to you, that is not a change from the flesh! And if you loan to someone, demanding and knowing you will get it back, that is not love! If you only treat people well that treat you well, you are still being led by the flesh, not the Spirit! That is the truth! You are being challenged! Jesus is challenging you to change from the ways of the flesh, to the ways of the Spirit! For the ways of the Spirit, is love! Amen.

Today, our Word is for those who follow Jesus. Jesus is teaching you to change, and let your actions toward other people to be driven by the Spirit, not by the flesh! Amen! For the ways of the Spirit, is love! Amen again! And Jesus lived His life driven by the Spirit; Jesus lived His life with actions that showed love. Hallelujah! And Jesus is teaching us that we must reflect His love for us, even in the way we treat our enemies. Glory Hallelujah! Now that is a challenge! Jesus is teaching us to love our enemies. And Jesus is teaching that we must change how we respond to our enemies, from the natural reactions of the flesh, to the righteous reactions of the Spirit! Glory Hallelujah! Jesus is teaching us that we must change the way we naturally treat people, to reflect the love that Jesus has when He treats people! Amen! This is not easy for any of us, for we are still in the flesh, but to treat people differently, we must become alive in the Spirit. For flesh treats people one way, while the Spirit treats people another way! Amen again! Jesus is teaching each of His followers, what His expectation is of you, now that you have accepted Jesus and received the Holy Spirit of God! Glory to God! Jesus is challenging you to change from the ways of the flesh, to the ways of the Spirit! For the ways of the Spirit, is love! Jesus is challenging you to be different from those who do not know Him! You should no longer be led by the flesh, nor treat people the same way as those who do not know Jesus! Amen! Our Word continues with Jesus guiding His followers, **"But love your enemies; do good to them, and lend to the without expecting to get anything back. Then your reward will be great, and you will be children of the Most High (God), because He is kind to the ungrateful and wicked."** Jesus is challenging us to love our enemies and treat them better than the world treats them! For great will be your reward; because you have allowed His Holy Spirit to lead you! Amen again! It is hard to love your enemies; when you are being led by the flesh! Your flesh will always treat your enemies differently, for that is the flesh! That is the truth! So you are being challenged! Jesus is challenging you to change from the ways of the flesh, to the ways of the Spirit! For the ways of the Spirit, is love! Amen.

Today, the Word of God is for those who follow Jesus. The Word of God is for you, and the Word of God is being spoken by Jesus! Jesus is teaching you to change, and let your actions toward other people to be driven by the Spirit, not by the flesh! Amen! For the ways of the Spirit, is love! Amen again! And Jesus lived His life driven by the Spirit; Jesus lived His life with actions that showed love. Hallelujah! And Jesus is teaching us that we must reflect His love for us, even in the way we treat our enemies. Glory Hallelujah! Now that is a challenge! Jesus is teaching us to love our enemies. And Jesus is teaching that we must change how we respond to our enemies, from the natural reactions of the flesh, to the righteous reactions of the Spirit! Glory Hallelujah! Jesus is teaching us that we must change the way we naturally treat people, to reflect the love that Jesus has when He treats people! Amen! This is not easy for any of us, for we are still in the flesh, but to treat people differently, we must become alive in the Spirit. For flesh treats people one way, while the Spirit treats people another way! Amen again! Jesus is challenging you to change from the ways of the flesh to the ways of the Spirit! For the ways of the Spirit, is love! Jesus is challenging you to be different from those who do not know Him! You should no longer be led by the flesh, nor treat people the same way as those who do not know Jesus! Amen! Jesus is challenging us to love our enemies and treat them better than the world treats them! For great will be your reward; because you have allowed His Holy Spirit to lead you! Amen again! And the Word of God concludes with Jesus saying to you, **"Be merciful, just as your Father (Almighty God) is merciful."** God has shown you great mercy! God has forgiven you of all your sins, and God has given you the greatest gift of all, eternal salvation! Hallelujah! Which you did not earn, nor can you pay it back! Glory Hallelujah! That is love! But mercy comes from the Spirit, not the flesh! God is merciful, and God is not flesh! Jesus is merciful, and Jesus is not flesh! And when Jesus was on earth wrapped in the flesh; He was merciful, because He was led by the Spirit! And that is the truth! So you are being challenged! Jesus is challenging you to change from the ways of the flesh, to the ways of the Spirit! For the ways of the Spirit, is love! Amen.

Today, Jesus is speaking to you! Jesus is challenging you to change from the ways of the flesh, to the ways of the Spirit! For the ways of the Spirit, is love! Jesus is challenging you to be different from those who do not know Him! You should no longer be led by the flesh, nor treat people the same way as those who do not know Jesus! Amen! Jesus is challenging us to love our enemies and treat them better than the world treats them! For great will be your reward; because you have allowed His Holy Spirit to lead you! Amen again! And God has shown you great mercy! God has forgiven you of all your sins, and God has given you the greatest gift of all, eternal salvation! Hallelujah! Which you did not earn, nor can you pay it back! Glory Hallelujah! That is love! Jesus is challenging you to show that level of love, even to your enemies. And that level of love can only come from the Spirit, not the flesh! And that is the truth! You are being challenged! Jesus is challenging you to change from the ways of the flesh, to the ways of the Spirit! For the ways of the Spirit, is love! Amen.

Day 259

"Now there have been many (appointed high) priests, since death prevented them from continuing in their role;

but because Jesus lives forever, He has a permanent priesthood.

Therefore He is able to save completely those who come to God through Him; because He always lives to intercede for them."

"Unlike the other high priests, Jesus does not need to offer sacrifices (according to Old Testament Law) day after day; first for his own sins, and then for the sins of the people. Jesus sacrificed for their sins once; for all, when He offered Himself (on the cross)."

(Hebrews 7:23-25 & 27)

In today's Scripture, the author of the letter to the Hebrews, who were primarily Jewish Christians, writes to explain the difference between the Jewish high priests and Jesus our High Priest. Amen! The Jewish people were accustomed to priests that were appointed to be high priests. And these high priests would represent themselves, and also the chosen people of God, by going to God with sacrifices, and asking for mercy for their sins. All of this was according to the Old Testament with God; and the Law that was delivered by Moses, to the people of God. Amen again! And this was not a custom, or merely a tradition; this was the Law as people knew it, and it was the Law that God commanded them to follow.

Hallelujah! But now God has delivered a New Covenant for His people, and that was always part of His plan. And that New Covenant has a new Law, and that is the Gospel of Jesus Christ! Glory Hallelujah! In this New Covenant, there is only One High Priest! Jesus! That was true when the author wrote the letter to the Hebrews, and that is true today! There is One High Priest, Jesus! There are priests in many religions today, but only One High Priest! Jesus! And all of us need to understand that! It does not matter what the religion is called, nor what the titles are in the religion. There is only One High Priest! Only Jesus can go to God to receive the gift of forgiveness of your sins; and the gift of eternal salvation with God! Jesus! Glory! Our Scripture begins with, **"Now there have been many (appointed high), priests, since death prevented them from continuing in their role; but because Jesus lives forever, He has a permanent priesthood."** Jesus is different than any other priest; because Jesus will always be alive, and in His role as High Priest! Amen! Our Word says that Jesus is always alive, **"Therefore He is able to save completely those who come to God through Him; because He always lives to intercede for them."** Jesus is always right there for you; to utilize His Priesthood to go to God on your behalf! Amen again! And the Word of God proclaims this about Jesus, our High Priest, that, **"Unlike the other high priests, Jesus does not need to offer sacrifices (according to Old Testament Law) day after day; first for his own sins, and then for the sins of the people. Jesus sacrificed for their sins once; for all, when He offered**

Himself (on the cross)." Jesus has already sacrificed "perfect blood' for your sins on the Altar of God. And that perfect blood was His blood! The perfect blood of Jesus is only required by God one time, and it will save your sins for eternity, when you accept Jesus as you High Priest and Savior! Hallelujah! There is only One High Priest! That only One High Priest is Jesus! And only Jesus can go to God to receive the gift of forgiveness of your sins; and the gift of eternal salvation with God! Jesus! Glory! Amen.

Today, our Scripture is speaking to Believers, and yet this is a message for all people. There is only One High Priest! That only One High Priest is Jesus! And only Jesus can go to God to receive the gift of forgiveness of your sins; and the gift of eternal salvation with God! Jesus! Glory! The Jewish people were accustomed to priests that were appointed to be high priests. That was according to the Old Testament with God; and the Law that was delivered by Moses, to the people of God. Amen again! But, Hallelujah! God has delivered a New Covenant for His people, and that was always part of His plan. And that New Covenant is the Gospel of Jesus Christ! Glory Hallelujah! And in this New Covenant, there is only One High Priest! Jesus! There may be priests in many religions today, but there still is only One High Priest! Jesus! It does not matter what the religion is called, nor what the titles are in the religion. There is only One High Priest! And that is the only High Priest that is appointed and recognized by God. Jesus! Glory! Our Scripture begins with, **"Now there have been many (appointed high) priests, since death prevented them from continuing in**

their role; but because Jesus lives forever, He has a permanent priesthood." Jesus is different than any other priest; because Jesus will always be alive, and in His role as High Priest! Amen! All priests who are flesh only will die. That is just a fact of life. However, Jesus was born of the spirit, wrapped in flesh! And Jesus's body defeated death; for His flesh never saw corruption in the tomb! In fact, Jesus's flesh walked the earth after His flesh died! Hallelujah! Then Jesus was raised into Heaven from earth, where He is today! Glory Hallelujah! So since Jesus never dies, He will always be our High Priest! And that is the truth! Amen! There is only One High Priest! That only One High Priest is Jesus! And only Jesus can go to God to receive the gift of forgiveness of your sins; and the gift of eternal salvation with God! Jesus! Glory! Amen.

Today, our Word is speaking to Believers; and yet this is a message for all people. There is only One High Priest! That only One High Priest is Jesus! And only Jesus can go to God to receive the gift of forgiveness of your sins; and the gift of eternal salvation with God! Jesus! Glory! God has delivered a New Covenant for His people, and that New Covenant is the Gospel of Jesus Christ! Glory Hallelujah! And in this New Covenant, there is only One High Priest! Jesus! There may be many in the world with the title of the high priest, but there still is only One High Priest! Jesus! And that is the only High Priest that is appointed and recognized by God. Jesus! Glory! Jesus is different than any other priest; because Jesus will always be alive, and in His role as High Priest!

Amen! Our Word says that Jesus is always alive, **"Therefore He is able to save completely those who come to God through Him; because He always lives to intercede for them."** Jesus is always right there for you; to utilize His Priesthood to go to God on your behalf! Amen again! Since Jesus is alive forever as you High Priest, He is always there for you to intercede for your sins, and keep your sins from a punishment of eternal death for you! Hallelujah! For you will continue to sin in this life, even after you accept Jesus and He washes away the sins that you had at that time. But you will keep sinning! And as long as you repent of your sins, Jesus steps in for you; so that your sin is forgiven! For Jesus is your High priest! Glory Hallelujah! There is only One High Priest! That only One High Priest is Jesus! And only Jesus can go to God to receive the gift of forgiveness of your sins; and the gift of eternal salvation with God! Jesus! Glory! Amen.

Today, the Word of God is speaking to Believers; the Word of God is speaking to you! Amen! There is only One High Priest! That only One High Priest is Jesus! Amen again! And only Jesus can go to God to receive the gift of forgiveness of your sins; and the gift of eternal salvation with God! Jesus! Glory! God has delivered a New Covenant for His people, and that New Covenant is the Gospel of Jesus Christ! Glory Hallelujah! And in this New Covenant, there is only One High Priest! Jesus! There may be many in the world with the title of high priest, but there still is only One High Priest! Jesus! And that is the only High Priest that is appointed and recognized by God. Jesus! Glory! Jesus is different than any other priest; because Jesus will always be alive and in His role as High Priest! Amen! Jesus is always right there for you; to utilize His Priesthood to go to God on your behalf! Amen again! And the Word of God proclaims this about Jesus, our High Priest, that, **"Unlike the other high priests, Jesus does not need to offer sacrifices (according to Old Testament Law) day after day; first for his own sins, and then for the sins of the people. Jesus sacrificed for their sins once; for all, when He offered Himself (on the cross)."** Jesus has already sacrificed "perfect blood' for your sins on the Altar of God. And that perfect blood was His blood! The perfect blood of Jesus is only required by God one time, and it will save your sins for eternity when you accept Jesus as you High Priest and Savior! Hallelujah! There is only One High Priest! That only One High Priest is Jesus! And only Jesus can go to God to receive the gift of forgiveness of your sins; and the gift of eternal salvation with God! Jesus! Glory! Amen.

Day 260

"In fact, when we were with you, we kept telling you that we would be persecuted. And it turned out that way; as you well know.

For this reason, when I could stand it no longer, I sent to find out about your faith. I was afraid that in some way the tempter (Satan) had tempted you, and that our labor had been in vain."

"Night and day we pray most earnestly that we may see you again and supply what is lacking in your faith.

Now may our God and Father Himself and our Lord Jesus clear the way for us to come to you."

(1 Thessalonians 3:4-5 & 10-11)

In today's Scripture, the great servant of Jesus, the Apostle Paul, is writing to Believers in the church of Thessalonica to encourage them at a time of separation from fellowship with the leaders of the church. Amen! Paul had been concerned because the church members had been abruptly cut-off from their normal leadership, guidance, and fellowship, and Paul was worried that without their normal support during a very difficult time of persecution for Believers in Jesus Christ, that their faith could be weakened by the temptations of the world. Amen again! For Satan attacks when Believers are separated from fellowship with other Believers; and when the Word of God is not consistently put into their hearts. Tell the truth! And today, we are also going through a time of persecution of the church; and separation from our normal fellowship activities with other Believers. Amen! And the servants of Jesus that normally teach us, lead us, and encourage us; are mostly physically separated from us. Amen again! The church is once again being challenged! But Hallelujah, we are being encouraged to reach out to each other, and pray for each other, so that our faith will be strengthened in a time of persecution. Glory Hallelujah! Our Scripture begins with the servant of Jesus reaching out to Believers to encourage them, saying that, **"In fact, when we were with you, we kept telling you that we would be persecuted. And it turned out that way; as you well know. For this reason, when I could stand it no longer, I sent to find out about your faith. I was afraid that in some way the tempter (Satan) had tempted you, and that our labor had been in vain."** As Believers, we know there will be persecution on earth for our faith in Jesus! So we need to reach out to each other during these difficult times, to encourage them and check on them. Amen! Our Word continues with the servant of Jesus saying to Believers, **"Night and day, we pray most earnestly that we may see you again and supply what is lacking in your faith."** And as servants of Jesus, we must pray with strength and consistency to God, so that He may increase the faith of Believers during these difficult times. Amen again! And the Word of God concludes with the servant of Jesus praying on behalf of the church, **"Now may our God and Father Himself and our Lord Jesus clear the way**

for us to come to you." We must pray to God for His mercy to see us through these difficult times of persecution for the church; so that the members of the church can once again come together to worship, study, and fellowship. Hallelujah! Our faith in Jesus will always keep us together as the family of God! Glory Hallelujah! So pray for each other that God our Father and our Lord Jesus will clear the way for us to come to each other in worship and fellowship again! Glory to God! Live in faith! Amen.

Today, our Scripture is speaking to Believers in Jesus Christ. Amen! We are being challenged to remain faithful through the persecution that the church is going through. Amen again! As Believers, we are never separated from Jesus; and we are never separated from God! Hallelujah! It does not matter what the persecution is! The world can keep us apart, but the world cannot keep us from being together! Glory Hallelujah! The Apostle Paul is writing to Believers to encourage them at a time of separation from fellowship with the leaders of the church. Amen! Paul was worried that without their normal support during a very difficult time of persecution for Believers in Jesus Christ, that their faith could be weakened. Amen again! For Satan attacks when Believers are separated from fellowship; and when the Word of God is not consistently put into their hearts. Tell the truth! Today we are also going through a time of persecution of the church; and separation from our normal fellowship activities with other Believers. Amen! And the church is once again being challenged! So we are being encouraged to reach out to each other; and pray for each other, so that our faith will be strengthened in a time of persecution. Amen again! Our Scripture begins with the servant of Jesus reaching out to Believers to encourage them, saying that, **"In fact, when we were with you, we kept telling you that we would be persecuted. And it turned out that way; as you well know. For this reason, when I could stand it no longer, I sent to find out about your faith. I was afraid that in some way the tempter (Satan) had tempted you, and that our labor had been in vain."** As Believers, we know there will be persecution on earth for our faith in Jesus! So we need to reach out to each other during these difficult times, to encourage them and check on them. Amen! Satan is busy, and will attack each of us, but have faith in Jesus, for Satan has already been defeated! Hallelujah! And no matter what the persecution is, our faith in Jesus will always keep us together as the family of God! Glory Hallelujah! So pray for each other that God our Father and our Lord Jesus will clear the way for us to come to each other in worship and fellowship again! Glory to God! Live in faith! Amen.

Today, our Word is speaking to Believers in Jesus Christ. Amen! We are being challenged to remain faithful through the persecution that the church is going through. Amen again! As Believers, we are never separated from Jesus; and we are never separated from God! Hallelujah! It does not matter what the persecution is! The world can keep us apart, but the world cannot keep us from being together! Glory Hallelujah! However, without our normal support during a very difficult time of persecution for

Believers and the church of Jesus Christ, our faith could be weakened, for Satan attacks when Believers when the Word of God is not consistently put into their hearts. Tell the truth! We are going through a time of persecution of the church; and separation from our normal fellowship activities with other Believers. Amen! And the church is once again being challenged! So we are being encouraged to reach out to each other; and pray for each other, so that our faith will be strengthened in a time of persecution. Hallelujah! As Believers, we know there will be persecution on earth for our faith in Jesus! So we need to reach out to each other during these difficult times, to encourage them and check on them. Amen! Our Word continues with the servant of Jesus saying to Believers, **"Night and day, we pray most earnestly that we may see you again and supply what is lacking in your faith."** And as servants of Jesus, we must pray with strength and consistency to God, so that He may increase the faith of Believers during these difficult times. Amen again! God hears your prayers, and frequent prayer changes things! Hallelujah! Pray constantly; for prayer also shows your faith. And it is our faith in Jesus that will always keep us together as the family of God! Glory Hallelujah! So pray for each other that God our Father and our Lord Jesus will clear the way for us to come to each other in worship and fellowship again! Glory to God! Live in faith! Amen.

Today, the Word of God is speaking to Believers in Jesus Christ. Amen! The Word of God is speaking to you! You are being challenged to remain faithful through the persecution that you, and the church are going through. Amen again! As a Believer, you are never separated from Jesus; and you are never separated from God! Hallelujah! It does not matter what the persecution is! The world can keep us apart, but the world cannot keep us from being together! Glory Hallelujah! However, without your normal support during a very difficult time of persecution for Believers and the church of Jesus Christ, your faith could be weakened. For Satan will attack you when the Word of God is not consistently put into your heart; and when you do not have the consistent support of other Believers during praise and fellowship. Tell the truth! So the church is once again being challenged! And you are being encouraged to reach out to other Believers; and pray for each other, so that their faith, and your faith will be strengthened during this time of persecution. Hallelujah! As a Believer, you know there will be persecution on earth for our faith in Jesus! And you are experiencing that today! So reach out to other Believers during these difficult times, to encourage them and check on them. Amen! As a servant of Jesus, you must pray with strength and consistency to God, so that He may increase your faith, and the faith of other Believers during these difficult times. Amen again! And the Word of God concludes with the servant of Jesus praying on behalf of the church, **"Now may our God and Father Himself and our Lord Jesus clear the way for us to come to you."** You must pray to God for His mercy to see us through these difficult times of persecution for the church; so that the members of the church can once again come together to worship, study, and fellowship. Hallelujah! Whatever the persecution is, Jesus has already defeated it! And the persecution that we are going through; cannot affect our relationship with God through our acknowledged faith! And our faith in Jesus will always keep us together as the family of God! Glory Hallelujah! So pray for each other that God our Father and our Lord Jesus will clear the way for us to come to each other in worship and fellowship again! Glory to God! Live in faith! Amen.

Today, our Scripture Guidance is for Believers in Jesus Christ. Amen! Our Scripture Guidance is for you! You are being challenged to remain faithful through the persecution that you, and the church are going through. Amen again! And to always remember that as a Believer, you are never separated from Jesus; and you are never separated from God! Hallelujah! It does not matter what the persecution is! The world can keep us apart, but the world cannot keep us from being together! Glory Hallelujah! As a Believer, you know there will be persecution on earth for our faith in Jesus! And you are experiencing that today! So reach out to other Believers during these difficult times to encourage them and check on them. Amen! As a servant of Jesus, you must pray with strength and consistency to God, so that He may increase your faith, and the faith of other Believers during these difficult times. Amen again! So today, pray to God for His mercy to see us through these difficult times of persecution; so that the members of the church can once again come together to worship, study, and fellowship. Hallelujah! Our faith in Jesus will always keep us together as the family of God! Glory Hallelujah! So pray for each other that God our Father and our Lord Jesus will clear the way for us to come to each other in worship and fellowship again! Glory to God! Live in faith! Amen.

Day 261

"What if some are unfaithful (to God)? Will their unfaithfulness nullify God's faithfulness (toward them)?

Not at all! Let God be true, and every human being a liar.

But if our unrighteousness brings out God's righteousness more clearly, what shall we say? That God is unjust in bring His wrath on us? (I am using a human argument.)

Certainly not! If that were so, how could God judge the world?"

(Romans 3:3-6)

In today's Scripture, the great servant of Jesus, the Apostle Paul, writes to the church in Rome present an understanding of the Gospel of Jesus Christ, God's plan of salvation for all people. Amen! In our particular Scriptures, Paul is explaining God's faithfulness to people. Amen again! In fact, Paul tells us that God is faithful to us, even when we are unfaithful to Him! Hallelujah! For all of us have sinned, and when you choose sin, you are being unfaithful to God! Tell the truth! Yet God, in his divine love and mercy, will still be faithful to His plan for you! Glory, Hallelujah, merciful God! God is not faithful to us because we are faithful to Him, nor is He faithful to us because we are worthy. God is faithful to us because He is God! And that is the forever truth! Glory to God! Our Scripture begins with, **"What if some are unfaithful (to God)? Will their unfaithfulness nullify God's faithfulness** (toward them)? Not at all! Let God be true, and every human being a liar." God is God! God has already written His plan for you, and God will be faithful to that plan! Amen! Our Word continues with, "But if our unrighteousness brings out God's righteousness more clearly, what shall we say? That God is unjust in bring His wrath on us? (I am using a human argument.) Certainly not!" God is God! God is righteous and just, and our unrighteousness can bring God's wrath, because God is just! Amen again! And the Word of God concludes that God is never unjust; because, "If that were so, how could God judge the world?" God is God! And it is because God is just; that He can and will, judge each person based on His righteousness! Hallelujah! God will be faithful in His plan for you; God will be faithful in what He says He will do, and God will be faithful and just when He judges you! God is God! Your unfaithfulness does not change God's faithfulness! Glory Hallelujah! Glory to God! Amen.

Today, our Scripture is speaking to all people. God is always faithful, whether you are faithful to Him or not! Amen! You are human, God is God! Amen again! Paul is explaining God's faithfulness to people. God is not like man. Man can be unfaithful and unjust, God cannot! Amen! For God is always God! Amen again! In fact, Paul tells us that God is faithful to us, even when we are unfaithful to Him! Hallelujah! For all of us have sinned, and when you choose sin, you are being unfaithful to God! Tell the truth! Yet God will still be faithful with His plan for you!

Glory, Hallelujah, merciful God! God is not faithful to us because we are faithful to Him, nor is He faithful to us because we are worthy. God is faithful to us because He is God! And that is the forever truth! Glory to God! Our Scripture begins with, **"What if some are unfaithful (to God)? Will their unfaithfulness nullify God's faithfulness (toward them)? Not at all! Let God be true, and every human being a liar."** God is God! God has already written His plan for you, and God will be faithful to that plan! Amen! God is faithful in His promises, whether you are unfaithful or not! God is not like you! There will be times in your life when you are unfaithful to God. Yet, God will be faithful in His plan for you; God will be faithful in what He says He will do, and God will be faithful and just when He judges you! God is God! Your unfaithfulness does not change God's faithfulness! Glory Hallelujah! Glory to God! Amen.

Today, our Word is speaking to all people. God is always faithful, whether you are faithful to Him or not! Amen! You are human, God is God! Amen again! Paul is explaining God's faithfulness to people. God is not like man. Man can be unfaithful and unjust, God cannot! Amen! For God is always God! Amen again! God is faithful to us, even when we are unfaithful to Him! Hallelujah! For when you choose sin, you are being unfaithful to God! Tell the truth! Yet God will still be faithful with His plan for you! Glory, Hallelujah, merciful God! God is not faithful to us because we are faithful to Him, nor because we are worthy. God is faithful to us because He is God! Glory to God! God is God!

God has already written His plan for you, and God will be faithful to that plan! Amen! Our Word continues with, **"But if our unrighteousness brings out God's righteousness more clearly, what shall we say? That God is unjust in bring His wrath on us? (I am using a human argument.) Certainly not!"** God is God! God is righteous and just, and our unrighteousness can bring God's wrath, because God is just! Amen again! God's punishment for our sins is true to His righteous divinity! It is clear that God is righteous when He is faithful to bring punishment to you when you are unrighteous! Hallelujah! Yet still, God will be faithful in His plan for you; God will be faithful in what He says He will do, and God will be faithful and just when He judges you! God is God! Your unfaithfulness does not change God's faithfulness! Glory Hallelujah! Glory to God! Amen.

Today, the Word of God is speaking to all people. The Word of God is speaking to you! God is always faithful, whether you are faithful to Him or not! Amen! You are human, God is God! Amen again! And therein is a big difference! God is not like man. Man can be unfaithful and unjust, God cannot! Amen! For God is always God! Amen again! God is faithful to us, even when we are unfaithful to Him! Hallelujah! For when you choose sin, you are being unfaithful to God! Yet God will still be faithful with His plan for you! Glory, Hallelujah, merciful God! God is not faithful to us because we are faithful to Him, nor because we are worthy. God is faithful to us because He is God! Glory to God! God is God! God has already written His plan for you, and God will be faithful to that plan! Amen! God is God! God is righteous and just, and our unrighteousness can bring God's wrath, because God is just! Amen again! And the Word of God concludes that God is never unjust; because, **"If that were so, how could God judge the world?"** God is God! And it is because God is just; that He can and will, judge each person based on His righteousness! Hallelujah! On Judgment Day, God will be just, and God will be righteous! And it is because of that, God will judge! And God will be faithful in His plan for you; God will be faithful in what He says He will do, and God will be faithful and just when He judges you! God is God! Your unfaithfulness does not change God's faithfulness! Glory Hallelujah! Glory to God! Amen.

Today, know that God is God! God is not like man. Man can be unfaithful, God cannot. God is faithful; for God is God! Man is not God, God is God! Amen! God is always faithful, whether you are faithful to Him or not! For God is always God! Amen again! God is faithful to us because He is God! Glory to God! God is God! God has already written His plan for you, and God will be faithful to that plan! Amen! God is God! God is righteous and just, and our unrighteousness can bring God's wrath, because God is just! Amen again! God is God! And it is because God is just; that He can and will, judge each person based on His righteousness! Hallelujah! God will be faithful in His plan for you; God will be faithful in what He says He will do, and God will be faithful and just when He judges you! God is God! Your unfaithfulness does not change God's faithfulness! Glory Hallelujah! Glory to God! Amen.

574

Day 262

"O God, do not remain silent; do not turn a deaf ear, do not stand aloof, O God.

See how your enemies growl, how your foes rear their heads.

With cunning the conspire against Your people; they plot against those you cherish."

"So pursue them with Your tempest and terrify them with Your storm.

Cover their faces with shame, Lord (God), so that they will seek Your Name."

(Psalm 83:1-3 & 15-16)

In today's Scripture, the author has written a psalm that is a prayer to God to crush the enemies that were against His people. Amen! The author is upset that God has not dealt with his enemies; and, in fact, seemed to have turned away from His people, and allowed the enemy to grow in power and control. Amen again! The author is impatient, and, frankly, frustrated; that God is not doing something about it, now! Tell the truth! And the author wants to see evidence that God is upset with these enemies, so that the enemies will bow down to God, and no longer be able to punish His people. Hallelujah! Yet, even through this frustration, the author realizes that the true victory belongs to God; and should be to glorify God. Glory Hallelujah! So even after showing frustration with God, and asking God to terrify the enemy, the author prays that the enemy will seek God! Glory to God! Amen! And this is relevant for God's people today, who have watched evil people of the world thrive, while utilizing their power in the world, to punish many of God's people. Amen again! And we are impatient! We are frustrated! And we want God to do something to our enemies, right now! So many Believers today are praying to God with an immediate expectation that God will do what we want Him to do, right now! While it is wonderful that we pray to God for His help, we must always understand that God has already planned all of this, according to His judgment and His timeline! And for His glory! So yes, pray to God to defeat your enemy; but also pray to God that your enemy turn to God, to be their God! Now that is victory over your enemy! When your enemy repents, seeks God, and becomes just like you, one of God's people! Glory to God! So, we are encouraged to pray to God; and we can even show frustration with God, but always remember it is God's judgment and His timeline! Hallelujah! And we should always pray that our enemy changes, and seeks God to be their God! Glory Hallelujah! Our Scripture begins with, **"O God, do not remain silent; do not turn a deaf ear, do not stand aloof, O God. See how your enemies growl, how your foes rear their heads. With cunning, they conspire against Your people; they plot against those you cherish."** When you desire God to do something, pray to God! If your enemies are after you, pray to God! If you are frustrated with God, pray to God! Pray to God and tell Him what is bothering you in your life! God wants His people to speak to Him in prayer! Amen! Our Word continues with a plea to God for His action against the enemy, saying to God, **"So pursue them with Your tempest and terrify them with Your storm. Cover their faces with shame, Lord (God),"** Pray to your Father, Almighty God, to attack your enemy! Pray to God to fight for you! Amen again! And finally, the Word of God concludes with why we should want God to fight our enemies, **"so that they will seek Your Name."** We should always pray to God with the understanding that the ultimate victory over the enemy; is to have the enemy realize that God is God! Pray that the enemy that God defeats, will now turn to God, and seek Him to be His God! Hallelujah! Glory to God! Amen.

Today, our Scripture is speaking to God's people. If you have accepted Jesus as your Lord and Savior, you are one of God's people. Amen! There are times when the enemy is pursuing you, and you have prayed to God for His help, and it has not happened yet. Amen again! In our Scripture, the author is upset that God has not dealt with his enemies; and, in fact, seemed to have turned away from His people and allowed the enemy to grow in power and control. Amen again! The author is impatient, and, frankly, frustrated; that God is not doing something about it, now! Tell the truth! And this is relevant for God's people today, who have watched evil people of the world thrive, while utilizing their power in the world, to punish many of God's people. Amen again! And we are impatient! We are frustrated! And we want God to do something to our enemies, right now! So many Believers today are praying to God with an immediate expectation that God will do what we want Him to do, right now! So, we are encouraged to pray to God; and we can even show frustration with God, but always remember it is God's judgment and His timeline! Hallelujah! Our Scripture begins with, **"O God, do not remain silent; do not turn a deaf ear, do not stand aloof, O God. See how your enemies growl, how your foes rear their heads. With cunning, they conspire against Your people; they plot against those you cherish."** When you desire God to do something, pray to God! If your enemies are after you, pray to God! If you are frustrated with God, pray to God! Pray to God and tell Him what is bothering you in your life! God wants His people to speak to Him in prayer! Amen! And pray that the enemy that God defeats, will now turn to God, and seek Him to be His God! Hallelujah! Glory to God! Amen.

Today, our Word is speaking to God's people. If you have accepted Jesus as your Lord and Savior, you are one of God's people. Amen! There are times when the enemy is pursuing you, and you have prayed to God for His help, and it has not happened yet. Amen again! The author is upset that God has not dealt with his enemies; and, in fact, seemed to have turned away from His people, and allowed the enemy to grow in power and control. Amen again! The author is impatient, and, frankly, frustrated; that God is not doing something about it, now! Tell the truth! And the author wants to see evidence that God is upset with these enemies, so that the enemies will bow down to God, and no longer be able to punish His people. Hallelujah! And today, God's people have watched evil people of the world thrive, while utilizing their power in the world, to punish people. Amen again! And we are impatient! We are frustrated! And we want God to do something to our enemies, right now! Many Believers today are praying to God with an immediate expectation that God will do what we want Him to do, right now! We are encouraged to pray to God, and we can even show frustration with God, but always remember it is God's judgment and His timeline! Hallelujah! When you desire God to do something, pray to God! If your enemies are after you, pray to God! If you are frustrated with God, pray to God! Pray to God and tell Him what is bothering you in your life! God wants His people to speak to Him in prayer! Amen! Our Word continues with a plea to God for His action against the enemy, saying to God, **"So pursue them with Your tempest and terrify them with Your storm. Cover their faces with shame, Lord (God),"** Pray to your Father, Almighty God, to attack your enemy! Pray to God to fight for you! Amen again! And pray that the enemy that God defeats, will now turn to God, and seek Him to be His God! Hallelujah! Glory to God! Amen.

Today, our Word is speaking to God's people. If you have accepted Jesus as your Lord and Savior, you are one of God's people. The Word of God is speaking to you! Amen! There are times when the enemy is pursuing you, and you have prayed to God for His help, and it has not happened yet. Amen again! You have watched evil people of the world thrive, while utilizing their power in the world, to punish people. Amen again! And you are impatient! You are frustrated! And you want God to do something to our enemies, right now! You have prayed to God with an immediate expectation that God will do what you want Him to do, right now! And you are encouraged to pray to God, and you can even show frustration with God, but always remember it is God's judgment and His timeline! Hallelujah! Pray to God and tell Him what is bothering you in your life! God wants His people to speak to Him in prayer! Amen! Pray to your Father, Almighty God, to attack your enemy! Pray to God to fight for you! Amen again! And finally, the Word of God concludes with why we should want God to fight our enemies, **"so that they will seek Your Name."** We should always pray to God with the understanding that the ultimate victory over the enemy; is to have the enemy realize that God is God! Pray that the enemy that God defeats, will now turn to God, and seek Him to be His God! Hallelujah! Glory to God! Amen.

Today, our Scripture Guidance is for Believers. While it is wonderful that we pray to God for His help, we must always understand that God has already planned all of this, according to His judgment and His timeline! And for His glory! So yes, pray to God to defeat your enemy; but also pray to God that your enemy turn to God, to be their God! When your enemy repents, seeks God, and becomes just like you, one of God's people! Glory to God! Now that is victory over your enemy! Amen.

Day 263

Then Jesus told this parable: "A man had a fig tree growing in his vineyard, and he went to look for fruit on it but did not find any.

So he said to the man who took care of the vineyard; 'For three years now I've been coming to look for fruit on this fig tree and haven't found any. Cut it down! Why should it use up the soil?'

'Sir', the man replied, 'leave it alone for one more year, and I'll dig around it and fertilize it.

If it bears fruit next year, fine! If not, then cut it down.'"

(Luke 13:6-9)

In today's Scripture, the great servant of Jesus, Luke, recalls to us the time that Jesus told people about repenting their sins, or perishing. Amen! Every single person who lives on earth must repent their sins through Jesus and be saved and have eternal life, or they will receive the punishment for their sins which is perishing to eternal death! Amen again! For God has given us an eternal plan of mercy through His Son Jesus, and all anyone has to do is repent and accept Jesus as their Savior. Glory! But Almighty God also gives each person free choice. You have the option of choosing Jesus, or rejecting Jesus. To choose Jesus, you must repent of your sins to God through Jesus, and ask to be forgiven and saved. Tell the truth! Amen! Or you can choose not to repent your sins to God through Jesus, and never asked to be forgiven for your sins, and you will perish into eternal damnation. And that is the truth! Amen again! Our Scriptures today are speaking to those who have heard the Word of God and the Gospel of Jesus, many times, but have not truly accepted Jesus. These are people who go to church, read the Word of God, look and speak like Believers, but have never accepted Jesus! For going to church does not save you! Reading the Bible does not save you! Looking and speaking like Believers does not save you! And this is very important; being from a family of Believers does not save you! You are lying to yourself, or you have been lied to! In fact, many people think they are saved because, as a child, you went in the front of the church; and confessed with your mouth, yet your heart did not know what you were confessing to! And that happens all the time! If you have not truly repented your sins to Jesus; and truly accepted Him as your Lord and Savior with your heart, you are not yet saved! God is trying to shake you today to wake up to this Truth! Hallelujah! And if this is you, Jesus is speaking this parable to you! Glory Hallelujah! Please listen with your heart, and truly accept Jesus so you can be saved! Glory! Our Scripture begins with, **Then Jesus told this parable: "A man had a fig tree growing in his vineyard, and he went to look for fruit on it but did not find any. So he said to the man who took care of the vineyard, 'For three years now, I've been coming to look for fruit on this fig tree and haven't found any. Cut it down! Why should it use up the soil?'** You have been in the church for years, listening to the Word of God, looking like a Believer. But God is looking, and God knows you are not saved! Amen! The Word continues with, **'Sir', the man replied, 'leave it alone for one more year, and I'll dig around it and fertilize it.'** Jesus is intervening for you! Jesus is saying to God, Father, please let me keep working on you! Jesus is saying on your behalf, Father, please give this person more time to repent, and be saved to everlasting life! Amen again! Yet the Word of God reveals the truth of those who do not accept Jesus after they have been fully fertilized by Jesus, that eventually Jesus will say about them what He says about the tree that was fertilized to bear fruit, proclaiming to Almighty God that, **'If it bears fruit next year, fine! If not, then cut it down.'"** At some point, you will run out of time to repent and be saved by Jesus! And at that time, if you have accepted Jesus, Hallelujah! You are saved! But if you have not, you will be cut down from the opportunity to be saved! And only God knows that time! Wake up! Leave the lie! God knows your heart, and so do you! Seek Jesus right now; ask for forgiveness of your sins, and ask Him to save you from perishing! Hallelujah, please! You are running out of time! And that is the truth! Amen.

Today, our Scripture is trying to get someone's attention. Our Scripture is speaking to those who have heard the Word of God and the Gospel of Jesus many times, but have not truly accepted Jesus. These are people who go to church, read the Word of God, look and speak like Believers, but have never accepted Jesus! For going to church does not save you! Reading the Bible does not save you! Looking and speaking like Believers does not save you! And this is very important; being from a family of Believers does not save you! You are lying to yourself, or you have been lied to! In fact, many people think they are saved because, as a child, you went in the front of the church; and confessed with your mouth, yet your heart did not know what you were confessing to! And that happens all the time! If you have not truly repented your sins to Jesus; and truly accepted Him as your Lord and Savior with your heart, you are not yet saved! God is trying to shake you today to wake up to this Truth! Hallelujah! And if this is you, Jesus is speaking this parable to you! Glory Hallelujah! Please listen with your heart, and truly accept Jesus so you can be saved! Glory! Our Scripture begins with, **Then Jesus told this parable: "A man had a fig tree growing in his vineyard, and he went to look for fruit on it but did not find any. So he said to the man who took care of the vineyard, 'For three years now, I've been coming to look for fruit on this fig tree and haven't found any. Cut it down! Why should it use up the soil?'** You have been in the church for years, listening to the Word of God, looking like a Believer. But God is looking, and God knows you are not saved! Amen! You are not saved because you go to church all the time! Too many church members fall for that lie! This may fool your Minister, your family, and the church congregation. But it does not fool you, and it certainly does not fool God! God sees that you have been in the church, and God is looking, but you still have do not show the fruit of salvation! Tell the truth! God sees that you are wasting away your time in church. Wake up! Leave the lie! God knows your heart, and so do you! Seek Jesus right now; ask for forgiveness of your sins, and ask Him to save you from perishing! Hallelujah, please! You are running out of time! That is the truth! Amen.

Today, our Word is trying to get someone's attention. Our Scripture is speaking to those who have heard the Word of God and the Gospel of Jesus, many times, but have not truly accepted Jesus. These are people who go to church, read the Word of God, look and speak like Believers, but have never accepted Jesus! For going to church does not save you! Reading the Bible does not save you! Looking and speaking like Believers does not save you! And this is very important; being from a family of Believers does not save you! You are lying to yourself, or you have been lied to! In fact, many people think they are saved because, as a child, you went in the front of the church; and confessed with your mouth, yet your heart did not know what you were confessing to! And that happens all the time! If you have not truly repented your sins to Jesus; and truly accepted Him as your Lord and Savior with your heart, you are not yet saved! God is trying to shake you today, to wake up to this Truth! Hallelujah! And if this is you, Jesus is speaking this parable to you! Glory Hallelujah! Please listen with your heart, and truly accept Jesus so you can be saved! Glory! You have been in the church for years, listening to the Word of God, looking like a Believer. But God is looking, and God knows you are not saved! Amen! The Word continues with, **'Sir', the man**

replied, 'leave it alone for one more year, and I'll dig around it and fertilize it.' Jesus is intervening for you! Jesus is saying to God, Father, please let me keep working on you! Jesus is saying on your behalf, Father, please give this person more time to repent, and be saved to everlasting life! Amen again! Jesus is keeping you alive, and every day you arise from your sleep, Jesus is asking God for the opportunity to continue to work on you. Jesus is fertilizing you! Wake up! Leave the lie! God knows your heart, and so do you! Seek Jesus right now; ask for forgiveness of your sins, and ask Him to save you from perishing! Hallelujah, please! You are running out of time! And only God knows that time! That is the truth! Amen.

Today, The Word of God is trying to get someone's attention. The Word of God is speaking to those who have heard the Word of God and the Gospel of Jesus, many times, but have not truly accepted Jesus. If this is you, the Word of God is speaking to you! Amen! You have been going to church, reading the Word of God, and to others; you look and speak like Believers, but You have never truly accepted Jesus! Amen again! For going to church does not save you! Reading the Bible does not save you! Looking and speaking like Believers does not save you! And this is very important; being from a family of Believers does not save you! You are lying to yourself, or you have been lied to! And right now, you are on the path to Hell! In fact, like many people, you may think that you are saved because, as a child, you went in the front of the church; and confessed with your mouth, yet you know that your heart did not know what you were confessing to! And that happens all the time! However, if you have not truly repented your sins to Jesus; and truly accepted Him as your Lord and Savior with your heart, you are not yet saved! And God is trying to shake you today, to wake you up to this Truth! Hallelujah! Jesus is speaking this parable to you! Glory Hallelujah! Please listen with your heart, and truly accept Jesus so you can be saved! Glory! You have been in the church for years, listening to the Word of God, looking like a Believer. But God is looking, and God knows you are not saved! Amen! Jesus is intervening for you! Jesus is saying to God, Father, please let me keep working on you! Jesus is saying on your behalf, Father, please give this person more time to repent and be saved to everlasting life! Amen again! Yet the Word of God reveals the truth of those who do not accept Jesus after they have been fully fertilized by Jesus, that eventually Jesus will say about them what He says about the tree that was fertilized to bear fruit, proclaiming to Almighty God that, **'If it bears fruit next year, fine! If not, then cut it down.'"** At some point, you will run out of time to repent and be saved by Jesus! And at that time, if you have accepted Jesus, Hallelujah! You are saved! But if you have not, you will be cut down from the opportunity to be saved! There will be a day that Jesus will stop fertilizing you, and at that time, God will look for the last time to see if you bear the fruit of salvation! This is a hard truth, but you better accept it! If you do not truly accept Jesus with your heart, you are going to hell forever! God is trying to help you right now! Wake up! Leave the lie! God knows your heart, and so do you! Seek Jesus right now; ask for forgiveness of your sins, and ask Him to save you from perishing! Hallelujah, please! You are running out of time! And only God knows that time! That is the truth! Amen.

Today, God is trying to get someone's attention! And you know if God is speaking to you! This is an urgent message, from God through Jesus! Amen! You know in your heart, that you have been living a lie! Everyone thinks that you have accepted Jesus, but you know that you have not! Amen again! This is the hard truth that you must accept, right now! For you are running out of time to repent your sins and accept Jesus with your heart! Jesus is still fertilizing you, intervening to keep you alive, because He loves you and does not want you to perish! Wake up! Leave the lie! God knows your heart, and so do you! Seek Jesus right now; ask for forgiveness of your sins, and ask Him to save you from perishing! Please listen with your heart, and truly accept Jesus so you can be saved! Glory! You have been in the church for years, listening to the Word of God, looking like a Believer. But God is looking, and God knows you are not saved! Amen! Jesus is intervening for you! Jesus is saying to God, Father, please let me keep working on you! Jesus is saying on your behalf, Father, please give this person more time to repent, and be saved to everlasting life! Amen again! Hallelujah, please! You are running out of time to repent and be saved by Jesus! There will come a time when Jesus will stop fertilizing you. And at that time, if you have accepted Jesus, Hallelujah! You are saved! But if you have not, you will be cut down from the opportunity to be saved! Wake up! Leave the lie! God knows your heart, and so do you! Seek Jesus right now; ask for forgiveness of your sins, and ask Him to save you from perishing! Hallelujah, please! You are running out of time! And only God knows that time! That is the truth! Amen.

Day 264

And Paul asked them, "Did you receive the Holy Spirit when you believed?" They answered, "No, we have not even heard that there is a Holy Spirit."

So Paul asked, "Then what baptism did you receive?" "John's baptism," they replied.

Paul said, "John's baptism was a baptism of repentance. He told the people to believe in the One coming after him, that is, in Jesus."

(Acts 19:2-4)

In today's Scripture, the Apostle Paul has arrived in Ephesus. There he found some people who appeared to be followers of Jesus, and stated that they had been baptized. Amen! Although Paul was pleased to hear this, as a servant of Jesus, he wanted to be sure that they had actually received Jesus. Amen again. For as a servant of Jesus, that servant needs to ensure that each person understands the Gospel of Jesus, including what the accepting of Jesus provides to them. Hallelujah. Our Scripture begins with, **And Paul asked them, "Did you receive the Holy Spirit when you believed?" They answered, "No, we have not even heard that there is a Holy Spirit."** God gives His children the Holy Spirit the moment that that person accepts Jesus! Amen! Our Word tells us that, **Then Paul asked them, "Then what baptism**

did you receive?" They replied, "John's baptism." The servant knew that they did not truly understand the Gospel of Jesus; or had truly been baptized. For they were not baptized in the name of Jesus! Amen again! And the Word of God proclaims that, **Paul said, "John's baptism was a baptism of repentance. He told the people to believe in the One coming after him, that is, in Jesus."** Man's baptism is worthless!! Hallelujah! And that is why God provides us with servants of Jesus; so that these servants can ensure that we understand the Gospel of Jesus! Glory Hallelujah! Today, there are many people who appear to be followers of Jesus but were baptized in the name of others! They were baptized for other reasons than Jesus. These people have not been baptized in the name of Jesus. They have not received the Holy Spirit. Our Scriptures are trying to help somebody! Hallelujah! Today, you are being asked, "What baptism did you receive?" Amen.

Today, our Scripture is speaking to those who attend church regularly and appear, or believe, that they are saved when they have not yet truly received Jesus. Amen! These people are misled or holding on to a lie! Amen again! And the servants of Jesus have a responsibility to ensure that each person truly understands what it is to be saved. Hallelujah! Do not be deceived! There are some people in the church that appear to be followers of Jesus, and intellectually know who Jesus is, yet not truly received Jesus, and have not yet received the Holy Spirit. Amen! This is a hard truth that must be uncovered; so that those who truly want to be saved, can be saved! Hallelujah! The Apostle Paul has arrived in

Ephesus, where he has come upon some people who appeared to be followers of Jesus; and stated that they had been baptized. Amen! Although Paul was pleased to hear this, as a servant of Jesus, he wanted to be sure that they had actually received Jesus. Amen again. For as a servant of Jesus, it is our responsibility to ensure that each person understands the Gospel of Jesus, including what the accepting of Jesus provides to them. Hallelujah. Our Scripture begins with, **And Paul asked them, "Did you receive the Holy Spirit when you believed?" They answered, "No, we have not even heard that there is a Holy Spirit."** God gives His children the Holy Spirit the moment that that person accepts Jesus! Honestly, ask yourself this question, did you receive the Holy Spirit? If not, then what baptism did you receive? Amen! Today, there are many people who appear to be followers of Jesus but were baptized in the name of others! They were baptized for other reasons than Jesus. These people have not been baptized in the name of Jesus. They have not received the Holy Spirit. Our Scriptures are trying to help somebody! Hallelujah! Today, you are being asked, "What baptism did you receive?" There are many people who appear to be followers of Jesus but were baptized in the name of others! They were baptized for other reasons than Jesus. These people have not been baptized in the name of Jesus. They have not received the Holy Spirit. Our Scriptures are trying to help somebody! Hallelujah! Today, you are being asked, "What baptism did you receive?" Amen.

Today, our Word is speaking to those who attend church regularly and appear, or believe, that they are saved, when they have not yet truly received Jesus. Amen! These people are misled, or holding on to a lie! Amen again! And the servants of Jesus have a responsibility to ensure that each person truly understands what it is to be saved. Hallelujah! Do not be deceived! There are some people in the church that appear to be followers of Jesus, and intellectually know who Jesus is, yet not truly received Jesus, and have not yet received the Holy Spirit. Amen! This is a hard truth that must be uncovered; so that those who truly want to be saved, can be saved! Hallelujah! The Apostle Paul has arrived in Ephesus, where he has come upon some people who appeared to be followers of Jesus; and stated that they had been baptized. Amen! Although Paul was pleased to hear this, as a servant of Jesus, he wanted to be sure that they had actually received Jesus. Amen again. For as a servant of Jesus, it is our responsibility to ensure that each person understands the Gospel of Jesus, including what the accepting of Jesus provides to them. Hallelujah. God gives His children the Holy Spirit! This is a question for each person reading this today! Did you receive the Holy Spirit? Honestly, ask yourself this question, did you receive the Holy Spirit? If not, then what baptism did you receive? Amen! Our Word tells us that, **Then Paul asked them, "Then what baptism did you receive?" They replied, "John's baptism."** The servant knew right away that they did not truly understand the Gospel of Jesus; or had truly been baptized, for they were not baptized in the name of Jesus! Amen again! Honestly, ask yourself this question, did you receive the Holy Spirit? If not, then what baptism did you receive? Our Scriptures are trying to help somebody! Hallelujah! Today, you are being asked, "What baptism did you receive?" There are many people who appear to be followers of Jesus, but were baptized in the name of others! They were baptized for other reasons than truly accepting Jesus. These people have not been baptized in the name of Jesus. They have not received the Holy Spirit. Our Scriptures are trying to help somebody! Hallelujah! Today, you are being asked, "What baptism did you receive?" Amen.

Today, the Word of God is speaking to those who attend church regularly and appear, or believe, that they are saved, when they have not yet truly received Jesus. If this is you, the Word of God is speaking to you! Amen! You have been misled, or you are holding on to a lie! Amen again! Do not be deceived! There are too many people in the church that appear to be followers of Jesus, and intellectually they know who Jesus is; yet they have not truly received Jesus, they and have not yet received the Holy Spirit. Amen! This is a hard truth that you must recognize about yourself; so that you can repent to Jesus, and truly be saved! Hallelujah! It is vitally important that you understand the Gospel of Jesus; and make a conscious choice with your heart, to accept Jesus as your Lord and Savior. Glory! And the moment that you truly accept Jesus, God will place His Holy Spirit inside of you! Hallelujah! That is the only way that anyone can receive the Holy Spirit. For when you accept Jesus, you become an adopted child of Almighty God, and God, your Father, gives His children the Holy Spirit! Glory Hallelujah! So you are being asked a question today! Did you receive the Holy Spirit? Honestly, ask yourself this question, did you receive the Holy Spirit? If not, then what baptism did you receive? Amen! Then you will know right away that you did not truly understand the Gospel of Jesus, nor had you been baptized in the Spirit. If you have not received the Holy Spirit of God, you were not baptized in the name of Jesus! Amen again! And that is the truth! And the Word of God proclaims that, **Paul said, "John's baptism was a baptism of repentance. He told the people to believe in the One coming after him, that is, in Jesus."** Man's baptism is worthless!! Hallelujah! And that is why God provides us with servants of Jesus; so that these servants can ensure that we understand the Gospel of Jesus! Glory Hallelujah! There are many people who appear to be followers of Jesus, but were baptized in the name of others! They were baptized for other reasons than truly accepting Jesus. These people have not been baptized in the name of Jesus. They have not received the Holy Spirit. And you may very well be one of those people! If you are one of those people, you need to understand that you are not yet saved! And our Scriptures are trying to help you! Hallelujah! But you have to ask yourself this question; "What baptism did I receive?" Amen.

Today, ask yourself do you have the Holy Spirit in you? It is not a difficult question to answer. You know, and God knows.

What baptism did you receive? Be sure that you are baptized in the One coming, that is, in Jesus. Amen! So honestly, ask yourself this question, did you receive the Holy Spirit when you were baptized? If not, then what baptism did you receive? Amen! Then you will know right away that you did not truly understand the Gospel of Jesus, nor had you been baptized in the Spirit. If you have not received the Holy Spirit of God, you were not baptized in the name of Jesus! Amen again! If you were baptized in any name other than Jesus, you do not have the Holy Spirit in you!!! Man's baptism is worthless!! Hallelujah! And that is why God provides us with servants of Jesus; so that these servants can ensure that we understand the Gospel of Jesus! Glory Hallelujah! On knowing this, be baptized in the name of the Lord Jesus! Jesus will place His hands on you, and the Holy Spirit will come on you! Hallelujah! Our Scripture Guidance is trying to save you from your own misunderstanding or a lie! So ask yourself this question, "What baptism did I receive?" Amen.

Day 265

From inside the (great) fish Jonah prayed to the Lord his God.

He said: "In my distress I called to the Lord, and He answered me. From deep in the realm of the dead I called for help, and You listened to my cry."

I said, "I have been banished from Your sight; yet I will look again toward your holy temple."

"When my life was ebbing away, I remembered you, Lord, and my prayer rose to you.

Those who cling to worthless idols turn away from God's love for them.

But I, with shouts of grateful praise, will sacrifice to You. What I have vowed, I will make good. I will say salvation comes from the Lord (God)."

And the Lord commanded the fish, and it vomited Jonah onto dry land.

(Jonah 2:1-2, 4, & 7-10)

In today's Scripture, the great servant of God, an unknown author, tells us the story of Jonah, a reluctant servant whom God has chosen to go to the great city of Nineveh and for Jonah to preach against Nineveh because of the wickedness that God had seen the people of Nineveh commit. Amen! But instead of doing what God told him to do, Jonah ran away from God! Hallelujah! But Jonah could never truly run away from God; for God is everywhere, and God sees you at all times! Glory Hallelujah! And God punished Jonah for disobeying Him and running away from Him. For when God tells you to do something, He expects you to do it! Amen! And today, God is speaking to someone through our Scriptures. Just like Jonah, God has told you to do something, and you are reluctant! Amen again! You are trying to run and hide from God, thinking that you will not have to do what God said. But again, just like Jonah, you cannot run away from God! Tell the truth! You cannot hide from God! God knows where you are! And that is the truth! In our Scripture passage, Jonah has been punished for disobeying God and running away from God. But hallelujah; Jonah understands his sin and repents to God! And God, being his merciful Father, has mercy on Jonah; and forgives Him, and ends Jonah's punishment. Amen! Merciful Father God! Our Scripture begins with, **From inside the (great) fish Jonah prayed to the Lord his God. He said: "In my distress, I called to the Lord, and He answered me. From deep in the realm of the dead, I called for help, and You listened to my cry." I said, "I have been banished from Your sight; yet I will look again toward your holy temple. When my life was ebbing away, I remembered you, Lord, and my prayer rose to you."** No matter what you have done, and no matter what your punishment is, seek God and repent! Remember, God is merciful, seek Him! Amen! Our Word continues with Jonah proclaiming to God that, **"Those** who cling to worthless idols turn away from God's love for them. **But I, with shouts of grateful praise, will sacrifice to You. What I have vowed, I will make good. I will say salvation comes from the Lord (God)."** When you repent to God for disobeying Him, you must also vow to Him that you will now obey Him! Amen again! And finally, after Jonah has repented of his disobedience to God; and vowed to now be obedient to God, the Word of God proclaims, **"And the Lord commanded the fish, and it vomited Jonah onto dry land."** Once you repent your sins and commit to God that you will be obedient, God is faithful to be merciful to you! Hallelujah! God commands you to be obedient to Him, and you can try to run, but you cannot hide! God sees you, and He will punish you for your disobedience. But glory to God; God is a merciful Father! You just have to repent and then be obedient to God's command, and God will show you His mercy! Amen!

Today, our Scripture is speaking to Believers who God has given a command. For whatever reason, you have been reluctant to be obedient! Amen! In fact, you have even turned away from God, hoping that God will leave you alone. Tell the truth! But you cannot run from God; you cannot hide from God, and God will not leave you alone! Amen again! God told Jonah to go to the great city of Nineveh to preach against them because of the wickedness that God had seen the people of Nineveh commit. Amen! But instead of doing what God has told him to do, Jonah ran away from God! Hallelujah! And God punished Jonah for disobeying

Him and running away from Him. For when God tells you to do something, He expects you to do it! Amen! And just like Jonah, God has told you to do something, and you are reluctant! Amen again! You are trying to run and hide from God, thinking that you will not have to do what God said. But you cannot run away from God! You cannot hide from God! God knows where you are! And that is the truth! Jonah was punished for disobeying God and running away from God. But hallelujah; now Jonah understands his sin and repents to God! And God has mercy on Jonah; and forgives Him, and ends Jonah's punishment. For God is a merciful Father! Our Scripture begins with, **From inside the (great) fish Jonah prayed to the Lord his God. He said: "In my distress, I called to the Lord, and He answered me. From deep in the realm of the dead, I called for help, and You listened to my cry." I said, "I have been banished from Your sight, yet I will look again toward your holy temple. When my life was ebbing away, I remembered you, Lord, and my prayer rose to you."** No matter what you have done, and no matter what your punishment is, seek God and repent! Remember, God is merciful, seek Him! Amen! God is always available to repent to, even if you feel your sin is unforgivable! God can forgive you for it! Hallelujah! You just have to repent to begin the process of seeking His mercy. Amen.

Today, our Word is speaking to Believers who God has given a command; and for whatever reason, you have been reluctant to be obedient! Amen! You have even turned away from God, hoping that God will leave you alone. But you cannot run from God; you cannot hide from God, and God will not leave you alone! Amen again! For when God tells you to do something, He expects you to do it! Amen! And just like Jonah, God has told you to do something, and you are reluctant! Amen again! You are trying to run and hide from God, thinking that you will not have to do what God said. But you cannot run away from God! You cannot hide from God! God knows where you are! And that is the truth! Jonah was punished for disobeying God and running away from God. Now Jonah understands his sin and repents to God! And God has mercy on Jonah; and forgives Him, and ends Jonah's punishment. For God is a merciful Father! No matter what you have done, and no matter what your punishment is, seek God and repent! Remember, God is merciful, seek Him! Amen! Our Word continues with Jonah proclaiming to God that, **"Those who cling to worthless idols turn away from God's love for them. But I, with shouts of grateful praise, will sacrifice to You. What I have vowed, I will make good. I will say salvation comes from the Lord (God)."** When you repent to God for disobeying Him, you must also vow to Him that you will now obey Him! Amen again! Too many Believers, myself included, often go to God through Jesus and ask for forgiveness, but do not vow to God to be obedient! Tell the truth! God will forgive you, but unless you vow to God that you will obey Him, you will fall into the same disobedience again! To truly move forward, you have to repent, and then be obedient to God's command to continue on the path to seek His mercy. Amen.

Today, the Word of God is speaking to someone who God has given a command; and for whatever reason, you have been reluctant to be obedient! Amen! If this is you, the Word of God is speaking directly to you! And you know it! You have even turned away from God, hoping that God will leave you alone. But you cannot run from God; you cannot hide from God, and God will not leave you alone! Amen again! For when God tells you to do something, He expects you to do it! Amen! God has told you to do something, and you are reluctant! Amen again! You are trying to run and hide from God, thinking that you will not have to do what God said. But you cannot! God knows where you are! And that is the truth! You are being punished right now for disobeying God and running away from God. You understand your sin, and now you must repent to God! And God will have mercy on you! For God is a merciful Father! No matter what you have done, and no matter what your punishment is, seek God and repent! Remember, God is merciful, seek Him! Amen! And when you repent to God for disobeying Him, you must also vow to Him that you will now obey Him! Amen again! Finally, after Jonah has repented of his disobedience to God; and vowed to now be obedient to God, the Word of God proclaims, **"And the Lord commanded the fish, and it vomited Jonah onto dry land."** Once you repent your sins and commit to God that you will be obedient, God is faithful to be merciful to you! Hallelujah! God will always be faithful to you even when you are unfaithful to Him. God is just and wants to have a merciful and righteous relationship with you, but when you have been disobedient, you have to seek God to fix it. And to do that, you just have to repent and then be obedient to God's command, and God will show you His mercy! Amen! For hallelujah and glory to God, God is a merciful Father! Amen.

Today, our Scripture Guidance is for someone who God has given a command to; and you do not want to do it. Amen! God commands you to be obedient to Him, and you can try to run, but you cannot hide! God sees you, and He will punish you for your disobedience. But God is a merciful Father! No matter what you have done, and no matter what your punishment is, seek God and repent! Remember, God is merciful, seek Him! Amen! When you repent to God for disobeying Him, you must also vow to Him that you will now obey Him! Amen again! And once you repent your sins and commit to God that you will be obedient, God is faithful to be merciful to you! Hallelujah! You just have to repent and then be obedient to God's command, and God will show you His mercy! Amen! For hallelujah and glory to God, God is a merciful Father! Amen.

Day 266

Then Jesus said to His disciples, "Whoever wants to be My disciple must deny themselves and take up their cross and follow Me.

For whoever wants to save their life, will lose it; but whoever loses their life for Me, will find it.

What good will it be for someone to gain the whole world, yet forfeit their soul? Or what can anyone give (to God) in exchange for their soul?

For the Son of Man is going to come in His Father's glory with His angels, and then He will reward each person according to what they have done."

(Matthew 16:24-27)

In today's Scripture, the great servant of Jesus, the Apostle Matthew, tells us of the time that Jesus told them about His upcoming death (verses 21-22). Amen. Peter told Jesus that this would never happen to Jesus! And Jesus rebuked Him! Amen again! For Jesus knew that it was not about glory in this life, but eternal glory with God in Heaven! Glory Hallelujah! So Jesus began to teach His disciples the importance of turning away from a focus on this life to follow Jesus and focus on everlasting life! Glory to God! Our Scripture begins with, **Then Jesus said to His disciples, "Whoever wants to be My disciple must deny** themselves and take up their cross and follow Me. For whoever wants to save their life, will lose it; but whoever loses their life for Me, will find it." To follow Jesus, you must love Him more than yourself and be prepared to be persecuted in this life to have everlasting life with God! Amen! Our Word poses this question to us from Jesus, saying, **"What good will it be for someone to gain the whole world, yet forfeit their soul? Or what can anyone give (to God) in exchange for their soul?"** You can gain everything this world has to offer, but if you do not follow Jesus, your soul will burn forever in hell! And nothing on earth will be an acceptable sacrifice to God to save your soul! Amen again! And the Word of God concludes with Jesus proclaiming this truth to all, **"For the Son of Man is going to come in His Father's glory with His angels, and then He will reward each person according to what they have done."** Jesus is coming again to bring His followers eternal salvation, and those who have not accepted Jesus, they will receive eternal damnation! For at that point, there is nothing any can do to alter their eternal destination! You will be judged! Hallelujah! You must follow Jesus on this earth; to follow Jesus to the Kingdom of God! Jesus is still teaching today! You must turn away from a focus on this life to follow Jesus and focus on everlasting life! Glory! Amen.

Today, our Scripture is trying to help someone in this life to follow Jesus and focus on everlasting life! Glory! Matthew tells us of the time that Jesus told them about His upcoming death. Amen! Peter told Jesus that this would never happen to Jesus!

Peter thought it was wrong for Jesus to talk about dying; because Peter felt that Jesus's life on this earth was too important for Him to die! And Jesus rebuked Him! Amen again! Jesus knew that it was not about glory in this life but eternal glory with God in Heaven! Hallelujah! So Jesus began to teach His disciples the importance of turning away from a focus on this life, to follow Jesus, and focus on everlasting life! Glory to God! And Jesus is teaching that to us today. Glory Hallelujah! Our Scripture begins with, **Then Jesus said to His disciples, "Whoever wants to be My disciple must deny themselves and take up their cross and follow Me. For whoever wants to save their life, will lose it; but whoever loses their life for Me, will find it."** To follow Jesus, you must love Him more than yourself and be prepared to be persecuted in this life to have everlasting life with God! Amen! This represents more than acknowledging and accepting Jesus with your head. This means to follow Him with your heart! To turn away from the desires of the world being your constant focus, and therefore stop living your life with your flesh in control of you. Hallelujah! To truly follow Jesus, your focus to live for the flesh must die; so that you can find a life focused on the Spirit! Amen! That is how you turn from Believer to one of Jesus's disciples! Glory Hallelujah! You must turn away from a focus on this life to follow Jesus and focus on everlasting life! Glory! Amen.

Today, our Word is trying to help someone in this life to follow Jesus and focus on everlasting life! Glory! Jesus told His disciples about His upcoming death. Amen! But Peter did not want to hear it, and Peter told Jesus that this would never happen to Jesus! Peter felt that Jesus's life on this earth was too important for Him to die! And Jesus rebuked Him! Amen again! Jesus knows that it is not about glory in this life but eternal glory with God in Heaven! Hallelujah! So Jesus began to teach His disciples the importance of turning away from a focus on this life to follow Jesus and focus on everlasting life! Glory to God! And Jesus is teaching that to us today. Glory Hallelujah! To follow Jesus, you must love Him more than yourself and be prepared to be persecuted in this life to have everlasting life with God! Amen! Our Word poses this question to us from Jesus, saying, **"What good will it be for someone to gain the whole world, yet forfeit their soul? Or what can anyone give (to God) in exchange for their soul?"** You can gain everything this world has to offer, but if you do not follow Jesus, your soul will burn forever in hell! And nothing on earth will be an acceptable sacrifice to God to save your soul! Amen again! That is why our focus on the desires of the world must change! Because as long as your focus on the desires of the world leads the way you live, Satan will use the temptations of the world to turn you away from Jesus! Tell the truth! And eventually, your focus on gaining the world; will turn you away from Jesus, and you could forfeit your soul! And what good would the gains of the world do you in eternity? So follow Jesus! Focus on Jesus! You must turn away from a focus on this life to follow Jesus and focus on everlasting life! Glory! Amen.

Today, The Word of God is trying to help someone in this life; to follow Jesus and focus on everlasting life! Glory! The Word of God is speaking to you! Amen! Jesus knows that it is not about glory in this life, but eternal glory with God in Heaven! Amen again! So Jesus is teaching you the importance of turning away from a focus on this life, to follow Jesus, and focus on everlasting life! Glory to God! To follow Jesus, you must love Him more than yourself and be prepared to be persecuted in this life to have everlasting life with God! Amen! For you can gain everything this world has to offer, but if you do not follow Jesus, your soul will burn forever in hell! And nothing on earth will be an acceptable sacrifice to God to save your soul! Amen again! And the Word of God concludes with Jesus proclaiming this truth to all, **"For the Son of Man is going to come in His Father's glory with His angels, and then He will reward each person according to what they have done."** Jesus is coming again to bring His followers eternal salvation, and for those who have not accepted Jesus, they will receive eternal damnation! For at that point, there is nothing any can do to alter their eternal destination! You will be judged! Hallelujah! There will come a time when our life on this earth in the flesh is over, and there will be no time left to make a decision on whether you will follow the world or follow Jesus. It will be too late! And you will be judged on who, or what, you followed on this earth. And that is the truth! That is why this is an urgent message to you! Your eternal destination depends on your decision to follow Jesus; or follow the world. Amen! You must follow Jesus on this earth; to follow Jesus to the Kingdom of God! Jesus is still teaching today! You must turn away from a focus on this life to follow Jesus, and focus on everlasting life! Glory! Amen.

Today, Jesus is speaking to you! Jesus wants you to follow Him, and focus on everlasting life! Focusing on this life will keep you from focusing on what is important, living your life for Jesus! When you live your life for Jesus; and follow Him, you are focused on your reward of eternal life with God! Glory to God! To follow Jesus, you must love Him more than yourself, and be prepared to be persecuted in this life to have everlasting life with God! Amen! For you can gain everything this world has to offer, but if you do not follow Jesus, your soul will burn forever in hell! And nothing on earth will be an acceptable sacrifice to God to save your soul! Amen again! For this is the absolute truth; Jesus is coming again to bring His followers eternal salvation, and for those who have not accepted Jesus, they will receive eternal damnation! For at that point, there is nothing any can do to alter their eternal destination! You will be judged! Hallelujah! You must follow Jesus on this earth; to follow Jesus to the Kingdom of God! Jesus is still teaching today! You must turn away from a focus on this life to follow Jesus and focus on everlasting life! Glory! So pick up your cross, and follow Jesus! Amen.

Day 267

"Each of you (Believers) should use whatever gift you have received to serve others (in the name of Jesus). as faithful stewards of God's grace in its various forms.

If anyone speaks, they should do so as one who speaks the very words of God. If anyone serves, they should do so with the strength God provides; so that in all things God may be praised through Jesus Christ. To Him be the glory and the power for ever and ever. Amen."

(1 Peter 4:10-11)

In today's Scripture, the great servant of Jesus, the Apostle Peter, talks to Believers about living for God, and serving Jesus to do the Will of God. Amen! Peter speaks to us about the gifts that God has given each Believer; so that they may serve Jesus and give glory to God! Amen again! This is such an important message to each Believer. You have been given gifts by God! Hallelujah! And these gifts were given to you so that you could praise God; by serving Jesus! Glory Hallelujah! God planned your gifts before you were born; so that when you accepted Jesus, you could begin to serve Jesus as praise to God! Tell the truth! God has always had a plan for you to serve Jesus! Peter is not talking to one Believer or a particular group of Believers, Peter is talking to all Believers! Amen! There is not one person who has accepted Jesus that God did not give gifts to, to serve Jesus as praise to God for saving that person! Amen again! God planned you to serve Jesus; with your service to Jesus to be praise to God for His gift of eternal salvation with Him. Glory! This is an urgent message, for time to serve Jesus is running out! And God did not save you through Jesus, for you to not serve Jesus! God saved you to serve Jesus, and bring glory to God! And that is the truth! Glory Hallelujah! This Scripture Guidance is for you! You have been saved from damnation through the blood of Jesus and God's plan of salvation for you. Amen! And God's plan for you includes you utilizing the gifts God gave you; to serve Jesus. Amen again! That is how God expects you to praise Him for saving you and bringing glory to Him. You and every single Believer is being challenged right now! Hallelujah! Our Scripture begins with, **"Each of you (Believers) should use whatever gift you have received to serve others (in the name of Jesus). as faithful stewards of God's grace in its various forms."** You have been given abilities and talents as gifts from God! And God expects you to use them to serve Jesus! For you have received God's grace, so be faithful to God and serve Jesus. Amen! Our Word continues with guidance on using your gifts when serving Jesus, saying to each Believer, **"If anyone speaks, they should do so as one who speaks the very words of God. If anyone serves, they should do so with the strength God provides;"** It does not matter what your gift is that God has given you; it is important, and to be utilized to serve Jesus with the strength and power that God will provide you! Amen again! And the Word of God concludes with why each

Believer should utilize their gifts to serve Jesus, **"So that in all things God may be praised through Jesus Christ. To Him be the glory and the power for ever and ever. Amen."** You should serve Jesus to praise God for saving you from the eternal death your sins have earned you! Hallelujah! And by serving Jesus, you give God glory! Glory Hallelujah! So you are being challenged! You have been given gifts by God to be utilized to serve Jesus; as your way of praising God for saving you! Glory! And by serving Jesus with your gifts and doing the Will of God, you bring glory to God! Glory Hallelujah! Give glory to God! Amen.

Today, our Scripture is speaking to each and every Believer in Jesus Christ. Amen! If you are a Believer, our Scripture is speaking to you! Amen again! God has given you gifts, and you are to use those gifts to serve Jesus by doing the Will of God for you! Hallelujah! And by serving Jesus, you give glory to God! Glory Hallelujah! The Apostle Peter is speaking to Believers about living for God and serving Jesus to do the Will of God. Amen! Peter speaks to us about the gifts that God has given each Believer; so that they may serve Jesus and give glory to God! Amen again! This is such an important message to each Believer. You have been given gifts by God! Hallelujah! And these gifts were given to you so that you could praise God; by serving Jesus! Glory Hallelujah! God planned your gifts before you were born; so that when you accepted Jesus, you could begin to serve Jesus as praise to God! God has always had a plan for you to serve Jesus! There is not one person who has accepted Jesus that God did not give gifts to, to serve Jesus as praise to God for saving that person! Amen! God planned you to serve Jesus; with your service to Jesus to be praise to God for His gift of eternal salvation with Him. Glory! This is an urgent message, for time to serve Jesus is running out! God saved you to serve Jesus, and bring glory to God! Glory Hallelujah! You have been saved from damnation through the blood of Jesus, and God's plan of salvation for you. Amen! And God's plan for you includes you utilizing the gifts God gave you; to serve Jesus. Amen again! That is how God expects you to praise Him for saving you and bringing glory to Him. You are being challenged, right now! Hallelujah! Our Scripture begins with, **"Each of you (Believers) should use whatever gift you have received to serve others (in the name of Jesus). as faithful stewards of God's grace in its various forms."** You have been given abilities and talents as gifts from God! And God expects you to use them to serve Jesus! For you have received God's grace, so be faithful to God and serve Jesus. Amen! So you are being challenged! You have been given gifts by God to be utilized to serve Jesus; as your way of praising God for saving you! Glory! And by serving Jesus with your gifts and doing the Will of God, you bring glory to God! Glory Hallelujah! Give glory to God! Amen.

Today, our Word is speaking to each and every Believer in Jesus Christ. Amen! If you are a Believer, our Word is speaking to you! Amen again! God has given you gifts, and you are to use those gifts to serve Jesus by doing the Will of God for you!

Hallelujah! And by serving Jesus, you give glory to God! Glory Hallelujah! Peter speaks to us about the gifts that God has given each Believer; so that they may serve Jesus and give glory to God! Amen! This is such an important message to each Believer. You have been given gifts by God! Hallelujah! And these gifts were given to you so that you could praise God; by serving Jesus! Glory Hallelujah! God has always had a plan for you to serve Jesus! There is not one person who has accepted Jesus that God did not give gifts to, to serve Jesus as praise to God for saving that person! Amen! God planned you to serve Jesus; with your service to Jesus to be praise to God for His gift of eternal salvation with Him. Glory! And your time to serve Jesus is running out! Amen again! God saved you to serve Jesus, and bring glory to God! Glory Hallelujah! And God's plan for you includes you utilizing the gifts God gave you; to serve Jesus. Amen! That is how God expects you to praise Him for saving you and bringing glory to Him. You are being challenged, right now! Hallelujah! You have been given abilities and talents as gifts from God! And God expects you to use them to serve Jesus! For you have received God's grace, so be faithful to God and serve Jesus. Amen! Our Word continues with guidance on using your gifts when serving Jesus, saying to each Believer, **"If anyone speaks, they should do so as one who speaks the very words of God. If anyone serves, they should do so with the strength God provides;"** It does not matter what your gift is that God has given you; it is important, and to be utilized to serve Jesus with the strength and power that God will provide you! Amen again! So you are being challenged! You have been given gifts by God to be utilized to serve Jesus; as your way of praising God for saving you! Glory! And by serving Jesus with your gifts and doing the Will of God, you bring glory to God! Glory Hallelujah! Give glory to God! Amen.

Today, the Word of God is speaking to each and every Believer in Jesus Christ. Amen! The Word of God is speaking to you! Amen again! God has given you gifts, and you are to use those gifts to serve Jesus by doing the Will of God for you! Hallelujah! And by serving Jesus, you give glory to God! Glory Hallelujah! This is such an important message to each Believer. You have been given gifts by God! Hallelujah! And these gifts were given to you so that you could praise God; by serving Jesus! Glory Hallelujah! God has always had a plan for you to serve Jesus! There is not one person who has accepted Jesus that God did not give gifts to, to serve Jesus as praise to God for saving that person! Amen! God planned you to serve Jesus; with your service to Jesus to be praise to God, for His gift of eternal salvation with Him. Glory! And your time to serve Jesus is running out! Amen again! God saved you to serve Jesus, and bring glory to God! Glory Hallelujah! And God's plan for you includes you utilizing the gifts God gave you; to serve Jesus. Amen! That is how God expects you to praise Him for saving you and bringing glory to Him. You are being challenged, right now! Hallelujah! God expects you to use them to serve Jesus! For you have received God's grace, so be faithful to God and serve Jesus. Amen! It does not matter what your gift is that God has given you; it is important, and to be utilized to serve Jesus with the strength and power that God will provide you! Amen again! And the Word of God concludes with why each Believer should utilize their gifts to serve Jesus, **"so that in all things God may be praised through Jesus Christ. To Him be the glory and the power for ever and ever. Amen."** You should serve Jesus to praise God for saving you from the eternal death your sins have earned you! Hallelujah! And by serving Jesus, you give God glory! Glory Hallelujah! So you are being challenged! You have been given gifts by God to be utilized to serve Jesus; as your way of praising God for saving you! Glory! And by serving Jesus with your gifts and doing the Will of God, you bring glory to God! Glory Hallelujah! Give glory to God! Amen.

Today, you are being challenged! God has saved you from eternal death, the moment you accepted Jesus as your Lord and Savior! And God has always planned for you to serve Jesus and do the Will of God. In fact, God gave you gifts of talent before you were born; so that you could do the specific Will that God has for you. This is God's plan for you to praise Him for saving you from eternal damnation, and bring glory to His Name! Hallelujah! You have been given gifts from God as part of His grace toward you, but are you using them? God expects you to use them to serve Jesus! For you have received God's grace, so be faithful to God and serve Jesus. Amen! It does not matter what your gift is that God has given you; it is important, and to be utilized to serve Jesus with the strength and power that God will provide you! Amen again! And you should serve Jesus to praise God for saving you from the eternal death your sins have earned you! Hallelujah! And by serving Jesus, you give God glory! Glory Hallelujah! So you are being challenged! You have been given gifts by God to be utilized to serve Jesus; as your way of praising God for saving you! Glory! And by serving Jesus with your gifts and doing the Will of God, you bring glory to God! Glory Hallelujah! You are running out of time! Use your gifts from God to serve Jesus to praise God for saving you from eternal damnation! Serve Jesus! Give glory to God! Amen.

Day 268

And the Lord (God) said to Joshua, "Today I will begin to exalt you in the eyes of all Israel, so they may know that I am with you, as I was with Moses."

Now when Joshua was near Jericho, he looked up and saw a Man standing in front of him with a drawn sword in His hand. Joshua went up to Him and asked, "Are You for us, or for our enemies?"

"Neither," He replied, "but as Commander of the army of the Lord (God) I have now come." Then Joshua fell face down to the ground in reverence, and asked Him, "What message does my Lord have for His servant?"

The Commander of the Lord's army replied, "Take off your sandals, for the place where you are standing is holy." And Joshua did so.

(Joshua 3: 7 & 5:13-15)

In our Scripture today, the great servant of God, Joshua, has continued on the mission that God has assigned him, after the death of Moses. Amen! His mission was to continue to lead the people of God to the Promised Land that God has promised them. Amen again! But to get to the Promised Land, the people of God had to fight many battles and conquer many cities along the way. However, the people were now without Moses, whom they trusted as their leader. Although God had now appointed Joshua to lead them, the people did not yet have confidence in Joshua. Amen! They knew that God was with Moses; because God worked so many miracles through Moses, but they had not yet seen God do great things through His new servant Joshua! Amen again! God new this, so God created divine intervention to validate to the people of God that Joshua was indeed the leader that God had chosen. Hallelujah! So first, God set up the crossing of the River Jordan on dry land, as He had done with Moses at the Red Sea, to show the people of God that God was with His servant. Hallelujah! Now, after crossing the River Jordan, the first big battle for God's people would be with the people of Jericho. But before God would again lead His servant, His servant Joshua had to show that He was with God! Amen! For God will be with His servants, but His servants must also commit to serving God! Amen again! Our Scripture begins with, **And the Lord (God) said to Joshua, "Today I will begin to exalt you in the eyes of all Israel, so they may know that I am with you, as I was with Moses."** Whatever God has assigned you to do, God will be with you, and God will show the people of God that He is with you! Amen! Our Word continues to tell us what happened to the servant of God, saying, **Now when Joshua was near Jericho, he looked up and saw a Man standing in front of him with a drawn sword in His hand. Joshua went up to Him and asked, "Are You for us, or for our enemies?" "Neither," He replied, "but as Commander of the army of the Lord (God), I have now come." Then Joshua fell**

face down to the ground in reverence, and asked Him, "What message does my Lord have for His servant?" God is there for you when you serve Him, but there will come a time when you have to show God that you are with Him! Amen again! And once the servant humbled himself and committed to God's Will, the Word of God says that, **The Commander of the Lord's army replied, "Take off your sandals, for the place where you are standing is holy."** And Joshua did so. You will have to commit to doing the Will of God; before He will continue to show that He is with you! Hallelujah! And God will continue to be with you as you serve Jesus and do the Will of God! Glory Hallelujah! Before God will lead you as a servant of Jesus to do His Will, you must humble yourself and commit to God! Then you will be on holy ground, in the presence of God! Amen.

Today, our Scripture is speaking to Believers. God wants you to be a servant of Jesus, and do the Will of God! Amen! You have been created and designed by God to do a mission that is the Will of God for you! Amen again! And God will be with you as you serve Jesus; however, before God is with you as you serve Jesus, you must humble yourself and commit to God! Hallelujah! Joshua had been selected by God to be His servant, and to deliver the people of God to the Promised Land. However, the people were now without Moses, whom they trusted as their leader. Although God had now appointed Joshua to lead them, the people did not yet have confidence in Joshua. Amen! They knew that God was with Moses; because God worked so many miracles through

Moses, but they had not yet seen God do great things through His new servant Joshua! Amen again! God knew this, so God created divine intervention to validate to the people of God that Joshua was indeed the leader that God had chosen. Hallelujah! So first, God set up the crossing of the River Jordan on dry land, as He had done with Moses at the Red Sea, to show the people of God that God was with His servant. Hallelujah! Now, after crossing the River Jordan, the first big battle for God's people would be with the people of Jericho. But before God would again lead His servant, His servant Joshua had to show that He was with God! Amen! For God will be with His servants, but His servants must also commit to serving God! Amen again! Our Scripture begins with, **And the Lord (God) said to Joshua, "Today I will begin to exalt you in the eyes of all Israel, so they may know that I am with you, as I was with Moses."** Whatever God has assigned you to do, God will be with you, and God will show the people of God that He is with you! Amen! When you are called by Jesus to serve Him and do the Will of God, God will lift you up in the eyes of the people to whom you are sent to! The Light of Jesus will shine through you, and God will put you in a situation that reveals that He is with you. Hallelujah! For you are doing the Will of God! Glory to God! And to serve the Will of God, you will be called by Jesus! And when you answer the call, God will be with you! Amen.

Today, our Word is speaking to Believers. God wants you to be a servant of Jesus and do the Will of God! Amen! You have been created and designed by God to do a mission that is the Will of God for you! Amen again! And God will be with you as you serve Jesus; however, before God is with you as you serve Jesus, you must humble yourself and commit to God! Hallelujah! Joshua had been selected by God to be His servant, and to deliver the people of God to the Promised Land. However, the people of God had not yet seen God do great things through His new servant Joshua! Amen again! So God created a divine intervention to validate to the people of God that Joshua was indeed the leader that God had chosen. Hallelujah! First, God set up the crossing of the River Jordan on dry land, as He had done with Moses at the Red Sea, to show the people of God that God was with His servant. Hallelujah! Now, the people knew that God was with Joshua and began trusting Joshua as a servant of God. Yet, the first big battle for God's people as they continued to march toward the Promised Land would be with the people of Jericho. Jericho was a strong, fortified city in the land of Canaan. But before God would again lead His servant, His servant Joshua had to show that He was with God! Amen! For God will be with His servants, but His servants must also commit to serving God! Amen again! And whatever God has assigned you to do, God will be with you, and God will show the people of God that He is with you! Amen! Our Word continues to tell us what happened to the servant of God, saying, **Now when Joshua was near Jericho, he looked up and saw a Man standing in front of him with a drawn sword in His hand. Joshua went up to Him and asked, "Are You for us, or for our**

enemies?" "Neither," He replied, "but as Commander of the army of the Lord (God), I have now come." Then Joshua fell face down to the ground in reverence and asked Him, "What message does my Lord have for His servant?" God is there for you when you serve Him, but there will come a time when you have to show God that you are with Him! Amen again! God is with you right now! So when you are called by Jesus, God is with you! But to serve Jesus, you must humble yourself! You must be willing to do whatever Jesus calls you to do before you know what your assignment is! Hallelujah! You must accept the call to serve Jesus, and then ask Him what it is He wants you to do! Glory Hallelujah! And when you accept and commit to Jesus, you have committed to God! Glory to God! Before God will lead you as a servant of Jesus to do His Will, you must humble yourself and commit to God! Amen.

Today, the Word of God is speaking to Believers. The Word of God is speaking to you! God wants you to be a servant of Jesus and do the Will of God! Amen! You have been created and designed by God to do a mission that is the Will of God for you! Amen again! And God will be with you as you serve Jesus; however, before God is with you as you serve Jesus, you must humble yourself and commit to God! Hallelujah! Joshua had been selected by God to be His servant and to deliver the people of God to the Promised Land. God created a divine intervention to validate to the people of God that Joshua was indeed the leader that God had chosen. Hallelujah! But before God would again lead

His servant, His servant Joshua had to show that He was with God! Amen! For God will be with His servants, but His servants must also commit to serving God! Amen again! And whatever God has assigned you to do, God will be with you, and God will show the people of God that He is with you! Amen! God is there for you when you serve Him, but there will come a time when you have to show God that you are with Him! Amen again! And once the servant humbled himself and committed to God's Will, the Word of God says that, **The Commander of the Lord's army replied, "Take off your sandals, for the place where you are standing is holy." And Joshua did so.** You will have to commit to doing the Will of God; before He will continue to show that He is with you! Hallelujah! Then, you will be in the presence of God; and God will continue to be with you as you serve Jesus and do the Will of God! Glory Hallelujah! Before God will lead you as a servant of Jesus to do His Will, you must humble yourself and commit to God! Amen.

Today, to serve the Will of God, you will be called by Jesus! And when you answer the call, God will be with you! But to continue to serve Jesus, you must commit to God, that you will do what Jesus has commanded you to do! To do that, you must humble yourself before God in the name of Jesus before you are given your assignment! Hallelujah! Then, you will be in the presence of God; and God will continue to be with you as you serve Jesus and do the Will of God! Glory Hallelujah! Before God will lead you as a servant of Jesus to do His Will, you must humble yourself and commit to God! Then you will be on holy ground, in the presence of God! Amen.

Day 269

"For (Jesus) Christ also suffered once for sins, the Righteous (One) for the unrighteous (all people); to bring you to God. Jesus was put to death in the body (flesh), but made alive in the Spirit."

"Therefore, since (Jesus) Christ suffered in His body, arm yourselves also with the same attitude; because whoever suffers in the body is done with sin.

As a result, they do not live the rest of their earthly lives for evil human desires, but rather for the Will of God."

(1 Peter 3:18 & 4:1-2)

In our Scripture today, the great servant of Jesus, the apostle Peter, is speaking to God's people about living for God, which requires the suffering of the flesh. Amen! To live your life for God, you must put away your desire to live for the flesh, which means your bodily (worldly) needs must suffer. Amen again! That is the suffering of the flesh; so that your flesh has less control over you, and your Spirit becomes more alive, allowing you to live your life focused more on living to please God. Hallelujah! This is a process for the rest of your life; to deny the desires of the flesh, and turn more to living your life for the desires of the Spirit! Glory to God! And Jesus is our example. For Jesus, while born and alive in the flesh while on earth, turned away from the desires of the flesh, and lived life completely for the Spirit. Even to the point of death, Jesus lived for the desires of the Spirit. And it is by His death; that we can be made born again, to be alive in a way that is Spirit. Amen! But we still have to choose. As long as you are alive on earth, you are in the flesh, and the flesh craves sin. Tell the truth! But hallelujah! Because Jesus died to pay a sacrifice to God for you, you are alive in the Spirit, and you can choose to pursue the desires of the Spirit! And that is the truth! Therefore, as a result, you can live for the Will of God! Glory Hallelujah! Our Scripture begins with, **"For (Jesus) Christ also suffered once for sins, the Righteous (One) for the unrighteous (all people); to bring you to God. Jesus was put to death in the body (flesh); but made alive in the Spirit."** Jesus suffered a murderous death for you, paying for your sins! And Jesus righteousness, gave you the opportunity to bring your unrighteous and sinful self, to God! Through your belief in Jesus, you have been re-born into the Spirit of God! Amen! Our Word tells each Believer this everlasting truth, **"Therefore, since (Jesus) Christ suffered in His body, arm yourselves also with the same attitude; because whoever suffers in the body is done with sin."** Jesus died for you; so that you can be washed and forgiven of your sins by Almighty God. So turn away from sin! Live your life with the same attitude as Jesus! Amen again! And the Word of God concludes with this message about Believers who have received forgiveness from God for their sins, **"As a result, they do not live the rest of their earthly lives for evil human desires, but rather for the Will of**

God." You do not have to live your life focused on sin; because you have been set apart as holy, and given the Holy Spirit of God, you can live for the plan that God has for you! Hallelujah! You can live your life to do the Will of God! Glory Hallelujah! Amen.

Today, our Scripture is speaking to Believers. Through your belief in Jesus as your Lord and Savior, you can now choose to live your life to please the Spirit! Hallelujah! You can choose to live your life to do the Will of God! Glory Hallelujah! The apostle Peter is speaking to God's people about living for God. Amen! To live your life for God, you must put away your desire to live for the flesh, which means your bodily (worldly) needs must suffer. Amen again! So that your flesh has less control over you, and your Spirit becomes more alive, allowing you to live your life focused more on living to please God. Hallelujah! Jesus has given you the ability to deny the desires of the flesh and turn more to living your life for the desires of the Spirit! Glory to God! Jesus is our example. For Jesus, while born and alive in the flesh while on earth, turned away from the desires of the flesh and lived a life completely for the Spirit. Even to the point of death, Jesus lived for the desires of the Spirit. And it is by His death; that we are born again, to be alive in a way that is the Spirit. Amen! But we still have to choose. As long as you are alive on earth, you are in the flesh, and the flesh craves sin. Tell the truth! But hallelujah, Jesus died to pay a sacrifice to God for you; so that you are now alive in the Spirit, and you can choose to pursue the desires of the Spirit! And that is the truth! Therefore, as a result, you can live for the

Will of God! Glory Hallelujah! Our Scripture begins with, **"For (Jesus) Christ also suffered once for sins, the Righteous (One) for the unrighteous (all people); to bring you to God. Jesus was put to death in the body (flesh), but made alive in the Spirit."** Jesus suffered a murderous death for you, paying for your sins! And Jesus's righteousness gave you the opportunity to bring your unrighteous and sinful self to God! Through your belief in Jesus, you have been re-born into the Spirit of God! Amen! Without Jesus, you cannot become righteous. So without Jesus, you cannot live for God! But with Jesus, you have been re-born! Jesus put your flesh to death, meaning that you are no longer a slave to the desires of the flesh. You are now alive in the Spirit! Hallelujah, thank you, Jesus! Glory to God! For Jesus did His part, now you must choose! How will you live the rest of your life? For the flesh, or for the Spirit? Amen.

Today, our Word is speaking to Believers. Through your belief in Jesus as your Lord and Savior, you can now choose to live your life to please the Spirit! Hallelujah! You can choose to live your life to do the Will of God! Glory Hallelujah! Amen! And to live your life for God, you must put away your desire to live for the flesh, which means your bodily (worldly) needs must suffer. Amen again! So that your Spirit becomes more alive, allowing you to live your life focused more on living to please God. Hallelujah! Jesus has given you the ability to live your life for the desires of the Spirit! Glory to God! Jesus is our example. For Jesus, while born and alive in the flesh while on earth, turned away from the desires of the flesh and lived a life completely for the Spirit. And by His death, we can be born again, to be alive in a way that is the Spirit. Amen! But we still have to choose. For as long as you are alive on earth, you are in the flesh, and the flesh craves sin. But hallelujah, Jesus died to pay a sacrifice to God for you; so that you are now alive in the Spirit, and you can choose to pursue the desires of the Spirit! Therefore, as a result, you can live for the Will of God! Glory Hallelujah! Jesus suffered a murderous death for you, paying for your sins! And Jesus righteousness, gave you the opportunity to bring your unrighteous and sinful self, to God! Through your belief in Jesus, you have been re-born into the Spirit of God! Amen! Our Word tells each Believer this everlasting truth, **"Therefore, since (Jesus) Christ suffered in His body, arm yourselves also with the same attitude; because whoever suffers in the body is done with sin."** Jesus died for you; so that you can be washed and forgiven of your sins by Almighty God. So turn away from sin! Live your life with the same attitude as Jesus! Amen again! This does not mean that you will be perfect, you will still sin! However, you can also choose to have an attitude to focus on living your life for the things of the Spirit! You can now choose to do the Will of God! And you will still sin, but you can now focus on doing the God that God has created you to do, you can do the Will of God! Glory to God! Jesus did His part, now you must choose! How will you live the rest of your life? For the flesh, or for the Spirit? Amen.

Today, the Word of God is speaking to you! Through your belief in Jesus as your Lord and Savior, you can now choose to live your life to please the Spirit! Hallelujah! You can choose to live your life to do the Will of God! Glory Hallelujah! Amen! And to live your life for God, you must put away your desire to live for the flesh, which means your body's (worldly) needs must suffer. Amen again! So that your Spirit becomes more alive, allowing you to live your life focused more on living to please God. Hallelujah! Jesus has given you the ability to live your life for the desires of the Spirit! Glory to God! For Jesus was born and alive in the flesh while on earth, yet turned away from the desires of the flesh, and lived life completely for the Spirit. And by His death, we can be born again, to be alive in a way that is the Spirit. Amen! But we still have to choose. But while you are alive on earth, you are in the flesh, and the flesh craves sin. But hallelujah, Jesus died so that through Him; you are now alive in the Spirit, and you can choose to pursue the desires of the Spirit! Therefore, as a result, you can live for the Will of God! Glory Hallelujah! For Jesus righteousness, gave you the opportunity to bring your unrighteous and sinful self, to God! Through your belief in Jesus, you have been re-born into the Spirit of God! Amen! Jesus died for you; so that you can be washed and forgiven of your sins by Almighty God. So turn away from sin! Live your life with the same attitude as Jesus! Amen again! And the Word of God concludes with this message about Believers who have received forgiveness from God for their sins, **"As a result, they do not live the rest of their**

earthly lives for evil human desires, but rather for the Will of God." You do not have to live your life focused on sin; because you have been set apart as holy and given the Holy Spirit of God, you can live for the plan that God has for you! Hallelujah! You can live your life to do the Will of God! Glory Hallelujah! Because Jesus died to put His perfect blood on the altar of God, God put His Holy Spirit inside of you, so you can now do the Will of God and live to please God! Glory to God! Jesus did His part, now you must choose! How will you live the rest of your life? For the flesh, or for the Spirit? Amen.

Today, you are being challenged! As a Believer in Jesus, you can now choose to live your life to please the Spirit! Hallelujah! You can choose to live your life to do the Will of God! Glory Hallelujah! Amen! And to live your life for God, you must put away your desire to live for the flesh, which means your body's (worldly) needs must suffer. Amen again! So that your Spirit becomes more alive, allowing you to live your life focused more on living to please God. Hallelujah! Jesus has made a way for you! Through your belief in Jesus, you have been re-born into the Spirit of God! Amen! Jesus died for you; so that you can be washed and forgiven of your sins by Almighty God. So turn away from sin! Live your life with the same attitude as Jesus! Amen again! You do not have to live your life focused on sin; because you have been set apart as holy, and given the Holy Spirit of God, you can live for the plan that God has for you! Hallelujah! You can live your life to do the Will of God! Glory Hallelujah! Jesus did His part;

now you must choose! How will you live the rest of your life? For the flesh, or for the Spirit? Amen.

634

Day 270

"Do you not know? Have you not heard? The Lord is the everlasting God, the Creator of the ends of the earth. He will not grow tired or weary, and His understanding no one can fathom.

He gives strength to the weary, and increases the power of the weak.

Even youths grow tired and weary, and young men stumble and fall.

But those who hope in the Lord will renew their strength. They will soar on wings like eagles; they will run and not grow weary, they will walk and not be faint."

(Isaiah 40:28-31)

In our Scripture today, the great servant of God, Isaiah, is speaking to the comfort of God's people. Isaiah states to God's people that each of His people has great benefits from God. Amen! And one of those benefits is that each of His people has the greatest resource for strength that there could ever be. For God is available to each of His people to give each one His strength! Amen again! Those who believe and trust in God, have a continuous source of strength and renewal. And Almighty, everlasting God is that source! Hallelujah! God is there for His children! God will faithfully give you His strength, if you seek Him for it! Amen! This is a benefit from God! But you must know and trust in God. And today, to know God; you must know and trust in Jesus! Amen again! And that is how you can receive God's strength, as a benefit from God! Glory Hallelujah! Our Scripture begins with, **"Do you not know? Have you not heard? The Lord is the everlasting God, the Creator of the ends of the earth. He will not grow tired or weary, and His understanding no one can fathom. He gives strength to the weary, and increases the power of the weak."** Don't you know that Almighty God your Father is always there for you; and is always strong for you! And as your Father, He will provide you with His strength to carry on in this world! But you must trust in Him! For your understanding is not His understanding! Amen! Our Word continues with, **"Even youths grow tired and weary, and young men stumble and fall."** All servants of Jesus will sometimes feel weak! All of God's children will sometimes feel weak in this sinful world! All of God's children will stumble and fall in this sinful world! Even the strongest of the servants of Jesus will get tired and suffer some defeats in this sinful world! All of us! Amen again! And finally, our Scripture says, **"But those who hope in the Lord will renew their strength. They will soar on wings like eagles; they will run and not grow weary, they will walk and not be faint."** No matter what troubles you have in this world, if you keep your faith in Jesus, Father God will renew you! And with the strength of God, you will fly; you will not grow weary serving Jesus, and you will not fall faint against the evil in this world! Hallelujah! So seek God; lean on His strength and fly, child of God, fly! Glory Hallelujah! Amen.

Today, our Scripture is speaking to God's children. There are times when God's children become weary. Living your life for God in a world of sin can sometimes wear you out. God knows this! You get tired of fighting and fighting and fighting, against the sin of this world and the enemies who are attacking you. Sometimes, you are so tired that you feel powerless and faint against it. God knows this too! Isaiah is speaking to God's people. Isaiah states to God's people that each of His people has great benefits from God. Amen! And one of those benefits is that each of His people has the greatest resource for strength that there could ever be. For God is available to each of His people to give each one His strength! Amen again! Those who believe and trust in God, have a continuous source of strength and renewal. And Almighty, everlasting God is that source! Hallelujah! God is there for His children! God will faithfully give you His strength, if you seek Him for it! Amen! This is a benefit from God! But you must know and trust in God. And today, to know God; you must know and trust in Jesus! Amen again! And that is how you can receive God's strength, as a benefit from God! Glory Hallelujah! Our Scripture begins with, **"Do you not know? Have you not heard? The Lord is the everlasting God, the Creator of the ends of the earth. He will not grow tired or weary, and His understanding no one can fathom. He gives strength to the weary, and increases the power of the weak."** Don't you know that Almighty

God your Father is always there for you; and is always strong for you! And as your Father, He will provide you with His strength to carry on in this world! But you must trust in Him! For your understanding is not His understanding! Amen! Our Scripture is encouraging us today!!! When you are tired, seek God! And He will give you His strength! Amen.

Today, our Word is speaking to God's people. Living your life for God in a world of sin can sometimes wear you out. God knows this! You get tired of fighting and fighting and fighting, against the sin of this world and the enemies who are attacking you. Sometimes, you are so tired that you feel powerless and faint against it. God knows this too! Isaiah states to God's people that each of us has great benefits from God. Amen! And one of those benefits is that we have the greatest resource for strength that there could ever be. Those who believe and trust in God, have a continuous source of strength and renewal. And Almighty, everlasting God is that source! Hallelujah! God is there for His children! God will faithfully give you His strength, if you seek Him for it! Amen! This is a benefit from God! But to know God, you must know and trust in Jesus! Amen again! And that is how you can receive God's strength as a benefit from God! Glory Hallelujah! Almighty God is always there for you; and is always strong for you! And as your Father, He will provide you with His strength to carry on in this world! But you must trust in Him! For your understanding is not His understanding! Amen! Our Word continues with, **"Even youths grow tired and weary, and young**

men stumble and fall." All servants of Jesus will sometimes feel weak! All of God's children will sometimes feel weak in this sinful world! All of God's children will stumble and fall in this sinful world! Even the strongest of the servants of Jesus will get tired and suffer some defeats in this sinful world! All of us! Amen again! God knows that! God knows that there will be days that are so difficult that even if you are young, you would grow tired and weary. God knows that there will be times when you will stumble and fall. God knows this! He knows when you are weary, so seek God for strength. Seek God for renewal. Seek God for power! Amen. God is your source! Our Word is encouraging us today!!! When you are tired, seek God! And He will give you His strength! Seek God! Amen.

Today, the Word of God is speaking to God's people. If you believe in Jesus as your Lord and Savior, the Word of God is speaking to you! Living your life for God in a world of sin can sometimes wear you out. God knows this! You get tired of fighting and fighting and fighting against the sin of this world and the enemies who are attacking you. Sometimes, you are so tired that you feel powerless and faint against it. God knows this too! But you have great benefits from God. Amen! Those who believe and trust in God have a continuous source of strength and renewal. And Almighty, everlasting God is that source! Hallelujah! God is your Father! Glory Hallelujah! God is there for His children! And God will faithfully give you His strength if you seek Him for it! Amen! This is a benefit from God! But to know God, you must know and trust in Jesus! Amen again! And that is how you can receive God's strength as a benefit from God! Glory Hallelujah! Almighty God is always there for you; and is always strong for you! And as your Father, He will provide you with His strength to carry on in this world! But you must trust in Him! For your understanding is not His understanding! Amen! All servants of Jesus will sometimes feel weak! All of God's children will sometimes feel weak in this sinful world! All of God's children will stumble and fall in this sinful world! Even the strongest of the servants of Jesus will get tired and suffer some defeats in this sinful world! All of us! Amen again! And finally, the Word of God says, **"But those who hope in the Lord will renew their strength. They will soar on wings like eagles; they will run and not grow weary, they will walk and not be faint."** No matter what troubles you have in this world, if you keep your faith in Jesus, Father God will renew you! And with the strength of God, you will fly; you will not grow weary serving Jesus, and you will not fall faint against the evil in this world! Hallelujah! Those who seek God, those who seek and trust the Lord, will renew their strength!!! They will renew their strength! The Word does not say maybe. If you seek the Lord, trust in the Lord, Almighty God will renew your strength! Amen. God, the Creator of all things, will touch you! And God will renew your strength! Hallelujah!!! Seek God! Amen.

Today, when you become tired, seek God! Today, when you become weary, seek God! Today, when you stumble and fall, seek

God! God will give strength to you, and God will increase your power! Seek God today, and you will have renewed strength. Seek God today, and you will soar on wings like eagles!!! Seek God today, and you will run and not grow tired or weary!!! In the name of Jesus, you have benefits from God, so use them! Seek God, and you will walk through this life and not be faint! So seek God; lean on His strength and fly, child of God, fly! Glory Hallelujah! Seek God today! Hallelujah!